Toward a History of Applied Economics

Toward a History of Applied Economics

Annual Supplement to Volume 32
History of Political Economy

Edited by Roger E. Backhouse
and Jeff Biddle

Duke University Press
Durham and London 2000

Printed in the United States of America
on acid-free paper. ISBN 0-8223-6485-9
This is the 2000 supplement to
History of Political Economy, ISSN 0018-2702.

Contents

Toward a History of Applied Economics

The Concept of Applied Economics: A History of Ambiguity and Multiple Meanings

Roger E. Backhouse and Jeff Biddle

The Concept of Applied Economics Historically Considered

The idea of "applied" economics, that is, the notion that there is a class of activities engaged in by economists that can properly be spoken of as the "application" of economics or political economy, has a fairly long history. Jean-Baptiste Say, in the introduction to his 1803 *Treatise*, spoke of applying the general principles of political economy to "ascertain the rule of action of any combination of circumstances presented to us." John Stuart Mill gave his 1848 compendium of political economy the title *Principles of Political Economy with Some of Their Applications to Social Philosophy*. Writing around the turn of the century, John Neville Keynes surveyed some of the meanings associated with the word *application* and the phrase *applied economics* in the writings of current and past economists. He argued that members of the "English school" such as Mill, John Elliott Cairnes, and Nassau Senior believed political economy to be a positive, abstract, deductive science; Keynes also argued that they maintained "a sharp line of distinction . . . between political economy itself and its applications to practice" (1917, 12). The English school believed it possible to construct a general body of theory through abstract reasoning, without wide knowledge of concrete economic facts.

We wish to thank Mary Morgan for her advice in organizing this project and for lengthy discussions on the themes discussed in this paper. We also wish to thank the *HOPE* team for their support and the participants in the conference for their assistance with the refereeing process. Roger Backhouse worked on this while holding a British Academy Research Readership for 1998–2000 and wishes to thank the British Academy for its support.

However, the process of applying this theory was a process of adjustment, of making allowances, of taking account of how factors excluded from consideration in the act of abstraction that accompanied theorizing would affect the operation of causes accounted for by the theory.[1] For this reason, application of theory, although not theorizing proper, was more likely to be successful when accompanied by careful observation and knowledge of specific experience.

Some sense about the ends toward which the English school would apply the principles of economics can be gathered from the language used by Neville Keynes and the authors he surveyed when talking about application. The word *application* was often coupled with the adjective *practical*; Keynes also spoke of applying the hypothetical laws of political economy to "the interpretation and explanation of concrete industrial facts." Economists frequently talked of application when discussing the advisability of making a conceptual distinction between the science of political economy, which involved discovery of the positive laws governing the production and distribution of wealth, and the art of political economy, which involved using those laws to address practical problems. As Keynes understood the writers who promoted this distinction, the goal of those engaged in the art of political economy would be to formulate maxims of conduct or rules of behavior for individuals and governments. When used in association with the idea of an art of political economy, then, applied economics was part of the process of formulating policy.

Keynes noted that not all economists agreed with the English school's view concerning the strict distinction between discovering principles and applying them, or between the positive science of economics and the normatively tinged art of political economy. Historicist and "inductivist" dissenters argued that the determination of the goals to be pursued through statecraft and the best means of pursuing them were all part of the science of economics and could not be separated from the process of discovering economic laws.

1. "When the principles of Political Economy are to be applied in a particular case, then it is necessary to take into account all the individual circumstances of that case; not only examining to which of the sets of circumstances contemplated by the abstract science the circumstances of the case in question correspond, but likewise what other circumstances may exist in that case, which not being common to it with any large and strongly marked class of cases, have not fallen under the cognizance of the science" (Mill 1877, 150).

Keynes himself came down on the side of the English school regarding the distinction between discovering principles and applying them—"theoretical and practical enquiries should not be systematically combined" (1917, 54)—and he accepted the idea that applied economics connoted the use of economic principles in the design of policy, as he proposed using the phrase *applied economics* in place of the phrase *art of political economy*. Keynes believed that talk of the art of political economy as a well-defined field of study promised too much. He felt that development of proper, reliable rules of action in most situations would involve so many noneconomic considerations as to make the relationship between the science of political economy and a field of endeavor devoted to discovering such rules tenuous at best. He thus argued that

> in lieu of such an art, we should then recognize special departments of political and social philosophy, dealing with practical questions, in which economic considerations are of material importance, for the discussion of which, therefore, economic knowledge is essential, and to the treatment of which economists will naturally turn their attention. (1917, 58)

But Keynes went on to acknowledge uses of the phrases *applied political economy* and *applied economics* in the literature of political economy that were unrelated to discovering maxims for behavior or designing policy:

> For a science may be applied in two ways: first, to the explanation of particular facts; secondly, to afford guidance in matters of conduct. The term applied economics or applied political economy has indeed been employed in three different senses: (a) in the sense suggested in the text [in association with the art of political economy]; (b) to designate the application of economic theory to the interpretation and explanation of particular economic phenomena, without any necessary reference however, to the solution of practical questions; (c) to mark off the more concrete and specialized portions of economic doctrine from those more abstract doctrines that are held to pervade all economic reasoning. (1917, 58–59)

Keynes then provided quotations from authorities, including William Stanley Jevons and Cairnes, intended to illustrate each of these senses. He also noted some disagreements between members of the English school over how widely the principles of economics could be applied, comparing Nassau Senior's argument that they could be applied (with proper adjustments and allowances) in all times and places, to Walter Bagehot's assertion that the principles of political economy applied only to well-developed commercial societies.

There were of course nineteenth-century economists besides those discussed by the elder Keynes who used and reflected upon the term *applied economics*. Léon Walras, for example, planned to organize his main work into volumes on "pure," "applied," and "social" economics. This corresponded to a distinction between what is true, what is useful, and what is just (see Jaffé 1983, 127). In using the term *true*, Walras referred to propositions that necessarily followed from the nature of things. Pure economics was a matter of logic. Applied economics considered ways to achieve given practical goals and involved forming a judgment about whether the reasoning of pure economics is relevant to the real world. Social economics also presumed pure economics, but dealt with a different range of questions than did applied economics. This conception of applied economics was also taken up by Vilfredo Pareto:

> We must begin by eliminating everything which is not essential and consider the problem reduced to its principal and essential elements. Hence we distinguish pure economics from applied economics. The first is represented by a figure which contains only the principal lines: by adding details the second is obtained. The two parts of economics are analogous to the two parts of mechanics: rational mechanics and applied mechanics. ([1906] 1971, 104)

He proceeds to make a further analogy, with pure and applied grammar.

This distinction between pure and applied economics is essentially the same as Senior's (1828, 36) distinction between the "practical" and "theoretic" branches of political economy. It is, however, given a strongly Cartesian twist, in that an analogy can be drawn between Walras's pure economic theory and Descartes's universal mathematics. One starts with the simplest and easiest of disciplines, mastering them before moving on, the assumption being that

> there must be some general science to explain everything which can be asked concerning measure and order not predicated of any special subject matter. This, I perceived, was called Mathesis Universalis. (Descartes, quoted in van Daal and Jolink 1993, 4)

This implies a clear relationship between pure and applied economics.

In choosing to juxtapose applied economics against "pure" economics, Walras and Pareto were echoing a terminology that was coming to be used more generally in science and mathematics. The origin of this terminology lay in nineteenth-century Germany, where the natural sciences were struggling to establish a place in universities alongside established humanistic and philological disciplines. When these disciplines became established, the ideology of purity became a means of preserving their autonomy (Ravetz 1973, 164). More generally, the distinction between pure and applied science arose out of the process whereby disciplines were institutionalized in the late nineteenth century. In German mathematics, for example, the professionalization of the subject was associated with what has been described as a "snobbish preference for pure mathematics over applications," and "purism" became an explicit creed of the professional (Grattan-Guinness 1997, 490). Pure science came to be seen as fundamental to applied science but to some extent separable from it.

It seems clear, then, that at least by the turn of the century, and probably earlier, it had become common for economists to talk and think in terms of applying or applied political economy/economics. The term was used at times without explanation, as if informed readers would know exactly what was being referred to, but there were also discussions of the exact nature of applied economics, the purposes for which it was applied, and its relationship to economics that was not applied. It is also obvious from Keynes's book, written at the time of the *Methodenstreit* in Germany and in England, that arguments over what it meant to apply economics, how to go about applying economics and to what end, and the distinction between applying economics and contributing to economic theory were part of much broader debates over the scope and method of political economy. Even within the English school, and within the circle of Cambridge economists of which the elder Keynes was a representative, one found different authors using the label *applied economics* to describe different classes of activities. There was, however, broad agreement among those authors on one matter. Application was something that one did with a previously existing body of theory or set of principles, one that could be developed through a method that was different from that used in applying it, and one whose nature was almost completely independent of whatever might occur in the process of applying it. To this extent, there was agreement on the Cartesian view of science that Walras and Pareto supported so much more explicitly.

There exists today among modern mainstream economists a similar shared understanding about what it means to apply economics, in that there is held to be a body of economic theory that is considered the "core" of the subject, and that applying economics involves reducing the degree of abstraction of this core theory in order to throw light on specific problems and situations. The reduction of abstraction can take several forms: attaching more-specific labels to variables and concepts that occur in the core theory; applying additional structure to the theory so that more-detailed conclusions can be drawn; attempting to provide numerical values for key parameters of the theory; interpreting specific real events as members of some general class of events with which the abstract theory purports to deal; and so on.

There are, no doubt, many reasons why this understanding, rather than any other, has come to dominate the profession. One possibility is that isolating theory from certain types of application fits in with a professional conservatism, enabling theorists to disengage (or at least to claim that they are disengaging) from politically or ideologically sensitive issues.[2] It was argued during the conference that the notion of a core that stands apart from applications offered a way to defend the discipline against the capture of applied fields by their constituencies—development economics by development agencies, labor economics by the unions, agricultural economics by the farmers, industrial organization by regulators, the economics of poverty by the poor, and so on. To answer such questions takes us beyond the scope of this essay, but these points are enough to emphasize that acceptance of this view of the core-applied relationship is not inevitable but has to be explained in terms of a specific historical context.

However, as was the case for the English school, *applied economics* in the modern mainstream literature may refer to a number of activities. In particular, uses of the phrase *applied economics* that refer to the interpretation or explanation of concrete facts live alongside uses referring to policy formation and evaluation. This is because the process of reducing abstraction that qualifies an activity as an application of economics in the mind of a writer may take place at any of several points along a continuum running from the most abstract versions of the core

2. Coats ([1980] 1993) argues this in the context of late-nineteenth-century U.S. economics.

theory to the most detailed analytical descriptions of particular situations or designs of particular economic policy measures. Models that result from applying (reducing the level of abstraction of) certain theoretical constructs may themselves be taken as "theory" that can be applied to certain questions or problems through further additions of structure and reductions of generality. For example, if the core theory is the theory of choice (say as described by a diagram comprising indifference curves and budget constraint), one level of application might involve labeling money and leisure as the goods, so as to obtain a theory of labor supply. The result of that application might itself be applied through the addition of structure, such as the incorporation of a nonlinear budget constraint reflecting wage structures, taxation, or social security provisions, or the placement of restrictions on the form of the preference relation. Further along the continuum, econometric techniques and data from a particular time and place might be used to attach numbers to parameters of the utility function or the labor supply function. Both the analytic results of the structurally supplemented labor supply model and the estimates produced by econometric research might be used to interpret specific events or to evaluate economic policy proposals.

It would be wrong to suggest, however, that the twentieth century has been marked by a gradual refinement of and consolidation about a modern variant of the English school conception of the relationship between economic principles and their applications. One frequently finds, in the twentieth-century literature, concepts of applied economics that are very different from the mainstream view we have just outlined. Two are especially important. The first is shared by economists who have denied that good theory can be formulated independently of the situations to which it is applied. This was true of the historicists of the nineteenth century, but also marks the thinking of many twentieth-century institutionalists. Wesley Mitchell's controversial presidential address to the American Economic Association in 1924, for example, spoke of economists in specialized fields such as banking, transportation, and labor problems who already found little use for the qualitative theories of Alfred Marshall and Jevons. He predicted that, when supplied with data from "real markets," economists would formulate their own theories about relationships between variables they could observe and measure and gradually change the complexion and content of economic theory (Mitchell 1937, 26–28). Milton Friedman shares Mitchell's view that useful theoretical concepts arise out of careful analysis of data, the classic example being his work on the consumption function, and that concepts based on no more than casual observation are unlikely to be very useful (Hirsch and de Marchi 1990, 43–45). For both of them, the process of inquiry involves a constant interplay of fact gathering and the formation of hypotheses.

The second concept is a consequence of the fact that economists do not necessarily practice what they preach.[3] Even economists who, if pushed on their beliefs about economic theory, would sound thoroughly orthodox, may in practice not use this theory when doing what they regard as applied economics. They may work at a more inductive, less formal level, not applying economic theory in any recognizable way. Both groups of economists may describe their work as "applied economics," but this is no more than a shorthand way of referring to economics that deals, or is purported to deal, directly with real-world problems. Thus Eli Devons (1961, 155) could write, "Although I have been an 'applied economist' for many years and have frequently tried to be introspective about my activities, I am, I fear, not yet able to give a clear and methodical account of what it is I am applying." He took "problems of applied economics" (such as distribution of industry or monopoly policy) as his starting point and discussed the extent to which economic theory could be used to shed light on them. The notion of applied economics was thus independent of any theory that might be applied. G. C. Allen, regarded by himself and others as an "applied economist," went even further, claiming that "whatever applied economics is, it is not the application of economic theory."[4]

Such views of applied economics, however, are difficult to disentangle from the mainstream view because of the variety of levels at which application can be made. At one extreme, one can argue that even to use concepts or language, of necessity more abstract than any concrete situation that may be analyzed, amounts to an application. What is applied need not be economic theory, as the term is conventionally understood, but something more basic. Thus within the category of economic theory, Devons distinguished between theoretical models, commonsense axioms, and theoretical concepts. The significance of this

3. This is related to McCloskey's (1986) point about the divergence between the official and unofficial rhetoric of economics. It can be argued, however, that it has little to do with "modernism" or "positivism."

4. Allen, in a personal communication with Denis O'Brien, who passed Allen's quotation on to Backhouse.

point is twofold: not only does it draw attention to the variety of ways in which the term *applied economics* can be used, but it also emphasizes the two-way interaction involved in the process of "application."

Applied Economics and the Sociology of Economics: Applied Fields

In the twentieth century, the idea that there is a distinct set of activities that can be labeled *applied economics* has come to be reflected in the institutional structure of the discipline as well as in the way economists have tackled specific problems. Writing in the 1940s, Joseph Schumpeter (1954, 23) referred to the applied fields in economics, offering a discussion of them that reflects the ambiguities involved in defining an application. He distinguished between five types of applied fields: (1) Fields that are considered part of general economics, but which are considered separately so that they can be treated in more detail. These include money and banking, trade, cycles, and location. (2) Fields that have, historically, preserved their independence from economics but are indispensable to economics and offer either instruments of economic analysis or opportunities for applying it. These include accounting, actuarial science, and insurance. (3) Fields that are based on public policy: agriculture, labor, transportation, "utilities," control of industry, and public finance. (4) Socialism, comparative systems, and population. (5) Area studies. Reflecting on this, Schumpeter commented,

> There is evidently no permanence or logical order to this jumble of applied fields. Nor are there definite frontier lines to any of them. They appear or vanish, they increase or decrease in relative importance, and they overlap with one another as changing interests and methods dictate. And . . . this is as it should be. (23)

Since Schumpeter wrote, this division of the subject into applied fields has become more thoroughly institutionalized, and it has increasingly come to mirror what we have identified as the modern mainstream view of applied economics (involving reductions in the level of abstraction of a core body of theory). The core consists of micro- and macroeconomics, with labor economics, development economics, monetary economics, public economics, and other types of applied economics existing around this core. Each of these has its own journals and conferences, is usually taught as a distinct course, and is populated by economists who engage more with other members of the same field than with economists in other fields. There is a clear hierarchy in that the core is regarded, along with necessary mathematical and statistical techniques, as an essential part of a training in economics, whereas applied fields can be left as optional choices for students.

The basic view that there is a theoretical core that can be applied seems so completely accepted as to be taken for granted in mainstream economics. It relies, however, on the discipline being dominated by theory that is believed to have specific characteristics. It is of very wide scope and can stand and be developed, to a large extent, independently of individual applications.[5] As with the overall meaning of applied economics, however, there exist in the profession differences of opinion regarding what theories belong in the core, where one draws the line between research that is contributing to the core and research that is applying the core, and the relative importance or significance of research on topics in the core versus applied economics research.

For example, the precise content of the core is subject to debate, as happens in individual institutions whenever teaching programs are negotiated. Take the example of macroeconomics. In the 1960s and 1970s, macroeconomics was clearly part of the core of the subject. The reasons for this were twofold: not only was macroeconomics regarded as sufficiently important to be an essential part of any economist's training, but it was also regarded as embodying a set of concepts and principles that could not be found in microeconomics—it was not reducible to microeconomics. With the advent of new classical macroeconomics and its successors, it became possible for macroeconomics to be regarded as no more than an application of microeconomics. This remained, however, sufficiently contested such that macroeconomics has remained within the core.

5. The exemplar for this type of theory is Samuelson 1947, in which the core is the theory of constrained maximization, which is then applied to the specific problems of the firm and the consumer. Samuelson is explicit that in applying the theory of constrained optimization to these two situations, all he needs is to change the labels and make minor changes to the structure. The notion of a fundamental theory supporting a variety of applications was an important part of the background of the group of mathematicians associated with Karl Menger's seminar in Vienna, including Abraham Wald, John von Neumann, and Oskar Morgenstern, who played an important role in the mathematization of economics in the 1930s and 1940s (Punzo 1991). See also Weintraub and Mirowski 1994 on the notions of pure and applied in Gerard Debreu's work.

That the boundary between core and application depends on more than simply the structure of the theory—that it depends on "social" factors as well as content—is illustrated by the fields of international economics and development economics. Development economics was, in the 1950s and 1960s, regarded by many, if not most, practitioners as not being an application of standard "core" microeconomic theory but as a field based on principles that differed from those used in the theory of developed economies (Peter Bauer and a few others dissented). Inhabitants of underdeveloped countries were assumed not to be imbued with the commercial mentality that was required for standard microeconomic theory to be applicable and hence a different theory was required. Yet, at least in developed countries such as England and the United States, development economics remained outside the core, as an applied field, because it was not regarded as sufficiently important to be part of every economist's training. It was acceptable for individual economists to ignore the problem of development and to focus on developed economies. With the advent of neoclassical techniques, on the other hand, the status of development economics as an applied field became much less ambiguous. Modern textbooks in development economics provide applications of core theory, along the lines sketched above, in a way that their predecessors did not.

International economics, however, was very much an applied field in that it was based on applying core microeconomic theory, adding structure by postulating more than one country. This was true of Heckscher-Ohlin-Samuelson trade theory and international monetary and macroeconomics as much as it is of the modern, imperfectly competitive theories of Avinash Dixit, Elhanan Helpman, and Paul Krugman, among others. In some institutions international economics has been regarded in this way, but it is also common, especially perhaps in Europe, for it to be regarded as part of the core. The additional structures that have to be introduced to explain problems in international economics are regarded as part of the core—to be applied—rather than as assumptions one brings in to apply the core theory. The core is an elastic concept that changes over time in response to both intellectual and outside influences.[6]

6. Joseph Remenyi's (1979) modified Lakatosian theory of "core demi-core interaction" offers a source of hypotheses and concepts for future research into the evolution of fields and their relationships with one another and to core research in economic theory.

Applied Economics and the History of Economic Thought

Near the beginning of his *History of Economic Analysis*, Schumpeter claimed that "we cannot confine ourselves to the history of 'general' economic analysis but shall have to keep our eye on developments in applied fields as well" (1954, 22). However, with certain major exceptions, notably money and banking, most histories of economic thought assign applied work a distinctly marginal place, with what the authors regard as pure theory being accorded the dominant role. One reason for this neglect is that the emergence of distinct applied fields, along with clear demarcations between applied and nonapplied work, is a twentieth-century phenomenon, while the main focus of most histories is on the nineteenth century and before. Thus, even after such an auspicious start, Schumpeter did not turn explicitly to applied fields for over nine hundred pages, his first passages on the contribution of the applied fields coming in his section titled "From 1870 to 1914 and Later" (944).[7]

Another perhaps more important reason lies in the specific conception of applied economics attributed above to both the classical writers and modern mainstream practitioners, one that involves a strict distinction between building theory and applying theory, with the former activity being regarded as more important from a scientific standpoint. The theory of value (with varying mixtures of distribution and growth) is central, for this covers the fundamental ideas about markets and competition on which all else depends. Developments in applied economics (at least those developments worthy of note) will simply follow and mirror developments in the theory. Related to this is a belief that applied economics is more ephemeral than theory.

The tendency to neglect applied economics in writing the history of economic thought matters, we suggest, for the following reason. A history of economic thought that focused on applied economics (leaving aside the details of precisely what we mean by the term) rather than on value and distribution could lead to a very different outcome from one that does not. It would have a different cast of "canonical works" and "great figures."[8] It also suggests an explanation of the puzzle as to why it is easier to tell the history of economic thought in a relativist way up

7. It is perhaps worth adding that this was among the sections unfinished and not typed at the time of Schumpeter's death.

8. See, for example, Backhouse 1994.

to 1870 than after that date. In the work of John Locke, Adam Smith, and even David Ricardo, theory is often embedded in application; that is, the explication of the "theory" or "model" runs in terms of some concrete question the author is addressing with the model. Thus, it is hard to discuss the theory without also discussing the "applied work," and these applied elements provide material for a relativist interpretation. In contrast, in the work of Walras, John Hicks, or Paul Samuelson, one more often finds the theory presented in a very abstract form, with the result that relativism has less to work with. Historians of economic thought have chosen, for whatever reason, to play down applied work after 1870. Adam Smith, for example, looks very different in the light of Albert Hirschman and Walt Rostow or even public choice or transition economics than in the light of Kenneth Arrow and Debreu. One can argue that he has as much, if not more, to say on applied problems of growth and development as do contemporary economists, whereas from the perspective of mathematical general equilibrium theory, his work cannot appear other than primitive.

The common, often implicit, justification for the neglect of applied economics is that it deals with issues that are by their nature ephemeral and therefore of less intrinsic interest today than theoretical ones. This may be correct, but it is an unacceptable justification for a historian to make. To understand the past it is necessary to understand the issues that were of concern at the time. Moreover, if economics, like other social sciences, is about understanding the contemporary world, it is by definition dealing with phenomena that in many cases will be ephemeral. So-called ephemera are a vital part of the subject, and to neglect them is to distort the history.

An attempt to write a history of applied economics, or to increase the focus on applied economics in writing the history of economics, should begin with a premise that was advanced in the first section of this introduction. This is the idea that the notion of applied economics itself is an object of historical investigation—that the meaning of the term *applied economics* and the perceived relationship between applied and nonapplied economics are subjects of negotiation and controversy at any point in time and have changed significantly over the past century.

When one gets to the twentieth century, in particular to the middle of the century, it becomes really crucial to focus explicitly on applied economics, both work labeled as *applied* by the research community of the time and work that has come to be regarded as applied. For, as noted above, in the works of many nineteenth-century writers, even those who maintained the desirability of separating theorizing from the application of theory, applied economics was often found side by side with nonapplied economics, making it difficult for the historian to avoid considering both. It is when one reaches the 1950s that any failure to focus explicitly on applied economics can lead to a seriously distorted picture in which the bulk of the discipline is neglected. The separation of theory from applied problems means that it becomes possible to write histories of, for example, general equilibrium theory that relate to no applied problems whatsoever. Even if one does discuss theory that is applied to practical problems, the increasing tendency to develop theory independently of discussion of empirical work, usually by developing theories in separate sections of an article,[9] means that it is possible to focus on the theory and to neglect the applications. Underlying all this, if one accepts that micro- and macroeconomics are fundamental, the result can easily be a neglect of numerous applied fields on the grounds (possibly mistaken) that once one understands the core, applied fields will fall into place. Thus as historians increasingly turn their attention to the twentieth century, it will become more and more important to keep focused on the history of applied economics.

A history of economics in the twentieth century that gives special attention to applied economics is likely to be an interesting one. We have sketched what we believe to be the currently dominant concept of applied economics and the way in which graduate training programs and the organization of the profession by fields have come to reflect and reinforce that concept. The story of the emergence of this state of affairs is bound to be a fascinating one, one that is intertwined with such subjects as the professionalization of the discipline and the transition "from interwar pluralism to postwar neoclassicism" (Morgan and Rutherford 1998). It will involve debates and conflicts between alternative views of applied economics that coexisted in the earlier decades of the century, including those that considered marketing, accounting,

9. This is illustrated by the survey of journal articles reported in Backhouse 1998, which shows that the format, now commonplace, of treating theory and application separately in articles on applied topics is a recent phenomenon in the leading academic journals. As late as 1950 such articles constituted no more than 3 percent of articles in the *AER*, *JPE*, and *QJE*, but they rose to 10 percent in 1960 (Backhouse 1998, 91). Such separation between theory and application involves the use of a more formal structuring of economic arguments than was normal in earlier periods.

and other elements of the curricula of the emerging business schools as fields of applied economics, and those that held that "whatever applied economics is, it is not the application of economic theory." The essays in this volume offer glimpses of what that story might look like and the sorts of research questions that may command the attention of those who attempt to write the story.

The Interplay of Facts, Theories, and Techniques

There is a conventional wisdom about the relationship between core theory and the applied fields among modern mainstream practitioners. It holds that workers wishing to shed light on some concrete situation do so by taking a previously developed theoretical model "off the shelf" and tinkering with it—adding structure to fit the situation, giving the abstract variables of the model more-specific labels, and so on. The direction of influence runs one way, in that the theory helps change and enrich our understanding of the situation, but the use of a model from the core in application does not alter the basic content of the core. In writing the history of applied economics it will be important to explore how often the actual relationship between theory and applied economics in the recent decades of this century has followed this pattern.

Warren Young's essay is in a sense a case study of this question and seems to provide an example of the conventional wisdom. In Young's story, we see Herbert Simon drawn to the question of the economic impact of atomic energy in part because it offers an opportunity to "apply" models of technological change in which he has developed an interest, although Simon ultimately concludes that more progress could be made by applying a different preexisting theoretical framework, that of activity analysis. Likewise, Walter Isard sees input-output analysis as the theoretical model best suited for exploring the macroeconomic impact of atomic energy. Young's narrative follows the decisions these men make as they attempt to translate the most salient features of the reality they are examining into forms that correspond to the categories of the models they have chosen to use, and the insights at which they arrive having made these translations.

Robert W. Dimand's article on applied game theory also deals with researchers who seem to embrace the modern understanding of application, and it underscores the notion that, within this conceptualization, application can be said to be occurring at several points along a continuum from highly abstract theorizing to very concrete description. The researchers surveyed by Dimand clearly see themselves as being involved in the application of game theory, in spite of the absence of statistical analysis, an explicit policy focus, or other characteristics that many might consider hallmarks of applied economics. Instead, their understanding of application is that of reducing abstraction, of redefining the "players," "payoffs," and "strategies" of "pure" game theoretic models as specific actors, actions, and consequences in particular social settings, even though the resulting models remain highly stylized representations of "reality."

The conventional wisdom about the relation of theory and application is fundamental to Thomas C. Leonard's chapter. Leonard briefly reviews over a century of controversy concerning whether the classical and then neoclassical theories of competitive markets "applied" to labor, that is, whether they enhanced understanding of the processes of wage and employment determination and whether they provided an appropriate guide for policy pertaining to the working class. This history provides a context for recent controversies over the minimum wage. Leonard argues that the reason why economists have been so resistant to the findings of David Card and Alan Krueger suggesting the absence of any effect of minimum-wage legislation on employment is that those findings raise doubts about core theory. Theory is there to be applied, in the sense that models can be fitted to data and policy conclusions can be drawn, but the relationship is one-way. If empirical data should challenge the general theory (as with Card and Krueger's results), the evidence is called into question. Applied economics is the application of a core of generally applicable economic theory. This creates a tension for labor economists such as Card and Krueger who adopt an empiricist approach in which data are fundamental and should influence the theories that economists hold, but whose work is based on applying standard theory.

In contrast, the essay by Robert S. Goldfarb and H. O. Stekler argues that there has been two-way interaction between theory and data leading to the testing of a core theoretical concept, rational expectations. Macroeconomics spawned an applied field—forecasting and the building of macromodels—which generated data on the performance of forecasters. This could then be used to test the assumption of rational expectations. What makes this a special case is that it is a case where the economic theories concerned are theories about what economists can, or cannot, do. Participants in the applied fields are themselves participants in the economies that they are seeking to model. On the other hand, while there has been no protest against the challenge to the rationality assumption implied by this work comparable to the protest against Card and Krueger's, economists have maintained the theory of rational expectations despite increasing evidence that the data on forecasters' performance do not support it. In this sense, therefore, the story told by Goldfarb and Stekler about forecasting supports the lessons that Leonard draws from the minimum-wage controversy.

It may be that the bulk of the stories of the application of economics in the modern era manifest the relationship between theory and application embodied in the conventional wisdom. If this is the case, the essence of these stories will comprise two main themes. The first will be the steps taken, or not taken, as economists modified a preexisting model and attempted to redescribe certain situations of interest in terms of that modified model. The second will be how such decisions influenced subsequent interpretations of, or policy responses to, those situations. These are important themes in Stephen J. Meardon's article, which reviews a century of attempts by economists to use mathematical models to understand and explain the geographic distribution of economic activity. Meardon's story often runs in terms of the tension between the questions these economists wanted to address and the tools, that is, models and modeling strategies, they wanted to use to address them. Judy L. Klein's essay on statistical quality control, however, reveals a different sort of relationship between pure theory and applied work, in which attempts by economists to solve practical problems ultimately led to innovations in core economic theory. Statistical quality control (SQC) began as an application of statistical theory to handle the very practical problem of minimizing the number of defective items emerging from a production process. The techniques of SQC were promoted by the government as a part of the war effort during World War II, and a number of prominent economists recruited for the war effort were given very practical SQC problems to solve. The results, in addition to more-efficient methods for testing artillery shells, included advances in statistical decision theory and a new way of thinking about the behavior of rational decision makers that began to show up in the postwar theoretical models that economists used.

Questions concerning the conventional wisdom about the relationship between economic theory and applied economics persist when we turn to the sociological dimension of applied economics and the historical questions surrounding the establishment of applied fields, each with its own journals, conferences, collegial networks, and so on. Several of the chapters in this volume look at questions concerning the emergence, development, and sometimes disappearance of such applied fields. Steven G. Medema and Pedro Nuno Teixeira examine instances in which applied fields grew up around attempts to use models derived from the core of neoclassical microeconomic theory to understand phenomena that had previously attracted relatively little attention from research economists. Teixeira describes how Gary Becker and Theodore Schultz's model of human capital became an organizing principle for a new field, the economics of education, and how the vicissitudes of the new field followed to some extent the fortunes of the human capital model in the theoretical literature. He is also careful to note the influence of external events such as macroeconomic trends on the development of the new field, and he makes the interesting point that early promoters of the "economic view" of education did not build a field by winning over an existing community of education researchers but by forging links to researchers in already established fields of economics. It is important to this story that the field involved the application of already existing "core" theory.

There is also a story to be told of how the idea behind the modern field of public choice came to be embodied in theoretical models and to motivate empirical research, and of the intellectual debates that accompanied this process. Steven G. Medema's article, however, is concerned more with how this idea became the basis of conferences, line items in the budgets of academic institutions, specialized training for graduate students in economics, and a journal—in short, of the institutional accoutrements of the large, self-conscious, self-perpetuating body of researchers that constitutes a modern field of applied economics.

While Teixeira and Medema offer examples of applied fields that arose from within economics, Bruce E. Kaufman's essay on personnel management offers a different picture, taken from the early years of this century, of how an applied field might originate. Kaufman makes the case that the research on personnel management, concerned with the actual and ideal policies of employers in dealing with their employees, was in its early years a field of applied economics. This is not because it involved the application of some well-defined economic theory to the study of the employment relationship, but because many of the initial researchers in the field were economists—they were members of the American Economic Association and of faculties in departments of economics. In the face of rising public interest in questions related to employer-employee relations, the participation of economists in the new field reflected the seemingly natural fit between such questions and the economists' traditional expertise in matters related to the labor force and the behavior of business enterprise. The story also involves a key individual in the person of John R. Commons and the demand for qualified instructors created by the rise of professional business schools. Kaufman's paper closes with a brief account of how the study of the employment relationship passed out of the hands of self-identified economists and suggests several tantalizing topics for future researchers in the history of applied economics, including the changing relationship over the course of the century between economics and "business" fields such as finance, accounting, and marketing, and the recent emergence of a new subfield of personnel economics based on the optimization/equilibrium framework of modern microeconomic theory.

Competing Conceptions of Applied Economics and the Applicability of Certain Economic Theories

Competing conceptions of applied economics confront each other most starkly when the article by Alexander Dow, Sheila Dow, and Alan Hutton and the essay by Robert W. Dimand are considered alongside each other. Dimand, as well as the economists whose work he discusses, accepts the mainstream conception of applied economics, according to which applied economics involves reducing the degree of abstraction of a theory, without necessarily going so far as to explain specific historical events. Alexander Dow and his colleagues argue that Scottish economics represented a tradition in applied economics that totally rejected such a view. In this tradition, the essence of economics, as synonymous with applied economics, is remaining in close touch with the real world, and it is hard to see how the game theory that Dimand discusses fits in at all. They contend that a variety of historical and institutional circumstances resulted in the persistence, in Scotland, of a tradition of applied economics that was very different from the one that came to dominate the profession at large during the twentieth century. The lesson to be drawn from their article is arguably that not only do the institutions of the profession influence the histories of applied fields, but they also affect the concept of applied economics itself.

The interaction between alternative conceptions of applied economics in a specific institutional setting, the Department of Applied Economics (DAE) at the University of Cambridge, is addressed in Flavio Comim's paper. Taking as his focus theories of economic growth, Comim shows how successive directors interpreted the "applied economics" of the department's title in very different ways, with significant consequences for the type of research that was undertaken. Richard Stone equated "applied" with "empirical," with the result that research was directed at measurement and the development of techniques for the analysis of statistical data. Under Brian Reddaway, applied economics meant a more practical, policy-oriented approach to economics, with greater skepticism about econometrics.

Comim places these differences over the concept of applied economics within the Cambridge DAE in the context of similar differences in the history of growth theory. For Roy Harrod and Evsey Domar, the pioneers of growth theory, application had to do with policy relevance. For the architects of neoclassical growth theory, such as Robert Solow, it meant quantifying economic theory, even if this involved exploring questions that had no direct relation to policy. This was also the case with the new growth theory, although this interpreted application in yet another way. Quantification (as in cross-sectional regressions) was much more loosely linked to theory than was the case with the "old" neoclassical economics.

Comim's essay is like Leonard's in demonstrating that such questions as whether one economic theory is more "applicable" than another, or whether an economic theory can usefully be applied, can be causes of open conflict in the community of economists. It seems likely that a history of applied economics will contain many examples of such conflicts, for in arguments between economists with competing approaches, a claim that one's research is more applicable is a claim that it is more useful, that it will provide more guidance in solving problems, that it is more worthy of the support and attention of the larger society. On the other hand, at least within the classical and the mainstream conceptions of economic science, there is a view that theory is more scientifically valuable to the extent that it is more general. Thus, we should not be surprised to see episodes in which bodies of research are denigrated for being too applied and others in which research is denigrated for not being sufficiently applicable.

Organization of the Volume and Directions for Further Research

There are many ways in which we could have grouped the chapters in this volume, as each can be viewed from several perspectives. We chose to start with a set of articles on what has happened when economists have applied their theories and analytical techniques to practical problems, in four very different contexts. Klein's essay describes a situation in which applications of statistical and economic theory took place at the behest of and for the narrow purposes of a client. In Young's chapter, on the other hand, the researchers examining the economic impact of atomic energy turned to the problem largely because of the way it fit into their own theoretical research agendas. Economic forecasting has long been an area to which it has been hoped economic theory could be fruitfully applied, but Goldfarb and Stekler examine an episode in the forecasting literature in which the main goal was to *test* a theory, rather than to apply a theory to produce better forecasts. Leonard's article on the minimum-wage debates is concerned with an example of the fairly common phenomenon of economists' applying a theory to draw conclusions regarding the impact of a government policy, and it provides an interesting study of the reaction in the community of economists when the empirical evidence raises real questions about the suitability of the theory for this task.

The papers in part 1 all make it clear that the interaction between theory and application is more complicated than one might first expect. But if applied economics does not connote a simple process using pre-existing theory to analyze a concrete problem, the question arises as to what else it might mean. The essays in part 2 address this, forcing readers to confront directly the idea of what we understand by applied economics. Comim uses the example of growth theory to explore how, as the literature developed and theories changed, so too did the concept of applied economics that underlay it. At some stages, application meant drawing policy conclusions, while at others it meant econometric estimation of theoretical models. Dow, Dow, and Hutton offer an example, in the Scottish tradition, of a particular institutional setup leading to the establishment of an approach in which economics was considered synonymous with what is conventionally considered applied economics. Dimand's chapter on early applications of game theory is not explicitly concerned with the meaning of applied economics, but in dealing with a literature that called itself application while appearing to fall squarely within the realms of economic theory, it raises the question of where the boundaries of applied economics lie.

Part 3 turns to the institutionalization of applied economics in the form of applied fields. By examining a body of research that was once considered an applied field of economics but gradually lost its identification with economics, Kaufman's study of the relationship between personnel management and labor economics in the early twentieth century reminds us that the arrangement of social science research into disciplines, applied fields, and subfields is subject to change over time. The essays by Teixeira and Medema, on the economics of education and public choice theory respectively, examine cases of a more recent phenomenon sometimes called "economic imperialism," in which economists apply neoclassical reasoning to research questions previously believed to fall within the bounds of other social sciences. In both cases an institutional manifestation of successful imperialism was the emergence of a new "applied field," with journals and well-defined networks of researchers. Meardon's article is a bit different in that it looks not at a particular self-defined field but at the history of attempts by economists to explain the particular phenomenon of the agglomeration of industry, attempts that were often represented as efforts to expand or redefine existing applied fields.

Although the essays in this volume cover much ground, they do not encompass the whole of the subject. There is, for example, more to be said about the following topics:

1. The impact of economists and economic research on the actual crafting of policy (the regulation of utilities, the design of social welfare policies, and so on).
2. The relations between economists working in government and business, whose role is solely to "do" applied economics, and economists in academia.
3. The evolving relationship between applied work and theory in macroeconomics.
4. The proliferation of institutionalized applied fields from the middle of the twentieth century.
5. The international transmission of applied versus theoretical work.

On many of these topics, there is, of course, already a significant literature. However, much remains to be done in using this literature to construct a history of economic thought in which applied economics is more central than it has been up to now.

Our hope is that the essays in this volume will provide a useful starting point for further research into the history of applied economics. They make considerable progress toward identifying the changing historical significance of the concept of applied economics and its varied and shifting meaning during the twentieth century. Equally important, the individual articles provide examples of what can be done in the area. They demonstrate clearly that the history of applied economics offers intellectual challenges equal to, if not greater than, those involved in more traditional topics for the history of economic thought.

References

Backhouse, Roger E. 1994. *Economists and the Economy: The Evolution of Economic Ideas*. 2d ed. Brunswick, N.J.: Transaction.

———. 1998. The Transformation of U.S. Economics, 1920–1960, Viewed through a Survey of Journal Articles. In *From Interwar Pluralism to Postwar Neoclassicism*, edited by Mary S. Morgan and Malcolm Rutherford. *HOPE* 30 (supplement): 85–107.

Coats, A. W. (Bob). [1980] 1993. The Culture and the Economists: Some Reflections on Anglo-American Differences. In vol. 2 of *The Sociology and Professionalization of Economics: British and American Essays*, edited by A. W. Coats. London and New York: Routledge.

Devons, Eli. 1961. Applied Economics: The Application of What? In *The Logic of Personal Knowledge: Essays Presented to Michael Polanyi on His Seventieth Birthday 11 March 1961* (no editor named). London: Routledge & Kegan Paul.

Grattan-Guinness, Ivor. 1997. *The Fontana History of the Mathematical Sciences*. London: Fontana.

Hirsch, Abraham, and Neil de Marchi. 1990. *Milton Friedman: Economics in Theory and Practice*. Brighton: Wheatsheaf.

Jaffé, William. 1983. *William Jaffé's Essays on Walras*. Edited by Donald A. Walker. Cambridge and New York: Cambridge University Press.

Keynes, John Neville. 1917. *The Scope and Method of Political Economy*. London: Macmillan.

McCloskey, Donald N. 1986. *The Rhetoric of Economics*. Brighton: Wheatsheaf.

Mill, John Stuart. 1877. *Essays on Some Unsettled Questions of Political Economy*. London: Longmans, Green and Co.

Mitchell, Wesley C. 1937. *The Backward Art of Spending Money*. New York: McGraw-Hill.

Morgan, Mary S., and Malcom Rutherford, eds. 1998. *From Interwar Pluralism to Postwar Neoclassicism*. Supplement to volume 30 of *HOPE*. Durham, N.C., and London: Duke University Press.

Pareto, Vilfredo. [1906] 1971. *Manual of Political Economy*. Translated by Ann S. Schwier. New York: Kelley.

Punzo, Lionello F. 1991. The School of Mathematical Formalism and the Viennese Circle of Mathematical Economists. *Journal of the History of Economic Thought* 13.1:1–18.

Ravetz, Jerome R. 1973. *Scientific Knowledge and Its Social Problems*. Harmondsworth, England: Penguin.

Remenyi, Joseph V. 1979. Core Demi-Core Interaction: Toward a General Theory of Disciplinary and Subdisciplinary Growth. *HOPE* 11.1:30–63.

Samuelson, Paul Anthony. 1947. *Foundations of Economic Analysis*. Cambridge, Mass.: Harvard University Press.

Schumpeter, J. A. 1954. *A History of Economic Analysis*. New York: Oxford University Press.

Senior, Nassau. 1828. An Introductory Lecture on Political Economy. *The Pamphleteer* 29:33–47. Reprinted in vol. 1 of *The Methodology of Economics: Nineteenth-Century British Contributions*, edited by Roger Backhouse. London: Routledge/Thoemmes Press, 1997.

van Daal, Jan, and Albert Jolink. 1993. *The Equilibrium Economics of Léon Walras*. London and New York: Routledge.

Weintraub, E. Roy, and Philip Mirowski. 1994. The Pure and the Applied: Bourbakism Comes to Mathematical Economics. *Science in Context* 7.2:245–72.

Part 1

Economic Techniques and Practical Problems

Economics for a Client: The Case of Statistical Quality Control and Sequential Analysis

Judy L. Klein

This is a case study of economics with a client orientation. The first major client encountered in our tale is the Bell Telephone System monopoly, which in the 1920s, 1930s, and 1940s utilized economic reasoning for reducing costs and improving the uniformity of its products that were manufactured at its Western Electric plant. Walter Shewhart, G. D. Edwards, Harold F. Dodge, H. G. Romig, and other Bell engineers devised statistical control charts and sampling plans to achieve average points of economic quality with limited variation about the optimum points. The second major client was the U.S. government, which during World War II hired economists and statisticians, including Harold Hotelling, Abraham Wald, Allen Wallis, and Milton Friedman, among others, to design procedures that would improve the quality of ordnance and lower inspection costs. With a client orientation you get "engineering economics"—economics tailored to solve a problem. It is economics that declares how a client should act. The declarative solution usually had to be in a form that people from a variety of backgrounds could follow—that necessitated communications embodied in numerical tables and data graphs rather than mathematical equations.

In the 1940s and 1950s "economic theory for a non-market economy," as RAND economist Charles Hitch (1958, 206) described it, was

I am grateful for feedback from Roger Backhouse, Jeff Biddle, Kenneth L. Campbell, Craufurd Goodwin, Albert Jolink, Leon Klein, Mary Morgan, Roy Weintraub, and participants at presentations of this article at the *HOPE* conference and the ECHE meeting in Paris in April 1999. I greatly appreciate a fellowship from the National Humanities Center that enabled me to research and write this article.

commonly practiced in the United States and Europe. Paul Homan (1946, 870) asserted that the analytical traits developed in economists' training were particularly suited to the state mobilization for war: "In this respect, the way opened for economists in wartime service was, in degree, quite beyond that for persons brought up in any other academic discipline except, perhaps, for physical scientists in various fields of research, especially that of atomic research." Homan argued that the wartime experience insured "a continuing large place for economists in the public service" (870).

During World War II, governments in several countries called upon professors from diverse disciplines to apply their knowledge. The U.S. government, for example, created the National Defense Research Committee in which scientists, mathematicians, statisticians, and economists worked together and with the military to improve the mechanisms of warfare. In his essay "Economic Reasoning and Military Science," Thomas Schelling (1960, 4) asserted that during World War II and the Cold War economists were called upon to practice the "science of economizing." It is relatively easy to make the case that such practice proved useful to the Allied war effort, and evidence of that is provided in this article. It is more difficult to discern whether wartime practice had a significant impact upon the nature of postwar economics.[1]

With regard to mathematics, J. Barkley Rosser (1988) and Jens Høyrup (1994) argue that the wartime work of mathematicians was mostly unpublishable common sense. It generally consisted of routine applications of elementary mathematics that resulted in no essential breakthroughs. As Høyrup sees it, the mathematics discipline gave more to the war effort than it received from the experience. Within a perceived context of a trade-off between applied and pure, Høyrup sees the war as a temporary detour down the applied route; the practice of wartime mathematics delayed and subsequently had little impact on theoretical developments after the war. Høyrup's thesis may well come to be disputed by other historians of mathematics, but I want to use his claim to provoke thought on whether economists' wartime applied work on statistical quality control was an unfruitful detour or whether it spurred developments in economic theory and statistical theory.

1. The impact of the wartime practice of economics is also explored in Mirowski forthcoming and Klein 1999a, 1999b.

The "economizing" that Schelling alluded to sounds like unpublishable common sense, but economists were forced to practice this in the contexts of statistical hypothesis testing, control engineering, and operational research. New approaches to decision theory, statistical theory, and strategy in game theory emerged from those enforced combinations. This is particularly evident in the example of sequential analysis crafted by Abraham Wald and enhanced by his colleagues in the Columbia Statistical Research Group, including Hotelling, Wallis, Friedman, George Stigler, Leonard Savage, J. Wolfowitz, and Frederick Mostellar. In his creation of a systematic sequential analysis to minimize sample size (for inspection or experimentation) subject to specified degrees of risk, Wald built on a radically new approach to choice within a context of uncertainty—*statistical decision*. The nineteenth century had been a golden age of statistical description. In the 1920s Jerzy Neyman, Egon Pearson, and Ronald Fisher, among others, formalized statistical inference. Wald's wartime application of the science of economizing to statistical inference fed into his postwar work on statistical decision functions. Prior to World War II, researchers used statistics to help them decide what to say; with statistical quality control, Walter Shewhart and Abraham Wald made significant steps in using statistics to tell us what to do.[2]

Statisticians have refined and continue to rely heavily on control charts, sequential analysis, and behavioristic statistics. Sequential analysis also served as a powerful metaphor in economic theorizing in the 1950s and 1960s. More significantly, Wald, Savage, and Wolfowitz built on this wartime challenge of telling a client what to do to construct a statistical theory of action that gave birth to the theory of optimal stopping and influenced theoretical developments in game theory, including a generalized statistical theory of the minimax solution in two-person, zero-sum games. I use this case study of economic reasoning applied to statistical quality control to explore the fertility of cross-disciplinary communication necessitated by problem solving for a client. I begin, however, not with the war economy but with another type of command economy—that within a large, vertically integrated monopoly seeking greater engineering efficiency in its mass production of telephone equipment.

2. Leonard Savage ([1954] 1972, 59) credits Wald with making major strides in replacing the "verbalistic by the behavioralistic outlook" in statistical theory.

Statistical Quality Control before World War II

Quality control, as opposed to *statistical* quality control (SQC), has a history that has been traced back to ancient civilizations (see, for example, Juran 1995), but the application of random sampling, normal probability distributions, and measurements of central tendency and dispersion to the control of quality in production is a twentieth-century phenomenon. There were isolated instances of a statistical approach to quality control as early as 1911.[3] The first major leap, however, into disciplined SQC came in the 1920s with the studies of Walter Shewhart at Bell Telephone Laboratories.[4] The starting point for Shewhart's suggestions for quality control in the 1920s and 1930s was the acknowledgment of "economic standards" such that the value of the benefit to the consumer of any modification in product and production was balanced with the cost of such modification. This determined how much variability should be left to chance. Shewhart argued that businesses should aim for only chance variation, that is, they should produce a uniform product "for which the differences between the units or groups were controlled by a complex system of non-assignable chance causes producing results independent of time" (Shewhart 1926b, 596). Shewhart was thus advocating that managers transform their production processes

3. See C. C. van Vechten's (1948) account of M. Provost's 1911 study of the French government's tobacco monopoly or the 1918 essay in *Engineering* titled "The Errors in Interchangeable Parts." G. S. Radford's 1922 book on statistical quality control describes the bell curve and a theory of errors, but does not advocate random sampling or time-series charting to achieve a stationary stochastic process. He also describes lessons on quality control from World War I (208).

4. As C. C. van Vechten of the Navy Bureau of Ordnance wrote in 1948, "Walter Shewhart is rightfully acknowledged to be the father of Modern Statistical Quality Control and indeed it is his child which has become the husky youngster that seems on the verge of something approaching a revolution in production methods" (5). Shewhart was not acting in isolation in the Bell system. The team concerned with inspection engineering in the 1920s and 1930s at Bell Laboratories and at the manufacturing arm of the Bell system, Western Electric's Hawthorne Works, included, among others, R. L. Jones, G. D. Edwards, Don Quarles, Harold F. Dodge, H. G. Romig, Paul Olmstead, Mary N. Torrey, A. B. Hazard, Joseph M. Juran, S. M. Osborne, and Walter Bartky (as a consultant) (see Dodge 1969, 77, 80). Fourteen videocassettes comprising a history of quality control and assurance at AT&T from 1920 to 1970 include interviews in 1988 and 1989 with Olmstead, Juran, Edwards Deming, Torrey, Bonnie Small, John Tukey, and others. The interviews touch on the following: the genius of Walter Shewhart; the cooperation and tension between the academic orientation of the mathematicians at Bell Labs and the practical orientation of the engineers at Hawthorne; the switch from colony organization of production to the product shop; the effect of the Great Depression on the Bell system; the context for key developments in statistical quality control; SQC in World War II; and the postwar Japanese interest in quality control.

into a stationary stochastic process that maintained a constant probability structure through time.[5]

Shewhart's use of the target practice metaphor to distinguish between "assignable" and "nonassignable" causes was reminiscent of many earlier treatises on statistical theory (see Klein 1997, 3–13) and portentous of the military use of this tool:

> Suppose a person were to fire one hundred rounds at a target. We know what probably would happen—the individual would not hit the bull's-eye every time. Possibly some of the shots would fall within the first ring, others, within the second ring, and, in general, the shots would be distributed somewhat uniformly about the center of the target. We have a more or less definite picture of some of the possible reasons why the individual would not hit the bull's-eye every time, but we probably cannot assign the reasons or causes for his missing the bull's-eye in any particular instance—the causes of missing are nonassignable. Suppose, however, that the individual tended to shoot to the right of the bull's-eye. Naturally we would conclude that there was some discoverable cause for this general tendency, e.g., we would feel that the observed effect could be assigned to some particular cause. (Shewhart 1926b, 593)

The goal of statistical quality control was to ferret out and eliminate product variation due to assignable causes that exceeded the variation that could have resulted from nonassignable causes. Shewhart asked, "When do the observed differences between the product for one period and that for another indicate lack of control due to assignable causes?"(1926b, 594). Shewhart argued that the engineer would find the answer through a graphical form of time series analysis. The economic statistician gets to the stationary process by eliminating seasonal variation and trends; so too does the quality control engineer.[6] Shewhart

5. The stationary stochastic process was not named as such until the work of Aleksandr Yakovlevich Khinchin and Herman Wold in the 1930s. Judy Klein (1997) documents the attempts by early-twentieth-century economic statisticians to transform time-series data into a "stationary" form, amenable to probability theory and immune to nonsense correlations. That groping toward the systematic construction of stationary stylized facts paralleled Shewhart's evangelical mission to render mass industrial production as stationary processes.

6. Abraham Wald, who made significant contributions to the theory of the decision-making process in quality control, was one of many statisticians in the first three decades of the twentieth century who investigated how to eliminate seasonal variation in economic time-series (see Wald 1936).

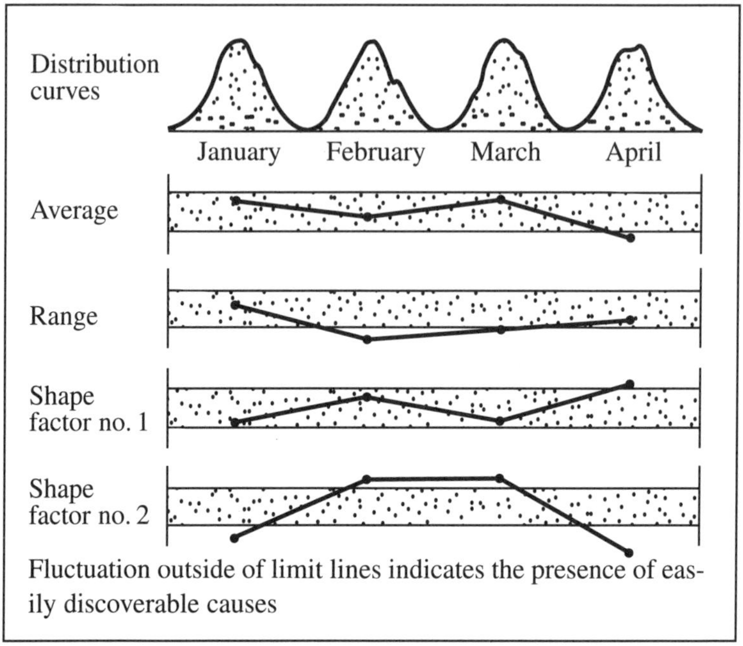

Figure 1 Shewhart's (1926a, 127) schematic representations for statistical control

argued that assignable seasonal variation could be spotted by monthly frequency polygons measuring some characteristic of quality in large samples (see figure 1) and trends could be spotted by tracking changes in the arithmetic mean and higher moments over time.

The transformation of the production process to a controlled, stationary process was to be guided and maintained primarily through the use of control charts, the first of which Shewhart unveiled at Bell Telephone Laboratories on 16 May 1924 (see Shewhart 1967, 72). Control charts tracked changes in mean, standard deviation or range, skewness, kurtosis, frequency distributions, and percent of defective parts over time. Each part of the chart indicated the average characteristic for a large sample and the limits of tolerance. The limit lines were "the engineer's fever thermometer" (Shewhart 1926a, 128). In many operations, the tolerable limits of the arithmetic mean of the smaller samples were three standard deviations above and below the mean for the large sample, so the 3-sigma standard became a rule of thumb. The statistician would construct the template of the control chart based on a large sample, then inspectors could track the characteristics from random samples taken at different periods of time. Any tracked observations that lay outside the limit lines indicated lack of control and the presence of serious assignable causes that would need investigation.[7]

This easily constructed and easily comprehended visual template became the archetypal weapon in the battle for control. As Colonel Leslie Simon, the director of army ordnance who figures large in our story, exclaimed,

> The control chart, when used with the average, $\overline{X}$, and the range, R, slays the hydra-headed dragon of complication; deflates the hobgoblin of fear-of-the-theoretical; and requires a minimum amount of labor in any large scale application of statistical technique.
>
> The control chart's usefulness inheres not only in its simplicity of application but also in its simplicity of concept. Almost any engineer will tell you that when test results differ too much from expected results (expected results, in general, being based on experience), there is either something wrong with the product or the test. If the engineer is honest, he will likely reflect a moment and add, "However, it is very difficult to tell when results differ *too much*." The control chart does just that—it tells simply and clearly and in an economic way, just when one should take action on the grounds that a set of test results differs too much from its predecessors. (Simon 1942, 314–15)

The joint committees from Bell Laboratories and the Hawthorne Works—Rating of Quality of Telephone Products, in the case of the former, and Inspection Statistics and Economy, in the case of the latter—proved to be fonts of innovation in statistical quality control. Out of the Bell system came the following: the Shewhart control charts; single and double sampling plans; the probability of acceptance (operating characteristic) curves; and the concepts of consumer risk, producer risk, average outgoing quality limit, average total inspection, and process average. In the AT&T (1989) oral history of SQC, Joseph Juran, Paul

7. In his statistical analysis of quality control, Shewhart said he was drawing on the accumulated knowledge from "four of our greatest physicists, Jeans, Gibbs, Planck and Lord Kelvin; four of our greatest mathematicians, LaPlace, Poisson, Charlier and Gauss; four of our greatest statisticians, Pearson [Karl], R. A. Fisher, Edgeworth and Yule; two of our greatest actuaries, Thiele and Gram and two of our greatest astronomers, Eddington and Kapteyn" (Shewhart 1926a, 126).

Olmstead, and Bonnie Small assert that although Shewhart's emphasis on variation and sampling and his distinctions between assignable and random causes got a good reception from the inspection engineers at Hawthorne Works, control charts were not used there in the 1920s or 1930s. According to Mary Torrey (AT&T 1989), control charts were used from 1924 onward by Bell Labs to determine the process average value and the minimum amount of inspection in order to construct sampling plans and tables, which were in turn used at Hawthorne Works. So much money was put into computing the Dodge-Romig tables for single and double sampling plans that from their introduction in 1929, they were considered confidential, proprietary information. In 1941, the U.S. military persuaded Bell Labs to publish the tables. Wartime exigencies also brought control charts to Hawthorne Works.

Until World War II, the Bell system was one of only a few U.S. manufacturers that implemented systematic random sampling for statistical quality control. Many companies had quality control programs, but these usually entailed 100 percent inspection of the finished product with the only action being acceptance or rejection. In 1937, International Business Machines boasted that "one out of every ten men in the Endicott plant is an inspector" ("Looking for Trouble" 1937, 539). Within a decade new devotees of statistical quality control would be boasting about how relatively little of their resources were devoted to inspection. Indeed Shewhart considered his vision to be as much about economics as it was about statistics, and the main stimulus to SQC in the Bell system had been the need to reduce inspection costs. Shewhart spoke of the "economic phases" of control, which included determining for each step in the process "the economic percentage rejection or tolerance" and the "the minimum amount of inspection which will suffice to give economic control of quality" (Shewhart 1928, 400). Shewhart's 1933 essay on the role of statistical method in economic standardization was the second paper in the first issue of the first volume of *Econometrica*. The role of economics in the Bell system's statistical quality control is also evident in the work of Shewhart's colleagues, G. D. Edwards (1928) and R. L. Jones (1927). Edwards named the equilibrium point of tangency between a unit cost and unit value curve for switching equipment (demanded by Bell's local exchanges and supplied by Bell's Western Electric) the point of "economic quality." He then derived the probability distribution curve of economic quality, which in turn was shaped by specifications for tolerances for defects. This was economics for a nonmarket economy. As Edwards explained it, "The basis of such standards within the Bell system is perhaps unique. Possible profit in the manufacture or sale of equipment plays no part in the determination. . . . Maximum utility for every dollar invested is the sole test" (Edwards 1928, 292).

Mass production by interchangeable parts had been around for decades (see Hounshell 1984). Shewhart, however, insisted that adding statistical method to mass production would give rise to both the only "scientific method for minimizing the cost of producing things to satisfy human wants" and the "*first critical and exhaustive investigation to find out if nature draws her samples at random*" (Shewhart 1939, 52, 73). Shewhart concluded that the data nature hands us are almost never random, but that the production process should be engineered in such a way to achieve random samples and the capacity for random assembly.[8] Statistical method plus mass production would generate "knowledge to be fed back into the process until we know enough to stay within a straight and narrow path" (Shewhart 1939, 106). The feedback loop creating the conditions for a random process oscillating about a constant mean within narrow limits would lead to three economies: a reduction in the cost of inspection, a reduction in the cost of rejection, and more efficient use of material (Shewhart 1939, 73).[9] For the Bell system engineers turned economists/statisticians, nature did not generally provide processes that were random or stationary, and capitalist industrial production did not inherently provide for the most efficient allocation of resources. These were "ought-to-be" states achieved through the active statistical control of mass production.

Shewhart's blend of economics, statistics, and engineering did get a good reception in Britain. Egon Pearson (1936, 1967) explained that the stimulus to British SQC came from Shewhart's visit to London in May 1932, during which Shewhart convinced several practicing industrialists to look into SQC. Within a year the Royal Statistical Society established the Industrial and Agricultural Research Section. Until the

8. In a similar vein, Harold Hotelling (1947, 177) argued that humans were unlikely to be able to draw the truly random samples required for proper statistical experimentation without the help of special equipment.

9. Shewhart's application of information flow in a feedback loop to a managerial scheme is remarkably early. It was only in 1932 that H. Nyquist published his work on negative feedback amplifiers in the *Bell Technical Journal*, and it was only after developments during World War II in control engineering that notions of feedback were generally applied to formal managerial approaches (see Klein 1999b).

war, however, much of the SQC research was relegated to the Rothamsted Agricultural Experimental Station, where Ronald A. Fisher had designed his statistical experimentation procedures, and the Cotton Industry Research Association, where L. H. C. Tippett worked on random sampling and quality of cotton yarn.

Control Charts and Munitions Testing

During World War II, U.S. ballistics testing and ordnance purchases generated far more practicing devotees of Shewhart's control charts than had been secured by market forces before the war.[10] Statistical quality control became a way of life for the military and those who supplied the military. One of the strongest advocates of statistical quality control in the United States Army was Colonel Leslie E. Simon, director of the ordnance department and director of the Ballistic Research Laboratory, Aberdeen Proving Ground. The strength of Simon's advocacy of SQC in procurement procedures will become evident in the next section, but two examples illustrate how ingrained statistical quality control became for military testing and operations.

Simon saw his ballistic testing as a measurement process, and like all good statisticians of his day he sought to make the process a stationary stochastic one:

> I believe that the Ordnance Department is the first to apply intentionally and systematically the control chart technique to the control of measurements. Ordinarily, one thinks of the arsenal as the manufacturers of defense products; but the Proving Ground turns out a product which is just as materially important as the munitions, and its product is *measurements*. If its flow is subject to assignable causes of variation, good munitions may be rejected and poor munitions accepted; if the range of variation of its measurements (accidental errors) is large, more rounds have to be fired in testing the product than if its measurements were more precise. In order to save valuable time and material, statistical methods are used in the control of the Proving Ground's product. (Simon 1942, 315)

10. U.S. direct involvement in World War II began, of course, with the Japanese attack on Pearl Harbor on 7 December 1941 and ended with the Japanese surrender on 14 August 1945. It is estimated that worldwide 18,767,000 civilians and 16,928,000 military personnel were killed in the war.

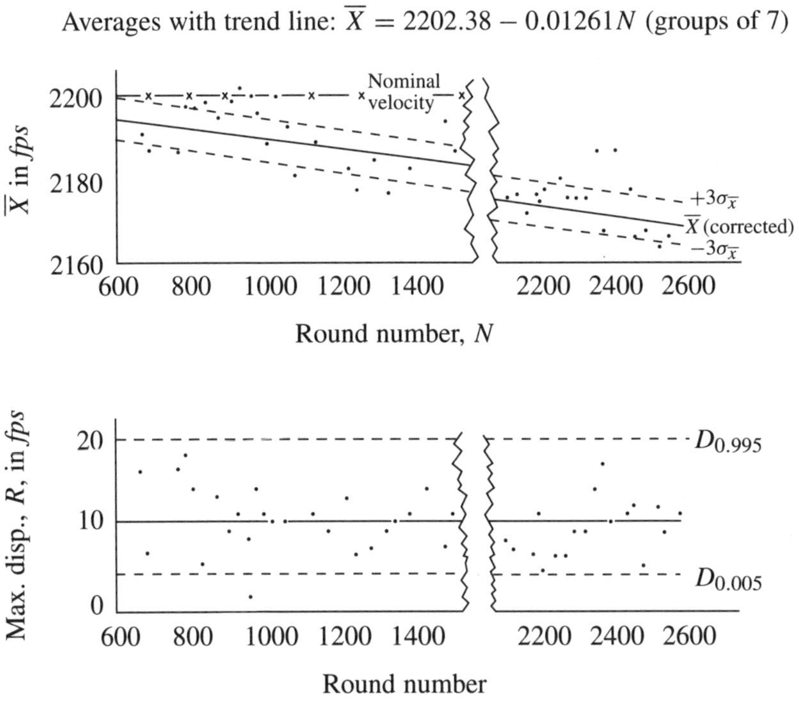

Figure 2 Simon's (1942, 316) control chart for the velocity of a gun over its test life cycle. Averages and dispersions for groups of 7.

With control charts, Simon (1942, 316) examined the "lives of guns that had been fired to the end of their test lives" to bring the calibration of guns used to test ammunition and the spacing of screens for velocity tests under statistical control (see figure 2).

A few years later, Simon sought to bring the artillery attack on Normandy under statistical control. Artillery ammunition was made in lots, it varied from lot to lot, and soldiers manning the guns usually fired experimental rounds to correct their aim for each new lot. For the attack on Normandy, it was impossible to supply units with ammunition lots of a large enough size to avoid the need for trial fires, which were out of the question for this surprise beach landing. In a dramatic tale Simon (1947) recounted how he and three other engineers flew to England to sample and sort ammunition until it was so uniform that trial fires would not be necessary to ensure accurate bombardment. Simon framed the problem in terms of the three causes of dispersion—establishment of powder charge, banding, and surface finish—and the two components of ammunition lots—powder lots and projectile lots. Simon concluded that the "economical solution of the problem is not that of sampling ammunition lots, as the artilleryman or ordinary engineer would suspect, but the sampling of the component powder lots and projectile lots" (1947, 277). Any lot that was out of control in terms of dispersion was discarded, but a difference in average value did not necessarily lead to rejection but rather to an assignment based on mean values. Simon and his team guided the sampling and sorting of a million rounds of 105mm ammunition at ammunition dumps throughout England. Within six weeks, 12 percent of the ammunition had been discarded and the usable ammunition had been sorted into three lots: white was expected to be on target according to standard firing tables, blue was expected to shoot over target, and red was expected to shoot short of the target (see figure 3; the "A," "B," and "C" ammunition refers to the white, blue, and red, respectively). The respective colors were painted on all boxes or crates of ammunition. Simon alleged that this sorting and sampling not only ensured that no Allied artillery ammunition fell on Allied troops, but it also "did much to change worried troops into confident and aggressive troops" (1947, 281).

Acceptance Inspection and Procurement

Procurement in World War II forced statistical quality control, which had before the war been confined to a few large corporations, onto every industry that supplied the U.S. war machine. The government achieved this enforcement through acceptance inspection, practice of SQC techniques in major military operations, education of corporate management in short university courses held nationwide, and in the development of new theories on sequential analysis and decision making through the Applied Mathematics Panel of the National Defense Research Committee.

Even before the war began, Colonel Simon was trying to persuade the military to adopt SQC. Simon argued that SQC would lead to greater uniformity of product, larger volume with no increase of costs, greater detection of trouble, useful documentation of quality in ordnance, and reductions in inspection and waste (Simon 1941).[11] In the early days

11. Simon's forecasts all proved accurate. At the initiation of SQC for ordnance purchases in September 1942, there were 42 ordnance inspectors per million dollars of material; by April

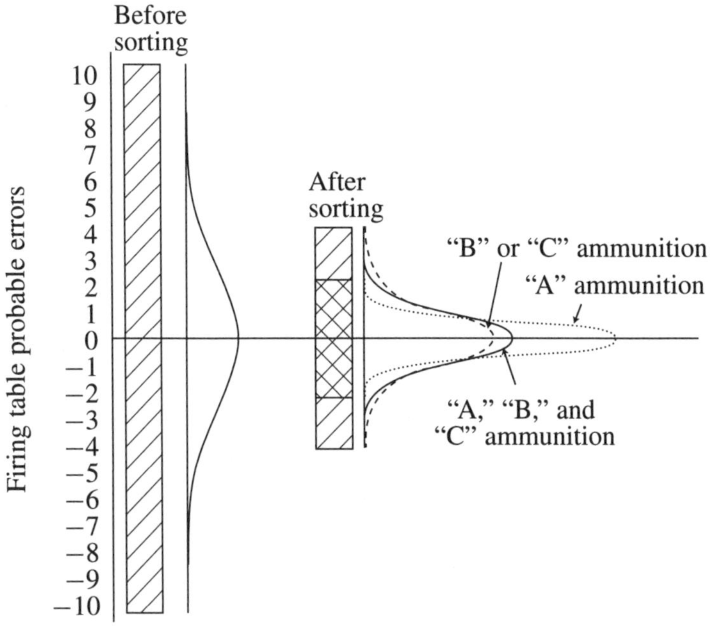

Figure 3 Simon's (1947, 279) schematic diagram of artillery ammunition before and after sorting for the attack on Normandy

of war emergency, the ordnance department of the United States Army adopted plans for acceptance sampling techniques and narrow quantitative tolerance limits. A major decision made in the emergency was that SQC would not be forced on suppliers through legislation but through the acceptance/rejection decisions of the ordnance department. District ordnance offices began implementation of SQC methods in September 1942 with the use of control charts in accepting armor plates. Within a few weeks, they were using sampling plans for a range of other ordnance materials. The navy, Quartermaster Corps, and Signal Corps soon followed suit.

The potential saving in scarce ordnance was the original incentive of the army's adoption of SQC methods. For many ordnance products, quality control tests inevitably led to the destruction of the product being

1943 only 12 inspectors per million dollars of ordnance were needed. Thus, despite a major increase in the flow of ordnance the number of inspectors declined from 20,000 to 13,000 (Safford 1946, 4).

tested. The adoption of SQC at proving grounds led, for example, to a 50 percent reduction in the total amount of ballistics testing necessary to judge the quality of armor plates. A similar approach to armor-piercing shot led to a 75 to 80 percent reduction in test rounds fired (Edwards 1942, 484). According to Warren Weaver, chief of the Applied Mathematics Panel, the sampling procedure recommended early in the war by the Columbia Statistical Research Group enabled the army to cut the portion of "Holy Moses" propellant destroyed in quality testing from 5 percent to 2 1/2 percent, thus achieving a savings of more than a million dollars a month (Weaver 1962, 617).

Army ordnance departments had used sampling before 1942. A sample from a manufacturer was tested and the sample was accepted or rejected. The innovations that Simon and other statisticians introduced in World War II were time-series analysis in the forms of control charts and accumulated knowledge from a large number of small samples and standard acceptance sampling plans. Under Simon's direction, the army ordnance department dug into its records and reorganized sample data by time and manufacturer. If control charts or sampling plans indicated that a manufacturer had statistical control over its process, the military reduced inspection of that manufacturer's product and allowed acceptance and payment before inspection took place on new shipments. The military encouraged economies and incentives, as Harold Dodge explained it, "by varying the quantity and severity of acceptance inspections in *direct* relation to the importance of the characteristics inspected, and in *inverse* relation to the goodness of the quality level as indicated by those inspections" (1969, 156).

Government Training of Quality Control Engineers

The military's acceptance inspection protocol was the chief way in which the government's use of statistical quality control influenced its application in the private sector. At the beginning of the war, the government placed inspectors in plants to assist in process inspection. By 1943, however, the government was insisting that its on-site employees would inspect only for acceptance, and manufacturers had to be responsible for their own quality control over process. The government, however, did provide clear specifications of acceptance limits, details of sampling inspection plans for each product, intensive courses in statistical quality control, and SQC manuals. Four examples of the latter include the War Department's *Guide for Quality Control, Control Chart Method of Analyzing Data, Chart Method of Controlling Quality during Production,* and *Ordnance Inspection Handbook on Standard Inspection Procedures, Quality Control.* The U.S. government applied acceptance sampling not only to munitions and ordnance but also to food, uniforms, office supplies, and communication equipment. The sampling plans for these items took into account the cost and importance of the material, and most were designed for 10 percent consumer risk (see, for example, Maack 1944).[12] By 1944, government expenditures represented one-half of all U.S. expenditures (see Cavin 1945), and the government was beginning to apply planning and quality control to civilian consumption goods.

Industrialists argued that the main impediment to statistical control over their own processes was lack of trained personnel (see, for example, "The Mathematical Manager" 1943). In response to demands from private suppliers for plant-based quality control engineers, the Office of Production Research and Development (OPRD) of the War Production Board and the National Defense Research Committee (NDRC) in early 1943 subsidized the eight-day training courses at various colleges and universities affiliated with the Engineering, Science and Management War Training Programs. By the summer of 1945, more than 8,000 persons from private industry had taken university courses, averaging fifty-seven semester hours, in SQC (Working 1945, 425). In contrast with the British government, which took the route of centralized consulting with a large staff, the U.S. government chose to help private industry through decentralized education directed by a permanent staff that never exceeded three.

The Carnegie Institute of Technology began offering evening courses in June 1941, but the prototype for intensive instruction came out of Holbrook Working and Edwin Olds's design for courses at Stanford.

12. In the Bell Labs schema, consumer risk was measured by the percent of lots accepted that were in essence defective, and producer risk was measured by the percent of good lots rejected. As Egon Pearson (1967, 83) noted, Shewhart's "emphasis on the need to measure producer's and consumer's risks also provided an unexpected practical illustration of Neyman's and my conception of the 'two kinds of error.'"

W. Edwards Deming, from the ordnance department, suggested the idea for the Stanford course to W. Allen Wallis, who had asked Deming how Stanford could help the war effort. Deming wrote, "You could accomplish a great deal by holding a school in the Shewhart methods some time in the near future" (letter from Deming quoted in Wallis 1980, 321). Wallis was soon called to Washington, but Deming taught the first course at Stanford in the summer of 1942 with Eugene Grant and Holbrook Working among the seventeen students. Within a few months, Ralph Wareham (from General Electric), Grant, Working, and Olds were teaching SQC courses. Working and Olds wrote an instructor's manual (1944) that was used in similar courses around the country. Working documented the breadth and success of the program in his 1945 paper in the *Journal of the American Statistical Association.*

Although the courses included explanations of acceptance sampling plans, their focus was on process quality control through the use of control charts. Working documented success stories that followed from these courses, including a reduction in variation in a critical dimension of ball bearings to one-fourth of that in precontrol chart days, a reduction in rejection rates in a steel foundry from 14 percent to 2 percent, and a saving of $125,000 annually through the use of a control chart on one aircraft assembly line (Working 1945, 425–26). To further persuade private manufacturers to adopt SQC, the government funded the publication of case studies written by former students who described the successful application of what they had learned in the intensive courses to their own production processes. The obligatory control chart in these case studies illustrated the before and after situations graduates encountered (see, for example, figure 4).[13] The government-educated civilian corps of quality control engineers became the kernel of a group that after the war would establish its own professional organization (American Society for Quality Control) and journal (*Industrial Quality Control*). In his 1980 account of the Columbia Statistical Research Group, Allen Wallis wrote, "Working and his colleagues brought about a significant increase in the productivity of American industry, for which he has not yet received proper recognition" (1980, 321).

13. The OPRD published at least ten quality control case studies. See, for example, the reports on John Deere Tractor (Fay 1945), Hoover Ball and Bearing (Trombly 1945), Lockheed (Crawford and Hammer 1945), and Radio Manufacture (Trowbridge and Clark 1945).

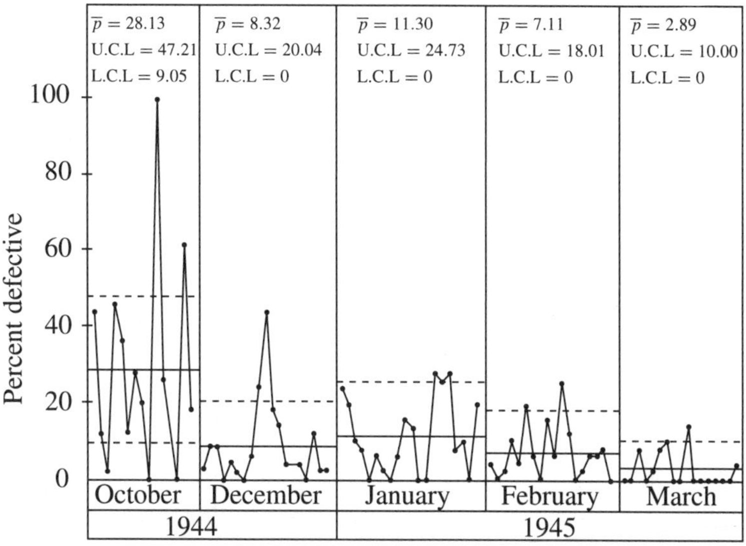

Figure 4 A John Deere control chart measuring the percentage of bushing nuts produced by an automatic screw machine that were defective. Fay (1945, 6) examined past data for this machine for October and started intervention to eliminate assignable causes in November. Within a few months John Deere had lowered the average percent defective from 28.13 to 2.89 percent. U.C.L.= upper control limit; L.C.L.= lower control limit.

The Statistical Research Group's Sequential Analysis

In the tale told so far, the U.S. government used SQC methods previously developed within the Bell system (e.g., Shewhart's control charts and Dodge and Romig's tables for single and double sampling plans) and encouraged their wide dissemination through procurement, publications, and courses. The government, however, through the Applied Mathematics Panel, was also responsible for the research and development of new theories and techniques that had major impacts on private industry and statistical and economic theory. In particular, military officers displeased with the large size of samples dictated by statisticians for proper testing of experimental guns turned to economists to devise a method of statistical testing that minimized the number of trials (and thus the costs of testing) necessary for given levels of consumer and producer risks (type 2 and type 1 errors respectively).

President Roosevelt had not appointed any mathematicians to the National Defense Research Committee when it was established in 1941. In the reorganization of 1942, however, the government decided that an Applied Mathematics Panel was necessary to complement the work of the scientists on the NDRC.[14] As Warren Weaver (1946, 5), chief of the Applied Mathematics Panel, reported, 53 of the panel's 194 studies during World War II were in the field of probability and statistics, including the development of statistical methods in inspection, sampling, and quality control. The larger umbrella organization of the Office of Scientific Research and Development also established contracts with Western Electric of the Bell system for help with statistical quality control for war procurement and manufacturing.

The chronology of the development of probability tests for sequential analysis illustrates the impact of government-funded applied mathematical research on industrial practice and the influence of an economic way of thinking on statistical theory. Sequential analysis grew out of the work of the Statistical Research Group at Columbia University that was headed by W. Allen Wallis and included Harold Hotelling, Milton Friedman, George Stigler, Leonard Savage, Frederick Mosteller, J. Wolfowitz, and Abraham Wald.[15] The Statistical Research Group (SRG) was

14. In her essay titled "The Mathematical Sciences and World War II," Mina Rees (1988) documents the applied work of mathematicians, including case studies from the AMP, wartime, and postwar computer programs, and the effects of wartime pursuits on the careers of mathematicians. Rees discusses immediate postwar strides made in linear programming for operations research through connections between George Dantzig's use of inequalities in complex problems of minimizing costs, George Stigler's study of subsistence costs, and T. C. Koopman's research in transportation theory. J. Barkley Rosser (1988) also discusses the applied work of mathematicians in World War II. With regard to the effect of the war effort on the mathematics discipline, Rees (1988, 280) quotes Churchill Eisenhart, who argued that the "essential service to American Mathematics was to help in making Applied Mathematics respectable." In a 1949 lecture titled "Some Recent Trends in Applied Mathematics," John H. Curtiss remarked, "It is further my guess that the mathematics courses in our universities and colleges may actually within a short time achieve a considerable measure of popularity formerly accorded only to the chemistry and economics courses. You will recall that it has been said that World War I was a chemists' war and that World War II was a physicists' war. There are those who say that the next world war, if one should occur, will be a mathematicians' war" (1949, 588).

15. For a discussion of some of the other research projects conducted by the Columbia Statistical Research Group, including those on game theory and experimental design, see Statistical Research Group 1947, Leonard 1991, and Mirowski 1991.

constituted on 1 July 1942 and disbanded on 30 September 1945. Wallis (1980) has provided those interested in the history of statistics and economics with a fascinating and thorough account of the SRG and the serendipitous development of their projects. The group included eighteen principals and sixty others, including thirty female computers who were generally mathematics majors from Hunter and Vassar. Recruiting for the group, according to Wallis, "was by the old-boy network pure and unabashed" (Wallis 1980, 325). Eight of the principals had studied or worked with Hotelling before the war. Wallis stressed the importance of the economic background of the principals:

> The fact that 7 of the 18 principals were primarily or secondarily economists—Bennett, Friedman, Hastay, Hotelling, Stigler, Wald and Wallis—unquestionably exerted a profound influence on the later statistical work of all members of the SRG, but especially on Savage's. It is, of course hard to separate the impact of the economists in SRG from the great influence on all statistical theory immediately after the war of game theory and decision theory, both of which are essentially economic theories. (Wallis 1980, 329)

In applying an economic way of thinking to statistical research, the SRG essentially developed an economics of experimentation and information. In reflecting on his wartime work with the SRG, Milton Friedman asserted that social scientists were more useful than natural scientists in wartime operations research:

> Social scientists were accustomed to working with lousy data, and wartime operational data certainly fitted that category. Natural scientists were accustomed to dealing with carefully controlled experimental data, and were often at a loss how to handle the kind of data turned out in wartime. (Friedman and Friedman 1998, 145)

Even in the context of controlled experimentation, however, the economists offered a perspective that resonated with wartime exigencies. The reports of the SRG frequently used the terms *optimal*, *efficiency*, *economy*, and *minimization of costs*. For example, in his modification of Shewhart's control charts for the air testing of bombsights, Hotelling frequently mentioned costs and trade-offs:

> In much quality-control work where individual inspection is cheap, inefficient statistical formulas are used frankly and deliberately when

> they are easy to calculate and to comprehend. The saving in computation represented by using the mean deviation instead of the standard deviation with many small batches may in some circumstances offset the increase of approximately one-eighth in the amount of inspection necessary to get the same accuracy. . . .
>
> Considerations of this kind should have no place where the unit cost is as great as that of dropping a bomb. Information acquired at such great expense should not be wasted by the use of inefficient statistical methods of combining the observations. . . .
>
> This plan may readily be adapted for efficient combination with experiments for determining the relative excellence of different models of sights and types of bombing, or for investigating other questions relating to bombing. Considerable economy in the total amount of bombing required should be obtainable by a proper design for experimenting simultaneously on various types of equipment and technique while at the same time carrying out the routine test bombing with full accuracy. (Hotelling 1947, 118, 140–41)[16]

Similarly, Milton Friedman introduced his report titled "Utilization of Limited Experimental Facilities when the Cost of Each Measurement Depends on Its Magnitude" with the following comment: "A primary objective in the statistical design of experiments is to maximize the amount of pertinent information obtained from a given amount of time, equipment, personnel, and supplies, or conversely, to minimize the cost of obtaining a given amount of information" (Friedman 1947, 321). With that objective in mind, Friedman used the mathematics of constrained optimization to design plans for metallurgical experiments that efficiently tested stress in alloys. The objective of the experiments was to recommend alloys for construction of blades for turbosuperchargers and gas turbines in high-temperature environments. Statistical techniques were only brought into play once the rapid progress of the early war years gave way to anomalies in the experiments designed to make further improvements: "Alloy A would test better than B, B than

16. William Kruskal (1980) asserts that although Hotelling's work had little direct impact on the bombsight testing program, it achieved major strides in the development of sophisticated control charts and multivariate statistical analysis. Hotelling modified the control chart for bivariate monitoring of errors in range as well as in deflection. Also, in meeting the challenge of testing the quality of complex equipment in a complex testing arena, Hotelling made use of the inverse of the estimated second-moment matrix to achieve an innovative algorithm for multivariate analysis of variance.

C, and then C would test better than A" (Friedman and Friedman 1998, 142). Friedman served as "a clearing agency for the results of the various experiments in progress, as an adviser on the statistical design of experiments, and as an analyst of the results" (142).[17] Once again, the economist's approach was optimization of the experimental process. By 1948, William Cochran was asserting in an Econometric Society report on recent developments in sampling theory that "the chief guiding principle in current research is that the object in taking a sample is to obtain estimates that have a minimum variance for a given cost, or alternatively a specified variance for minimum cost" (1948, 71).

The prime example of the Statistical Research Group's economics of statistical testing was their articulation of a sequential analysis of statistical hypothesis testing. In his 1980 essay, Wallis reproduced a 1943 memorandum to Wald and a 1950 letter to Warren Weaver that tell the story of the development of sequential analysis. The short description that follows draws on the 1950 letter and Warren Weaver's account in the Columbia Oral History interviews. According to Weaver, Captain Garret L. Schuyler in navy ordnance had confided to him that

> it's no good to go to a statistician and ask him to design an experiment to test shells, because they will design an experiment which is so long, which is so costly and which uses up so much of your shells that you've lost the war before you get the test over. (Weaver 1962, 619)[18]

Schuyler, however, found that economists trained in statistics were receptive to his concerns about minimizing cost while ensuring adequate sampling for quality control. According to Wallis, their investigation into sequential analysis was triggered in early 1943 by a comment from Captain Schuyler on how to compare test results from a new method of firing naval shells with an old method of firing:

17. It was in the course of Friedman's experiments with high-temperature alloys that his skepticism of multiple regression began. He booked forty hours on the unique Mark I computer at Harvard and obtained estimates of metallurgical parameters that fit the data well. Using the regression results he designed two new alloys (F-1 and F-2) that failed miserably in the subsequent MIT lab tests (see Friedman and Friedman 1998, 144, and Friedman and Schwartz 1991).

18. Weaver explained that he left out the profanity that apparently gilded Schuyler's every sentence.

> He brought up the problem of the necessary sample size for comparing two percentages and gave me a memorandum prepared for him on that subject by a certain John von Neumann. I had never before heard of the von Neumann fellow, but the memorandum was obviously very smart for a man who apparently knew little about statistics. (Wallis 1980, 325).

In further conversations, Schuyler was amazed by the large sample size that Wallis insisted was necessary for comparing percentages in ordnance testing. "A wise and seasoned ordnance expert," Schuyler argued, "would see after the first few thousand or even few hundred [rounds] that the experiment need not be completed, either because the new method is obviously inferior or because it is obviously superior beyond what was hoped for" (Wallis 1980, 325).[19]

Schulyer's challenge was initially taken up by Wallis and Friedman, who approached the problem of errors in hypothesis testing with the goal, so strongly cultivated in the economics discipline, of efficient allocation of scarce resources. As statisticians of the day saw it, there were two types of errors in testing the hypothesis that the new method of firing was better than the old. The first type of error was accepting the hypothesis that the new method was better than the old when it was not. The second type of error was rejecting that hypothesis when it was true. According to Abraham Wald's account,

> It was conjectured by W. Allen Wallis and Milton Friedman jointly that sequential tests would have far reaching consequences for the theoretical foundations of statistics, beyond their immediate practical applications, and that in a sense they are more efficient than the current best tests, i.e. the "most powerful" tests. More precisely, it was conjectured that there exists a sequential test that controls the errors of the first and second kind to exactly the same extent (has exactly the same α and β) as the current most powerful test, and at the same time

19. Three centuries before, a gambler asked Galileo Galilei to confirm logically his seasoned intuition that the probability of a ten being thrown with three dice was greater than that for nine, even though both could be made from the same diversity of numbers (see Galilei [1642] 1962, 195, and Klein 1997, 145). Galileo calculated that the probability of a ten being thrown was .125 and that of a nine was .116, a difference of only .009. His pursuit of this query led to new reasoning on probability theory. The challenge Schuyler posed to Wallis was similar: embody the intuition of the seasoned inspector into a mathematical formula that could give rise to standard guidelines to green inspectors so that they too could tell when to stop the test firing before wasting precious ammunition and time.

requires an expected number of trials considerably smaller than the number of trials required by the current most powerful test procedure. It was this conjecture of Friedman and Wallis which gave the author the incentive for carrying out the present investigation. (Wald 1943, 5–6)

Friedman and Wallis posed the idea of such a test to Wald, who in March and April 1943 devised a sequential probability ratio test.[20] This test established a decision protocol for each additional observation and signaled at what point the sampling procedure could be terminated with the researcher confident that the inspection was sufficient. With each new observation, the inspectors decide whether they now have enough information to accept the hypothesis, or whether they can now reject it, or whether they have to keep seeking further information.

In September 1943 the Statistical Research Group published a classified Applied Mathematics Panel report by Wald on sequential analysis and in July 1943 published a report by H. A. Freeman on applications. The navy, through John Curtiss, suggested that levels of the actual count of defectives as a function of sample size would be more practical than likelihood ratios. The military audience also called forth a format that replaced, where possible, equations with tables (sampling plans) and charts. This algorithmic tailoring for practical inspection and testing in the military ensured that sequential sampling plans were not only more

20. Wallis (1980, 325) recounts his and Friedman's agonizing over the decision as to whether to turn the idea over to someone with more strength in mathematical statistics.

The idea behind sequential analysis was not entirely new. As Wallis described it, Wald "simply sequentialized" the Neyman-Pearson likelihood ratio. Wald explained that Dodge and Romig's (1929, 1941) sampling plans and Harold Hotelling's (1941) experimental determination of the maximum of a function could be seen as forerunners to sequential analysis. One finds conjecture on endogenous sample size in early debates. For example, in his Royal Statistical Society discussion of his quality control investigation on light bulbs in the British General Electric Laboratories, Bernard Dudding stated, "It will be obvious that as the knowledge of the variations in quality of the product accumulates, so the engineer directing the work could better determine where to fix his rejection limits, and how many specimens to include in his sample batch in order that the money spent in testing and re-testing should be the minimum, consistent with the risk of passing material below the safe level" (quoted in Pearson 1934, 144). In the AT&T (1989) oral history of quality control, Joseph Juran explains that he and Dodge independently invented the notion of minimum inspection per lot. Juran says that during World War II, "that concept got latched onto by a number of the professors of statistics and the like. They had a wonderful time digging into minimum inspection per lot trying to squeeze the last drop of blood out of the minimum." The significant and unique contribution that Wald made was the sequential probability ratio test and the formal analysis that supported it.

efficient in minimizing sample size, but they were also often simpler to use with fewer on-the-job calculations needed, compared with previous sampling plans.

George Barnard, who around the same time was trying to develop a sequential procedure for sampling in British industry, asserted that many engineering inspectors "untutored in the theory of statistical hypothesis" had been in essence practicing sequential analysis. According to Barnard, "Sequential theory only makes precise these common-sense procedures" (1946, 3). The Statistical Research Group's mathematical derivation of a probability ratio test and complements to that, such as the operating characteristics curve, were, however, not examples of "unpublishable common sense" that Høyrup (1994) alleges comprised most of the output of wartime mathematics. Publication of the theory and applications of sequential analysis took many forms, including Wald's journal articles in the *Journal of the American Statistical Association* (1945a), *Annals of Mathematical Statistics* (1945b), and *Econometrica* (1947a), and books by Wald (1947b) and the SRG (1948). The reports to the Applied Mathematics Panel remain the most lucid accounts of the prescribed practice, as opposed to the theory. An illustrative example given in AMP report 30.2R describes the sequential procedure for testing the quality of some protective material:

> A certain protective material is satisfactory if it is completely perforated by not more than 15 percent of cal. 30 AP M2 bullets fired at normal obliquity for 1 foot range. It is not acceptable if the percentage is 30 or more. The user is willing to take 2 chances in 100 of accepting bad material and 1 chance in 100 of rejecting good material. (Statistical Research Group 1945, 2.21)

These a priori specifications of acceptable quality tolerance (.15), unacceptable tolerance limit (.30), and type 2 error or "consumer risk" ($\beta = .02$) and type 1 error or "producer risk" ($\alpha = .01$) were plugged into formulas or mapped onto nomograms. The calculations were used to determine either a tabular sampling plan or the intercepts and the slope of the parallel lines for graphic analysis.[21] In the illustrative example in figure 5, the first seven shots do not perforate the protective armor. There

21. The Special Devices Division, Office of Research and Inventions of the Navy, even designed machines dedicated only to sequential analysis: "For each item inspected, the inspector presses one key of two keys, depending on whether the item is defective or satisfactory, and a signal is given when a decision is reached" (Statistical Research Group 1945, 2.04).

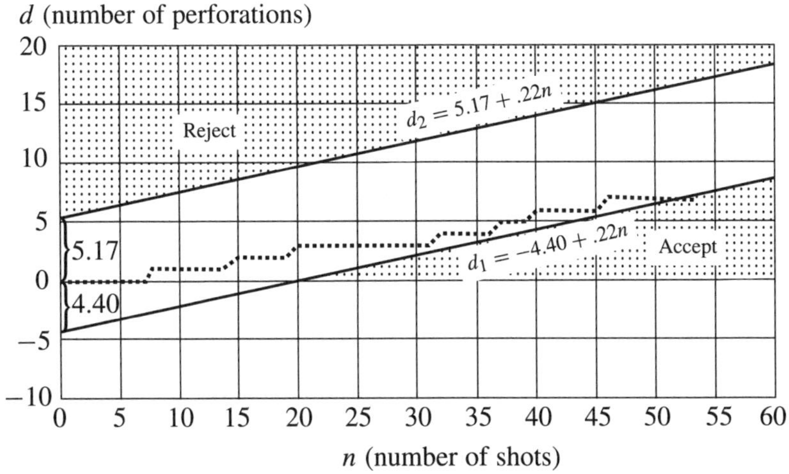

Figure 5 Graph of sequential procedure for inspecting protective material, from the Statistical Research Group's (1945, 2.24) AMP report on applications of sequential analysis

is, however, perforation on shots 8, 15, 20, 32, 37, 40, and 46. With each shot the inspecting team plotted the results of the accumulated sample information (follow the dotted line from 0 to 53) and saw whether their new coordinate fell in the rejection, acceptance, or continue-firing region of the graph. With the fifty-third shot, the sample was declared to be acceptable and the test firing ceased.

Wald's procedure was a plan of action that preserved statistical quality control while minimizing the number of observations. As Wald described it in a Columbia Statistical Research Group report to the Applied Mathematics Panel,

> The effect is as if we were to use the data as they come in for redetermining continuously the necessary number of trials. Thus, the sequential test automatically leads us to make few trials where the deficiency or superiority of the lot is so great as to be apparent from a small amount of data, and leads us to make many trials when the lot is on the margin of acceptability.
>
> For a wide class of problems sequential tests are more efficient and more economical than those now in use, in the sense that they give equally sound conclusions with, on the average, a smaller amount

> of data (or more reliable conclusions with, on the average, the same amount of data). A remarkable feature of sequential tests is that even when the lot tested actually is at the margin of acceptability, as the tests now in use assume it to be, a sequential test is (if applicable) more efficient and economical than the best existing tests. In fact the ratio of superiority in most cases is in the neighborhood of two-to-one. And from the preceding paragraph, it is clear that the superiority of sequential tests is even greater when the lot tested is not near the margin. (Wald 1943, iv–v)

In the case of sequential analysis, persuasion was as potent as investigation in evoking new forms of mathematical reasoning and graphic analysis. It behooved the SRG to convince the military that sequential analysis was usually more efficient for acceptance inspection than the single and double sampling plans that had previously guided almost all major procurement. Graphs are generally more effective than equations in the political arithmetic of persuasion, and in this case the operating characteristic curves and the average sample number curves (see figure 6) were important complements to the sampling tables and charts. Milton Friedman was instrumental in deriving these visions of persuasion that also enabled those constructing their own sampling plans to judge the relative protection of possible plans and to compare typical sample sizes for specified levels of protection. According to Wallis's recollection, Friedman noticed that each time four a priori specifications (see the specifications of tolerance and risk levels for protective material described above) were put into the testing algorithm, only three parameters (two intercepts and the slope for the two parallel lines) emerged:

> Friedman was the first to point this out and he naturally asked, "Where is the vanished parameter?" More specifically he pointed out that there must be many combinations of the original four parameters which lead to the same final set of three. Now, finding all of the sets of four that lead to a given set of three amounts to finding what the probabilities of acceptance are for all possible lot qualities, which is what is known as the operating characteristic curve. Its complement is called the power function. . . . At any rate this opened up a whole new range of activity for Wald's theoretical abilities, and a whole new spurt in theoretical developments. (Wallis 1980, 327).

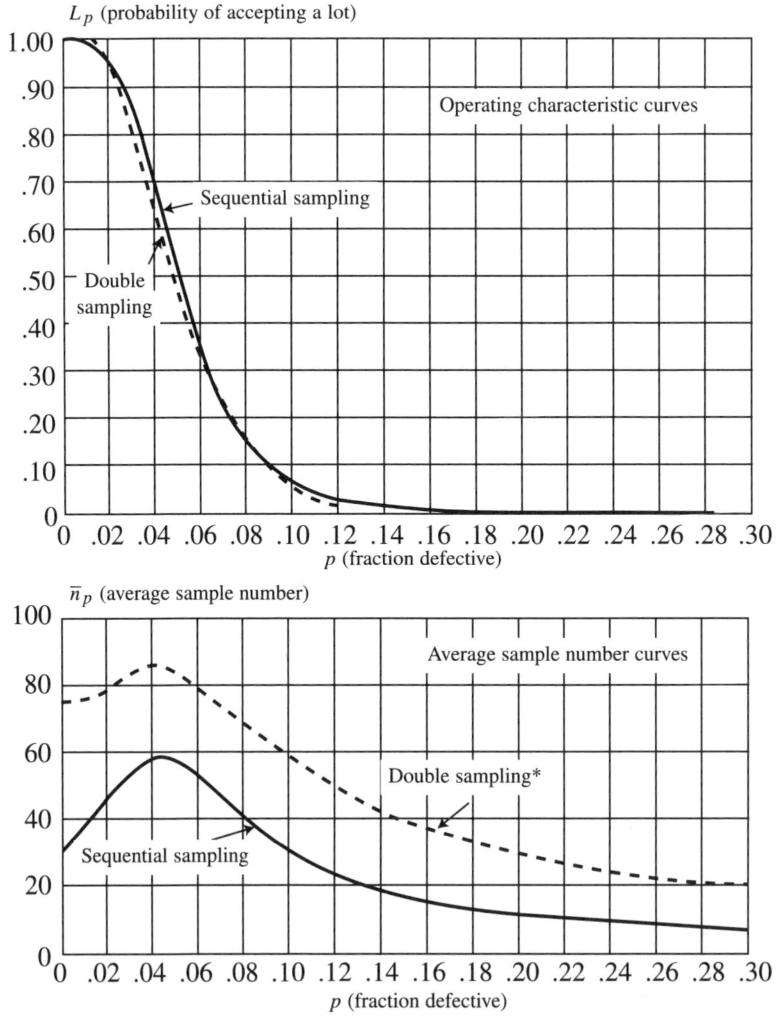

Figure 6 A comparison of sequential and double sampling inspection. Sequential sampling plan defined by $p_1 = .02$, $p_2 = .09$, $\alpha = .05$, $\beta = .10$. Double sampling plan defined by $n_1 = 75$, $n_2 = 150$, $c_1 = 3$, $c_2 = 5$; $N = 800$–1,299. The operating characteristic curve enables the researcher or inspector to gauge the level of protection in a sampling plan chosen based on specification of risks and tolerance limits. The OCC is then used to determine the average sample size that would come from sampling according to those specifications. The ASN curves were used to illustrate that for a similar level of protection, sequential sampling inevitably led to a smaller required sample size than double or single sampling (Statistical Research Group 1945, 2.27).

*Assuming items are examined one at a time and the lot is rejected as soon as $c_2 + 1$ defects are found.

Duly persuaded, the navy rapidly adopted sequential plans for acceptance inspection. The result was a dramatic reduction in necessary resources devoted to inspection. For example, in the summer of 1945, the Quartermaster Corps reported:

> We have had a 40% increase in workload in the past six months with a 5% increase in personnel. . . . I do not believe there is any doubt but that the use of [sequential] sampling plans has assisted us greatly in carrying this load.
>
> That this saving of inspection was by no means due to superficiality of coverage is borne out by figures showing a considerable improvement in quality following introduction of sequential sampling plans. (Enrick 1946, 12)[22]

The potential benefit to the military was deemed so valuable that the reports on sequential analysis were classified as "Restricted" under the Espionage Act.[23] Within months of Wald's formulation of a sequential probability ratio test, the government was applying this decision-making protocol on acceptance inspection to thousands of suppliers, and private sector demand for access to information on this procedure escalated. In March 1945, after one year of secret testing of sequential sampling procedures, the quartermaster general asked the National Defense Research Committee to declassify and widely disseminate the information on sequential process control so that private contractors could practice it and increase the quality and quantity supplied to the military while reducing their waste and their production costs. The reports on sequential analysis were immediately made public. They were to be the only AMP reports declassified during the war. By October 1945, at least 6,000 firms reported sampling plans based on sequential analysis; that number had been increasing at a rate of 500 a month by the end of the war (Weaver 1946, 5). Sixteen years later, Warren Weaver remarked:

22. Wallis said that some of the credit that has subsequently been given to sequential analysis for the improvements in the Quartermaster Corps should have been given to the stern leadership of a Colonel Rogow: "Sequential analysis became the opposite of a scapegoat: something to which all credit should be attached, so that it would not be necessary to say that they were simply doing what could have been done twenty years sooner" (Wallis 1980, 327).

23. Wallis (1980) discusses the irony that Wald's work was classified even though he was an enemy alien and thus had no clearance to read classified material. His contribution did, however, lead to his being one of the few enemy aliens to receive U.S. citizenship during the war.

> From that moment to this, there have been not only several large volumes written about sequential analysis, there have been I suppose hundreds of research papers. It turned out to be the beginning of a whole new field of statistical analysis. It was born of the war. It was born of the destructive testing of military explosives. It was born partly in the mind of Captain Schuyler, partly in the minds of Alan Wallis and his colleagues, and to a very large extent, in the mind of Professor Wald. (Weaver 1962, 621)

Postwar Production

In his essay "The Meaning of Discipline," Max Weber wrote, "The discipline of the army gives birth to all discipline. The large-scale economic organization is the second great agency which trains men for discipline" (1946, 261). Several large manufacturing corporations maintained and enhanced their disciplined statistical control over production processes even when U.S. military consumption dramatically declined at the end of the war. One case study (Brumbaugh 1945) of a large manufacturer (who chose to remain anonymous) illustrates the dramatic change brought about by closer tolerances and increased inspection. In 1942, the firm in question had to convert to 100 percent war production of a product similar to what they had been producing. They stored a sizable inventory of their final goods and parts that had been produced for the private market in a warehouse for the duration of the war. When production for the civilian market resumed near the end of the war, they decided to use their old inventory to gain an edge in the market. The chief inspector was startled by the results of his quality check on the piece parts produced before the war. As figure 7 makes clear, prewar production had been out of statistical control—dispersion in prewar samples was much greater than in war samples. Less than 14 percent of the prewar inventory could be assembled without rework, and 20 percent had to be totally scrapped. The author of the case study, Martin Brumbaugh, noted, "This inventory of piece parts can be made into marketable product only by setting up a small machine shop in the assembly area and then relying entirely upon selective assembly. This will be a costly procedure which is warranted solely on the basis of market advantage" (1945, 12). That business, like many others, had grown accustomed to the more efficient random assembly without reworking that had been cultivated by government insistence on uniform product, narrow tolerances, and sampling inspection.

As Theodore Brown wrote in the *Harvard Business Review* a few years after the war ended,

> Statistical quality control or, more simply quality control has been called the greatest advance in manufacturing during the last quarter century. Whatever may be the truth of this opinion, the fact is that many progressive companies such as Sheaffer Pen, Gillette Safety Razor, International Harvester, Ford Motor, and General Electric have installed quality control methods and are firm in the belief that their use secures better products, reduced costs, and improved worker relations. (1951, 69)

Not all businesses, however, followed suit. Joseph M. Juran (1995), who had worked on quality control in the Bell system, asserts that the tremendous pent-up demand for consumer goods in the face of great shortages immediately after the war destroyed the cost-effectiveness of many quality control programs. Also, as Mark Jahn (1992) points out, the war had shifted the emphasis from controlling manufacturing processes toward acceptance inspection.

In his AT&T oral history interview (1989), W. Edwards Deming asserted that lack of attention to process explained the reason for the failure of statistical quality control to fully revolutionize postwar American industry: "It died away after the war—just was gone—because people did not understand processes. They didn't understand management as a process." For Deming, part of the blame lay with the statisticians who emphasized Neyman and Pearson's "enumerative" solution to "analytic" problems. The Neyman-Pearson approach was fine in answering questions of how much, how many—that is, sampling in acceptance inspection—but useless for predicting what was the best method. It offered no "deep insight into the stability of a system."[24] Shewhart, on the other hand, had focused on the "capability of a process" and had argued

24. In a similar vein, George Box of the Center for Quality and Productivity Improvement at the University of Wisconsin–Madison recently criticized the placement of statistics in the mathematical sciences rather than the experimental or industrial sciences: "The present training of many statisticians renders them competent to *test* a tentative solution to a problem once it has been reached but not to take part in the long, painstaking and often exciting job of discovering that solution. In other words they are not equipped to take part in the process of investigation itself. . . . Mathematics has once more succeeded in killing the dynamic features of this kind of experimentation and analysis. In particular one listens to many discussions

that there is "no knowledge without prediction." According to Deming, "The only job for management and government is prediction." Deming said that even he did not fully own up to the importance of process until the 1950s. By that time it was Japanese rather than American industry that was most receptive to this view of statistical quality control.

In 1946, Japanese manufacturers organized the Union of Japanese Scientists and Engineers and made contact with inspection engineers on detail in Japan from Bell Telephone Laboratories. In 1950, the Japanese union brought Deming over to teach courses in statistical quality control (see Deming 1967, 1982; AT&T 1989; and Nonaka 1995). The courses, according to Deming, differed from the U.S. wartime courses in that top managers were involved, Japanese industrialists were desperate to improve their market share, and all participants had studied calculus. In 1954, Juran also began a series of courses in Japan. Japanese engineers, including Kaoru Ishikawa and Genichi Taguchi, also visited Shewhart at Bell Laboratories in 1958 and 1962. By the time of Taguchi's second visit to Bell Laboratories in 1980, however, the Japanese were teaching the Americans rather than vice versa (see Godfrey 1986, Ishikawa 1980, and Taguchi 1981). The American loss of market share to the Japanese forced U.S. manufacturers to once again take an interest in statistical quality control, this time with a new buzzword—*statistical process control.* Within this renewed emphasis on process, the control chart became an analytical tool for experimenting with changes to the production process—control engineers generated disturbances to study the capabilities of processes.

Postwar Theory

Before concluding about the interactions of economic theory and statistical quality control, I want to take stock of key points raised so far.

1. Combining an applied welfare economics, theories on statistical variation, and management practice, Bell system inspection engineers articulated the concept of processes under statistical control. A process under statistical control was one that generated a product that was uniform as manifested in a mean and a variance that remained constant no matter what time segment a sample was

of the generation of fixed designs in fixed regions in known variables which have dubiously 'optimal' properties" (1996, 4, 6).

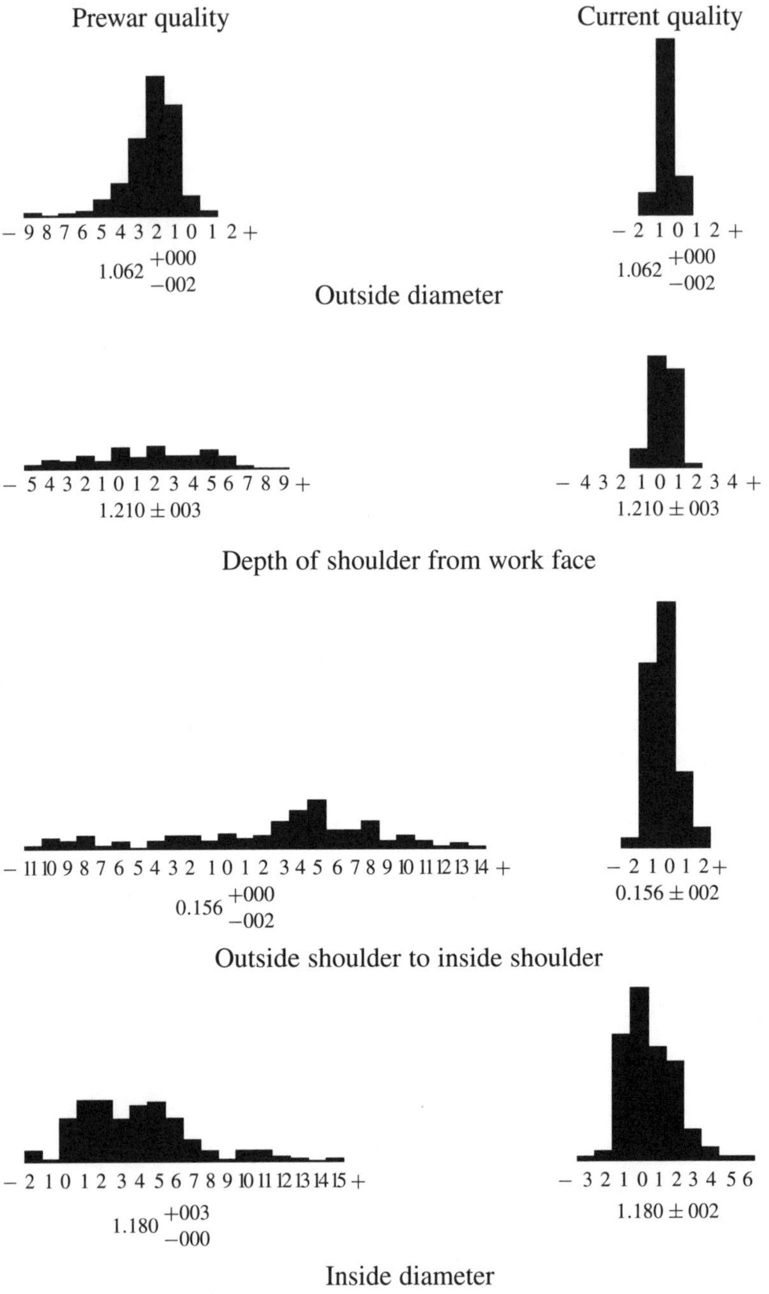

Figure 7 Quality of stored inventory of parts produced before the war compared with wartime parts (Brumbaugh 1945, 11)

selected from. This abstraction was shaped in the 1920s, a few years before mathematical statisticians articulated the concept of the stationary stochastic process.

2. The Bell engineers' attempts to eliminate seasonal variation and trends in the phenomena of production processes paralleled the attempts of economic statisticians to eliminate seasonal variation and trends in their observations of phenomena.
3. There was also a parallel with statistical theory in the articulation of producer risk and consumer risk that corresponded to type 1 and type 2 errors in the Neyman-Pearson probability scheme for testing hypotheses.
4. Institutionalized incentives for static mathematical theory on the one hand and dynamic practice on the other generated constructive tension. The culture of Bell Labs stressed the investigation of mathematical validity and encouraged publication in academic journals. The culture of the Hawthorne Works at Western Electric demanded effective, operational rules of thumb on processes; energy directed to external publication was seen as a misuse of resources. During World War II, civilian statisticians working for the National Defense Research Committee, including those in the Statistical Research Group at Columbia University, used probability theory to generate proofs, equations, and likelihood parameters. When permitted, they usually published results in the *Annals of Mathematical Statistics*. The military, on the other hand, insisted on a user-friendly, practical orientation. In both the Bell system and the World War II government cases, the communicative bridge between theory and practice was a visual algorithm—control charts, sampling tables, graphs of sequential procedure, or operating characteristic curves.
5. Although Shewhart's invention of the control chart preceded the Dodge-Romig and sequential sampling tables, businesses and government agencies in the 1930s and 1940s usually gave priority to acceptance sampling inspection rather than process control. In the 1950s in Japan and the 1970s in the United States, inspection engineers and applied statisticians revitalized Shewhart's focus on process.
6. Major developments in statistical quality control occurred in climates of imperfect competition such as the vertically integrated monopoly of the Bell system, the ordnance departments of military

> services, and the government/industry embraces of postwar Japan. In these cases, cost minimization was a major stimulus to statistical quality control, and economic theory provided the structure for determining the ideal points that ought to be achieved. This application of engineering economics led to an economizing of testing resources and to more stable processes producing uniform products.

We have seen how business and government employment of hundreds who could apply the "science of economizing" led to changes in production, procurement, and inspection procedures. Was this concerted application of economics at the expense of theoretical developments in the discipline as Høyrup (1994) has argued was the case for wartime employment of mathematicians? During World War II, hundreds of economists, statisticians, and scientists were hired to pool their expertise to tell a client what to do. A major product of this client orientation was a statistical theory of decision-making processes that seeded postwar developments in systems analysis, game theory, and behavioristic statistics.[25]

The impact of this client orientation on subsequent statistical theory is clear. Hundreds of articles and books have been written on sequential analysis, entire graduate courses are now devoted to the subject, and there is an academic journal titled *Sequential Analysis*. After the war, Wald made further abstractions on the optimum character of the sequential probability ratio test, connected his theory on sequential analysis to the random walk, applied his "economizing" to the process of estimation itself, and demonstrated that optimization of decision functions, which weighted loss and took into consideration costs of experimentation, could serve as a starting point for tackling almost any statistical problem (see Wald 1948, 1949, and Wolfowitz 1952). In his brief overview of the legacy of Wald's sequential probability ratio test, Donald Darling (1976) discusses subsequent developments in open-end tests

25. Statistical quality control constructs a systematic process that leads to decisions. It is thus closely related to the philosophy and practice of operations research that grew out of World War II and early Cold War military research. In his essay "Quality Control and Operations Research" (1957) Paul Olmstead examines the similarities and differences between the nature, contexts, and applications of the two decision processes. Philip Mirowski (forthcoming), Esther-Mirjam Sent (1998), and Judy Klein (1999a, 1999b) also discuss the impact of World War II developments in operations research and control engineering on the economics discipline and on military funding of economics research during the Cold War.

and the theory of optimal stopping. Darling asserts that the statistical pursuit of stopping time that maximizes some payoff is now intimately related to mathematical theories of martingales and dynamic programming. In his report on the foundations of behavioristic statistics, Jerzy Neyman (1971) speaks to pre-Wald notions of sequential procedures embodied in the work of Walter Bartky at Bell Labs and post-Wald developments by George Barnhard, Herbert Robbins, Donald Darling, and Charles Stein. While acknowledging the major step taken with Wald's sequential probability ratio test, Neyman points out that Wald had focused only on the economy of sequential tests over those of fixed sample size, and the full potential arising from the admission of infinitely dimensional sample space was not realized until two decades later. In his *Foundations of Statistics*, Leonard Savage, who had worked with Wald in the SRG during the war, explains how Wald's statistical decision theory built on Jerzy Neyman's call for the mathematical statistical study of "inductive behavior" in opposition to mere "inductive inference" ([1954] 1972, 159). Jacob Marschak (1946, 109) asserted that whereas von Neumann and Morgenstern's work on game theory had established that being an "economic man" implied being a "statistical man," Wald had established that "statistical man" must be an "economic man."

Paul Samuelson declared that Wald's development of sequential analysis would have made him a likely candidate for a Nobel Prize in statistics had there been such an award. Samuelson explained, "Not only has Wald's theory been thrown into immediately practical form, but in addition he was able unknowingly to make numerous contributions to the classical problem of 'gambler's ruin,' upon which much time has been spent by such immortals as Huyghens, James Bernoulli, De Moivre, Lagrange, Laplace and others" (Samuelson 1950, 142). Indeed, Samuelson (1948) devoted some of his own research time to mathematical investigation of the links between sequential analysis, gambler's ruin, and other problems of conditional probability.

Sequential analysis also became an analogy that economists applied to technological change and decision making. For example, Zvi Griliches, referring to Wald's work, used the analogy of the inverse relationship between the necessary sample size and the difference between the population means to explain how differences in the rate of acceptance of hybrid corn were related to differences in the profitability of switching from openly pollinated seed to a hybrid seed (1957, 516).

Similarly, Kenneth Arrow (1958, 5–6) saw Wald's theory of sequential analysis as a useful analogy for describing learning with positive and negative feedback or for modeling the strategy of firms making choices in the face of uncertainty.[26] The government's enforcement of statistical quality control and the sampling plans that came from the military's attempts to minimize cost also influenced the economic theories of the firm (see Cooper 1951) and of nonprice competition (see Chamberlin 1953).

It was, however, in the theoretical areas of strategy, gaming, and risk taking that the Statistical Research Group's work on sequential analysis had the most impact. Prior to World War II, Wald (1939) had articulated notions of weight, loss, and risk within a mathematical decision space. Independently of John von Neumann and Oskar Morgenstern, Wald had demonstrated that the risk function of a minimax solution was constant.[27] In his prewar work on statistical decision functions, however, all the observations were drawn from cross-sectional samples. Wald's wartime work on statistical quality control forced him to think of decision making as a process in time and to construct samples in which information accumulated sequentially and subsequently added to the costs of experimentation. After the war, Wald and SRG colleagues Wolfowitz and Savage blended this sequential accumulation of information with Bayesian statistical theory on a priori distributions, mathematical functions that embodied both risk and costs of experimentation, and von Neumann and Morgenstern's work on two-person, zero-sum games (see, for example, Wald and Wolfowitz 1950).[28] Wald added the choice of relying on the outcome of a random generator (e.g., a pair of dice) to

26. In his presidential address to the Econometric Society, Arrow (1957) also drew on Wald's theories of sequential analysis and statistical decision strategy to argue that the paucity of appropriate economic time-series data meant that the government could not solve sequential decisions problems to the extent that optimal automatic rules would be better than discretionary policy.

27. In *General Equilibrium Analysis* (1993) Roy Weintraub explores Wald's prewar experience in Vienna and discusses his encounters with game theory and his contributions to mathematical economics. Savage saw Wald's application of the minimax principle to statistical decisions on a level of importance with Thomas Bayes's work: "It is the only rule of comparable generality proposed since Bayes' was published in 1763" (Savage 1951, 59). Thomas Ferguson (1976) provides historical context for exploring the significance of Wald's statistical decision model and its connection with game theory.

28. In Wald's statistical decision theory, the two-person game was played between the statistician and "nature," and the loss function was the negative of the payoff function that had been specified by von Neumann and Morgenstern.

other options facing any decision maker. Wald applied statistics to game theory and game theory to statistics and generalized the minimax solution to the case of infinite sets of strategies. Complementary to Wald's theory of statistical action, Savage championed normative, behavioristic statistics and sequential thinking. For example, in a debate with Maurice Allais on irrationality revealed by experiments (the Allais paradox), Savage suggested a quasi-empirical test of rationality where with each new situation that tests an initial set of normative preferences, the holder of these preferences must decide whether to maintain the preferences or to adjust the preferences in light of the new challenge to those preferences (see Savage [1954] 1972, 102).

Wald had hoped that the 1950 publication of his treatise *Statistical Decision Functions* would inspire many to take up the work of statistical action. The research program on statistical decisions, however, was cut short by the death of Wald and his wife in an airplane crash in India in December 1950. In memorial articles and in book reviews written after his death, Morgenstern (1951), Wolfowitz (1952), Gerhard Tintner (1952), Savage (1951), and Lindley (1951) summarized Wald's postwar theoretical achievements that his work on statistical quality control stimulated.

Superficially at least, this appears to be a tale of applied economics inspiring new developments in decision theory, statistical theory, and economic theory. Wald's postwar work certainly has the trappings of theory rather than application. Reviewers, for example, described the "formidable" and "impenetrable" mathematics of Wald's postwar publications that could encompass four different topologies on one page. Wolfowitz (1952, 4) explains that although Wald never lost sight of the fact that "there was a question to be answered and a decision to be made," his very abstract mathematical approach did not easily lend itself to specific applications. If one, however, looks at the first footnote in all of Wald's postwar publications on statistical decision functions, one sees that the paymaster was the Office of Naval Research. In contrast with the specific tasks handed to the Statistical Research Group during World War II, Wald's research funded by the navy during the Cold War was not directed to the solution of specific problems. The navy, however, was a client paying for research on how to decide what to do. At the command of the Bell system before the war, the U.S. government during the war, and the United States Navy after the war, Shewhart, Wald, and their colleagues applied principles of political economy to "ascertain the rule of action" that Jean-Baptiste Say alluded to in his treatise of 1803.[29] The outcomes were statistical theories of decision making that, within a framework of reducing costs of inspection or experimentation, attempted to control production and prescribe optimal behavior.

References

Arrow, Kenneth J. 1957. Statistics and Economic Policy. *Econometrica* 25.4:523–31.

———. 1958. Utilities, Attitudes, Choices: A Review Note. *Econometrica* 26.1:1–23.

AT&T. 1989. *A History of Quality Control and Assurance at AT&T, 1920–1970.* Fourteen videocassettes containing interviews with Paul Olmstead, Joseph Juran, W. Edwards Deming, Mary Torrey, Bonnie Small, John Tukey, and others.

Barnard, George A. 1946. Sequential Tests in Industrial Statistics. *Journal of the Royal Statistical Society* 8 (supplement): 1–26.

Box, George E. P. 1996. Scientific Statistics, Teaching, Learning, and the Computer. In *COMPSTAT Proceedings in Computational Statistics, 12th Symposium Held in Barcelona Spain, 1996*, edited by Albert Prat. Heidelberg: Physica-Verlag.

Brown, Theodore H. 1951. Quality Control. *Harvard Business Review* 29.6:69–80.

Brumbaugh, Martin A. 1945. A Report on Pre-War Quality. *Industrial Quality Control* 2.2:11–12.

Cavin, J. P. 1945. Aspects of Wartime Consumption. *American Economic Review, Papers and Proceedings* 35.2:15–36.

Chamberlin, Edward H. 1953. The Product as an Economic Variable. *Quarterly Journal of Economics* 67.1:1–29.

Cochran, William G. 1948. Recent Developments in Sampling Theory in the United States. *Econometrica* 16:71–77.

Cooper, W. W. 1951. A Proposal for Extending the Theory of the Firm. *Quarterly Journal of Economics* 65.1:87–109.

Crawford, James R., and C. Preston Hammer. 1945. *Statistical Quality Control at Lockheed.* Office of Production Research and Development, Quality Control Reports, vol. 9. Pittsburgh: Carnegie Institute of Technology.

Curtiss, J. H. 1949. Some Recent Trends in Applied Mathematics. *American Scientist* 37:587–88, 618, 620, 622, 624.

29. See the reference to Say on the first page of Backhouse and Biddle's introduction. The client orientation determined the specific nature of the rules of action. In Cold War military strategy, severely shaped by the actions of two nuclear-armed superpowers, the zero-sum, two-person game had great appeal (see Mirowski forthcoming). Thus the minimax solution was useful and, in the absence of multiple equilibria, the Nash equilibrium was uninteresting. Game theory eventually thrived outside the military-funded research programs (see Dimand in this volume), but the zero-sum, two-person game with the minimax solution lost dominance to a much more general reasoning.

Darling, Donald A. 1976. The Birth, Growth, and Blossoming of Sequential Analysis. In *On the History of Statistics and Probability*, edited by D. B. Owen. New York: Marcel Dekker.

Deming, W. Edwards. 1967. What Happened in Japan? *Industrial Quality Control* 24 (August): 89–94.

———. 1982. *Quality, Productivity, and Competitive Position*. Cambridge: Massachusetts Institute of Technology, Center for Advanced Engineering Study.

Dodge, Harold F. 1969. Notes on the Evolution of Acceptance Sampling Plans. *Journal of Quality Technology* 1:77–88, 155–62, 225–32.

Dodge, Harold F., and H. G. Romig. 1929. A Method of Sampling Inspection. *Bell System Technical Journal* 8:613–31.

———. 1941. Single Sampling and Double Sampling Inspection Tables. *Bell System Technical Journal* 20:1–61.

Edwards, G. D. 1928. Standard Quality. *Bell Telephone Quarterly* 7:292–303.

———. 1942. Quality Control of Munitions. *Army Ordnance* 23.135:482–85.

Enrick, Norbert L. 1946. The U.S. Army Quartermaster Corps' Use of Sequential Sampling Inspection. *Industrial Quality Control* 2.5:12–14.

The Errors in Interchangeable Parts. 1918. *Engineering* 105 (January 4): 18.

Fay, E. L. 1945. *An Application of Statistical Quality Control at the John Deere Tractor Company*. Office of Production Research and Development, Quality Control Reports, vol. 8. Pittsburgh: Carnegie Institute of Technology.

Ferguson, Thomas. 1976. Development of the Decision Model. In *On the History of Statistics and Probability*, edited by D. B. Owen, 333–46. New York: Marcel Dekker.

Freeman, Harold A. 1943. Sequential Analysis of Statistical Data: Applications. Applied Mathematics Panel Report 30.2, Columbia University.

———. 1945. Sequential Sampling Inspection for Attributes. *Industrial Quality Control* 2 (September): 3–7.

Friedman, Milton. 1947. Utilization of Limited Experimental Facilities when the Cost of Each Measurement Depends on Its Magnitude. In *Techniques of Statistical Analysis for Scientific and Industrial Research and Production and Management Engineering*, edited by Churchill Eisenhart, W. A. Hastay, and W. Allen Wallis. New York: McGraw-Hill.

Friedman, Milton, and Rose Friedman. 1998. *Two Lucky People: Memoirs*. Chicago: University of Chicago Press.

Friedman, Milton, and Anna J. Schwartz. 1991. Alternative Approaches to Analyzing Economic Data. *American Economic Review* 81:48–49.

Galilei, Galileo. [1642] 1962. Sopra le Scoperte dei Dadi. Translated by E. H. Thorne. In *Games, Gods, and Gambling*, edited by Florence David. London: Charles Griffin.

Godfrey, A. B. 1986. The History and Evolution of Quality in AT&T. *AT&T Technical Journal* 65.2:9–20.

Griliches, Zvi. 1957. Hybrid Corn: An Exploration in the Economics of Technological Change. *Econometrica* 25 (October): 504–22.

Hitch, Charles. 1958. Economics and Military Operations Research. *The Review of Economics and Statistics* 40.3:199–209.

Homan, Paul T. 1946. Economics in the War Period. *The American Economic Review* 36.5:855–71.

Hotelling, Harold. 1941. Experimental Determination of the Maximum of a Function. *Annals of Mathematical Statistics* 12:23.

———. 1947. Multivariate Quality Control, Illustrated by the Air Testing of Sample Bombsights. In *Techniques of Statistical Analysis for Scientific and Industrial Research and Production and Management Engineering*, edited by Churchill Eisenhart, W. A. Hastay, and W. Allen Wallis. New York: McGraw-Hill.

Hounshell, David A. 1984. *From the American System to Mass Production, 1800–1932: The Development of Manufacturing Technology in the United States.* Baltimore: Johns Hopkins University Press.

Høyrup, Jens. 1994. *In Measure, Number, and Weight.* Albany: State University of New York Press.

Ishikawa, Kaoru. 1980. *Guide to Quality Control.* Tokyo: Asian Productivity Organization.

Jahn, E. Mark. 1992. A History of Statistical Process Control. Ph.D. diss., San Diego State University.

Jones, R. L. 1927. Quality of Telephone Materials. *Bell Telephone Quarterly* 6 (January): 32–46.

Juran, J. M., ed. 1995. *A History of Managing for Quality: The Evolution, Trends, and Future Directions of Managing for Quality*. Milwaukee: ASQC Quality Press.

Klein, Judy L. 1997. *Statistical Visions in Time: A History of Time Series Analysis.* Cambridge: Cambridge University Press.

———. 1999a. Controlling Gunfire, Inventories, and Expectations with the Exponentially Weighted Moving Average. Unpublished. Mary Baldwin College.

———. 1999b. Economic Stabilization Policies and the Military Art of Control Engineering. Unpublished. Mary Baldwin College.

Kruskal, William H. 1980. First Interactions with Harold Hotelling; Testing the Norden Bombsight. *Journal of the American Statistical Association* 75:331–35.

Leonard, Robert. 1991. War as a "Simple Economic Problem": The Rise of an Economics of Defense. In *Economics and National Security*, edited by Craufurd D. Goodwin. *HOPE* 23 (supplement): 261–83.

Lindley, D. V. 1951. Review of Statistical Decision Functions. *Journal of the Royal Statistical Society, Series A* 114.2:250–53.

Looking for Trouble: Quality Control of International Business Machines. 1937. *American Machinist* 81 (June): 539–43.

Maack, Jack G. (Lt.). 1944. Sampling Plan Developed by QM for Woolen Textiles. *Textile World* 94:88–89.

Marschak, Jacob. 1946. Neumann's and Morgenstern's New Approach to Static Economics. *Journal of Political Economy* 54.2:97–115.

The Mathematical Manager. 1943. *The Industrial Bulletin of Arthur D. Little, Inc.* 194 (November): 4.

Mirowski, Philip. 1991. When Games Grow Deadly Serious: The Military Influence on the Evolution of Game Theory. In *Economics and National Security*, edited by Craufurd D. Goodwin. *HOPE* 23 (supplement): 227–55.

———. Forthcoming. *Machine Dreams: Economics Becomes a Cyborg Science*. New York: Cambridge University Press.

Morgenstern, Oskar. 1951. Abraham Wald. *Econometrica* 19.4:361–67.

Neyman, Jerzy. 1971. Foundations of Behavioristic Statistics. In *Foundations of Statistical Inference*, edited by V. P. Godambe and D. A. Sprott. Toronto: Holt, Rinehart and Winston.

Nonaka, Izumi. 1995. The Recent History of Managing for Quality in Japan. In *A History of Managing for Quality*, edited by J. M. Juran. Milwaukee: ASQC Quality Press.

Olmstead, Paul S. 1957. Quality Control and Operations Research. *Bulletin of the International Statistical Institute* 35:355–64.

Pearson, Egon S. 1934. Sampling Problems in Industry. *Journal of the Royal Statistical Society*, supplement, 1.2:107–51.

———. 1936. Statistical Method and Industry in Great Britain. *Journal of the American Statistical Association* 31:361–66.

———. 1967. Some Notes on W. A. Shewhart's Influence on the Application of Statistical Methods in Great Britain. *Industrial Quality Control* 24 (August): 81–83.

Radford, G. S. 1922. *The Control of Quality in Manufacturing*. New York: Ronald Press.

Rees, Mina. 1988. The Mathematical Sciences and World War II. In part 1 of *A Century of Mathematics in America*, edited by Peter Duren, with the assistance of Richard A. Askey and Uta C. Merzbach. Providence, R.I.: American Mathematical Society. (Copyright 1988; reprinted with corrections in 1989.)

Rosser, J. Barkley. 1988. Mathematics and Mathematicians in World War II. In part 1 of *A Century of Mathematics in America*, edited by Peter Duren, with the assistance of Richard A. Askey and Uta C. Merzbach. Providence, R.I.: American Mathematical Society. (Copyright 1988; reprinted with corrections in 1989.)

Safford, H. F. 1946. The U.S. Army Ordnance Department's Use of Quality Control. *Industrial Quality Control* 2.4a:4.

Samuelson, Paul A. 1948. Exact Distribution of Continuous Variables in Sequential Analysis. *Econometrica* 16.2:191–98.

———. 1950. Recent Texts on Mathematical Statistics. *Review of Economics and Statistics* 32.2:139–43.

Savage, Leonard J. 1951. The Theory of Statistical Decision. *Journal of the American Statistical Association* 46 (May): 55–67.

———. [1954] 1972. *The Foundations of Statistics*. New York: Dover Publications, Inc.

Schelling, Thomas C. 1960. Economic Reasoning and Military Science. *American Economist* 4.1:3–13.

Sent, Esther-Mirjam. 1998. Engineering Dynamic Economics. In *New Economics and Its History*, edited by John B. Davis. *HOPE* 29 (supplement): 41–62.

Shewhart, Walter A. 1926a. Finding Causes of Quality Variation. *Manufacturing Industries* 11:125–28.

———. 1926b. Quality Control Charts. *Bell System Technical Journal* 5:593–603.

———. 1928. Economic Aspects of Engineering Applications. *Journal of the Franklin Institute* 205 (March): 395–405.

———. 1933. The Role of Statistical Method in Economic Standardization. *Econometrica* 1.1:23–35.

———. 1939. Application of Statistical Method in Mass Production. In *Proceedings of the Industrial Statistics Conference Held at MIT, September 8–9, 1938*. New York: Pitman Publishing.

———. 1967. The First Shewhart Control Chart. *Industrial Quality Control* 24 (August): 72.

Simon, Leslie E. 1941. On the Initiation of Statistical Methods for Quality Control in Industry. *Journal of the American Statistical Association* 36:53–60.

———. 1942. Application of Statistical Method to Ordnance Engineering. *Journal of the American Statistical Association* 37:313–24.

———. 1947. Sampling and Sorting Ammunition for the Attack on Normandy. *American Society for Quality Control Conference Papers* 1:275–81.

Statistical Research Group, Columbia University. 1945. *Sequential Analysis of Statistical Data: Applications*. SRG Report 255, AMP Report 30.2R. New York: Columbia University Press.

———. 1947. *Selected Techniques of Statistical Analysis*. Edited by Churchill Eisenhart, W. A. Hastay, and W. Allen Wallis. New York: McGraw-Hill.

———. 1948. *Sampling Inspection: Principles, Procedures, and Tables for Single, Double, and Sequential Sampling in Acceptance Inspection and Quality Control Based on Percent Defective*. Edited by H. A. Freeman, Milton Friedman, Frederick Mosteller, and W. Allen Wallis. New York: McGraw-Hill.

Taguchi, Genichi. 1981. *On-Line Quality Control during Production*. Tokyo: Japanese Standards Association.

Tintner, G. 1952. Abraham Wald's Contributions to Econometrics. *Annals of Mathematical Statistics* 23.1:21–23.

Trombly, Russell C. 1945. *An Application of Statistical Quality Control at the Hoover Ball and Bearing Company*. Office of Production Research and Development, Quality Control Reports, vol. 6. Pittsburgh: Carnegie Institute of Technology.

Trowbridge, Fred, and John T. Clark. 1945. *Statistical Quality Control in Radio Manufacture*. Office of Production Research and Development, Quality Control Reports, vol. 5. Pittsburgh: Carnegie Institute of Technology.
van Vechten, C. C. 1948. Historical Note. *Industrial Quality Control* 4.6:5.
Wald, Abraham. 1936. *Berechnung und Ausschaltung von Saisonschwankungen*. Vienna: Verlag von Julius Springer.
———. 1939. Contributions to the Theory of Statistical Estimation and Testing Hypotheses. *Annals of Mathematical Statistics* 10:299–326.
———. 1943. *Sequential Analysis of Statistical Data: Theory*. Columbia University: Applied Mathematics Panel Report 30.1.
———. 1945a. Sequential Method of Sampling for Deciding between Two Courses of Action. *Journal of the American Statistical Association* 40:277–306.
———. 1945b. Sequential Tests of Statistical Hypotheses. *Annals of Mathematical Statistics* 16.2:117–86.
———. 1947a. Foundations of a General Theory of Sequential Decision Functions. *Econometrica* 15.4:279–313.
———. 1947b. *Sequential Analysis*. New York: Wiley.
———. 1948. Optimum Character of the Sequential Probability Ratio Test. *Annals of Mathematical Statistics* 19:236–39.
———. 1949. Statistical Decision Functions. *Annals of Mathematical Statistics* 20:165–205.
———. 1950. *Statistical Decision Functions*. New York: Wiley.
Wald, Abraham, and J. Wolfowitz. 1950. Bayes Solutions of Sequential Decision Problems. *Annals of Mathematical Statistics* 21:82–89.
Wallis, W. Allen. 1980. The Statistical Research Group, 1942–1945. *Journal of the American Statistical Association* 75:320–30.
Weaver, Warren. 1946. Summary. In *Mathematical Studies Relating to Physical Research*. Vol. 1 of *Summary Technical Report of the Applied Mathematics Panel*. Washington, D.C.: NDRC.
———. 1962. *The Reminiscences of Warren Weaver*. Interview with Barbara Land. Columbia University: Oral History Research Office.
Weber, Max. 1946. *From Max Weber: Essays in Sociology*. Edited and translated by H. H. Gerth and C. Wright Mills. New York: Oxford University Press.
Weintraub, E. Roy. 1993. *General Equilibrium Analysis*. Ann Arbor: University of Michigan Press.
Wolfowitz, J. 1952. Abraham Wald, 1902–1950. *Annals of Mathematical Statistics* 23.1:1–13.
Working, Holbrook. 1945. Statistical Quality Control in War Production. *Journal of the American Statistical Association* 40:425–47.
Working, Holbrook, and Edwin G. Olds. 1944. *Manual for an Introduction to Statistical Methods of Quality Control in Industry: An Outline of Lectures and Exercises*. War Production Board, Office of Production Research and Development.

Atomic Energy and the Application of Early Models of Technological Change in Economics, 1946–1954

Warren Young

On Labor Day 1954, President Eisenhower initiated construction of Shippingport, the first commercial U.S. nuclear power plant. Almost a decade previously, however, the "economic question" of atomic energy had arisen and treatment of it gained momentum as the tools of economic theory and analysis were refined and applied in the attempt to assess "possible economic effects of atomic energy" (May 1947, 58). These tools ranged from Herbert Simon's application of the short-run general equilibrium models of Griffith Evans and Kenneth May and their extension to include technological change (Evans 1934; May 1946, 1947; Simon [1947] 1948, 1947b, 1947c), to linear activity analysis models as utilized by Simon in his chapters (1950a, 1950b) in the 1950 Cowles Commission volume *Economic Aspects of Atomic Power* (Schurr and Marschak 1950; Simon 1951). Moreover, comparative cost and regional input-output models were also applied, as manifest in the work of Walter Isard, John Lansing, and Vincent Whitney (Isard and Lansing 1949; Isard 1951; Isard and Whitney 1952a, 1952b).

The object of this article is to illustrate how the question of the potential economic impact of nuclear power *induced* the refinement of existing theoretical techniques of economic analysis. As I will try to show, the application of economic theory to the case of atomic energy

I wish to thank Professor Herbert Simon for access to his papers and his recollections. Research was supported by the Royal Economic Society and Bar Ilan University. Thanks also to referees and editors for helpful comments and constructive criticism. Correspondence may be addressed to the Department of Economics, Bar Ilan University, Ramat Gan, Israel; e-mail: youngw@mail.biu.ac.il.

illustrates a number of fundamental issues when "applying" economics. The first relates to the application of general economic models to real-world problems. In the case of atomic energy, as will be seen, there was a split between economists who were concerned with the *logic* of a general model (Simon) and economists concerned with the *details* of the particular situation to which a general model is applied (Isard). The second issue relates to the obstacles faced by economists—such as Simon and Isard—who attempted to assess the economic impact of the new atomic power technology by applying "pure" models—whether general equilibrium, activity analysis, or input-output approaches; how they decided which aspects of the new technology were relevant; and how this affected the results they obtained.

Briefly put, then, this article is a case study of what can be called the common pattern that emerges when existing theoretical, general, or abstract economic models are refined and applied. In our case, as will be seen, Simon was at first interested in the economics of technological change, refining the Evans-May general equilibrium framework to try to comprehend, in a general way, the impact of a change in technology on the economy as a whole (Simon 1947a), and only later saw the introduction of atomic energy as a means by which to pursue his interest. Isard, for his part, had become interested in the economics of the electric power industry, at first basing his analysis of the impact of atomic energy upon conventional comparative cost estimates and then—after refining Wassily Leontief's input-output approach to an interregional model—also applying this technique to the problem of atomic energy.

In the first part of the article, therefore, the approaches taken by Simon ([1947] 1948, 1947b, 1947c) assessing the possible economic effects of atomic energy are presented. These were based, as noted above, on the earlier models of Evans (1934) and May (1946, 1947). Before I discuss Simon's extension of the models of Evans and May, I will survey those early models in order to understand Simon's application of Evans-May general equilibrium models of technological change. In the second part of the essay, the development of Simon's approach to activity analysis is outlined, and it is shown that he applied this approach in his contribution to the Cowles volume on atomic energy (Schurr and Marschak 1950), a year before it was published in the Koopmans volume (Simon 1951). In the third part of the article, Simon's application of activity analysis (Simon 1951) to assess the possible existence of "trigger effects" of technological change will be discussed. The fourth section compares the Cowles-Simon approaches to those of the Isard-Lansing-Whitney studies over the period 1949–52 (Isard 1948; Isard and Lansing 1949; Isard and Whitney 1949a, 1949b, 1952a, 1952b). The final section provides Simon's own retrospective view of his early contributions based upon an interview with him conducted in 1993.

Evans, May, and Simon: From General Equilibrium Models of Technological Change to Estimating Possible Economic Effects of Atomic Energy

In *Models of Bounded Rationality*, which dealt with economic analysis and public policy, Herbert Simon related how he came to construct models of technological change based upon the earlier work of, in particular, Griffith Evans (1934) and Kenneth May (1946, 1947) (Simon 1982, sec. 3, 261–65). As Simon explained (1982, 261),

> I began to work on the economics of technological change more or less by accident. In the late 1940s, among my teaching responsibilities at Illinois Institute of Technology was a course in American history. At this same time, I was renewing and deepening my acquaintance with economic theory by attending staff seminars of the Cowles Commission at the University of Chicago. My reading of history led me to wonder whether one could give an account, in economic terms, of the gradual transformation of America from a rural to an urban society.
>
> To this end, I constructed a classical, two-sector general equilibrium model along the lines that had been pioneered by Griffith Evans and his students (particularly Kenneth May . . .) into which I introduced technological change by altering the parameters of the production relations and solving the resulting problem in comparative statics (Simon, 1947). Evans had already discovered [Evans 1930] the power of second-order conditions for maxima and minima as tools for determining the signs of coefficients, thus anticipating Samuelson's use of them in the *Foundations* (1947) . . . it was through the work of Evans and his students, to which I was exposed while I was at Berkeley from 1939 to 1942, that I learned to use this tool.

Simon continued:

> In 1947 . . . Jacob Marschak and Sam Schurr in the Cowles Commission were undertaking a study of the prospective economic effects of atomic energy. Marschak invited me to join the atomic energy study with the responsibility for developing a methodology for evaluating the macro-economic effects of the availability of atomic power.
>
> My first approach to this problem was to develop macromodels with a single production function (sometimes a general one, sometimes of the Cobb-Douglas type), but with provision for changes in birth and death rates of the work force as well as changes in the technical coefficient and the quantity of capital. Here again it was the work of Kenneth May that suggested this way of formulating the problem, providing me with a very useful framework for my thinking about the atomic energy question. . . . Using this kind of model, I developed a working paper that was published only as an abstract [Simon (1947) 1948] and is here reproduced [in *Models*] in full for the first time. (1982, 263)

Simon's extension of Evans and May actually proceeded as follows. His paper was originally titled "On the Economic Effects of Technological Change" (Simon 1947b) and it was influenced directly by May's 1947 paper, as will be shown below. The original paper was revised, with a new title, "Some Economic Effects of Technological Change," and presented as Cowles Commission Staff Paper no. 202 and discussed at the Cowles Commission discussion meeting on 12 July 1947 (Simon 1947c). Among the prominent economists present at this meeting were Abba Lerner, Kenneth Arrow, Leonid Hurwicz, Tjalling Koopmans, Jacob Marschak, Schurr, and Kenneth May himself, along with Evsey Domar, who composed the minutes of the meeting, but more about this below. Only after this did Simon present his paper at the Chicago meeting of the Econometric Society on 27 December 1947 at a session chaired by Marschak. The title of the paper remained the same—"Some Economic Effects of Technological Change"—and an abstract of it appeared in the report of the Chicago meeting in *Econometrica* in April 1948 (Simon [1947] 1948, 199–200). It was finally published, with significant revisions and additions (but still with the same title), in *Models* (1982, 281–306). Before going on to discuss Simon's extension in detail, a brief discussion of the models of Evans and May is called for.

Evans's 1934 *Econometrica* paper titled "Maximum Production Studied in a Simplified Economic System" was based upon his earlier book, *Mathematical Introduction to Economics* (1930). In his paper Evans proposed, in effect, what May later called a "two industry simplified economic system" (May 1946, 285), the object of which was to determine maximum output of consumption goods for a given level of employment in consumption and capital goods sectors. As May noted, in Evans's model "all capital goods produced are used up in the same period and hence" the output of consumption goods "is the net output." On this basis, in May's "one-industry model" (1946), he stated that "it seems reasonable to identify" the output of consumption goods with aggregate output (1946, 287–88).

In his 1947 *Econometrica* paper "Technological Change and Aggregation," May extended his analysis from a one-sector model with technological change to a general equilibrium macromodel including such change. He directly proceeded to discuss "the effect on the aggregate production function of changes in the production functions of the micromodel" at this point, presenting Evans's (1934) two-sector general equilibrium model as his "micromodel." This was a six-equation model with "one degree of freedom," in May's terminology—"i.e. the number of variables minus the number of independent equations relating them" was equal to one (1947, 52 n. 6)—which in order to be solved required defining the level of employment as the independent variable (May 1946, 287), such that the solution to the micromodel in terms of employment "determines the macromodel" (1947, 55–56).

May then went on to derive a "relation between functions holding for all values" of employment in the range he considered for his two-sector model (1947, 57–58). He then gave as an example of this application the case where "a technological change occurs, so that output increases in both industries by the same percentage . . . the percentage being independent of employment" (58). According to the results of his model, "the percentage increase in aggregate output is *greater* than [the percentage increase in output in both industries] by an amount dependent on employment and the functions involved" (58). May concluded, "It appears that technological change has a cumulative effect in the aggregate and that extreme care must be exercised in drawing conclusions about over-all effects from data on particular firms" (58). Interestingly enough, at this point in his paper, May noted that "in the discussion of possible economic effects of atomic energy there has been a tendency to ignore the interrelations of industries and hence to underestimate aggregate effects" (58 n. 16). Now, as this paper was also to appear as a Cowles Commission paper, May was here directly referring to the work then being undertaken by Simon for the Cowles Atomic Energy Project led by Marschak and Schurr. And thus it is not surprising that in his draft paper, later presented at the July 1947 Cowles discussion meeting—which May attended—Simon cited this passage verbatim (Simon 1947b, 4 n. 1). Simon, however, took issue with May's position, as will be discussed below. The importance of Simon's extension of Evans and May on the *theoretical* level, however, does not match either the significance of its application to the "atomic energy question," as he put it, or of the results he obtained regarding the potential macroeconomic impact of the introduction of atomic energy, and it is to this that I now turn.

In his original 1947 draft paper "On the Economic Effects of Technological Change" (1947b), Simon attempted to obtain, in his words, "some estimates of the magnitude of the direct effect upon national income of the introduction of cheap atomic energy . . . by studying simple economic models." He proposed introducing "the change in energy costs" via "a change in the production function for energy." To this end, Simon adopted the Evans-May methodology by first presenting "a rather general model" based upon a micromodeling approach, then reducing it "to a macromodel of aggregates," and finally examining "certain special cases of the macromodel" (1947b, 1). In other words, what Evans, May, and Simon did was to specify sector-specific production functions so as to derive an aggregate production function from them. They then went on to attempt to derive, in turn, general statements about how changes in the production function of an individual sector would affect, or could be modeled as changes in, the aggregate production function itself.

The significant result he presented in the first section of his paper, in his view, was "*that the effects of technological changes in different industries are additive*" (1947b, 3; emphasis added). The problem facing Simon was that in May's previous study of the problem, May had "warned that ignoring the interrelations of industries may lead to an underestimate of aggregate effects" since, based on his analysis, May "argue[d] that it appears that technological change has a cumulative effect in the aggregate." The issue, then, as Simon wrote, was "how can the possibility, which May foresees, of cumulative effects, be reconciled with our result that the effects are additive?" (1947b, 4). In his view, "the contradiction is apparent rather than real," as in *both* models the incremental change in output in the "consumption good industry," which Simon termed (dy/y), will be larger than the incremental *parametric* change in the state of technology of the consumption good industry (1947b, 3–4).

For Simon, however, "this is a rather inconsequential point. . . . the real issue is whether technological change in an economy of *n* industries can be estimated correctly from a model in which some of these industries are represented collectively only as aggregates" (1947b, 4). Simon went on to generalize his results from micromodels of a two-industry and three-industry economy to a macromodel, concluding that "it appears, then, that the effects of technological change in an economy can be studied by means of a macromodel, without concern for cumulative effects, provided that *k* is properly interpreted," *k* in Simon's terms being the parametric change in the state of technology, that is, the "technological change of magnitude *k*" (5–6).

In the second section of his original draft paper, Simon specifies his energy-based macromodel, again using the Evans-May methodology. In this four-equation macromodel, output of consumption goods is dependent on the aggregate factor of production for consumption goods and "the quantity [of energy] employed in the entire economy," which Simon terms E. The output of E is dependent on the aggregate production factor for capital goods and the state of technology. He then derived an equation for the incremental change in output resulting from technological change based upon the proportion of the value of energy production to the output of consumption goods, which he called VE/VY, and the incremental parametric value of the technological change, *k*, that is, the percentage change in the productivity of the power industry. Then he said, "Since VE/VY can ordinarily be determined for any economy from available statistics, it will be interesting to calculate the values of dY/Y *corresponding* to the various values of" *k* (1947b, 7). At this point, he provided a table for the values of dY/Y, given VE/VY and *k*.

In his 1982 version, Simon summarized his 1947 estimate "of the increase in production of consumption goods that might result from technological improvements in the electric power industry," that is, the effects of atomic energy. As he wrote (1982, 288),

> At an average price of 1.5 cents per KWH [kilowatt-hour], the value of the 280 billion KWH electric power generated in the United States

> in 1944 (including power generated in industrial plants for their own use) was about 4.2 billion dollars. The total national income in the same year was 160 billion dollars. Hence $(VE/VY) = .026$. An increase in productivity of five per cent in the power industry (a cost reduction of about .75 mills per KWH) would therefore lead to a percentage increase in the national income of $5 \times .026 = .13$. Stated in other terms, each one mill reduction in power costs would increase the national income by about one-sixth of one percent. This result holds strictly, of course, only for cost reductions of small magnitude.

Now, in the first revised version of his original 1947 draft paper, which he called "Some Economic Effects of Technological Change," presented at the Cowles Commission discussion meeting on 12 July 1947, Simon went further than the static Evans-May approach by suggesting the superimposition of a long-term dynamic model on the static model of technological change, as recounted in the minutes of the meeting compiled by Domar (Domar 1947; Simon 1947c). As Domar reported, Simon pointed out that the Evans model included "only short run effects" and that "long-term effects stemming from capital accumulation, population growth etc. are equally important." According to Domar's minutes,

> The speaker [Simon] indicated how these might be studied by superimposing a long-term dynamic model on the static model. The variables in the long-term model would include real income, capital, the work force etc. It was shown that for one simple model of this sort, the long-term effect of a technological change could be measured, and would bear a definite relation to the short-term effect. (Domar 1947)

Domar then recounted the equational structure of Simon's "long-term dynamic model" (1947, 2). And Simon's 1947 dynamic equational system was reproduced, almost verbatim, in his 1982 version of the paper (1982, 296–98).

The abstract of Simon's "Christmas paper" ([1947] 1948; Young 1998) as it appeared in the report of the Chicago meeting of the Econometric Society published in *Econometrica* gave a quite detailed account of the results of his original 1947 paper, which, as I have shown, was seen and discussed at the time by some of the most prominent economists of this century—and this, in contrast to the impression Simon gives in *Models* (1982, 263), as if his 1947 paper had a "limited audience."

The significance of his 1947 paper is seen in its initial estimates of the economic impact of atomic energy on the national income of the United States, and this in comparison to Simon's contribution to the 1950 Cowles study.

At this point, however, we must distinguish between the 1947 calculations made by Simon, which were based on his Evans-May type approach, and his calculations that appeared in the 1950 Cowles volume, which were based upon his application of activity analysis to the problem of atomic energy. Indeed, in the 1950 Cowles volume, Evans and May are not mentioned at all, even in the bibliography! In any event, Simon's 1950 "resource savings" calculations are much more sophisticated and not simply "back of the envelope stuff," being equational systems based upon his activity analysis approach, which, as he put it, assessed "the effect of a technological change on total income" by measuring "the changes in income consequent upon technological changes" (Simon 1951, 262, 267). Interestingly enough, however, the overall results Simon obtained were quite similar to those he obtained in 1947; but more about this in the next section.

Simon's Approach to Activity Analysis, 1947–50: The Potential "Resource Saving Effect" of Atomic Energy

Simon developed his own approach to activity analysis to assess the effect of technological change on total income in general and applied it to what he called the potential "resource saving effect" of ostensibly cheaper electricity to be generated by atomic energy. And this, because as he came to realize, his "first approach to the problem"—based upon an Evans-May type model—was itself somewhat problematic, or, as he put it, the models he used were too sensitive to demographic assumptions and thus gave "iffy results" (1982, 263–64). He continued:

> Not being satisfied with relying too heavily upon these classical dynamic models, I sought another approach to estimating the macroeconomic effects of atomic energy, finding a useful technique in the linear programming and activity analysis formalisms just then being developed by Koopmans and Dantzig. (264)

In other words, Simon came to realize that the "new" technique of activity analysis would be better suited not only for calculating resource savings but also for analyzing trigger effects. George Dantzig, by devising the "Simplex Method" in 1947 (Dantzig 1951), had opened the way for the practical application of activity analysis. Between 1947 and 1950, therefore, Simon changed from the Evans-May approach to applying activity analysis to the potential resource saving effect of atomic energy, using it in his 1950 contribution to the Cowles volume (e.g., chap. 13, "The Effects of Atomic Power on National or Regional Economies"), that is, a year *before* his 1951 paper in the Koopmans volume. While Simon did present a version of his paper on 27 December 1947 at the meeting of the Econometric Society as noted above, Marschak had earlier received detailed comments on Simon's approach to resource saving from H. J. Barnett, an expert in the field of energy economics. He raised a number of questions and issues which were to be taken up by Simon in later revisions. Among these were queries relating to possible differences in replacement of existing power plants with atomic plants by privately owned as against government-owned public utilities and the life of the power plant. But the most striking of Barnett's questions related to the problem of resource saving due to substitution resulting from cost reduction and the effect of population growth in relation to technological change and capital utilization and growth. Indeed, as Barnett put it, the entire problem that Simon was trying to solve would change if augmentation of demand (through growth in population, changes in tastes, or fuller utilization of resources) and other technological changes were assumed (Marschak to Simon, 9 December 1947, Simon Papers). And it was these points that probably brought Simon to the realization that he needed a broader approach than Evans-May, one that would not be sensitive to "demographic assumptions" and would enable not only resource savings calculations but also take into account the possible effects of changes in processes, that is, trigger effects.

A month later, on 8 January 1948, Marschak, Schurr, and Simon met to discuss Simon's chapters for the Cowles Project Report and additional issues regarding atomic power and its economic effects to be considered by Schurr. According to the minutes of this meeting as recorded by Marschak, dated 9 January (Simon Papers, Atomic Energy), they decided to take up Barnett's points both on the need for short-term calculation of national resource savings and that regarding resource saving due to substitution effects using constant factor ratios, realistic constants, and arithmetical presentation of the effects of hypothetical variations. Two weeks before this, as noted above, Simon had presented what Marschak called Simon's "Christmas paper," titled "Some Economic Effects of Technological Change," at the Chicago meeting of the Econometric Society. Over the next six months, Simon further refined and extended the theory he presented in this paper by developing the notion of what he called the "trigger effects of technological change"; but more about this below.

On 29 June 1948, Marschak again wrote Simon regarding his contribution to the Cowles study on atomic energy. He wrote,

> Your chapter on "Effects of Inventions Upon the Economy of a Region" seems to me to literally cry out for mathematical presentation. I mean not only the parts dealing essentially with the theory as presented in your Christmas paper last year; and not only the new passage on "trigger effects"; but also the sections on the various "multipliers." (Simon Papers, Atomic Energy)

The "mathematical presentation" or technique that Simon turned to was activity analysis. A year later, Marschak once again wrote Simon, enclosing the draft conclusion of Schurr's forthcoming articles in the *Bulletin of Atomic Scientists* (*BAS*) and *Harvard Business Review*, along with his editorial suggestions as project coordinator for the Cowles study. Marschak wrote,

> It seems to me that Sam discussed the economic effects in . . . steps which are similar to but possibly not identical with some of your "degrees of approximation." . . . "Resource saving" = power cost reduction times old demand for power. Effect of changes in process and/or location; this is your trigger effect. (Simon Papers, Atomic Energy)

On 2 August 1949, Simon replied to Marschak and accepted Marschak's interpretation of Schurr's definitions regarding resource saving and trigger effects (Simon Papers, Atomic Energy). Attached to his letter, Simon provided his estimate of "the overall income effect":

> We are now in position to estimate the overall income effect (including both the effect of increased demand and the resource-saving effect previously calculated) of a $2\frac{1}{2}$ mill reduction in the cost of electricity. We do this under the assumption of a demand elasticity of 1 for industrial uses of electricity, and an elasticity of 2 for non-industrial uses. The total increase in national income attributable to the reduction in

> cost of electricity is equal to the amount of reduction ($2\frac{1}{2}$ mills per KWH) times the total demand for electricity *after* thc cost reduction has taken place. That is, the income effect is equal to the savings in resources due to the cost reduction, in producing this larger quantity of electricity.

He added the following in a note:

> This method of measuring the income effect can be given precise theoretical justification under the assumption that new technological processes are not introduced as a result of the cost reduction. If new processes are introduced which are economical under the new electricity prices, but were not economical with the higher prices, then our estimating method exaggerates the income effect.

Simon went on:

> In 1946, consumption of electricity totaled 240 billion KWH. With the demand elasticities assumed above, we have seen that industrial consumption would be increased by about 40 billion KWH, and non-industrial consumption about 13 billion KWH, thus increasing total consumption to about 293 billion KWH. The total increase in national income would then be 293 × 2.5 million dollars, or approximately 730 million dollars. This is two-fifths of one per cent of the national income.

In the 1950 Cowles volume, Simon revised this calculation slightly, estimating the increase in industrial consumption to be some 45 billion KWH, and nonindustrial consumption to be some 25 billion KWH, so that total consumption would be increased to 310 billion KWH (rather than the 293 billion in his note to Marschak of 2 August 1949). As Simon wrote (1950b, 231), "The total increase in national income would then be no more than 310 × 2.5 million dollars, or approximately 775 million dollars. This is 2/5 of 1% of the national income."

Simon and the Search for Trigger Effects of Technological Change: The Case of Atomic Energy

In *Models* (1982), Simon recounted how he and the directors of the Cowles "atomic energy project," Marschak and Schurr, were concerned with the possible trigger effects of technological change. As Simon recalled (1982, 264),

> In the atomic energy project, we were particularly concerned with the possibility that there might be a "trigger effect"—that a cost-reduction in energy might cause a great burst of growth in some industry that was hardly visible before cheap energy arrived on the scene.

How, then, did Simon proceed in his search for trigger effects? In an early piece on the problem, written in 1948 and titled "'Trigger Effects' of Technological Change," Simon wrote,

> The effects of the improvement in a production process may be divided into two classes: (1) the saving in resources because smaller quantities of the factors of production are required for a given output; (2) substitution effects, because the reduction in cost of production makes it profitable to substitute the product in question for other products as factors in other production processes (or consumption goods). Where a particular factor of production plays only a small role in the economy—where the total value of the factor is only a small part of the total income of the economy, and of the cost of producing any good—the substitution effect will be insignificant, and the total effect will be approximately measured by the resource-saving. (Simon Papers, Atomic Energy)

Simon continued on to question whether trigger effects had actually ever been important historically, but was still unwilling, at this point, to rule them out entirely. He then wrote that

> the possibility of a trigger effect hinges upon the existence or discovery of a production process for some good that uses very large quantities of the cheapened factor and very small quantities of other factors per unit of output. This process may only become economically reliable when the factor in question is substantially cheapened, but the cheapening, by permitting the process to be used, may cause widespread substitution.

Simon concluded as follows:

> We suppose, then, two factors of production, and two production processes. We assume further, that in any one process, the two factors are required in fixed proportions, but that these proportions are quite

> different for the two processes. If the cost of the one factor is fixed, how will the cost of the product vary with the cost of the other factor?

In his contribution to the Cowles volume, Simon dealt with the issue of possible short-run trigger effects of atomic energy in detail (1950b, 232–37) before going on to deal with possible "long-term repercussions" of "the cheapening of power" (237–39). Simon first presented the position that "it may be argued that past data on the elasticity of demand for electricity cannot safely be projected into the future because at some lower price of electricity important 'trigger effects' may appear," going on to say that "by 'trigger effects' we mean very large increases in the demand for electricity produced by small changes in its price and occurring in some new, possibly yet unknown, applications of electricity." He continued that "in answering this contention, we need not deny that lower electricity prices might bring about an enormous increase in the consumption of electricity, and that in certain price ranges the elasticity of demand for electricity might be much greater than our estimates from historical data." He then said, "But our present interest is primarily in the effect of such changes upon the national income" (1950b, 232). Thus, after analyzing in detail the case of a specific industry, he wrote that there were "a number of possibilities of trigger effects" at the level of *specific industries* and continued as follows:

> But our present analysis shows that strong "trigger effects," so far as national income is concerned, would be produced only by the discovery of some process that used electricity in very large quantities per unit of output, and the other factors of production in very small quantities per unit of output. Since we have no reason to expect that new applications of electricity will not require a substantial capital investment per unit of output (quite apart from the investment required to produce electricity) *the prospect is not at all bright for revolutionary changes in technological process that would completely invalidate our methods of estimating possible income effects.* (1950b, 234; emphasis added)

Simon concluded that as regards the potential macroeconomic effect of atomic energy on the U.S. economy, "the principal short-run effect upon an economy like that of the United States would be a moderate increase in productivity, and a consequent increase in income," but "it does not seem likely that it will be more than 1%" (1950b, 246).

Following from his work on atomic energy, in his paper "Effects of Technological Change in a Linear Model" that appeared in the volume edited by Koopmans (*Activity Analysis of Production and Allocation*), Simon (1951) formally dealt with the problem of how "to measure the changes in income consequent upon technological changes" (267). According to him, there were two cases of technological change. In the first, "the technological change may not alter the lists of scarce factors and economical activities" (267). In the second, "when the effects of a technological change . . . include changes in the lists of economical activities or scarce factors . . . we shall call them 'trigger effects'" (268). He went on to formally identify, within the framework of "activity analysis" at the microeconomic level of a specific industry, the elements in technological changes that bring the economy to shift from one set of "economic activities" to another, which he termed "trigger" changes or "trigger effects." According to Simon, the *measured relative magnitude* of the technological change reflected the "resource-saving effect," while the change in level of a *specific activity* "resulting from the technological change" reflected the "substitution-effect" (269).

Simon then went on to produce empirical estimates ("in advance of the change") of the income effect of a technological change of known magnitude (269–70). He identified two kinds of trigger effects. The first was "through technological improvement of an activity," such that "this activity becomes economical and replaces a previously economical activity . . . which now becomes uneconomical." The second was "through changes in the technological coefficients of an economical activity" so that "through changes in the relative availability of the factors, a previously uneconomical activity . . . becomes economical and replaces a previously economical activity" (271). He then gave examples of these two types. Simon then attempted to develop a "procedure for estimating the magnitude of the income effect of a technological change that produces" the second type of trigger effect, which he termed "a derived trigger effect"; this, in his view, was "more complicated than the estimation procedures" for the first case of technological change mentioned above, but he did not provide any empirical estimates. In any event, his concern that there would be trigger effects of atomic energy at the macroeconomic level was indeed misplaced, for as he later wrote in *Models* (1982, 264),

> We tried hard but without any success to identify candidate industries for triggering. When we failed to find any, I received substantial additional assurance from the results of the activity analysis formulation, which showed that such trigger effects, however spectacular they might be for the industry concerned, *would be unlikely to have major macroeconomic consequences. (This conclusion from the theory was reinforced by our empirical analysis, which showed that the reduction in energy costs by the use of atomic energy was going to be, at best quite modest*). (emphasis added)

In the version of the 1947 Christmas paper reproduced in *Models*, Simon noted the resemblance between his approach to analyzing the impact of technological change and those used by Leontief (1936, 1937) in his input-output analysis. Interestingly enough, about the same time Isard was involved in his own research on the economic implications of atomic power, which would eventuate in an attempt to apply a multiregional I-O model to gauge the economic impact of atomic power (1948, 1952a, 1952b). And it is to the contributions of Isard and his colleagues regarding the assessment of the potential economic effect of "atomic power" that I now turn.

The Cowles and Isard-Lansing-Whitney Studies: Applications of Comparative Cost and Regional Input-Output Models

Isard published some preliminary results of his research on the economic impact of nuclear power in an article in the 1948 *Quarterly Journal of Economics*. The first point he made was that "political and security solutions of the atomic energy problem may well run counter to the economic ones. If so, the former in all probability will override the latter" (1948, 204). The second point was that with regard to cheaper electricity generation resulting from atomic power "the direct effect upon national income through the labor freed for other pursuits . . . would be noticeable but nothing dramatic. The direct gain would at most be expressed in terms of a few percent" (213–14).

In this article, Isard also cited some preliminary results of the Cowles Project as published by Marschak (1946) and Schurr (1947) in the *BAS*, but did not critically comment on them. Rather, he wrote that "alternative computations, arriving at the same conclusion have been carried out" by Marschak and Schurr (Isard 1948, 214 n. 6) and concluded his 1948 article by saying that "it appears unlikely that atomic energy will have a revolutionary impact upon world and national economies" (227).

A year later, Isard published two articles with Whitney directed at a more general readership. The first was titled "Atomic Power Politics" (1949b), the second "Atomic Power and Economic Development" (1949a). In the latter paper, they attacked Schurr's conclusions regarding the cost of generating electricity in atomic power plants—drawn from the earlier costing studies of Thomas (1946) and Condliffe (1946)—as "optimistic" (74). Isard's critique was based on a research paper he had written with Lansing titled "Comparisons of Power Costs for Atomic and Conventional Steam Stations" published in the August 1949 issue of *Review of Economics and Statistics*. This article, and its addendum, constituted a detailed critique of the Cowles cost estimates and technique, as manifest in Schurr 1947, 1949 and Menke 1947. Moreover, Isard and Lansing mentioned the problem of public and private discount rates in atomic power projects and, most important, raised the issue of government *subsidization* of atomic power (1949, 221, 224–25). In "An Addendum on the Cowles Commission Estimates," Isard commented in detail "upon the long awaited atomic power cost estimates of the Cowles Commission" as they appeared in Schurr (July 1949). According to Isard, Schurr either "ignored" the cost estimates of Thomas or "made errors in the adjustment of the Thomas figure to a 50 percent plant factor" (Isard and Lansing 1949, 227). He went on to say that the Cowles results reflected a "major inconsistency" regarding the question of "economies of scale," for while Cowles *rejected* "any significant economies of scale," the basis for its *cost* calculations—the Condliffe report (1946)—had, according to Isard, assumed economies of scale (Isard and Lansing 1949, 227).

Isard continued on to say that the Cowles long-term cost estimate, which was derived "on the assumption that the investment per kilowatt in atomic electricity would ultimately be as low as the investment in ordinary thermal electricity" (Schurr 1949, 465), was based upon a "quite arbitrary hypothesis" (Isard and Lansing 1949, 227). He went on to say that he had "pointed out the virtue of thinking in terms of goals rather then specific cost estimates" (1949, 227). Moreover, in a note he said "our paper was made available" to Cowles "in December 1948"

(227 n. 13). Isard concluded, "In short, in introducing unnecessary assumptions by employing specific cost estimates as it has, the Cowles Commission uses a poor technique, one that can easily be misleading and in fact has been" (228).

In April 1952, Isard and Whitney published an article titled "Atomic Power and Regional Development" in the *BAS* (1952b), which preceded their book, *Atomic Power: An Economic and Social Analysis* (1952a), published the same month. In their book, they went into the early costing methodology of Thomas and Condliffe in great detail and again criticized the Cowles results, which were *specific* cost estimates (1952a, 48–49). In their concluding chapter, titled "Atomic Power—Prospect and Retrospect," Isard and Whitney (1952a, 217) wrote, "To a considerable extent, the future of commercial atomic power will depend on its cost relative to alternative sources of power. Obviously, subsidization is one way by which its cost may, in specific circumstances, be lowered." Reactions to their volume were on the whole favorable, with most observers acknowledging the difference in technique and method of analysis, while at the same time pointing out the overall similarity with the Cowles results as regards the macroeconomic consequences of atomic energy (Mullenbach 1953; Katzin 1953; Dahl 1953; Brown 1953). And it is at this point that I turn to what Isard and Lansing called the "the application of a new methodological approach," that is, "'input-output analysis,' from the point of view of atomic power" (Isard and Lansing 1952a, 119).

Isard had published his seminal paper "Interregional and Regional Input-Output Analysis: A Model of a Space-Economy" in the November 1951 issue of the *Review of Economics and Statistics*. His work was an extension of Leontief's work from 1936 onward on developing I-O models (Leontief 1936, 1951). In his attempt at applying I-O analysis to the case of nuclear energy, Isard focused upon "the assessment of indirect effects of atomic power." Indeed, his 1952 *BAS* article with Whitney referred to the conclusions in their book, indicating the necessity for the application of I-O analysis in the following terms (Isard and Whitney 1952b, 120):

> We have already made clear our conclusion that the direct effects of atomic power on industrial development will not be revolutionary. It is the indirect effects, which so far have not been subjected to analysis, which are likely to be really consequential.

However, as they admitted, not only was the technique only in the very early stages of its development, but the regional empirical data were also lacking.

Isard and Whitney then went on to hypothetically analyze the economic development of "semi-developed region X" by using I-O analysis in a case where "the introduction of relatively cheap atomic power makes it feasible to establish an iron and steel works with an annual output valued at $1,000,000" (1952b, 120–21). They then asked, "How will this affect other industries in terms of such factors as output and employment?" going on to say that "here the traditional location analysis found in our own book and in that of the Cowles Commission is of limited ability" (121). Using a hypothetical I-O table, Isard and Whitney performed a numerical *gedankenexperiment* and also outlined its limitations accordingly (121–24). They concluded by saying that "even if the lack of validity of any present estimates of cheap atomic power is taken into account, it is easy to overemphasize the probable role of atomic power in economic development through a failure to comprehend the extreme complexity of the process. . . . the ability of a region to become industrialized, given cheap atomic power, may be made to appear greater than it is by the necessary inability of the existing theoretical models to allow for the kind of obstacles inevitably found in the real situation" (124).

To sum up, then, the major differences in applications between the Cowles and Isard groups related to their respective techniques and methods of analysis. In the former case, activity analysis was used and specific cost estimates generated; in the latter case, at first, comparative cost estimates were approximated, but afterward cost goals were substituted when multiregional I-O analysis was applied. Isard and his coauthors believed, like the Cowles group, that the impact of atomic power would not be large. However, as seen above, they were very critical of the Cowles estimates and approach, in particular their estimates of how much it would reduce energy costs. They also argued that I-O analysis was the proper way to think about what they termed the "indirect effects" of atomic power, albeit having to admit that neither the data nor the technique was, as of then, sufficient for quantitative analysis. It must be remembered, however, that it was Simon who first noticed the similarities between his *initial* approach and that of Leontief (Simon 1982, 285), something that may have given the lead to Isard to shift his own emphasis from comparative cost estimates to I-O analysis accordingly.

"A New World with Free Energy," or "Cassandra": The Cowles and Isard Studies in Retrospect

In a November 1993 interview, Professor Simon gave his recollections of his input into the Cowles volume and his relationship with Marschak, Schurr, and others, including colleagues in the areas of atomic physics and nuclear engineering. As Simon recalled, when he first arrived at the conservative results regarding the macroeconomic implications of atomic power, both Marschak and Schurr "pressed him hard" with regard to the possibility of trigger effects. According to Simon's recollection, Marschak said that he "must be sure that there were not any indirect effects" that were not included in his models. In the end, Marschak and Schurr were "a bit more optimistic" regarding atomic power, but "they didn't try to enforce the party line" with regard to Simon. As Simon put it, his move from differential equations and Cobb-Douglas (Evans-May type) models in his Christmas paper (December 1947) to a "linear model" based on the approach of "activity analysis" was the result of the fact that he "tried to look hard at and for trigger effects," that is, based upon *discrete analysis*, although he was unsuccessful in his search, as noted above. In any event, regarding the possibility of trigger effects, Simon made the important point in his interview that trigger changes were based upon the assumption of an economy at full employment equilibrium, something that was not clearly stated in the earlier accounts.

With regard to the position taken by the industrial-scientific community to the Cowles volume and its economic projections, Simon made the point that the physicists he knew who were involved with the atomic power program had "no great confidence in economists" and their prognostications due to the "hubris effect." Simon recalled that even prior to Eisenhower's "Atoms for Peace" program, the scientists at General Atomics, where he was economic consultant, were "very enthusiastic" seeing a "new world with free energy" and were just not willing to listen to a "Cassandra" going "on about economic cost." He recalled that there was "no great reaction to the Cowles volume," at least not in the industrial-scientific community with which he had contact. Simon also recalled his contacts with the academic community at the University of Chicago. As he put it, during the war he was friendly with and even "living with physicists," especially the codirector (along with Enrico Fermi) of the Chicago Atomic Pile Project, Nobel Laureate physicist Leo Szilard. Simon knew about the atomic pile and recalled that as early as 1943 he thought about "what free energy would mean" even "before he thought about the costs of producing it." At this time, it was the "topic of academic conversation" at the University of Chicago, as "so many people were involved in the project." Indeed, Simon stressed that he was "originally influenced" by the 1946 Smyth report, with its stress on "free energy" and its assertion that "1 atom equaled *a lot of energy*" (emphasis added). But, after consulting with his friend, the noted nuclear engineer Richard Meier, Simon realized early on that Meier was right when he asserted that in terms of "engineering economics, nuclear reactors will cost more" than conventional power stations because the "costs of heat exchange were not cheaper." The major point Simon stressed in the interview was that the issues of nuclear waste disposal and decommissioning were not included in the Cowles volume since it was an "at best analysis," and at the time there was no information beyond the Smyth report (Smyth 1946). Simon said that in his view the "physicists were amazingly cavalier about disposal problems" and recalled Glenn Seaborg, later chairman of the Atomic Energy Commission, "exuding goodwill and confidence and pooh-poohing the problems of atomic energy." This, in Simon's view, was the major problem in the development of the atomic power program, as "the technological change was introduced *before being able to solve the problem of disposal*."

Now, these early approaches were, in effect, worst case scenarios provided by economists who were essentially assessing the effects of a technology that had not even produced electricity. It is not surprising, therefore, that their economic prognostications were not heeded by the community of scientists, engineers, businesspersons, public officials, and politicians who made up what I have elsewhere called the "nuclear-industrial complex," for the combination of political considerations and pecuniary interests simply outweighed the Cassandra-like warnings of Simon, Isard, and others regarding the macroeconomics of atomic energy (Young 1998). Indeed, perhaps the problem is not the reception of the Cowles-Isard studies, but their nonreception by the economics community. Both the Cowles and Isard volumes were not cited in subsequent costing and cost-benefit studies. For, even after microeconomic-based cost-benefit analysis was applied to atomic power projects for generating electricity, the macroeconomic efficacy of atomic energy in the United States and elsewhere was not called into question, but that is another story (see Young 1998).

References

Brown, A. J. 1953. Review of *Atomic Power: An Economic and Social Analysis*, by W. Isard and V. Whitney. *Manchester Guardian* 9 (January): 2.

Condliffe, J. 1946. Atomic Energy: Its Future in Power Production. *Chemical Engineering* 53 (October): 125–33.

Dahl, R. 1953. Review of *Atomic Power: An Economic and Social Analysis*, by W. Isard and V. Whitney. *Annals of American Academy* 285 (January): 190.

Dantzig, G. 1951. Maximization of a Linear Function of Variables Subject to Linear Inequalities. In *Activity Analysis of Production and Allocation*, edited by T. Koopmans. New York: Wiley.

Domar, E. 1947. Cowles Commission Discussion Meeting, Minutes: 105, 12 July. In Simon Papers, Atomic Energy.

Evans, G. 1930. *Mathematical Introduction to Economics*. New York: McGraw-Hill.

———. 1934. Maximum Production Studied in a Simplified Economic System. *Econometrica* 2 (January): 37–50.

Isard, W. 1948. Some Economic Implications of Atomic Energy. *Quarterly Journal of Economics* 62 (February): 202–28.

———. 1950. Review of *Economic Aspects of Atomic Power: An Exploratory Study*, by S. Schurr and J. Marschak. *Nation* 171, 16 (December): 657.

———. 1951. Interregional and Regional Input-Output Analysis: A Model of a Space-Economy. *Review of Economics and Statistics* 33 (November): 318–28.

Isard, W., and J. Lansing. 1949. Comparisons of Power Costs for Atomic and Conventional Steam Stations. *Review of Economics and Statistics* 31.3:217–26.

———. 1949. [written by Isard] An Addendum on the Cowles Commission Estimates. *Review of Economics and Statistics* 31.3:217–26.

Isard, W., and V. Whitney. 1949a. Atomic Power and Economic Development. *Bulletin of Atomic Scientists* 5.3:73–79.

———. 1949b. Atomic Power Politics. *The Yale Review* 38.3:398–409.

———. 1952a. *Atomic Power: An Economic and Social Analysis*. New York: Blakiston Press.

———. 1952b. Atomic Power and Regional Development. *Bulletin of Atomic Scientists* 8.4:119–24.

Katzin, L. 1953. Review of *Atomic Power: An Economic and Social Analysis*, by W. Isard and V. Whitney. *Bulletin of Atomic Scientists* 9.4:152.

Leontief, W. 1936. Quantitative Input and Output Relations in the Economic System of the United States. *Review of Economic Statistics* 18.3:105–25.

———. 1937. Interrelation of Prices, Output, Savings, and Investment. *Review of Economic Statistics* 19.3:109–32.

———. 1951. *The Structure of the American Economy, 1919–1939*. New York: Oxford University Press.

Marschak, J. 1946. The Economic Aspects of Atomic Power. *Bulletin of Atomic Scientists* 2.5–6:8–9.

May, K. 1946. The Aggregation Problem for a One-Industry Model. *Econometrica* 14 (October): 285–98.

———. 1947. Technological Change and Aggregation. *Econometrica* 15 (January): 51–63.

Menke, J. 1947. Nuclear Fission as a Source of Power. *Econometrica* 15 (October): 314–34.

Mullenbach, P. 1953. Review of *Atomic Power: An Economic and Social Analysis*, by W. Isard and V. Whitney. *American Economic Review* 43 (June): 460.

Schurr, S. 1947. Economic Aspects of Atomic Energy as a Source of Power. *American Economic Review: Papers and Proceedings* 37.2:98–108.

———. 1949. Atomic Power in Selected Industries. *Harvard Business Review* 27.4: 459–79.

Schurr, S., and J. Marschak. 1950. *Economic Aspects of Atomic Power: An Exploratory Study*. Princeton, N.J.: Princeton University Press, for the Cowles Commission.

Simon, Herbert. Papers. Carnegie-Mellon University Library.

———. [1947] 1948. Some Economic Effects of Technological Change. Paper presented at the Chicago meeting of the Econometric Society, 27 December 1947 (known as the Christmas paper), as reported in *Econometrica* 16.2:199–200. In Simon Papers, Atomic Energy.

———. 1947a. Effects of Increased Productivity upon the Ratio of Urban to Rural Population. *Econometrica* 15 (January): 31–42.

———. 1947b. On the Economic Effects of Technological Change. In Simon Papers, Atomic Energy.

———. 1947c. Some Economic Effects of Technological Change (Cowles Commission Staff Paper no. 202), as reported in minutes of Cowles Commission discussion meeting, 105, 12 July 1947, recorded by E. Domar. In Simon Papers, Atomic Energy.

———. 1948. "Trigger Effects" of Technological Change. In Simon Papers, Atomic Energy.

———. 1950a. Atomic Power and the Industrialization of Backward Areas. Chap. 14 in Schurr and Marschak 1950.

———. 1950b. The Effects of Atomic Power on National or Regional Economies. Chap. 13 in Schurr and Marschak 1950.

———. 1951. Effects of Technological Change in a Linear Model. In *Activity Analysis of Production and Allocation*, edited by T. Koopmans. New York: Wiley.

———. 1982. *Models of Bounded Rationality: Economic Analysis and Public Policy*. Cambridge, Mass.: MIT Press.

Smyth, H. 1946. *Atomic Energy for Military Purposes*. Princeton, N.J.: Princeton University Press.

Thomas, C. 1946. Nuclear Power. In *The International Control of Atomic Energy*, 121–27. Washington, D.C.: Government Printing Office.

Young, W. 1998. *Atomic Energy Costing*. Norwell and Boston, Mass.: Kluwer Academic Press.

Why Do Empirical Results Change? Forecasts as Tests of Rational Expectations

Robert S. Goldfarb and H. O. Stekler

The term *applied economics* probably has as many meanings as there are schools of thought in economics. Whatever its meaning, many applied economics fields include literatures involving empirical evidence. Labor economists have estimated labor supply elasticities; industrial organization economists have worried about measures of market power; economists studying addictive behavior estimate price elasticities of demand for cigarettes; public finance economists analyze whether cutting capital gains taxes will raise revenues; trade economists measure trade elasticities; those interested in business cycles estimate interest rate elasticities. Empirical activity has not been limited to measuring important parameters. Economists working in applied fields have also provided empirical evidence to support or refute particular propositions, models, theories, and frameworks.[1]

While many of the empirical examples cited above involve applied fields with a microeconomic orientation, this article focuses on an empirical literature that is associated with macroeconomic theory and then "fed back" on that theory's literature in an interesting way. The story proceeds through a number of sometimes overlapping stages. In the first stage, macroeconomics spawned the applied fields of economic

We wish to thank Roger Backhouse, Jeff Biddle, Bryan Boulier, David Ribar, Chris Snyder, Warren Young, and an anonymous referee for helpful comments and suggestions.

1. Examples include, What is the evidence for pure versus impure altruism? For the Phillips curve? For "competitive" wage determination? For economists' being more selfish than others? For airline markets' being "contestable"? For the proposition that raising the minimum wage lowers employment? For the idea that the more concentrated an industry is, the higher are its profits? For diminishing returns to R and D?

forecasting and empirical macromodel building. In the second stage the forecasting field generated data (and a literature) about forecaster performance. In the third stage, these forecasting records were used to test the rational expectations idea, a central assumption of recent macroeconomic theorizing. In a final stage overlapping the previous one, the concepts developed to test the rationality assumption fed back to the forecasting field, providing enhanced procedures for evaluating and improving actual forecasts.

The purpose of this essay is twofold: first, to provide a historical narrative about the rationality of forecasts, and then to develop historical/methodological insights from this narrative. The history is of special interest not only because of the centrality of the rational expectations assumption in macroeconomic analysis, but also because the results produced by this empirical literature as it developed over time were convoluted and contradictory. In the process of our discussion we pose four questions:

1. What is the historical pattern of support for rational expectations in this empirical literature?
2. How can one explain the conflicting empirical results in this historical record?
3. In the face of these conflicting results, how can one evaluate the "cumulative weight of the evidence" from this testing literature as it proceeds?
4. Did this empirical testing literature feed back onto the forecasting and macrotheory literature?

Macroeconomics, Forecasting, and Expectations: A Brief Historical Narrative

The field of macroeconomics as we know it had its inception with the 1936 publication of Keynes's *General Theory*. However, even in the late 1950s, there were still graduate programs that covered macroeconomics topics in courses called National Income Analysis, Monetary Theory, and Business Cycles, suggesting that macroeconomics per se was not recognized everywhere as a separate field. And it was only in 1956 that the *American Economic Review* first introduced the classification of Income and Employment Theory into its book review section.

Models and Forecasting

The development of macroeconometric models can be traced to Jan Tinbergen's (1939) seminal work. The new macroeconomic theory provided the underlying framework, and new econometric techniques, based on Cowles Foundation research, provided an additional stimulus for the development of these models. L. R. Klein's (1950) model built on this framework and was the first in a series of such models designed to explain and predict the behavior of the U.S. economy.

Prior to econometric forecasting of the economy, other techniques were used to make economic predictions. As early as 1938, the National Bureau of Economic Research had identified indicators that were useful for predicting turning points in the U.S. economy (Mitchell and Burns 1938). However, the formal evaluation of the performance of alternative forecasting techniques came later. Charles Roos (1955) described and compared alternative methods; Sidney Alexander (1958) evaluated some of the NBER methodology; Henri Theil (1958) presented a methodology for evaluating quantitative predictions; Victor Zarnowitz (1967) undertook the first analysis of quantitative judgmental forecasts; and H. O. Stekler (1968) produced a comprehensive comparison of the then-existing U.S. econometric models.

Expectations Concepts

One of the most challenging topics in macroeconomics during the 1950s and 1960s was to determine how individuals formed their expectations about economic variables. The two main competing concepts were extrapolative versus adaptive expectations. The literature abounds with studies that sought to determine which of these was superior. In the extrapolative expectations case, the expected value of an economic variable (X_{et}) was the value that was observed in the most recent period (X_{t-1}) adjusted for a change in the trend ($X_{t-1} - X_{t-2}$):

$$X_{et} = a_0 + a_1 X_{t-1} + a_2(X_{t-1} - X_{t-2}).$$

There were a variety of assumptions about the values of the a_i. Originally, it was assumed that $a_0 = 0$ and $a_1 = 1$, while a_2 could take on either positive or negative values. If a_2 was positive and the trend was extrapolated, individuals would be expecting the observed trend to continue in the future. If that coefficient was negative, the past trend would be expected to reverse itself and the expectations were called regressive.[2]

In contrast, the theory of adaptive expectations asserts that next period's expected value of a variable equals the last observed value plus a correction for last period's forecast error:

$$X_{et} = X_{t-1} + a_1(X_{et-1} - X_{t-1}).$$

An obvious problem with this way of determining expectations is that if the variable has a trend, there will be systematic biases. In addition to these possible biases, both the extrapolative and adaptive theories were backward looking. In the first case, the expectations depended upon the most recent past and how the past changed, while the adaptive expectations were geometrically weighted averages of past observations. What was needed was a theory of expectation formation that was forward looking.

The Rational Expectations Concept

John Muth's (1961) theory of rational expectations provided just such a forward-looking explanation of the way individuals form their views about the future. Muth argued that expectations about an economic variable were rational if they were formed in the same way as the world was generating the actual values of that variable:

$$X_t = a_0 + a_1 X_{et} + e_t.$$

For the forecasts to be rational, they must be unbiased, and the errors must be uncorrelated with any information known at the time that the expectations were formed. The specific statistical tests for unbiasedness are presented in the next section.

Muth is credited with the development of the theory of rational expectations that is now incorporated into macroeconomic modeling, but this idea was actually developed in a microeconomic framework. It was associated in particular with a dynamic cobweb model for analyzing agricultural supply functions.[3] It is also interesting to note that many early microeconomic studies did not find rational expectations

2. If a_0 and a_2 were 0 and $a_1 = 1$, the expectations were called static. Lovell 1986 contains a useful discussion of additional competing expectations concepts.

3. Muth (1961, 320) states that "this prediction formula has been used by Nerlove . . . to estimate the supply elasticity of certain agricultural commodities."

formulations empirically successful (see Lovell 1986). This of course raises the issue of why the rational expectations hypothesis was adopted in the macrotheory literature, when the microeconometric literature suggested skepticism.

Muth's concept about expectations formation was not immediately incorporated into macroeconomic theorizing or into empirical tests of this hypothesis using macroeconomic variables such as GNP or the CPI. Michael Lovell (1986, n. 1) suggests that it was only incorporated into the macromodels after economists recognized that this concept had policy implications. Partly in response to the widespread incorporation of this hypothesis into theoretical and empirical macromodels, a literature developed that tested the rationality hypothesis using economic forecasts.

Testing for Rational Expectations

Before proceeding with the history of this literature, we must explain the concepts involved. While there are other ways of testing the rational expectations hypothesis, we are concerned here with the literature that has focused on the rationality of forecasts of economic variables. In order to empirically test the rationality hypothesis using these forecasts, the characteristics associated with that hypothesis had to be enumerated and a set of statistical procedures developed.

The two main concepts are weak and strong rationality. Weak rationality means that the forecasts are unbiased—that is, that individuals do not make systematic errors—and also do not fail the weak form informational efficiency tests. A regression like (1), estimated by OLS, is usually used to test for bias. In (1) F represents a forecasted value of an economic variable while A represents its actual value (outcome). There is no bias if the coefficients (a, b) in equation (1) are 0 and 1, respectively:

$$A_t = a + bF_t + e_t \tag{1}$$

and the errors of the regression are serially uncorrelated. Sometimes the test is applied to each of the coefficients individually, but most often the F distribution is used in testing the joint hypothesis that $a = 0$ and $b = 1$. In addition, weak form informational efficiency requires that the forecast errors $(A_t - F_t)$ be uncorrelated with past forecast values or errors. If this condition is not fulfilled, then there exists information in the past observations that could have been utilized for the new forecast. This information would certainly have been available to the forecaster when the new forecast was generated.

In the case of multiperiod predictions, the assumptions associated with OLS might not hold. The error terms of multiperiod predictions might be serially correlated because the cumulative changes have overlapping quarters in common. In this case the regression equation (1) must be estimated by a different statistical procedure, general method of moments (GMM), but the tests for bias, after the coefficients have been estimated, remain the same, while the informational efficiency test is concerned with the moving average order of the error terms.

Turning from weak to strong rationality, the latter requires that weak rationality be achieved and that the forecast error not be correlated with *any* other information known at the time that the prediction is prepared. If there is a correlation, the forecaster has not efficiently utilized these data. Thus, whereas weak form rationality involves only information about the forecasted variable itself, strong form rationality broadens the forecaster's information requirements to the universe of potentially useful economic time-series.

With a myriad of series available whenever a forecast is prepared, it is impossible to definitively test whether or not an individual has efficiently utilized *all* available information. One researcher using a particular sample of data series might find that strong rationality is not rejected, while another researcher, using a different set of data series, rejects this rationality hypothesis. A conceptual answer to this dilemma is suggested by G. S. Maddala (1991), but, as a practical matter, it is hard to actually apply.[4]

A History of Tests Using Livingston Price Forecast Data

An empirical literature using macroeconomic forecasts to test the rationality hypothesis began appearing in 1969. In that literature, various sets

4. "The question of what variables should be included in the information set I_{t-1} actually depends on costs and benefits. It is true that past values of the variable being forecast are readily available and should be in the information set. But the same cannot be said of other variables. Agents with economically rational expectations will set the marginal cost equal to the marginal benefit of acquiring information. In practice, however, since these costs and benefits are difficult to observe, it is hard to say what the information set I_{t-1} ought to be" (Maddala 1991, 324–25).

of forecasts were examined to determine whether or not those predictions were rational. This testing literature produces a meandering and convoluted set of results over time, failing to quickly produce a clear and unambiguous answer about rationality.

We will document this time pattern by examining a set of studies that used a single database, the Livingston surveys of economists' expectations. The Livingston surveys are the price (and GNP) forecasts of economists collected by Joseph Livingston. (Livingston began collecting the data in 1947; after his death, the Federal Reserve Bank of Philadelphia assumed responsibility for the survey.) Between 1970 and 1989 eleven published papers used this data set to investigate the rationality of price forecasts. The empirical results and conclusions derived from this series of studies have varied. In some cases the expectations were judged to be rational, only for this conclusion to be called into question by other parts of the same study, or by the next study.

Stephen Turnovsky (1970) is the first to use these data to analyze how expectations were formed. He is concerned not only with the rationality of the forecasts but is also interested in determining whether the adaptive and/or extrapolative theories might explain the formation of price expectations six and twelve months ahead.

His analysis suggests that none of the theories is able to explain the formation of expectations for the period 1954–64, but all of the theories fit the data better for the period 1962–69, with the extrapolative theory favored over the adaptive. The tests for the rationality of the expectations yield conflicting results. The null that the 1954–64 forecasts were rational is rejected for all of the data. For the years 1962–69 the hypothesis that the expectations are unbiased is not rejected for the six-month predictions but is rejected for the twelve-month forecasts.[5]

The subsequent papers that use the Livingston forecasts do not test the adaptive and extrapolative theories of expectation formation but concentrate on testing whether forecasts are rational. The statistical methodology of these studies also differs from Turnovsky's. Turnovsky, as well as James Pesando (1975), for example, use Muth's concept that a rational forecast should be generated by the same process that produces the actual outcomes. They assume that an autoregressive process based on current and past price changes determines future price changes.

5. Turnovsky used equation (1) but did not apply the F test. He only examined the two coefficients in the equation separately.

Consequently for the forecasts to be rational they must incorporate all of the information contained in the previously observed rates of inflation. Thus the one-period-ahead forecasts would be efficient if the coefficients of the autoregression explaining the actual price levels in period t did not differ from the autoregression which explained the one-period-ahead price forecasts for period $t - 1$. However, the evaluation procedures differ from Turnovsky to Pesando. Pesando explicitly compares the coefficients of the two autoregressions, using a Chow test. Multiperiod forecasts would be consistent (and thus rational) if they were generated by the same process, that is, Wold's chain principle of forecasting.

Pesando analyzes both the six-month and twelve-month forecasts for two time periods: 1959–69 and 1962–69. For both time periods, the null hypothesis that the six-month forecasts are rational is not rejected; the opposite results are obtained for the twelve-month predictions.

Despite the difference in evaluation procedures from Turnovsky to Pesando, their results for the years 1962–69 agree with each other (both studies do not reject rationality for six months, but do for twelve months). The findings for the other time periods cannot be compared because the time periods that are examined are different in the two studies. Nevertheless, at the time that Pesando published his paper, economists could not have derived definitive conclusions about the rationality of the price forecasts because the results of the six- and twelve-month predictions do not agree.

Pesando's interpretation of his own findings contains an interesting twist. He suggests that the failure to reveal rationality may indicate that the expectations measured in the Livingston data "are not those of the market as a whole, on the maintained hypothesis that market forecasts must, indeed, be rational" (1975, 856). While he supports this possibility by citing studies that equity markets are efficient, the argument itself reveals how intuitively appealing the rational expectations hypothesis was to observers. If the data do not fit rational expectations, too bad for the data!

John Carlson (1977) also worries about the Livingston data, but in a way different from Pesando. Carlson argues that previous studies display "a pattern of uncritical acceptance of the data as copied out of the newspaper columns" (28) and that the data require a crucially different interpretation than the previous studies provide. The previous studies assumed that the December levels of the CPI were known at the time that the economists made their predictions of the level of this variable for June and December of the following year. In actuality, when the forecasts were made, only the October figures were known. Thus, economists were, in fact, making predictions of the value of the CPI eight and fourteen months in the future instead of six and twelve months as had previously been assumed. Therefore, these forecasts had to be compared with the actual changes that occurred over eight- and fourteen-month periods rather than over a half year or a year. The methodology that was used earlier thus introduced a bias because the actual base level for December could be different from what the economists might have assumed it to be.

When Carlson uses the data adjusted for the fact that the forecasts are for eight and fourteen months, his findings conflict with one of Pesando's conclusions. The shorter-term forecasts are no longer rational.[6] From Carlson's results, all mean CPI forecasts, short and long, reject the rationality hypothesis, and we would seem to have a definitive conclusion. Unfortunately, a definitive conclusion has not in fact been obtained, since the mean wholesale price forecasts made by the same group of economists do not reject the rationality hypothesis. Carlson suggests that it is extremely unlikely that the forecasts are rational in one case and irrational in the other.[7]

The next study by Donald Mullineaux (1978) argues that the methodology used by Pesando and Carlson was inappropriate. Both used the Chow test, but that test requires that the error variances of the realized inflation and the predicted inflation equation be identical. This assumption is unlikely to be satisfied, since the variance of a set of forecasts is usually smaller than the variance of the set of outcomes. Mullineaux then suggests an alternative test which does not require this assumption. To determine whether the forecasts incorporate all of the information contained in the past history of the variable, he regresses the forecast error on past values of prices. All the coefficients should be 0 if the rationality hypothesis holds. Otherwise, there is information in the history of the series that has not been exploited.

Using this procedure, Mullineaux runs tests for two time periods, 1959–69 and 1962–69, using two sets of data, Pesando's and Carlson's.

6. This finding applies to the time period 1959–69. Carlson did not replicate Pesando's other time period.

7. Carlson also suggests that expectations may be formed differently during periods with different inflation rates.

For the six-month Pesando data from 1959–69, the null of rationality is rejected. For the eight-month Carlson data for the same period, it is not rejected. For the twelve-month Pesando and fourteen-month Carlson data 1959–69, the null is not rejected. For 1962–69 the null is not rejected using either set of data for either of the forecast horizons. Again there is no definitive conclusion because some forecasts are rational and others are not. It is also worth noting that Mullineaux's findings contradict several of the Carlson and Pesando results.

Rather than discussing the seven remaining Livingston-based studies in detail, we provide brief summaries of their results in table 1. The evidence in table 1 and the previous text discussion of four earlier studies document conflicting findings within and across the eleven studies based on the Livingston data.

The existence of conflicting findings is also reflected in the comments of contributors to this literature. For example, Stephen Figlewski and Paul Wachtel (1981, 1) observe that

> there is presently little agreement over what the data show about expectations formation. Depending on the time period examined, the estimation technique employed, and the version of the data series tested, different researchers have interpreted their evidence as supporting rational expectations, contradicting rationality or pointing towards an adaptive or extrapolative expectations scheme.

Recall that the first of our four questions posed early in this article was, What is the historical pattern of support for rational expectations in this empirical literature? One answer to this question is that the *individual* Livingston-based studies *never* provided consistent support for the rational expectations hypothesis.

Interpretation of the Conflicting Evidence

Our chronological summary of empirical studies indicated that a particular study often displayed conflicting results. Moreover, the results of one study frequently contradicted other earlier studies. To distinguish among these conflicting results, we use the terms *contradiction* and *flip-flop*. Contradictions arise when a single study contains conflicting findings about rationality. For example, a study might find that the one-period-ahead forecasts may look "rational," while the two-period-ahead forecasts do not. Contradictions also occur when contemporaneous

Table 1 Rationality studies of price/inflation forecasts, 1979–89

Study	Data Time Period	Forecast Horizon	Statistical Methodology	Results	Relationship to Prior Studies
Pearce 1979	1959–75	8–14 months	Fits ARIMA to CPI data; uses recursive estimate from ARIMA to compare to Livingston.	Livingston errors are larger; not rational.	Contradicts some prior efficiency results.
Figlewski and Wachtel 1981	1947–75	8 months	Pooled cross-sectional time series. *F* test on coefficients.	Rejects null of unbiasedness; errors autocorrelated.	No previous pooled cross-sectional time series studies.
Brown and Maital 1981	1961:IV to 1977:IV	6–12 months	Hansen-Hodrick estimation procedure for multiperiod estimates; joint tests on coefficients.	Null not rejected for CPI or WPI.	Results about bias conflict with conclusions of previous studies.
Hafer and Resler 1982	1959–69; 1959–78	8–14 months	Livingston data disaggregated into 6 groups; uses Mullineaux procedures, but Hansen-Hodrick not used for 14 months.	Efficiency null rejected for 5 of 6 groups (8 months); consistency (14 months) null not rejected for 5 of 6 groups.	No previous studies with this disaggregation, but study gives contradiction between 8- and 14-month results.
Schroeter and Smith 1986	June 1948–December 1981	8–14 months	Uses Carlson data; Hansen-Hodrick procedure to correct Brown-Maital results; *F* test for joint null on coefficients.	CPI forecasts not rational; WPI rationality not rejected.	Contradiction between CPI, WPI results; conflicts with previous Brown-Maital results for CPI forecasts.
Bryan and Gavin 1986	1956:I to 1980:I	Quarterly	Uses Hansen-Hodrick to correct earlier study on Michigan data. *F* test for joint null on coefficients.	Livingston surveys not rational; null for Michigan not rejected.	Contradiction between Michigan, Livingston results.
Batchelor and Dua 1989	1956–66:I; 1966:II–1977:IV; 1978–83	6 months; year	Includes both Michigan and Livingston data. Corrects Bryan-Gavin; uses different MA process; *F* tests for joint null on coefficients.	Forecasts are rational in most periods.	Conflicts with some of previous Livingston data studies, not with previous Michigan data studies.

Note: For the data time periods, "1961:IV" means the fourth quarter of 1961, "1977:IV" means the fourth quarter of 1977, etc.

studies using different data sets yield opposing conclusions about rationality. Flip-flops occur when a later study using the same database conflicts with the findings of prior papers.

The studies using the Livingston forecasts exhibit both of these characteristics. For example, Turnovsky's study produces a contradiction, since it contains conflicting findings about rationality depending on the horizon of the forecasts. Pesando obtained results identical to Turnovsky's and thus generated the same contradiction. The Carlson study contains both a flip-flop and a contradiction. His results reversed those of Pesando—the flip-flop—and were internally inconsistent, since results about the CPI and WPI did not agree. Similarly, Mullineaux's results represent a contradiction (since some forecasts are rational, others are not) and a flip-flop (since several of the Carlson and Pesando results are reversed). Finally, the last column of table 1 indicates that six of the seven studies described there involve contradictions or flip-flops or both.

The second question we posed initially asked, How can one explain the conflicting empirical results in this historical record? It is impossible to identify all of the factors that "caused" a specific conflicting result. However, the text discussion and the presentation in table 1 of the seven Livingston-based studies identify a number of important contributing factors. One clearly significant cause was variation in statistical methods. Mullineaux (1978), for example, argues that the methods used in two previous papers were incorrect; applying a different method, he gets different results. The use of Hansen-Hodrick (1980) procedures (see table 1) is another example of changed econometric procedures. A second contributing factor is disagreement over what data are appropriate. Carlson's (1977) argument that forecasters are making eight-month rather than six-month predictions is the major example. Both of these factors fit under the rubric that "the data-processing method can affect the results."

What does not fit under that rubric is that there are contradictions within an individual study: different forecast horizons generate different rationality results, or WPI data say one thing while CPI data say something else. What causes these within-study contradictions remains an open question. Two potential explanations are (1) that forecasters can incorporate information about the current situation into their current quarter forecasts, so their current quarter forecasts are "better" than their distant quarter predictions, and (2) that individual forecasters might find it more difficult to forecast the CPI than the WPI, perhaps because they have specific knowledge about particular components of the WPI.

What about the "Weight of the Evidence"?

Faced with these contradictions and flip-flops, what about the "weight of the evidence"? That is, can a historian of ideas determine whether, at various dates after 1970, empirical studies suggested and implied a prevailing view about the rationality of these forecasts? Could definitive inferences have been drawn from these results, or would the conclusion instead have had to be that "the results are indeterminate"? The Figlewski-Wachtel quote above suggests it would have been difficult to find a determinate result in 1981. By 1986, however, Lovell was able to make a stronger summary statement. He argues that his survey of the empirical literature shows that "a number of empirical studies of expectations (are) not supportive of the commonly invoked rational expectations hypothesis" (1986, 120). This statement appears in a section of his paper titled "Implications—Should the Facts Be Allowed to Spoil a Good Story?"

The statistical technique known as meta-analysis allows new light to be shed on this question. This technique for systematically "combining" empirical results provides a way to investigate what the weight of the evidence might have been at various points in the history of this empirical literature. In a companion paper (Goldfarb and Stekler 1999), we have shown how this technique might be applied to this literature. Because our companion paper addresses the technical problems involved in using that technique, here we present only some of the weight-of-the-evidence results.

Our meta-analysis encompasses a total of thirty price forecast studies from 1970 to 1998. In addition to the Livingston data studies discussed above, these studies use forecast data sets from the Michigan Survey Research Center, ASA/NBER, the Blue Chip Economic Indicators, and the Money Market Surveys; the studies also used forecasts of econometric models or forecasting services.[8]

8. The Michigan Survey Research Center collects forecasts of consumers. The ASA/NBER survey collects predictions of professional forecasters and is now called the Survey of Professional Forecasters. The Blue Chip Economic Indicators is a consensus forecasting service run by Bob Eggert; once a month this service conducts a telephone survey to obtain the forecasts of prominent economists in major U.S. business and financial institutions. Money Market

Meta-analysis allows us to statistically test whether the results of separate studies, taken together, provide a verdict about the hypothesis of rationality. Since this weight of the evidence may have changed at various points over the history of this literature, we performed a separate meta-analysis for every relevant year over the period. That is, we performed an additional meta-analysis for every year in which a new study was published, since its publication changed the available stock of studies. Thus, for example, our meta-analysis for 1986 only includes the studies that had been published as of 1986.

A striking advantage of a chronological series of meta-analyses is that one can gauge whether a new study or group of studies is important enough to cause a *reversal* in the weight of the cumulative evidence from the literature.[9] That is, it allows a historian to determine whether the addition of a new study to the existing literature causes a change in the meta-analysis verdict rendered by that literature. The procedure for conducting a meta-analysis is described in the appendix.

To carry out a meta-analysis, it is necessary to establish a null hypothesis. A simple approach would be to test the null that all forecasters are rational. The difficulty here is that the null hypothesis—all forecasters are rational—is arguably too stringent a test of rational expectations. Observers such as Steven Sheffrin (1983) have noted that some individuals may not have strong incentives to prepare accurate forecasts displaying rational expectations. Suppose some forecasters lack these incentives, but most do not. Then the hypothesis that all forecasters are rational might be rejected, but the hypothesis that, say, 90 percent of forecasters are rational might not be. To deal with this problem, our companion paper tests three alternative nulls: (1) all forecasters are rational; (2) 90 percent of forecasters are rational; and (3) 80 percent of forecasters are rational. Here we present in detail only the results from the null that

---

Surveys is a weekly survey of sixty U.S. securities dealers that collects their predictions of changes in economic variables to be announced in the near future. (The survey of the CPI predictions is conducted two weeks prior to the publication of the actual CPI number.)

9. The notion that conflicting evidence may emerge to challenge an existing weight-of-the-evidence view in various empirical economics literatures has been studied elsewhere. Goldfarb (1997) has identified more than twenty empirical literatures that display this kind of conflict as the literature ages, and Bradford De Long and Kevin Lang (1992) provide evidence that is also consistent with the existence of this phenomenon. These earlier studies are not based on the kind of meta-analysis we do here, however. Moreover, the reversals identified in the current study require an actual change in the weight of the evidence, whereas the two earlier papers cited above only require "some" conflicting evidence rather than an entire reversal of the weight of the evidence.

90 percent of forecasters are rational. As we shall see, these results lie between the findings associated with the other two hypotheses.

Meta-analysis Findings

Table 2 presents a chronology of meta-analysis findings for the null hypothesis that 90 percent of forecasters are rational. It lists every year from 1970 to 1998 in which the publication of new studies from all sources—not just the Livingston surveys—would have allowed a new meta-analysis. The meta-analysis results are tabulated in each listed year for forecasts at three possible time horizons: one quarter ahead, two quarters ahead, and four quarters ahead. For each of these forecast horizons there are three columns: column A shows the number of independent observations available for a meta-analysis; column B presents the number of these observations for which the null (that the particular forecasts were rational) was rejected; and column C displays the probability that the column B numbers could have been obtained by chance if 90 percent of the forecasts were in fact rational. Thus, a very low probability is required in row C to reject the null that 90 percent of forecasters are in fact rational.

We now illustrate how this procedure might be used to determine what the weight of the evidence was in every year represented in our table. Consider the first-quarter results. Until 1985 the probabilities in column C for the first quarter remain above .05. That is, until 1985, the null that 90 percent of forecasters are rational could not be rejected at the 5 percent level. From 1985 through 1989, the null could be rejected because probabilities fall below .05. From 1990 through 1997, this result is reversed, and the null could once again not be rejected. In 1998, it could again be rejected. That is, based on chronological meta-analyses of current-quarter forecasts, the weight of the cumulative evidence *reverses* three times over the twenty-eight years from 1970 through 1998. However, since the number of observations prior to 1985 is small, that period should be given less attention; there are two reversals from 1985 through 1998.

Using the period from 1985 on, neither the results from the six-month span nor the four-quarter results display any reversals, although reversals do take place if the period before 1985 is included. Two other interesting features of these results are that (1) in some years (1991 and 1995), the meta-analyses reject rationality for some horizons but not others and

(2) some studies can have a very large effect on the cumulative weight of evidence, single-handedly causing reversals. Thus, for example, a study by Zarnowitz (1985) changes the one-quarter and four-quarter meta-analysis results (compare the 1985 row of table 2 with the previous [1982] row), and a study by Anthony Davies and Kajal Lahiri (1998) reverses the current-quarter meta-analysis results.

Comparing results using the three different null hypotheses yields the following summary findings. First, there are reversals—that is, changes in the results from the cumulative weight of the evidence—no matter which null is used. Second, despite these reversals, the six- and twelve-month results from 1985 on consistently reject rationality for all three nulls. Third, the one-quarter results show considerably more ambiguity from 1985 on, varying depending on which of the three hypotheses is used. The "all forecasters" criterion consistently rejects rationality for the one-quarter forecasts, the 80 percent criterion consistently does not reject the rationality of the one-quarter forecasts, and (as we have seen) the 90 percent criterion is in between the other two, reversing itself several times with respect to the one-quarter results.

The meta-analysis yields the following conclusion about our current state of knowledge: if any forecasts are rational, it is only for the current quarter, and even there the evidence is mixed. It also suggests an answer to the third of our questions posed at the outset: In the face of conflicting results, how can we evaluate the cumulative weight of the evidence as this testing literature developed? Our answer is that meta-analysis provides a potentially useful technique for evaluating the weight of the evidence when there are conflicting empirical results. Among its strengths are its ability to identify any reversals in the weight of the evidence that might arise as the literature proceeds. Nevertheless, even this technique cannot completely resolve the conflicting results in this literature on testing for rational expectations.

Additional Historical and Methodological Implications

Question 4 inquired about feedback loops from the testing literature to the forecasting literature. Such a feedback does indeed exist. Using forecasts to test for rationality has led to improvements in the methodology for judging predictions and therefore potentially to increased forecast accuracy. These methodological improvements resulted from applying

Table 2 Examination of the rationality of inflation forecasts (90% criterion)

	Current Quarter			Six Months (Two-Quarter Span)			Annual (Four-Quarter Span)		
Year	Number of Independent Cases (A)	Number of Rejections of Null of Rationality (B)	Probability that Number of Rejections Could Have Been Attained by Chance[a] (C)	Number of Independent Cases (A)	Number of Rejections of Null of Rationality (B)	Probability that Number of Rejections Could Have Been Attained by Chance[a] (C)	Number of Independent Cases (A)	Number of Rejections of Null of Rationality (B)	Probability that Number of Rejections Could Have Been Attained by Chance[a] (C)
1970	—	—	—	1	0	n.a.	1	1	n.a.
1975	—	—	—	1	0	n.a.	1	1	n.a.
1977	—	—	—	2	1	.269	3	1	.375
1978	3	2	.057	5	3	.024	6	3	.043
1979	3	2	.057	5	4	.002	6	4	.005
1981	3	2	.057	3	1	.375	3	0	1.000
1982	4	2	.103	8	5	.002	3	0	1.000
1985	86	25	<.001	87	42	<.001	82	51	<.001
1986	86	25	<.001	87	43	<.001	82	52	<.001
1987	87	25	<.001	87	43	<.001	82	52	<.001
1988	93	25	.001	87	43	<.001	82	52	<.001
1989	93	25	.001	89	43	<.001	86	52	<.001
1990	74	12	.386	89	43	<.001	86	52	<.001
1991	74	12	.386	89	43	<.001	105	57	<.001
1992	74	12	.386	89	43	<.001	108	59	<.001
1993	74	12	.386	89	43	<.001	108	58	<.001
1995	75	13	.288	89	43	<.001	108	58	<.001
1998	60	17	.004	89	43	<.001	108	58	<.001

[a] The probability indicates the significance level at which the hypothesis of rationality can be rejected. Thus a low probability number (such as .001) indicates that the null of rationality *can* be rejected.

the strong form rationality tests in forecast evaluations. These tests investigate whether all available information has been utilized in generating those forecasts.

A set of forecasts must be compared against some standard to determine whether they can be improved. It had been customary to use naive or time-series predictions as this benchmark. This procedure assumed that these benchmark predictions were the best available alternative forecasts. More recently, forecast evaluations have asked, "Was there any information available that would have improved the forecast?" (Joutz 1988). This is exactly the strong form rationality test. Thus, the process of testing for the rationality of forecasts resulted in the improvement of forecast evaluation techniques. Moreover, if subsequent forecasts incorporate useful information that had not previously been included, their quality would be improved.

Which brings us back to question 1: What is the historical pattern of support for rational expectations in this empirical literature? We noted earlier that the eleven Livingston data studies exhibited conflicting results that did not provide clear support for the rational expectations assumption. Moreover, Lovell, writing in 1986, concludes that the literature to that point is not supportive of rational expectations.

But what about the meta-analysis answer to that same question, which is based on a larger number of studies over a longer period? It clearly indicates that at no point over the time span of this testing literature does the cumulative weight of the evidence provide consistent support for a rational expectations assumption.

The obvious follow-up question would seem to be, Why does this empirical evidence appear to have had little or no impact on the acceptability of the rational expectations assumption? We can only suggest some alternative (and not necessarily mutually exclusive) explanations for this apparent lack of impact. First, viewed from the meta-analysis perspective, it took a long time for this seemingly contradictory literature to come to a stable weight-of-the-evidence conclusion. Our results do not stabilize until 1985. Moreover, while a meta-analysis giving this result could have been done in 1985, the fact is that meta-analysis procedures were not applied to this literature before our 1999 work. Thus, one might well argue that these results are not widely known even now. This leaves open the question of why Lovell's 1986 negative conclusion about empirical support for rational expectations seems to have had little effect. Second, testing a theory by its assumptions runs afoul of well-known Friedmanesque ideas (Friedman 1953) of how to test a theory.[10] Third, even in the absence of these Friedmanesque qualms, one might decide that forecasts measured by surveys are not the most desirable test case for rational expectations. At a more specific level, we have seen that Pesando at least was suspicious of the Livingston data in particular. Fourth, one may have misgivings about meta-analysis techniques in general, or about the application of meta-analysis to this particular literature.[11] Fifth, there may be other tests of rational expectations frameworks that do not get such negative results. Sixth is a well-known Kuhnian claim from the philosophy of science: a theory is never defeated by facts alone, no matter how devastating, but only by another theory. This claim seems to apply especially well to economics.[12] It remains to be seen whether our meta-analysis results, if they come to be accepted as statistically defensible, will have any effect on the willingness of researchers to keep using rational expectations assumptions.

Appendix

Description of Meta-analysis Procedures

Meta-analysis proceeds in the following way. Suppose we have six studies investigating the rationality of forecasts. Each study uses data for a different forecaster, so the six studies are arguably independent. Five of the studies find, at the 5 percent level of significance, that the null of rationality cannot be rejected. One of the six does reject. The meta-analysis takes this count of the number of rejections and then uses the

10. After citing a Prescott version of the Friedman argument applied to rational expectations, Sheffrin notes that "Prescott somewhat understates the value of the survey data. Researchers have not used the survey data to evaluate all the implications of the rational expectations hypothesis but simply to test if the hypothesis bears any resemblance to actual reported expectations. If every survey (including those that examined individual responses) revealed that expectations were totally at odds with the realized time series, then an unbiased scientific investigator would not put much faith in a research program based on rational expectations" (1983, 23).

11. See our companion paper (Goldfarb and Stekler 1999) for some discussion of problems with meta-analysis and with this application. One specific problem is that individual studies often lump together the forecasts of more than one forecaster and then test the rationality of that "average" forecast. It is not hard to envisage situations in which the average forecast is not rational, but a large percentage of the underlying individual forecasts might be.

12. The statement in the text is a paraphrase of a statement by Albert O. Hirschman (1970, 62). Hirschman is in turn quoting Paul Streeten, who is paraphrasing Thomas Kuhn (1962).

binomial distribution with $p = .05$ to see whether this many rejections could have been obtained by chance. This tests the null that *all* forecasters are rational; a very low probability (below .05) of obtaining this result by chance would reject the null of rationality. Since the likelihood of one rejection of the null in six "tries" (one rejection in six studies) occurring by chance is .265, the null of rationality cannot be rejected at conventional levels of significance. Only a much lower probability of this number of rejections happening by chance could lead to a meta-analysis rejection of the null of rationality.

In applying meta-analysis to this literature, we had to do the following:

1. Carefully specify what studies could legitimately be combined into a meta-analysis. An intuitively appealing rule is that only independent studies should be combined, as opposed to reiterations or clones of previous studies.[13] The idea is to avoid double-counting or double-weighting virtually identical studies. For example, consider two studies, the second becoming available one year after the first. The second study incorporates all the data in the first study, plus one extra year of data, and employs the same techniques to analyze the data. These two studies are not independent, and the second study appears to supersede the first. We would only include the second study in our meta-analysis. Since we do a chronological series of meta-analyses, some studies leave our sample as later studies with longer data series or superior statistical techniques become available.
2. Carefully specify what null hypotheses might be meaningful. This led to our using alternative null hypotheses, as described in the text.

References

Alexander, Sidney. 1958. Rate of Change Approaches to Forecasting. *The Economic Journal* 68.270:288–301.

13. The issues here are related to the more general concerns about checking versus replicating versus reproducing research results discussed in Backhouse 1997. While our focus is narrower than Backhouse's, our criterion for including studies seems consistent with his statement of what constitutes "new econometric studies": "to count as new, a study has to involve some significant difference from the old studies, in the same way that replication in natural science experiments involves more than an exact repetition of an old experiment" (Backhouse 1997, 143).

Backhouse, Roger. 1997. *Truth and Progress in Economic Thought*. Cheltenham, England: Edward Elgar.

Batchelor, Roy A., and Pami Dua. 1989. Household versus Economist Forecasts of Inflation: A Reassessment. *Journal of Money, Credit, and Banking* 21.2:252–57.

Brown, Bryan W., and Shlomo Maital. 1981. What Do Economists Know? An Empirical Study of "Expert" Expectations. *Econometrica* 49.2:491–504.

Bryan, Michael F., and William T. Gavin. 1986. Models of Inflation Expectations Formation: A Comparison of Household and Economist Forecasts. *Journal of Money, Credit, and Banking* 18.4:539–44.

Carlson, John A. 1977. A Study of Price Forecasts. *Annals of Economic and Social Measurement* 6.1:27–56.

Davies, Anthony, and Kajal Lahiri. 1998. Reexamining the Rational Expectations Hypothesis Using Panel Data on Multiperiod Forecasts. In *Analysis of Panels and Limited Dependent Variable Models*, edited by C. Hsiao, K. Lahiri, H. H. Pesaran, and L. F. Lee. Cambridge and New York: Cambridge University Press.

De Long, Bradford, and Kevin Lang. 1992. Are All Economic Hypotheses False? *Journal of Political Economy* 100.6:1257–72.

Figlewski, Stephen, and Paul Wachtel. 1981. The Formation of Inflationary Expectations. *Review of Economics and Statistics* 3.1:1–10.

Friedman, Milton. 1953. The Methodology of Positive Economics. In *Essays in Positive Economics*. Chicago: University of Chicago Press.

Goldfarb, Robert S. 1997. Now You See It, Now You Don't: Emerging Contrary Results in Economics. *Journal of Economic Methodology* 4.2:221–44.

Goldfarb, Robert S., and H. O. Stekler. 1999. Testing for Rationality: Would Meta-analysis Help? Mimeo.

Hafer, R.W., and David H. Resler. 1982. On the Rationality of Inflation Forecasts: A New Look at the Livingston Data. *Southern Economic Journal* 48.4:1049–56.

Hansen, Lars-Peter, and R. J. Hodrick. 1980. Foreign Exchange Rates as Optimal Predictors of Future Spot Prices: An Econometric Analysis. *Journal of Political Economy* 88.5:829–53.

Hirschman, Albert. 1970. *Exit, Voice, and Loyalty*. Cambridge: Harvard University Press.

Joutz, Frederick L. 1988. Informational Efficiency Tests of Quarterly Macroeconometric GNP Forecasts from 1976 to 1985. *Managerial and Decision Economics* 9.4:311–30.

Klein, L. R. 1950. *Economic Fluctuations in the United States, 1921–1941*. New York: Wiley.

Kuhn, Thomas. 1962. *The Structure of Scientific Revolutions*. Chicago: University of Chicago Press.

Lovell, Michael C. 1986. Tests of the Rational Expectations Hypothesis. *American Economic Review* 76.1:110–24.

Maddala, G. S. 1991. Survey Data on Expectations: What Have We Learnt? In *Macroeconomics and Econometrics*. Vol. 2 of *Issues in Contemporary Economics*, edited by Marc Nerlove. New York: NYU Press.

Mitchell, Wesley C., and Arthur F. Burns. 1938. *Statistical Indicators of Cyclical Revivals*. Bulletin 69. New York: National Bureau of Economic Research.

Mullineaux, Donald J. 1978. On Testing for Rationality: Another Look at the Livingston Price Expectations Data. *Journal of Political Economy* 86.2:329–36.

Muth, John F. 1961. Rational Expectations and the Theory of Price Movements. *Econometrica* 29.3:315–35.

Pearce, Douglas K. 1979. Comparing Survey and Rational Measures of Expected Inflation. *Journal of Money, Credit, and Banking* 11.4:447–56.

Pesando, James E. 1975. A Note on the Rationality of the Livingston Price Expectations. *Journal of Political Economy* 83.4:849–58.

Roos, Charles F. 1955. Survey of Economic Forecasting Techniques. *Econometrica* 23.4:363–95.

Schroeter, John R., and Scott L. Smith. 1986. A Reexamination of the Rationality of the Livingston Price Expectations. *Journal of Money, Credit, and Banking* 18.2:239–46.

Sheffrin, Steven. 1983. *Rational Expectations*. Cambridge: Cambridge University Press.

Stekler, H. O. 1968. Forecasting with Econometric Models: An Evaluation. *Econometrica* 36.3/4:437–63.

Theil, Henri. 1958. *Economic Forecasts and Policy*. Amsterdam: North Holland.

Tinbergen, Jan. 1939. *Statistical Testing of Business Cycle Theories II: Business Cycles in the United States of America, 1919–1932*. Geneva: League of Nations.

Turnovsky, Stephen J. 1970. Empirical Evidence on the Formation of Price Expectations. *Journal of the American Statistical Association* 65.332:1441–54.

Zarnowitz, Victor. 1967. *An Appraisal of Short-Term Economic Forecasts*. New York: National Bureau of Economic Research.

———. 1985. Rational Expectations and Macroeconomic Forecasts. *Journal of Business and Economic Statistics* 3.4:293–311.

The Very Idea of Applying Economics: The Modern Minimum-Wage Controversy and Its Antecedents

Thomas C. Leonard

Disagreements among economists rarely breach the academy's walls. The recent minimum-wage controversy is a significant exception. At first glance, all the sound and fury is a puzzle.[1] Minimum-wage effects, at least for current U.S. magnitudes, are small potatoes.[2] Of several more important policy concerns—entitlement reform, health insurance, CPI calculation, for example—none has generated anything like the vituperation that has characterized the minimum-wage controversy. But if the minimum-wage controversy is not especially important to the economy, it is very important to economics, and, thereby, to the status of economics as a policy science.

Correspondence may be addressed to Professor Thomas C. Leonard, Department of Economics, Fisher Hall, Princeton University, Princeton, NJ 08544; e-mail: tleonard@princeton.edu. I am grateful to Jeff Biddle, Bob Goldfarb, an anonymous referee, and participants in the 1999 *HOPE* conference on the history of applied economics for helpful comments on an earlier draft of this material.

1. In the wake of Card and Krueger 1995, one Nobel laureate intoned, "I tremble for my profession" (Miller 1996). Another made reference to "camp-following whores" (Buchanan 1996). A third eminence called Card and Krueger's main interlocutors, David Neumark and William Wascher, "heroes" (Barro 1996).

2. Even a 27 percent increase in the U.S. minimum wage (from \$3.35 to \$4.25, in 1990 and 1991) affected only about 8 percent of the labor force, and these workers were concentrated in the retail trade and food service sectors. Ignoring employment effects, Card and Krueger estimate that \$5.5 billion was transferred to low-wage workers, only 0.2 percent of total U.S. annual earnings (1995, 277). Card and Krueger estimate that if firms had passed along all of the labor cost increases to consumers, prices would have increased (once and for all) only about 0.3 percent (393).

The reason, I want to argue, is that the core of modern economics—neoclassical price theory—is seen to be at stake. In particular, minimum-wage research has come to be seen as a test of the applicability of neoclassical price theory to the determination of wages and employment. The modern minimum-wage controversy is not just a technical quarrel over the sign and magnitude of wage-elasticity coefficients; it is the latest chapter in a longstanding methodological dispute over whether and in what domains neoclassical price theory can be said to properly apply. One does not make opposition to minimum wages a disciplinary litmus test, unless there is something this important at stake.[3]

The modern minimum-wage controversy engages economists because it brings to light methodological issues ordinarily submerged in the course of normal science. I present a history of the economics of minimum wages designed to illuminate two such issues: (1) does prevailing theory explain and predict the determination of wages and employment, and (2) by what means do economists decide when explanation and prediction are successful?

The history—really three vignettes—is designed to show, first, that the current debate is a modern-dress version of an old family argument in economics. Second, it provides some evidence for my claim that the minimum-wage controversy is not merely a substantive disagreement among labor specialists, but also a recurring touchstone for methodological debate about the application of economics.

What Is the Modern Minimum-Wage Controversy About?

The modern minimum-wage controversy derives from a recent literature in empirical labor economics, which argues, foremost among several claims, that moderate increases in mandated minimum wages do not lead to adverse employment outcomes for low-wage workers.[4] Many of these findings are collected or summarized in David Card and Alan Krueger's

3. George Stigler said in 1976 that "one evidence of professional integrity of the economist is the fact that it is *not* possible to enlist good economists to defend . . . minimum wage laws" (Stigler 1982, 60).

4. Card and Krueger say that their "strongest and most important finding" is the absence of disemployment effects from moderate increases in minimum wages (1995, 387). The qualifier "moderate" is important. No economist believes that fixing a wage floor at $100 per hour would not create disemployment. Card and Krueger also recognize that the intensity of the minimum-wage debate is out of proportion to its economic importance (1995, 395).

influential 1995 book, *Myth and Measurement: The New Economics of the Minimum Wage* (hereafter cited as *Myth*).

The current controversy arises because "the new economics of the minimum wage" is at odds with neoclassical price theory, which predicts disemployment, and with a generation of time-series econometric research, which consistently finds evidence of disemployment effects. *Myth*'s findings are also at odds with what most U.S. economists, especially labor economists, believe (Whaples 1996). Card and Krueger understand this; indeed, they expressly conceive of their project as a refutation of neoclassical price theory's predictions and of the econometric evidence adduced in support (1995, 396–97).

Following the contemporary emphasis, I focus on employment and welfare effects: do minimum-wage increases disemploy low-wage workers, and do minimum-wage increases, on balance, help low-wage workers? Later I take up the less emphasized but essential matter of distribution: To what extent do workers affected by minimum-wage legislation live in poor or near-poor households?[5]

The Neoclassical Theory of Minimum-Wage Effects

The neoclassical theory is familiar. Mandated minimum wages are treated as any other price floor. If the mandated wage exceeds the market-clearing wage, then, given a downward-sloping labor demand curve, firms reduce the quantity of labor demanded. The magnitude of the reduction depends upon the wage increase and the wage elasticity of labor demand, but the direction of change is unambiguous. Welfare effects also depend upon the wage elasticity of demand. Some workers will receive the higher wage and are better off. Other workers, those whose product is worth less than the new minimum, will be laid off, or will work fewer hours. If the quantity of labor refers to employment, then the wage gains of those who keep their jobs must be traded off against the wage losses of those who lose their jobs.[6]

5. Poor and near-poor families are those with incomes at or below 1.5 times the U.S. poverty level.

6. Suppose, for example, that the wage elasticity of demand is −0.2 and that the minimum-wage increase is 10 percent. This implies that 2 percent of workers (if L is employment) will lose their jobs, and that 98 percent will get a 10 percent raise, meaning that affected low-wage workers collectively realize income gains of 7.8 percent [(0.98)(0.1) − (.02)(1.00)]. By implication, minimum wages will help the class of affected workers when the wage elasticity

Disemployment is a logically *necessary* result if one assumes that (1) firms maximize profits and (2) the low-skilled labor market is competitive, that is, that firms have no monopsony power (Kennan 1995). Neoclassical theory can accommodate a weakening of assumption 2. If labor markets are monopsonistic, firms exercise their market power and pay a wage lower than workers' marginal revenue product (MRP_L). Monopsonistic firms offer higher wages to attract new hires, which leads to costlier labor expenditures (more pay to the inframarginal workers) and inefficiently low employment.

In principle, then, a judiciously chosen minimum wage (set between monopsony wage and MRP_L) can increase employment and efficiency. In practice, however, labor economists traditionally regard monopsony as an empirical curiosum (Brown 1988, 134 n. 1).[7] Individual low-wage firms typically employ a small percentage of the low-wage work force (Brown, Gilroy, and Kohen 1982, 489), so monopsony power is seen as limited in practice.[8]

Neoclassical economics is less able to accommodate a weakening of the profit-maximization assumption, which is more fundamental. With few exceptions (see, for example, Prasch 1996), contemporary economists maintain the profit-maximization assumption, generally reverting to monopsony models derived from efficiency-wage explanations.

If some firms pay more than the going wage, and profit maximization is assumed, then the only remaining explanation is that some firms find it profitable to pay above the going rate, which defines an efficiency-wage explanation (Krueger and Summers 1988). Efficiency-wage accounts propose that wages can exceed MRP_L when (1) higher wages bring forth greater worker productivity, a reversal of the traditional causality,

---

is less elastic than −1.0. But there are two important caveats. First, not all affected workers get a 10 percent raise; those between the old and new minima get a smaller increase. Second, wage elasticities generally derive from studies that calculate employment effects for entire demographic groups, not just for the minimum-wage workers within those groups. Thus, an elasticity estimate such as −0.2 measures the effect of minimum-wage increases on the employment of some group (say, teenagers), which includes higher-wage (hence unaffected) workers, and thereby underestimates the employment effects on the lowest-wage workers. (These points are due to Neumark, Schweitzer, and Wascher 1998, 3–4).

7. Robert Whaples finds that "six out of seven labor economists believe that 'few American workers are employed in monopsonistic labor markets'" (1996, 726).

8. Even with monopsony power, the range of employment-increasing wage increases is limited. A minimum set above the MRP_L at the monopsonist's profit-maximizing output also results in disemployment.

(2) there is an informational asymmetry such that firms cannot readily monitor worker effort, and (3) firms have high recruitment and turnover costs (the last is emphasized by Card and Krueger 1995, 373–79). Since profit maximization and perfect competition entail disemployment with higher minima, it is not surprising that, historically, both assumptions recur in arguments against and for the minimum wage.

History of Minimum-Wage Legislation and Its Economics

The idea of administered wages is ancient. Wage payments to laborers were conventional and noncontractural long before the industrial revolution and the concomitant rise of freely contracting labor. But the idea of administered wages as a legal means of improving the lot of the urban working poor has its origins in nineteenth-century reform movements, especially in the United Kingdom. Minimum wages were connected to mid-Victorian-era trade union movements and were an important item on the Fabian socialist agenda to "democratize" unregulated industries and improve working conditions (Webb and Webb [1897] 1920).[9]

The first laws setting wage floors, as against a fixed wage or an output-price peg, have their origin in Australasia. The District Conciliation Boards of New Zealand, established in 1894 principally for arbitration of labor disputes, had statutory authority to set minimum wages (Douglas 1919, 701). The first independent legal agencies designed specifically for setting minimum wages were established by the 1896 Factory and Shops Act, enacted by the state of Victoria to fix minimum wages in "sweated" industries (701).[10] Britain passed the Trade Boards Act of 1909, which likewise set minimum wages in several industries deemed to be "sweating."

9. A minimum wage means only that workers cannot legally accept a wage below it. Higher wages are legal. How and in what settings the minimum is to be fixed is more ambiguous, as the compelling but vague term *living wage* suggests. See Pigou 1922.

10. Definitions of "sweating" vary. Reporting on the 1888–90 investigation of "sweated industries" by a select committee in the British House of Lords, Beatrice Webb offers the following definition: "Lord Derby and his colleagues decided that sweating was no particular method of remuneration, no particular form of industrial organization, but certain conditions of employment—viz., unusually low rates of wages, excessive hours of labor, and unsanitary workplaces. When we get any one of these conditions in an exaggerated and extreme form, . . . then we may say, that the labor is sweated, and that the unfortunates are working under the sweating system" (cited in Holcombe 1910, 574).

The late-nineteenth-century minimum-wage movement in the United States was originally voluntarist in spirit. Organizations like the National Consumers League hoped, by information provision and moral suasion, to persuade consumers to avoid firms that paid especially low wages to workers—a minimum wage was seen as a moral rather than a legal standard (Kelley 1912). State legislation overtook their efforts. Massachusetts (1912) was the first, followed a year later by Wisconsin, Minnesota, Washington, Oregon, California, Colorado, Nebraska, and Utah (see Millis 1914).

Some laws empowered supervisory boards to determine minimum wages; others directly fixed minima by statute. In all cases, the states' laws, unlike their British Commonwealth precursors, applied to women and minors only. Until the advent of a federal minimum in 1938, men were deemed outside such paternal protection, in light of the U.S. Constitution's explicit protection of the right to free contract.[11]

Stretching back into the classical era is the question of whether a general theory—that of free markets and how they determine price and quantity—can be applied to matters of wage and employment determination. In other words, is it the case, as Adam Smith said, that the market for men is like the market for goods, so that there exists a "labor market" in which wages are determined as prices are in other markets? At least as early as John Stuart Mill, we see a further application of this application: what does the general "free market" model, as applied to the workers and employers' behavior, tell us about the effects of a particular policy measure, the wage floor?

Mill's 1848 political economy text has a recognizably modern argument on employment effects. Ignoring the peculiarities of Mill's wages-fund doctrine, which he had yet to abandon, the outline of the neoclassical disemployment argument is present 150 years ago. Said Mill:

> If law or opinion succeeds in fixing wages above this [competitive] rate, some laborers are kept out of employment; as it is not the intentions of the philanthropists that these should starve, they must be provided for. (1848, 432)

Minimum wages will disemploy some workers, says Mill, and something must be done to help the newly disemployed. But, whatever is done

11. For a brief history of the dramatic political events leading up to the Fair Labor Standards Act (FLSA), see Grossman 1978.

to help—public assistance, for example—will create a disincentive to work.

Mill points to the now familiar efficiency cost of all interventions—the tension between alleviating poverty and providing incentives to work. If laid-off workers receive a guaranteed income, then there is no incentive to work unless the minimum wage is well above this level. But if the minimum is so set, previously viable jobs are eliminated, which is wasteful (Kennan 1995).

The disemployment argument is in place, as is a familiar theme of British political economy: unintended policy consequences. The sundry social reform movements of nineteenth-century Britain generally regarded Mill's late classical economics as a kind of vulgar laissez-faire, a mere ratification of the raw excesses of Victorian industrial capitalism. But Mill was an ardent social reformer. He quarreled not with the goal of meliorating adverse free-market outcomes, but with the efficacy of policy instruments such as a legal minimum.

Henry Sidgwick (1886) shared Mill's skepticism regarding the net benefits of government interventions, especially utopian socialist schemes (see Hutchison 1953, 53–54). And Sidgwick was at pains to distinguish British political economy from more truly laissez-faire approaches, such as Claude-Frédéric Bastiat's. British political economy does not argue that low-wage workers get what they deserve, but that well-intentioned interventions may do more harm than good. Says Sidgwick:

> You can make it illegal to employ a man under a certain rate of wages, but you cannot secure his employment at that rate, unless the community will undertake to provide for an indefinite number of claimants work remunerated at more than its market value; in which case its action will tend to remove, to a continuously increasing extent, the ordinary motives to vigorous and efficient labor. (1886, 631)

In an 1897 article by Alfred Marshall, the disemployment argument is also quite clear: "[The academic economist] must for instance analyse the methods which people are tempted to take for securing a high minimum wage . . . and must show which of them will have indirect effects that will cause workingmen as a whole a loss greater than the benefit. . . . ordinary people do not see that the means most commonly advocated . . . would impoverish all" (1897,128). Here, in an address to the inaugural meeting of the Cambridge Economics Club (29

October 1896), we also find Marshall elevating efficiency as the badge of the academic economist. The economist must fight conventional wisdom on minimum wages, says Marshall, not because one disagrees with the goal of alleviating poverty among the working poor, but because minimum wages do more harm than good (1897, 129).

The Marshallian theory of minimum wages finds its most thorough and lucid exposition in a 1907 essay by H. B. Lees Smith; it is a remarkable paper written in partial response to minimum-wage arguments in Sidney and Beatrice Webb's *Industrial Democracy* ([1897] 1920). I present Lees Smith's argument truncated and translated into modern argot, but it bears reading in the original.

At the outset, Lees Smith assumes that productivity is independent of cost: "we may assume for the present that the efficiency of both wage-earners and employers is the same before and after the enactment of the minimum" (1907, 504). He notes that statutory coverage may be partial or total, taking partial coverage first.

If the minimum is actually binding, higher labor costs must be funded from reduced expenditures on other inputs, higher output prices, or lower profits (504). Take reduced expenditures first. If other inputs such as skilled labor are substitutes, and they generally are, then a binding minimum will *increase*, not decrease, their prices and expenditures thereon, which eliminates other input costs as a means of funding higher costs of low-skilled labor (505).

If, alternatively, output prices are increased to fund higher low-skilled labor costs, then output demand will fall, unless such demand is perfectly inelastic. And, if firms and workers are already optimizing, the reduction in output quantity demanded will entail an inefficient reallocation of inputs to other uncovered sectors (506). Thus, present in Lees Smith is the law of demand and the assumption of profit maximization:

> A rise in the price of the commodity will lead to a decrease in the demand for it. This means that a certain amount of the labor and capital hitherto employed in the production of the commodity must seek other occupations. But this is likely to involve both the laborers and the employers in a loss. *Employers and laborers were presumably occupied where, with such choices as they had, they thought they would do the best for themselves.* . . . It is no kindness to the workers in a trade to merely turn them out. (506; emphasis added)

Finally, increased wages may be funded out of profits. But if profits are diminished by higher labor costs, capital will migrate to more remunerative sectors. This will occur unless the covered sector's output market is so uncompetitive that supranormal profits can fund the higher labor costs, a claim nowhere made by minimum-wage proponents.

Thus, each possible alternative entails low-skilled labor being disemployed. With universal coverage, the same outcome obtains, only low-skilled labor becomes unemployed or leaves the labor force. Concludes Lees Smith: the disemployment verdict of "pure theory" is clear. Lees Smith fully anticipates the neoclassical argument, as exemplified by Stigler 1946.

I do not wish to suggest that political economists were uniformly opposed to minimum wages. Not only is it anachronistic to assume that economics was, around 1900, a uniform or even professionalized discipline, but, all along the way, there were those who denied that late-classical and then Marshallian models applied to labor markets. F. D. Longe (1894), who was one of the first to challenge Mill's wages-fund doctrine, dissented, as did a number of American Institutionalists, notably John R. Commons, who helped draft the first Wisconsin minimum-wage statute.

Perhaps the most conspicuous proponents of minimum wages in this era are Beatrice and Sidney Webb. Sidney Webb (1912) offers an especially useful counterpoint to Lees Smith 1907.

Webb argues that, for the least productive workers, wages are not determined by labor productivity. He says, "The wages of the lowest grade of labor are fixed, not by 'worth' in any sense—not even the possible 'value in exchange'—of the individual laborer, but (as we nowadays sadly concede) largely by the urgent necessities of the 'marginal' man, or, rather, the 'marginal' woman" (1912, 990). By implication, either low-wage firms are not profit maximizing, or they find it profitable, along efficiency-wage lines, to hire workers whose productivity is very low.

Webb makes recourse to both claims. At one point he says that "a Legal Minimum positively increases the productivity of the nation's industry, by ensuring the surplus of unemployed workmen shall be exclusively the less efficient workmen . . . [which] is plainly not the case under 'free competition'" (979). For this to be true, firms cannot be, *ex ante*, profit maximizing, so Webb is offering, in rough form, an early version of the "shock-therapy" argument.

Arguing in the alternative, Webb also makes an efficiency-wage argument. "To put it plumply," he says, "if the employers paid more, the labor would be worth more" (990). Why might higher productivity follow higher wages? At one point Webb argues that affected firms will be obliged to innovate—"[the minimum wage] acts as a constant incentive to the further improvement of the manual laborers, the machinery and the organizing ability used in industry"—implicitly assuming, as against Lees Smith, that factor substitution would not, on balance, work against low-skilled workers (985). Webb also argues that if the minimum were to increase wages above subsistence, laborers will be physically stronger and thus more productive. This latter claim requires that firms had failed to perceive that a wage above subsistence would increase profitability.

What we observe, then, is that Webb takes issue with the key ideas in Lees Smith's account, not least profit maximization and perfect competition. Webb also argues, at least implicitly, against the law of demand. Where Lees Smith insists that higher output prices will entail lower output quantity demanded, Webb suggests that "the community [consumers] would willingly pay more for it, and yet consume as much, or nearly of much of it as it now does" (990).

I do not wish to suggest that Webb and Lees Smith would have described their disagreement solely in terms of profit maximization and labor market structure. The hope, rather, is that this sketch suffices to show that the leading contemporary issue in minimum-wage economics—employment effects—is already being debated in familiar terms around the turn of the century. The disemployment account is recognizable in Mill 150 years ago, and, in the sense of considering the labor-market conditions under which disemployment does and does not obtain, is almost fully formed 90 to 100 years ago.

What is missing from the minimum-wage arguments of this era is empirical evidence. The evidence for the successful application of economics to labor markets is entirely theoretical—that is, based on appeal to reason and logic. Clearly, U.S. data became available only following the states' minimum-wage legislation. But what is striking through much of the twentieth century is the extent to which the application of economics to labor markets remains almost entirely theoretical. George Stigler's landmark paper, for example, presents only a few stylized facts for evidence, admitting that "no precise estimate of the effects of the minimum wage upon aggregate employment is possible" (1946, 361).

The mid-twentieth-century debate recapitulates many of the old arguments about whether the general theory of competitive markets, now full-blown neoclassical price theory, is applicable to labor markets. But, here our second theme emerges: the role of empirical evidence as the arbiter of which theory (if any) is indeed applicable. The marginalist controversy and the economics of minimum wages come together in the person of Richard Lester.

Minimum Wages and the Marginalist Controversy

Richard Lester, the labor economist to whom Card and Krueger dedicate their book, argued that firms do not always maximize profits and that labor markets generally are not competitive. Lester's conclusion was based on surveys of manufacturing CEOs who did not know marginal costs and revenues, and on wage surveys, which found a wide variance in wages paid to production workers of roughly equal productivity (Lester 1946a, 1946b). Lester read ignorance of marginal magnitudes as implying that firms do not maximize profits; and he read the unexplained wage variation as suggesting that firms do not take wages as given.

Lester was not the first to argue that firms do not maximize profits,[12] but his work generated a volley of neoclassical responses, an exchange which has come to be known as the marginalist controversy. Some responses were directed at Lester's challenges explicitly (Machlup 1946, 1947; Stigler 1947) and others more indirectly (Alchian 1950; Friedman 1953).[13] It was Lester's investigation of labor markets, and his strong conclusions, that gave rise to a withering exchange on the nature of economic theory and on the role of empirical evidence in testing theories and their implications.

That labor research was the occasion for the methodological dispute we ordinarily associate with the marginalist controversy is not coincidence. Lester and other institutionally minded labor economists of the mid-century era—especially John Dunlop, Clark Kerr, and Lloyd

12. R. L. Hall and C. J. Hitch (1939,18) interpret their interviews of businessmen as arguing that firms do not equate marginal revenues and marginal costs, but use rules of thumb for marking up average costs.

13. Lester's rejoinder to Machlup 1946 (itself a reply to Lester 1946a) and reply to Stigler 1946, the neoclassical locus classicus, are found in Lester 1947.

Reynolds (DKLR)—practiced a kind of labor economics that differed significantly from the neoclassical labor economics that later predominated (Freeman 1989, 317–42). The DKLR method was built around institutional expertise, detailed case studies, and surveys of management and workers. They surely resented what they regarded as neoclassical theory-tropism: relative indifference to empirical work, and hostility to survey questionnaires in particular (Machlup 1946).

Related, and perhaps more important, DKLR rejected the neoclassical model's assumptions of profit maximizing and perfect competition, at least for empirical purposes.

> The labor market is not a bourse; wage rates are typically quoted prices. (Dunlop 1944, cited in Freeman 1989, 330)

> The labor market is by nature an imperfect instrument. . . . all kinds of wage distortions exist even under non-union conditions. (Reynolds and Taft 1956, 168, cited in Freeman 1989, 319)

> Reasoning about labor markets as though they were commodity markets seems to be an important explanation for erroneous conclusions on such matters as minimum wages. (Lester 1947, 146, responding to Stigler 1946)

> A [competitive market–determined wage structure] is a useful norm for theoretical speculations but an unstable departure point for empirical studies. (Kerr 1977, 46, cited in Freeman 1989, 318)

In short, DKLR disagreed with the neoclassical presumption that labor markets, especially the determination of wages and employment, operate no differently than do goods markets.

The controversy following Lester's challenge had methodological consequences that reverberate still. Fritz Machlup's 1946 response to Lester 1946a was important less for its argument that Lester's survey methodology was sloppy, than for its methodological claim that profit maximization is not a descriptive claim but a useful fiction. Managers may not know marginal magnitudes, nor need they be calculating on all conceivable margins. But their habits and routines can be thought of as learned strategies that themselves derive from a goal of profit maximization. Methodologically, it is *as if* firms maximize profits (Machlup 1946).

Alchian (1950) added a natural selection story to the gap that Machlup opened between intent and effect. Whether or not firms intend to maximize profits, Alchian argued, a Darwinian business environment ensures that surviving firms will be maximizing profits, as underperforming firms are weeded out by competition. It is a competitive output market structure that creates profit maximizing behavior, albeit as a by-product rather than as the necessary goal of firms.

Milton Friedman's famous paper (1953) borrowed elements from both Machlup 1946 and Alchian 1950. With Machlup, Friedman embraced the *as if* method, which he inflated into a grander claim: theoretical assumptions need not be true. While it is clearly unrealistic to assume that billiard players solve systems of differential equations when making shots, it is useful for prediction, says Friedman, to pretend that they do. Friedman goes so far as to make "unrealistic" (read: false) assumptions into a theoretical virtue: "The more significant the theory, the more unrealistic the assumptions" (1953, 14).

From Alchian, Friedman carries over the idea that an agent's intent is unimportant; economics should be seen not as a theory of motivational states but of market outcomes. Friedman concedes that firms need not intend to maximize profits, but boldly argues that this does not matter methodologically. Theories are to be judged not by the truth or falsity of their assumptions, but, rather, by the success of their predictions. The assumption that firms consciously optimize is false, he concedes, but the prediction that only profit-maximizing firms will survive in the long run is empirically accurate.

Methodologically, the realism-of-assumptions debate is something of a muddle. Our focus is on the role of empirical results in adjudicating among competing theories. Much turns on whether one sees assumptions as restricting the applicability of the theory—a domain assumption—or whether one sees assumptions' truth or falsity as negligible for theoretical purposes, such as prediction (Musgrave 1981).

If we regard the assumption of competitive labor markets as a domain assumption, then the disemployment prediction obtains *only* when the assumption is true, that is, only when labor markets are competitive. Stigler's reply to Lester 1946a at one point reverts to just this domain-assumption interpretation (1947, 155).[14] Alternatively, one can predict

14. Joan Robinson, parenthetically commenting on the minimum-wage debate, connects the matter of assumptions to the Marshallian-era version of the controversy: "This [monopsony] analysis may throw light on the dispute between Marshall and Mr. and Mrs. Webb upon the

disemployment regardless of whether the competitive-market assumption is true or not, a negligibility assumption. If the power of firms to set wages below MRP_L is negligible, then the falsity of the assumption will not much matter because, ceteris paribus, the disemployment prediction will still be borne out. This is Friedman's interpretation of how assumptions work in economics.

Both readings have important implications for application. Since Stigler agrees that assumptions constrain the applicability of theory, then it is clearly important that assumptions not be too restrictive; otherwise, there is nothing to apply to. But Stigler, of course, does not really attend to the question of whether maximization and competition are overly restrictive assumptions. As we have seen, his own contribution offers only limited empirical evidence. And he is quite dismissive of Lester's attempt to empirically test the key assumptions.

In any event, it was Friedman's reading that carried the day: economists need not worry about the truth or falsity of assumptions; only predictive accuracy matters. By implication, empirical work should be confined to testing the predictions of theory.[15] Testing of assumptions, of the kind that Lester has undertaken, can be dismissed as methodologically beyond the pale.

Although Friedman prevailed, his methodological injunction—empirically test theoretical predictions—went mostly unheeded. With few exceptions (e.g., Peterson 1957), the relative lack of mainstream empirical work on minimum-wage effects persists well into the 1970s. Robert Goldfarb's survey (1974) of the minimum-wage literature finds that the empirical support for disemployment effects, especially for adults (ages twenty and up), who have generally composed the majority of low-wage workers, is quite limited. With the exception of teenage employment, it is not hyperbole to suggest that, in the Nixon era, the basis for professional priors was essentially unchanged from that of three generations earlier.

'marginal productivity theory' of wages (see [Marshall's] *Principles*, 705). It seems to have arisen because Mr. and Mrs. Webb failed to realized the implications of the assumptions of perfect competition, while Marshall failed to recognize the extreme unreality of those assumptions" (Robinson [1933] 1950, 300–301 n. 2).

15. I do not take up Friedman's implicit claim that theoretical components are separable, that is, that there is a meaningful distinction between theoretical assumptions and theoretical implications.

Empirical Evidence on Employment Effects of Minimum Wages

The empirical literature grew rapidly with the expansion of time-series econometric techniques. Roughly twenty-five papers are reviewed in Charles Brown, Curtis Gilroy, and Andrew Kohen's (1982) survey. Goldfarb (1981) reports empirical progress, especially with regard to distribution effects.

Most empirical papers in this period make use of a regression with something like the following specification:

$$Y = f(MW, D, X_1 \ldots X_n),$$

where Y is labor force status (e.g., labor force participation ratio, employment-population ratio, unemployment rate), MW is some measure of the minimum wage,[16] D is a business cycle variable to account for changes in aggregate economic activity, and X_i is an exogenous variable controlling for labor supply, school enrollment, participation in the armed forces, and so on (Brown, Gilroy, and Kohen 1982, 497). Some specifications add a time trend as well (see Mincer 1976). There are different functional forms to the specifications, but nearly all studies use Current Population Survey (CPS) data.

Brown, Gilroy, and Kohen summarize the literature as follows: teenage employment-rate elasticities are on the order of −0.1 to −0.3, but "the lower half of that range is to be preferred." For young adults (ages 20–24), the effect of the minimum wage on employment is "negative and smaller" than that for teens. But Brown, Gilroy, and Kohen are careful to say that "uncertainty about the effects on [older] adults is a serious gap in the literature . . . ," echoing Goldfarb 1974 (1982, 524). These conclusions generally comport with contemporaneous surveys and collections (Rottenberg 1981; Report of the Minimum Wage Study Commission 1981; Eccles and Freeman 1982).

The uncertainty surrounding adult employment effects notwithstanding, the disemployment prediction seems comfortably consolidated by the 1980s (Alston, Kearl, and Vaughan 1992). There may have been

16. "The key variable, minimum wage, has generally been measured by the ratio of the nominal legal minimum wage to average hourly earnings weighted by coverage, as devised by Kaitz (1970). Ratios of minimum wage rates to average hourly earnings are calculated for each industry, weighted by the proportion of workers covered. These are combined into an index in which the weight for each industry ration is the number of persons employed in the industry as a percentage of total employment" (Brown, Gilroy, and Kohen 1982, 499).

quibbles about the exact magnitude of disemployment effects, but none about whether they existed (Deere, Murphy, and Welch 1995, 232). Indeed, there was very little empirical work on minimum wages undertaken during the mid-eighties. What changed?

First, the few new time-series estimates which did incorporate data from the eighties seemed to suggest that employment elasticities with respect to minimum wages were becoming more inelastic. Second, while the nominal value of the federal minimum wage stayed at $3.35 per hour between 1981 and 1990, several states raised their minima, which created a research opportunity for cross-sectional studies. Finally, the increase in income inequality during the 1980s spurred political action for redistributive measures. In the nineties, minimum-wage research revived, and with dramatic consequences.

The "New" Economics of Minimum Wages and Its Critics

I emphasize two lines of attack that Card and Krueger mount on the neoclassical account. First, they present cross-sectional evidence from four studies—most famously from the New Jersey–Pennsylvania (NJ-PA) fast food experiment—which finds that the employment elasticity of the minimum wage is positive, or at least nonnegative. Of *Myth*'s seven analyses of employment effects, one shows zero effect and six show positive effects, but only two of these are significantly different from 0 at the 0.05 level (1995, 388).

Second, and less well known, Card and Krueger review the established econometric literature and judge it altogether inadequate. They conclude that previous findings are unreliable, tainted by publication bias and specification search. Paul Osterman calls this aspect of *Myth* "a damning indictment of how labor economics has been practiced over the past three decades" (1995, 839). Card and Krueger offer their own empirical approach—"natural experiment" and "model-free empiricism"—as evidentially superior to earlier econometric studies.

Card and Krueger's Evaluation of Previous Empirical Work

Card and Krueger (CK) review earlier empirical work on minimum-wage effects and judge it inadequate and tendentious. CK replicate and extend some earlier work, finding that employment elasticities attenuate when more recent years are included. A meta-analysis of previous time-series estimates concludes that earlier work is corrupted by publication bias and specification search.

CK argue that time-series estimates, over time, involve larger and larger samples, which, ceteris paribus, should increase t-statistics. If the additional data in newer studies are independent of the older data, "then a doubling of the sample size should result in an increase in the absolute value of the t-ratio of about 40 percent" (1995, 187).[17] If the t-statistics do not increase with sample size, then, CK suggest, something is fishy. Using the time-series studies reviewed in Brown, Gilroy, and Kohen 1982, CK find that the t-statistics are, in fact, declining in sample size (188).[18]

CK also conduct a related meta-analysis that compares the relationship between the estimated coefficients of employment elasticity with their respective standard errors, for the same set of time-series studies. If the estimated coefficients (b) are truly unbiased, CK argue, then there should be no systematic relationship between them and their respective standard errors (se). If, on the other hand, editors will only publish studies with robust test statistics ($t > 2$, say), then this publication bias should be reflected in the meta-analysis, given that $t = b/se$. Plotting "implicit" standard errors against the coefficients, CK find a rather good fit (for $b = 2se$), with only two or three exceptions, suggesting a problem with independence (1995, 191).

From this meta-evidence, CK offer three possible explanations. One explanation is that structural change made the employment effects of minimum wages decline over time. But structural change calls into question the validity of time-series work to begin with. The alternative

17. Card and Krueger note the lack-of-independence problem that occurs with time-series data more generally, but point out that previous authors themselves assume independence following adjustments for serial correlation in errors and similar procedures.

18. Actually, they plot the absolute value of the t-statistic against the square root of the degrees of freedom, or $(n - k)^{1/2}$. The rationale is explained by Kennan 1995. The t-statistic in a regression with n observations on k explanatory variables satisfies the equation $t^2(n - k) = r^2/(1 - r^2)$, where t is the t-statistic of a regressor and r is the partial correlation coefficient between this regressor and the dependent variable. As the sample size increases, r converges to its population value, assuming stationarity of the partial correlation, so t must grow at the same rate as the square root of $n - k$ (Kennan 1995, 1963).

explanations are specification search and publication bias. CK argue that the early literature was contaminated by a preference (on the part of data-mining researchers and biased editors) for statistically significant results that comported with the disemployment predictions of the neoclassical model.

The econometric specifications which became standard were chosen, CK suggest, because they produced the desired negative sign and got the t-statistics above 2. Later researchers tended to reuse these specifications. Because true statistical significance was overstated in the earlier research, however, more recent work (presumably not so susceptible to temptation) discovered weaker effects (1995, 192–93). Three of Finis Welch's studies are singled out by CK as examples of this econometric malpractice.

Natural Experiments and "Model-Free" Empiricism

Myth is notable for its emphasis on natural experiments (NE) and, more generally, the idea of "model-free" empirical work. CK take the NJ-PA study as their most important result, precisely because they believe that its setting is closest to the ideal of the randomized controlled experiments of the "hard" sciences. They imply that an NE, even if an imperfect substitute for a randomized controlled experiment, is evidentially superior to traditional econometric techniques.

The New Jersey–Pennsylvania (NJ-PA) study compares employment responses in the fast-food market in New Jersey and eastern Pennsylvania to increases in the minimum wage (New Jersey raised its state minimum from \$4.25 to \$5.05, while Pennsylvania's remained at \$4.25). The "experiment" compares the employment effects on affected workers against the Pennsylvania "control" group. If all differences between New Jersey and Pennsylvania remain unchanged before and after the minimum-wage increase, then any employment (E_{it}) "difference in differences" (DD) can be attributed to the minimum-wage effects, as follows:

$$DD = (E_{\mathrm{NJ2}} - E_{\mathrm{PA2}}) - (E_{\mathrm{NJ1}} - E_{\mathrm{PA1}}),$$

where period 1 is February 1992 (before the new minimum takes effect in April 1992) and period 2 is November 1992. Neoclassical theory predicts that, ceteris paribus, employment in New Jersey should fall relative to employment in Pennsylvania, that is, that *DD* will be negative. CK, however, find it to be positive.[19]

CK sometimes make extravagant claims regarding the significance of this finding, even as they are careful to acknowledge the relative weaknesses of NEs. First, NEs do not randomly assign subjects into treatment and control groups, which is essential for attributing any differential outcomes to the minimum wage exclusively. Minimum-wage legislation is the outcome of a political process, and states that enact minimum wages may differ from those that do not; they may have more robust economic growth, for example (1995, 23). Second, NEs are not "blind." Subjects know when they are (or are not) being treated. Third, NEs require ceteris paribus. Any current differences between treatment and control groups must persist in the absence of the minimum-wage intervention (e.g., both groups should exhibit identical rates of growth) (23).

CK are confident that these departures from classical experiments are small relative to the advantage NEs provide over traditional econometric approaches. The NE approach is "model free" in that its results do not hinge on a particular econometric specification or, therefore, upon the theoretical assumptions that underwrite a given specification. And, at least in principle, NEs can reduce the incentive for specification search, the temptation to fit the model to the data.

Replies to Card and Krueger

The replies to *Myth* are too numerous to document fully, a measure of its influence. Professional critics have focused less on the nature than on the execution of CK's empirical methods, especially in the famous NJ-PA study.

The most serious replies are as follows: (1) the survey is poorly designed as reflected in the noisy data that result (Kennan 1995; Welch 1995); (2) the study is not a proper NE, particularly with respect to the control group (Hamermesh 1995; Kennan 1995; Welch 1995); (3) results are short run only (Hamermesh 1995); (4) employment increases should mean higher output and lower output prices, but CK find evidence of higher output prices (Brown 1995); and, most conspicuously,

19. Employment is measured in full-time equivalents (FTEs), where a part-time worker is counted as 0.5 FTE. The results: 2.7 = [21.0 – 21.2] – [20.4 – 23.3].

(5) results cannot be replicated and are contradicted when superior data are employed (Neumark and Wascher 1995).[20]

Low-wage employers may well have already adjusted to the New Jersey minimum-wage increase before it took effect in April 1992, given that the statute passed in 1990. Or their adjustment may have occurred after the second survey. And the replication by David Neumark and William Wascher (1995) does contradict CK's original work.[21] And CK's most important result—that employment in New Jersey increases relative to employment in Pennsylvania—obtains principally because employment fell in Pennsylvania, the control. It is, John Kennan argues, "like having a drug trial in which the drug has no effect but the placebo makes people sick" (1995, 1958).

Conclusion: The Very Idea of Applying Economics

The "new" economics of the minimum wage is not really new at all. Although Card and Krueger do not mention it, their method of natural experimentation has direct empirical antecedents in a little-known statistical literature developed in the 1910s and 1920s. There are large repositories of "before and after" employment data collected by the U.S. Bureau of Labor Statistics and by various state agencies.[22] And Card and Krueger's empiricism and their monopsony explanation have acknowledged affinities with the DKLR approach. But two things do distinguish the contemporary controversy: (1) the substantive emphasis on employment effects and (2) the methodological emphasis on empirical work as the arbiter of successful theoretical application.

As the debate over minimum wages increasingly stresses its role as a test of the applicability of price theory to labor markets, there is a concomitant emphasis on employment effects. Reactions by nonspecialists to *Myth* are almost entirely in this vein. Said one Nobel laureate:

20. A more detailed account is available in Leonard 1997, 268–73.

21. Card and Krueger 1998 replies to Neumark and Wascher 1995.

22. Kennan 1995 instances a remarkably detailed study of minimum-wage effects in Oregon (Obenauer and von der Nienburg 1915), which begins, "Does the establishment of a legal minimum wage for women do more harm than good to the women it is designed to assist?" and which presents employment and wage data for tens of hundreds of affected girls and women. The BLS published eleven bulletins on minimum-wage issues prior to Obenauer and von der Nienburg 1915, and there are detailed data in numerous state publications, such as National Industrial Conference Board 1927.

> Just as no physicist would claim that "water runs uphill," no self-respecting economist would claim that increases in the minimum wage increase employment. Such a claim, if seriously advanced, becomes equivalent to a denial that there is even minimal scientific content in economics, and that, in consequence, economists can do nothing but write as advocates for ideological interests. (Buchanan 1996)

Labor specialists are less intemperate but equally preoccupied with disemployment. *Myth* examines many consequences of minimum wages, but CK themselves make central their own findings and their critique of previous econometric work on employment effects.

The emphasis on employment has crowded out a crucial, and answerable, policy question: Do minimum wages reduce poverty? A desire to help the working poor, of course, lies at the root of minimum-wage policy. An obviously relevant question is, Are affected workers poor? (Stigler 1946).[23] The surprising answer is, generally, no. The reasons for a positive but weak relationship between minimum wages and household income are well understood and well documented (Gramlich 1976).

The relationship is weak when low-wage workers are members of nonpoor households (teens, say), or when households have nonwage income, or when households have no workers at all. Low-wage workers are more likely to be in poor families than are all workers, but the great majority of low-wage workers are not poor. Ralph Smith and Bruce Vavrichek (1987) found that 75 percent of affected workers in 1985 were neither poor nor near-poor. CK's own distribution analysis finds that only 30 percent of affected workers live in poor and near-poor families (1995, 280). In other words, over two-thirds of income redistributed by minimum-wage increases—even assuming zero disemployment—will go to individuals in families neither poor nor near-poor.

Myth concludes, "We believe that our findings suggest a reorientation of policy discussions away from the efficiency aspects of the minimum wage and toward distributional issues" (393). But, at the same time, CK are obliged to say that the minimum wage is a "blunt instrument" for redistributing income to poor families and find that "the effect of

23. Not all economists accept alleviation of poverty as the goal of minimum wages. Some argue that flattening the income distribution is worthwhile for its own sake, and others suggest that progressive income redistribution stimulates aggregate demand, owing to a higher propensity to consume in lower-income households (Prasch 1996).

the minimum wage on the *overall* poverty rate of adults is statistically undetectable" (1995, 285, 280; see also Burkhauser, Couch, and Wittenberg 1996).[24] Even if one believes that minimum-wage increases do not disemploy low-wage workers, or is prepared to suffer disemployment as a cost of redistribution, it is significant that minimum wages do so little for the goals of poverty reduction or progressive income redistribution. The evidence on distribution—where the data are comparatively reliable and uncontroversial—has been completely overshadowed by the emphasis on whether the disemployment prediction obtains.

The methodological emphasis on empirical work as the arbiter of successful theoretical application is also new to the contemporary period. Friedman (1953), we have seen, made testing of theoretical predictions the paramount goal of economic science, but only in the contemporary controversy does empirical work actually assume this role. CK are explicit: they regard their work not merely as four papers contributing to a large empirical literature, but as "a simple and direct test of the kind of theoretical reasoning that economists routinely apply to other, more complicated phenomena" (1995, 397).

Some are prepared to renounce *Myth* on a priori grounds. Evidence that says "water runs uphill" is to be rejected on its face. But labor is the quintessentially empirical field in economics. Labor economists take pride in their willingness to submit theoretical claims to the tribunal of empirical evidence. In other corners of economics, such as macroeconomics, says Richard Freeman, "the evidentiary base is sufficiently diffuse to allow economists with different priors to reach different conclusions—to make a lawyer's case as it were" (1995, 831). But, Freeman argues, not so in minimum-wage research, where changes occur in discrete exogenous jumps, and evidence permits far less scope for "disparate interpretation" (831).

Nearly all labor specialists in the controversy, critics and supporters alike, take for granted (at least nominally) that attempts to apply theory must be tested by empirical evidence. CK's valedictory to *Myth* says that "although many economists may disagree with our interpretation of the findings in this book, we hope that they will at least agree on the value of testing the implications of standard economic theory, and on the validity of our empirical approach" (1995, 399). Their hope has been met. I can

24. A minimum wage can help only the employed. Card and Krueger (1995, 305) estimate that about two-thirds of adults in poor families do not work at all. Burkhauser, Couch, and Wittenberg (1996, 551) estimate that fully one-quarter of poor families have no working adults.

locate no serious objection, even among CK's strongest critics, to the idea of empirical evidence as testing theory or to the evidential virtues of natural experiments. But a methodological ambivalence persists. If all agree that the data should be decisive, no one agrees on *when* the data are decisive.

I conjecture that the ambivalence regarding empirical testing has two sources. One is methodological. To answer the key substantive question—do *Myth*'s results refute price theory's disemployment prediction?—one must know the answer to a prior methodological question: what evidence constitutes a refutation? If *Myth* really offers "a simple and direct test" of neoclassical price theory, then one must know what counts as a simple and direct test. Without methodological argument, still less consensus, there are no ready means for evaluating CK's claim.

The other source of ambivalence derives from a residual unease with the robustness of the empirical evidence on disemployment. The evidence for adults, we have seen, was never as strong as that for teenage workers. Furthermore, CK's most contentious claim—that the entire empirical literature before circa 1990 is contaminated by econometric malpractice—has gone virtually unrebutted. The silence is fairly deafening. The only paper to directly take issue with CK's extraordinary indictment is Neumark and Wascher 1996.[25]

Finally, good evidence on minimum-wage effects is hard to obtain, even given the relatively advantageous NE setting, as Kennan 1995 points out. Even ignoring legal noncompliance and survey measurement error, there are thorny problems. First, employers can respond to wage increases by reducing nonpecuniary compensation—health insurance, training, pleasant work environment, scheduling flexibility, discounts on goods and services. This simply rearranges the composition of the worker's pay packet and should not affect employment (Kennan 1995). Second, employers might reduce hours without reducing employment, so measuring employment will miss changes in labor demand. Third, affected workers already have highly volatile employment patterns. The noise in the employment data makes it difficult to disentangle changes

25. Neumark and Wascher (1996) examine *Myth*'s meta-analysis of the time-series literature and argue that CK's results are better explained by structural change than by publication bias leading to specification search. Parameter values changed, they say, producing spurious evidence of publication bias. Neumark and Wascher do not consider the implications of structural change for the validity of time-series evidence.

caused by statutory minima from those caused by confounding factors—the proverbial needle-in-the-haystack problem (Kennan 1995).

All of these empirical challenges are well known to labor researchers. But they are troubling. Methodologically, the belief that empirical evidence "decides" when theory applies obviously has less force when the evidence tends to be equivocal. Substantively, if the evidence for minimum-wage effects is equivocal—when, according to its producers, it offers the best of empirical opportunities—then what does this imply about the quality of evidence in economics more generally?

Herein lies a basic disciplinary tension. Modern labor economics is empirical. Indeed, in some respects, *Myth* can be read as an empiricist manifesto—go forth and test, and if the data are inconvenient for the theory, so much the worse for theory. But modern labor economics is also, unlike its mid-century variant, firmly neoclassical (Freeman 1989, 318). Price theory, like its predecessors, has the goal of producing a general theory of economic behavior, which places the determination of wages and employment comfortably within its purview—markets are markets are markets. And a general theory that does not apply in one domain is not a general theory. These twin disciplinary ambitions—to be an empirical policy science, and to have a general theory of economic behavior—can clearly come into conflict, especially when, as with minimum wages, compelling evidence meets core theoretical belief.

The economist's dilemma is as follows: do I reject the evidence or reject the application of theory? Most respondents to *Myth* have chosen the first option—some on principle, but most on grounds that the new evidence is too fragile to justify abandoning core doctrine. Still others argue that more evidence is required. Kennan says:

> *Myth and Measurement's* lasting contribution may well be to show that we just don't know how many jobs would be lost if the minimum wage were increased to $5.15, and that we are unlikely to find out using more sophisticated methods of inference on the existing body of data. What is needed is more sophisticated data. (1995, 1964)

More sophisticated data are surely desirable. But the conflicting ambitions of economics will continue to manifest themselves in recurring controversy, at least until the data are so sophisticated that economists routinely answer methodological questions such as, What evidence would convince you that your theory is refuted?

References

Alchian, Armen. 1950. Uncertainty, Evolution, and Economic Theory. *Journal of Political Economy* 58.3:211–21.

Alston, Richard, J. R. Kearl, and Michael Vaughan. 1992. Is There a Consensus among Economists in the 1990s? *American Economic Review Papers and Proceedings* 82.2:203–9.

Barro, Robert. 1996. Higher Minimum Wage, Higher Dropout Rate. *Wall Street Journal*, 11 January, A14.

Brown, Charles. 1988. Minimum Wage Laws: Are They Overrated? *Journal of Economic Perspectives* 2.3:133–45.

———. 1995. Comment for review symposium on *Myth and Measurement: The New Economics of the Minimum Wage*, by David Card and Alan Krueger. *Industrial and Labor Relations Review* 48.4:828–30.

Brown, Charles, Curtis Gilroy, and Andrew Kohen. 1982. The Effect of the Minimum Wage upon Employment and Unemployment. *Journal of Economic Literature* 20.2:487–528.

Buchanan, James. 1996. Commentary on the Minimum Wage. *Wall Street Journal*, 25 April, A20.

Burkhauser, Richard, Kenneth Couch, and David Wittenberg. 1996. "Who Gets What" from Minimum Wage Hikes: A Re-estimation of Card and Krueger's Distributional Analysis in *Myth and Measurement: The New Economics of the Minimum Wage. Industrial and Labor Relations Review* 49.3:547–52.

Card, David, and Alan Krueger. 1995. *Myth and Measurement: The New Economics of the Minimum Wage*. Princeton, N.J.: Princeton University Press.

———. 1998. A Reanalysis of the Effect of the New Jersey Minimum Wage Increase on the Fast-Food Industry with Representative Payroll Data. NBER Working Paper no. 6386. Cambridge, Mass.: NBER.

Deere, Donald, Kevin Murphy, and Finis Welch. 1995. Employment and the 1990–1991 Minimum-Wage Hike. *American Economic Review Papers and Proceedings* 85.2:232–43.

Douglas, Dorothy. 1919. American Minimum Wage Laws at Work. *American Economic Review* 9.4:701–32.

Dunlop, John. 1944. *Wage Determination under Trade Unions*. New York: Augustus M. Kelley.

Eccles, Mary, and Richard Freeman. 1982. What! Another Minimum Wage Study? *American Economic Review Papers and Proceedings* 72.2:226–32.

Freeman, Richard. 1989. *Labor Markets in Action*. Cambridge: Harvard University Press.

———. 1995. Comment for review symposium on *Myth and Measurement: The New Economics of the Minimum Wage*, by David Card and Alan Krueger. *Industrial and Labor Relations Review* 48.4:830–34.

Friedman, Milton. 1953. The Methodology of Positive Economics. In *Essays on Positive Economics*. Chicago: University of Chicago Press.

Goldfarb, Robert. 1974. The Policy Content of Quantitative Minimum Wage Research. *Industrial Relations Research Association Proceedings*: 27:261–68.

———. 1981. The Context of Recent Research. In *The Economics of Legal Minimum Wages*, edited by Simon Rottenberg. Washington, D.C.: American Enterprise Institute.

Gramlich, Edward. 1976. Impact of Minimum Wages on Other Wages, Employment, and Family Incomes. *Brookings Papers on Economic Activity*, no. 2:409–51.

Grossman, Jonathan. 1978. Fair Labor Standards Act of 1938: Maximum Struggle for a Minimum Wage. *Monthly Labor Review* 101.6:22–30.

Hall, R. L., and C. J. Hitch. 1939. Price Theory and Business Behavior. *Oxford Economic Papers*, no. 2:13–45.

Hamermesh, Daniel. 1995. Comment for review symposium on *Myth and Measurement: The New Economics of the Minimum Wage*, by David Card and Alan Krueger. *Industrial and Labor Relations Review* 48.4:835–38.

Holcombe, A. 1910. The British Minimum Wages Act of 1909. *Quarterly Journal of Economics* 24.3:574–77.

Hutchison, Terrence. 1953. *A Review of Economic Doctrines 1870–1929*. Oxford: Clarendon Press.

Kelley, Florence. 1912. Minimum-Wage Laws. *Journal of Political Economy* 20.10:999–1010.

Kennan, John. 1995. The Elusive Effects of Minimum Wages. *Journal of Economic Literature* 33.4:1950–65.

Kerr, Clark. 1977. *Labor Markets and Wage Determination*. Berkeley: University of California Press.

Krueger, Alan, and Lawrence Summers. 1988. Efficiency Wages and the Interindustry Wage Structure. *Econometrica* 56.2:259–93.

Lees Smith, H. B. 1907. Economic Theory and Proposals for a Legal Minimum Wage. *Economic Journal* 17.68:504–12.

Leonard, Thomas. 1997. The Reason of Rules in the Intellectual Economy: The Economics of Science and the Science of Economics. Ph.D. diss., The George Washington University.

Lester, Richard. 1946a. Shortcomings of Marginal Analysis for Wage-Employment Problems. *American Economic Review* 36.1:62–82.

———. 1946b. Wage Diversity and Its Theoretical Implications. *Review of Economics and Statistics* 28.3:152–59.

———. 1947. Marginalism, Minimum Wages, and Labor Markets. *American Economic Review* 37.1:135–48.

Longe, F. D. 1894. The Coal Strike and a "Minimum" Wage. *The Economic Journal* 4.13:25–34.

Machlup, Fritz. 1946. Marginal Analysis and Empirical Research. *American Economic Review* 36.4:519–54.

———. 1947. Rejoinder to an Antimarginalist. *American Economic Review* 37.1:148–54.

Marshall, Alfred. 1897. The Old Generation of Economists and the New. *Quarterly Journal of Economics* 11.2:115–35.
Mill, John Stuart. 1848. *Principles of Political Economy with Some of Their Applications to Social Philosophy*. Boston: Little & Brown.
Miller, Merton. 1996. Commentary on the Minimum Wage. *Wall Street Journal*, 25 April, A20.
Millis, H. A. 1914. Some Aspects of the Minimum Wage. *Journal of Political Economy* 22.2:132–55.
Mincer, Jacob. 1976. Unemployment Effects of Minimum Wages. *Journal of Political Economy* 84.4, part 2: 87–104.
Musgrave, Alan. 1981. "Unreal Assumptions" in Economic Theory: The F-Twist Untwisted. *Kyklos* 34.3:377–87.
National Industrial Conference Board. 1927. *Minimum Wage Legislation in Massachusetts*. New York: NICB.
Neumark, David, Mark Schweitzer, and William Wascher. 1998. The Effects of Minimum Wages on the Distribution of Family Incomes: A Non-Parametric Analysis. NBER Working Paper no. 6535. Cambridge, Mass.: NBER.
Neumark, David, and William Wascher. 1995. The Effect of New Jersey's Minimum Wage Increase on Fast-Food Employment: A Reevaluation Using Payroll Records. NBER Working Paper no. 5224. Cambridge, Mass.: NBER.
———. 1996. Is the Time-Series Evidence on Minimum Wage Effects Contaminated by Publication Bias? NBER Working Paper no. 5631. Cambridge, Mass.: NBER.
Obenauer, Marie, and Bertha von der Nienburg. 1915. Effect of Minimum-Wage Determinations in Oregon. *Bulletin of the U.S. Bureau of Labor Statistics*. Number 176. Washington, D.C.: U.S. Government Printing Office.
Osterman, Paul. 1995. Comment for review symposium on *Myth and Measurement: The New Economics of the Minimum Wage*, by David Card and Alan Krueger. *Industrial and Labor Relations Review* 48.4:839–42.
Peterson, John. 1957. Employment Effects of Minimum Wages, 1938–1950. *Journal of Political Economy* 65.5:412–30.
Pigou, A. C. 1922. Trade Boards and the Cave Committee. *The Economic Journal* 32.127:315–24.
Prasch, Robert. 1996. In Defense of the Minimum Wage. *Journal of Economic Issues* 30.2:391–97.
Report of the Minimum Wage Study Commission. 1981. Washington, D.C.: U.S. House of Representatives.
Reynolds, Lloyd, and C. Taft. 1956. *The Evolution of the Wage Structure*. New Haven, Conn.: Yale University Press.
Robinson, Joan. [1933] 1950. *The Economics of Imperfect Competition*. London: Macmillan.
Rottenberg, Simon, ed. 1981. *The Economics of Legal Minimum Wages*. Washington, D.C.: American Enterprise Institute.

Sidgwick, Henry. 1886. Economic Socialism. *Contemporary Review* 50 (November): 620–31.

Smith, Ralph, and Bruce Vavrichek. 1987. The Minimum Wage: Its Relation to Incomes and Poverty. *Monthly Labor Review* 110.6:24–30.

Stigler, George. 1946. The Economics of Minimum Wage Legislation. *American Economic Review* 36.3:358–65.

———. 1947. Professor Lester and the Marginalists. *American Economic Review* 37.1:154–57.

———. 1982. *The Economist as Preacher and Other Essays*. Chicago: University of Chicago Press.

Webb, Sidney. 1912. The Economic Theory of a Legal Minimum Wage. *Journal of Political Economy* 20.10:973–98.

Webb, Sidney, and Beatrice Webb. [1897] 1920. *Industrial Democracy*. London: Longmans, Green.

Welch, Finis. 1995. Comment for review symposium on *Myth and Measurement: The New Economics of the Minimum Wage*, by David Card and Alan Krueger. *Industrial and Labor Relations Review* 48.4:842–49.

Whaples, Robert. 1996. Is There a Consensus among American Labor Economists? *Journal of Labor Research* 17.4:725–34.

Part 2

The Concept of Applied Economics

On the Concept of Applied Economics: Lessons from Cambridge Economics and the History of Growth Theories

Flavio Comim

This article examines one important episode in the history of applied economics—the history of growth theories—in order to illustrate the historical nature of the concept of applied economics. First, this episode is discussed from the perspective of the theorists' views of the applied dimension of their theories and then from the perspective of the work carried out at the Department of Applied Economics (DAE) of Cambridge University. I emphasize the divergences concerning economists' understanding of the proper use of economic theory, divergences that might ultimately reveal the influence of distinct practices and institutional environments.

The history of growth theories provides a good field of inquiry for a discussion of divergences and disagreements about concepts of applied economics. Walt Rostow (1990) argued that the applied dimension of growth theories has often meant different things to different theorists; for instance, he pointed out that some theorists have not considered measurement and testing as applied economics in the history of growth theories. Similarly, Amartya Sen (1970) observed that at the early stages of growth theories, theorists (perhaps having the cases of Roy Harrod, Trevor Swan, and Robert Solow in mind) seemed to be more interested in doctrinal debates and in solving measurement problems than in defining the field of application of their theories. Later, the task

I am very grateful to Roger Backhouse, Geoff Harcourt, Jeff Biddle, and Mary Morgan for their valuable comments. I also would like to express my gratitude for suggestions received from the participants at the 1999 *HOPE* conference. Any errors and omissions are my responsibility.

of applying growth theories was devolved to the field of econometrics, a development that has, to a certain extent, resulted in the isolation of the theoretical from the practical aspects of these theories. And yet, as suggested by Solow (1997), the applied side of growth theories appears consistently to have exerted much influence on the development of theories. How can we explain the diversity of conceptualizations of applied economics in the history of growth theories? Should we simply accept that among the competing approaches—which have employed different conceptions of applied economics—there is one correct concept and that all the others are pursuing (or have pursued) misguided lines of research?

In view of the divergences concerning the assessment of the application of growth theories, it is argued here that there are several concepts of applied economics, that these concepts are historically determined (rather than subjected to a fixed and stable relation between "pure" and "applied" economics), and that competing approaches have employed different conceptions of applied economics in the elaboration of their criteria of assessment of other growth theories. This argument is illustrated by two case studies: (1) a discussion of how growth theorists have understood the term *applied economics* and (2) an analysis of the type of work done at the DAE.

To elaborate: the paper discusses different conceptions of applied economics that have been assumed by formal growth theorists. The investigation is narrowed by concentrating on the main theorists of each important historical period in the development of formal growth models, with emphasis on the work carried out at the University of Cambridge. An objection to this line of inquiry might be that the theoretical differences between competing concepts of applied economics are not relevant to an understanding of the actual application of those concepts and that only an investigation of their use could reveal their actual influences. In order to explore this possibility, a case study is provided by an examination of the empirical and applied work conducted by the DAE since its founding in 1945.

The Concept of Applied Economics

Debates about the applied dimension of growth theories have been a constant characteristic of this field. Theoretical and doctrinal discord in the literature has revealed different conceptions of applied economics, based on different practices and interests. The evidence seems to corroborate the view that what constitutes an application is historically contingent and that the historical nature of applied fields cannot be described from the perspective of the conventional view of applied economics as characterized in the introduction to this volume. Evidence provided by the history of growth theories suggests that application of theories and models is not a one-way procedure. It involves rather a diversity of uses that are better understood from a historical perspective. As observed by James Mirrlees (1973, xxi), one of the morals from the history of growth theory is that "one should criticise the uses of the models, not the models alone." According to Mirrlees (xii–xvi), some of the uses to which growth models have been put are:

1. The Historical: to discuss historical events from a new perspective;
2. The Predictive: to raise conjectures about future changes in behavior or in policy;
3. The Interpretative: to make sense of information provided by economic systems;
4. The Revelatory: to demonstrate previously unsuspected possibilities;
5. The Philosophical: to provide empirical support for theoretical issues;
6. The Institutional: to analyze institutional issues, such as monetary and public finance issues;
7. Estimation: to provide tools for estimating parameters, which might be put to further uses;
8. The Exploratory: to assist communication of ideas in a nonauthoritarian way.

Although Mirrlees does not relate any of the uses in particular to alternative styles of argument, this possibility must be considered. (I call *style* a way of organizing arguments, a language; it usually refers to the use of mathematics or the use of words as a way of conveying an argument. Thus, alternative styles of arguments will refer to alternative ways of developing an argument by either following mathematical or ordinary-language logic.) In the same way that, for example, more-mathematical models may be better prepared for producing quantitative results, it is possible that more-descriptive models may be better prepared for handling historical situations and interpreting information from real-life economic systems. Indeed, it seems that different concepts of applied economics are expected to be associated with different styles of argument, which in turn are related to different uses. Mirrlees indirectly adresses the relation between styles and uses for growth models when he discusses the relation between uses and their relevance. As he puts it:

> A more interesting observation is that some uses depend much more on leaps of intuition than others—and must, from that point of view, be more open to criticism. If a growth model is used to demonstrate a possibility, or contradict a conjecture, it normally requires little credulity to see the general relevance of the result. When, on the other hand, a particular model is used for evaluating policy in a particular country, the relation of model to reality is the central justification. (1973, xxvi)

Hence, models should be seen not only in relation to the uses to which they might be put—because these uses define the standards against which the models must be assessed—but also according to the styles of argument to which they are related. When a growth model (mathematical in style), intended to provide exclusively quantitative estimates of certain growth variables, is assessed in terms of any other use, it may face problems. For example, there is no reason why endogenous growth models, formulated in order to test convergence predictions among countries, must comply with other alternative uses of growth models, such as the institutional. Likewise, there is no necessary reason why a growth model elaborated with the intention of providing predictions should be assessed from, for example, a historical perspective. It is logically possible that a model, formulated in order to raise conjectures about future changes in policy, would not be able to make sense of historical events from a new perspective. Thus, models should be assessed according to their intended uses and styles of argument. But, how can the above mentioned different uses of growth models serve distinct conceptions of applied economics?

A good illustration of contrasting conceptions of applied economics is provided by the views of Frank Hahn (1971) and Sen (1970) in the introduction to their respective collections of growth papers. Hahn (1971, vii) says of growth literature that while "it would be singularly unwise to use the present theory alone in analysing some past episode, or perhaps even in formulating present policies, it certainly does not mean that it has all been a waste of time." According to him, the study of equilibrium paths is important because it might constitute a first step in understanding actual paths. He does not seem to be bothered by his own acknowledgment that "in particular the essential 'stationariness' of steady state at once suggests that such constructions may be quite unable to capture the rich process of actual economic growth" (viii). Rather, when criticizing Harrod and Joan Robinson for being faithful to John Maynard Keynes's belief in the difficulties of sustaining a viable rate of return on investment over time, he claims that "modern steady-state theory is not about a world of disappointed expectations, unwanted capacity and speculative hoarding. It is like the theory of the equilibrium of a frictionless pendulum, a theory which, it should be remarked, physicists have found it useful to study" (xii). Thus, it appears that when referring to the applied dimension of growth theories, Hahn does not have in mind economic history or the provision of basic guidelines for economic policy or, least of all, the explanation of growth histories.

A different conception of applied economics is suggested by Sen's comments on the practical importance of growth theories, according to which

> with this immensely practical motivation it would have been natural for growth theory to take a fairly practice-oriented shape. This, however, has not happened and much of modern growth theory is concerned with rather esoteric issues. Its link with public policy is often very remote. It is as if a poor man collected money for his food and blew it all on alcohol. (1970, 9)

It must be noted that Sen is criticizing not modern growth theory per se but the discordant harmony between the theory and practice of growth models; not the style of argument developed by growth theorists but the mismatch between style and the uses to which the arguments are put. He is arguing that as long as growth theories are not in a "fairly practice-oriented shape," they cannot be applied. Thus, it appears that when referring to the applied dimension of growth theories, Sen has in mind the provision of practical guidelines for public policies. In contrast to Hahn's view, it is clear that Sen privileges the historical, predictive, and institutional uses of growth models in Mirrlees' list. Hahn's and Sen's different conceptions of applied economics are merely an illustration of deeper divergences that have been found originally in the history of growth theories.

Growth Theorists' Views of Applied Growth Theory

A more systematic investigation of the different conceptions of applied economics held by growth theorists could be carried out by contextualizing their views within each historical period in the development of formal growth models. Following Rostow (1990), Sen (1970), Henry Wan (1971), and Solow (1996), these periods may be classified as (1) Pioneering of Growth Theory, 1936–57; (2) Old Neoclassical Growth Theory, 1956–66; (3) Old Keynesian Growth Theory, 1956–70; and (4) New Growth Theory, 1986–present. To some extent, the dates are arbitrary; they merely refer to the years when some of the most important contributions have been presented. Similarly, the categories are arbitrary; they merely purport to represent along broad lines taxonomic differences already present in the growth literature. Here, emphasis is given to the interpretation of these periods as sets of different activities representing distinct uses of growth models that are associated with theorists' different views on the concept of applied economics.

The Pioneering period, defined by the contributions of Harrod (1939) and Evsey Domar (1946), represented an attempt to integrate Keynesian macroeconomic analysis with elements of economic growth, focusing on the necessary conditions for a dynamic equilibrium between savings and investment. Harrod argued that a steady-state growth would be achieved only if G_A, the growth rate determined by population growth and technical progress, was equal to G_W, where G_W, the warranted rate, satisfied the equality $G_W = s/v$ ($s =$ the saving rate, and $v =$ desired capital/product quotient). According to Harrod, there was no reason for the equality to hold. Similarly, Domar pointed out a chronic tendency to underinvestment which would prevent this equality from holding. This model specification led Harrod and Domar to predict the instability of growth in capitalist economies.

The Old Neoclassical Growth Theory period, defined by the contributions of Solow (1956) and Swan (1956), was characterized by the use of the neoclassical form of the production function in growth theories. The production function assumed constant returns to scale, diminishing returns to each input, and nonzero elasticity of substitution between the inputs. The dynamics in the Solow-Swan model were determined by exogenous elements, namely, the rate of population growth n and the changes in the level of technology, represented by shifts of the production function. The fundamental differential equation of the Solow-Swan model was $Dk = s \cdot f(k) - (n + \delta) \cdot k$, where Dk = the change in the capital stock per capita over time, s = the saving rate, $f(k)$ = the production function, δ = the depreciation rate for the capital/labor rate, and k = the capital/labor rate. The steady state was achieved when $Dk = 0$, that is, when gross investment per person $s \cdot f(k)$ was equal to the effective depreciation rate for the capital/labor ratio. The assumption of continuous substitution possibilities between inputs guaranteed that the capital/labor rate would adjust to satisfy the steady-state condition. This adjustment with equilibrium opposes Harrod's and Domar's predictions of growth instability.

The Old Keynesian Growth Theory period, defined by the contributions of Nicholas Kaldor (1957, 1960) and Joan Robinson (1956, 1962), meant a revival of Keynesian ideas in the economic growth literature. Whereas Kaldor, through a series of six papers between 1954 and 1962 emphasized macroeconomic aspects of growth, Robinson stressed the choice of techniques and methodological aspects of growth theories. Kaldor's growth theories consisted of (1) a saving function, including a distribution theory of profit and wage shares that replaced the marginal productivity theory of distribution; (2) a theory of full employment, assuming firms with price-making power; and (3) a technical progress function, where the rate of growth of per capita output was an increasing function of the rate of growth of per capita capital. Robinson's growth theories consisted of (1) open models, where she analyzed the effects of investment decisions and constraints on the investment level, and (2) closed models, where she discussed under which conditions full employment could be maintained within alternative growth patterns. Both Kaldor and Robinson criticized the neoclassical theory of distribution and stressed in their models that investment determined savings, that marginal saving propensities out of profit and wages were different, and that technical progress was not entirely exogenous.

Finally, the New Growth Theory period, beginning with the work of Paul Romer (1986) and Robert Lucas (1988), was based on models with spillovers of knowledge across producers and external benefits of human capital, which implied increasing returns to investment in a broad class of capital goods. Subsequently, R and D theories were incorporated in order to explain technological advance and imperfect competition. Diffusion of technology models provided results similar to the ones presented by the Solow-Swan model. The key element that underlies New Growth theories is the global absence of diminishing returns to capital.

This family of models is also known as endogenous growth theories. In the case of the model constructed by Romer (1990), endogenous growth is generated by externalities from the declining costs of inventing new products. Optimum growth rates are achieved by a proper allocation of labor between production and research. Representative household utility is maximized subject to monopoly pricing and research spillovers.

In what follows, the theorists' conceptions of the applied dimension of their theories are examined.

Pioneering Period

The most important references in the Pioneering period are Harrod (1936, 1948) and Domar (1946, 1957). At this early stage, the notion of applying growth theory seems to have been closely related to the provision of rough guidelines for economic policy, but the issue of application did not receive special attention from theorists. In Harrod's article of 1939, the applied side of his model involves exclusively manipulation of the "warranted rate" through the use of permanent anticycle policies which would influence expectations and investment (the capital/product quotient v could be interpreted as a simple accelerator quotient). The empirical dimension of the applied side is downplayed. As Harrod puts it (1939, 26), "It should be noticed that the instability theory makes the empirical verification of the acceleration principle more arduous." Similarly, Domar (1946) barely discusses the application of his model, limiting himself to brief comments on its policy consequences, which consist basically of supporting compensatory measures of public policy required to increase investment.

However, in the transitional period toward the next stage in the history of growth theory, Domar (1957) acknowledges that for the attainment of a "workable theory of growth" a middle ground between general treatises and highly simplified symbolic models must be achieved. He advocated the inclusion of less tractable variables and emphasized the criterion of reliability as a precondition for the successful use of growth models. Caution was involved in the use of different theories, despite their apparent relevance. As he argued (1957, 13), "The use of growth models as a practical guide to economic development is enticing, but the pitfalls are deep indeed." Objections were raised not against the use of models per se but against the use of models without due caution.

Domar (1957) provides a good illustration in support of the idea that different uses of growth theories are related to different styles of argument. He discusses the view that continuous government borrowing might result in ever-rising public debt requiring increasing taxes. In order to demonstrate his argument he constructs numerical examples and examines the behavior of the tax rate over time under alternative assumptions. Although the tables are meant only as illustrations, he describes them as "experiments" (1957, 41). Having assumed the values of the main parameters such as the propensity to save and the fraction of national income borrowed by the government, he calculates the evolution of the tax rate and the ratio of debt to national income for given original values of debt and income. Then, alternative cases are discussed and different policies are examined according to different circumstances. Ultimately, his "applied economics" lies in a descriptive and numerical (as opposed to quantitative, since it avoids measurement or estimation) style of argument which involves different thought experiments. Application here concerns the establishment of theoretical outcomes that could provide a rationale for successful growth policies.

This was also Harrod's view of applied economics. He seems to have maintained throughout his life the view that "we shall continue in confusion until growth theory has progressed further and been able, in consequence, to formulate well based principles in applied economics that policy makers can understand and act upon" (1973, 101). Harrod conceived of growth theory as the "political economy" dimension of his dynamic theory (see Young 1989, 181–82), encompassing a greater range of factors than the ones that can be specified by statistical measurement.[1] Therefore, the applied dimension of his theories comprised a certain looseness compatible with historical, predictive, interpretative, and institutional uses of growth models.

1. For more on Harrod and the development of the growth research program, see Warren Young's *Harrod and His Trade Cycle Group* (1989), which argues that Harrod's lifetime objective of making Keynes's theories dynamic meant to him an extension of the validity and applicability of Keynes's approach. Young quotes a letter that Harrod sent to Keynes (6 July 1938) in which Harrod notes that "Tinbergen may be doing very valuable work in trying to reduce this part of theory to quantitative terms. . . . The matter has a personal interest as well as a purely academic one to me. . . . I make a statement about the 'acceleration principle.' Then Tinbergen comes and says that the facts do not suggest that it had the influence I ascribed to it. Surely one ought *not* to leave the matter there. To Tinbergen, the statistics merely suggest a negative result. To me, if I applied his technique, they might *suggest* a refinement of my concepts or a restressing of the importance of one at the expense of the other. I confess all this frightens me a little" (Young 1989, 154).

The Old Neoclassical Growth Theory Period

The period of Old Neoclassical Growth Theory, comprising the growth theory of the 1950s and 1960s, meant initially a move from the vague and policy-laden notion of applied economics to a more quantitative and empirical approach toward the application of growth theories. The original papers of Solow (1956, 1957) and Swan (1956), with distant ancestors in Ramsey 1928 and Meade 1936, have given rise to a theoretical framework in which the stability of growth equilibrium (in one-sector models) was guaranteed through a simple adjustment mechanism of factor substitution, which made possible the use of statistical techniques. It was in this context that the concept of applying a theory became very closely associated first with measurement and then with using econometrics in order to report (estimating, not testing) empirical regularities and provide predictions for policy making. Solow (1997, xiii) justifies the applied dimension of his approach, arguing that "it was the introduction of some technological flexibility that had opened up growth theory to a wider variety of real-world facts and to a closer connection with general economic theory." The important point here is that the Solow-Swan neoclassical model influenced not only theorists' ideas about the determinants of economic growth, but also their conception of applied economics.

For instance, Solow's (1957) application of his model to U.S. data for the period 1909–49, with the objective of isolating shifts of the aggregate production function from movements along it, provided the foundation for work such as Griliches 1963, 1967, Jorgenson 1966, and Jorgenson and Griliches 1967, all four of which produced (1) a measurement of changes in the total factor productivity (TFP) and in the quantities of output and input and (2) an agenda for correcting errors in the measurement of output and for incorporating the measurement of input into a unified social accounting framework.[2] After the literature on "growth accounting" and measurement problems, the applied dimension of growth theories was manifested in the elaboration of econometric models. Policy issues were addressed but were kept at a very abstract

2. It is interesting to note that Solow's justification for his measurement exercises draws on an issue of taste and usefulness of results. As he puts it, "Either this kind of aggregate economics appeals or it doesn't. Personally I belong to both schools. If it does, I think one can draw some crude but useful conclusions from the results" (1957, 312).

level.[3] A good illustration of this concept of applied economics is given by Edward Denison (1967), who emphasized the quantitative nature of economic growth by arguing that "the subject of economic growth is inherently comprehensive and quantitative. The author is persuaded that it will not advance far without both comprehensiveness and quantitative measurement" (1967, 3). Although he claims that the classification of sources of growth provided by his study is useful for appraisal of policy actions, he points out that he does not really try any appraisal in his work. This is illustrative of what might be called the quantitative view of applied economics.

Broadly speaking, it might be said that application here entails the quantification of certain concepts and/or variables previously identified and contextualized by theories. The operational definitions are very dependent on theoretical guidelines, and the task of applied economists consists of gathering and analyzing predetermined empirical evidence. The sort of practices and activities involved by this conception of applied economics privileges a mathematical style of argument and revelatory, philosophical, and estimation uses of growth models.

The Old Keynesian Growth Theory Period

Subsequently, contributions such as those by Kaldor (1955–56, 1958), Kaldor and Mirrlees (1961–62), and Joan Robinson (1956, 1962) advocated a different conception of applied economics, echoing Alfred Marshall.[4] For Marshall (1920), the application of economics implied the isolation of a particular situation and the conjunction of all the different aspects related to that situation. As he argued (1920, 33), "The direct pursuit of practical aims leads us to group together bits of all sorts of knowledge, which have no connection with one another except for

3. As Solow (1997, 77) observes, "Any theory that says something about the real world is likely to have implications for policy. But it is only good sense to realize that an abstract theory, like the one I have been developing, can only say abstract things about economic policy. At the very beginning, I described the aggregative theory of growth as a parable. You expect a parable to have a moral, but hardly to contain concrete instructions for the conduct of life. So here, when I talk about policy implications, I have to stay at roughly the same level of abstraction as the theory on which they are based."

4. Kaldor does not discuss his views on the meaning of applying economics in his early work (1957, 1961–62 [with Mirrlees], 1964) on growth. References are found in his late work. Therefore, in what follows his views on applied economics are presented with no assessment of the consistency of his views throughout the years.

the immediate purposes of the moment." Within this perspective the role of statistical analysis is limited to an input into the general framework of the application of a theory, where the main objective is to provide concrete guidelines for historically determined situations.

Kaldor (1955–56) argued that the basic difficulty with the neoclassical approach to growth and distribution lay in the meaning of capital as a factor of production. He criticized the quantitative approach of the applied dimension of neoclassical economics, arguing that capital could not be measured either in terms of value or in physical units.[5] He proposed a new referential unit for an empirical assessment of his theories that was meant to avoid the quantitative bias present in neoclassical applied economics. According to Kaldor,

> Since facts, as recorded by statisticians, are always subject to numerous snags and qualifications, and for that reason are incapable of being accurately summarised, the theorist, in my view, should be free to start with a "stylised" view of the facts—i.e. concentrate on broad tendencies, ignoring individual detail, and proceed on the "as if" method, i.e. construct a hypothesis that could account for these "stylised" facts, without necessarily committing himself to the historical accuracy, or sufficiency, of the facts or tendencies thus summarised. ([1958] 1989, 230)

From this perspective, Kaldor's "Causes of the Slow Rate of Economic Growth in the United Kingdom" ([1966] 1989) and "The Case for Regional Policies" ([1970] 1989) can be seen as examples of his applied economics: they both start by establishing the basic stylized facts from empirical evidence, develop the theoretical background that explains those facts, and conclude with suggestions for economic policies. It is interesting to note that in comparing some contentions about the causes of the slow rate of growth in the United Kingdom he observes that "the difficulty about them [the causes] is that with one or two possible exceptions, they are not capable of being tested, and there is no way in which their individual role could in any way be quantified" ([1966] 1989, 283). Despite his use of regression equations as part of his argument, he draws ultimately on stylized facts built from historical evidence. Similarly, in

5. In terms of value, measurement requires the existence of a rate of interest, which in turn would assume the value of the capital to be measured. In physical terms, such an exercise would require the isolation of two identical situations differing only in their quantities of capital (or labor) in precise numerical relationship (Kaldor 1955–56).

his paper on the case for regional policies, he argues that the principle of cumulative causation privileges a theoretical mechanism (endogenous factors resulting from the process of historical development) that explains stylized facts better than the neoclassical argument based on exogenous differences in resource allocation. It might then be suggested that Kaldor's applied economics was shaped in a form that allowed him to feel more comfortable with the use of economics in real and historical systems where the quantification strategy could not provide the uses of economic models he was aiming for. Perhaps it is for this reason that he blames the "great exercise" of mathematical economists which "made the theory a *less usable tool* than it was thought to have been in its early and crude state before the full implications of general equilibrium had been so thoroughly explored" ([1974] 1989, 399; emphasis added). Kaldor, in his *Essays on Economic Policy* (1964), explicitly acknowledges that the papers included

> belong to the field of "applied" rather than "pure" economics—they concern the application of economic theory to issues of economic policy. . . . But the particular issues of economic policy, and the manner in which economists tackle them, are even more ephemeral than the theoretical ideas that form their background. Moreover, their consideration often involves a detailed analysis of the economic situation of some particular country at some particular time, which makes their perusal tedious reading once that situation has passed into history. (1:vii)

Application for Kaldor was then closely related to the historical and institutional uses of growth models and to a style of argument—the opposite of the Solow-Swan style—which allowed the discussion of particular and ephemeral issues. As a concrete example of his conception of applied economics, Kaldor ([1944] 1964) examined the consequences of full employment policies on the revenue and expenditures of public authorities. It is interesting to note that his statistical analysis was contextualized according to the historical circumstances present in Great Britain in 1938 and divided into the periods of prewar and postwar Britain. Moreover, he seemed to be concerned not only with the logical aspects of economic policy—as seemed to be the case with Harrod-Domar models—but also with the practical methods available in order to achieve effective and practicable policies (see Kaldor [1944] 1964, 27–28).

An explanation for Kaldor's concept of applied economics might be found in his claim that economists must use theories that embody significant features of the world economy as a first step to applying economics. He argued that "most abstract economic models postulate a 'closed system,' but they *apply the conclusions reached to open systems*, such as national economies, without being fully aware of the inconsistencies involved in this procedure" ([1977] 1989, 426–27; emphasis added). Therefore, the concept of applied economics he sponsors through his theoretical and applied work is one that minimizes, in his own terms, the inconsistencies involved in the application of closed-system results to open systems, events, or situations.

Joan Robinson held a concept of applied economics similar to Kaldor's. She repeatedly criticized neoclassical growth theories for not allowing discussion of historical, that is, time related, issues. For instance, criticizing Meade's growth theory she claimed ([1971] 1979, 312) that when all equipment is made of one physical substance, important distinctions, such as distinctions between long and short periods, cannot be discussed. She also raised the point that the quantification of economic concepts turned concepts that originally were *ex ante*, such as the production function, into *ex post* ones. The argument was that when the production function was estimated, it could only reflect the choices that had been made. *Ex ante* aspects of the production function, in particular the influence of factor prices on allocative choices, cannot be discussed with production functions that have been estimated/quantified. Her wider critique of the quantitative principle behind the statistical side of applied economics was that "not all economic concepts can be reduced to strictly quantitative terms" and that "mathematical logic is a powerful tool of thought, but its application in economic theory generally seems to consist merely of putting circular elements into algebra" (1979, 115, 116–17).

According to Robinson, a theory in order to be applied needed to have its foundations in historical time. She observed that "a system of simultaneous equations need not specify any date nor does its solution involve history. But if any proposition drawn from it is applied to an economy inhabited by human beings, it immediately becomes self-contradictory" ([1974] 1979, 49). It is interesting to note that a large part of Robinson's critique of neoclassical growth theory was due to a different view concerning the applied dimension of growth models. According to her definition of applied economics (1980, 90), "To construct models that cannot be applied is merely an idle amusement. It is only by interpreting history, including the present in history, that economics can aspire to be a serious subject." She meant by "historical time" almost what Kaldor meant by "stylised facts": an empirical realm defined by a particular place, at a particular date, under particular circumstances.[6] "Particular" here does not need to be associated with "individual" situations. A set of circumstances, once connected by a common history, would qualify as "particular."

Another characteristic of Robinson's concept of applied economics was its intrinsic relation with policy issues. Because she believed that "discussion of an actual problem cannot avoid the question of what should be done about it; questions of policy involve politics" ([1977] 1979, 1), she equated the use of theory with policy issues and value judgments. By sponsoring a policy-oriented concept of applied economics, critical of measurement attempts of all growth variables and of models which, in her view, ignore history, historical time,[7] and judgments of value, Robinson was engaged in a conflict with other growth theorists, such as Solow, whose nature was essentially practical rather than theoretical. She was very critical, for example, of Solow's aggregation procedures and imputation of growth rates to contributing factors, due to their lack of applicability. Indeed, as remarked by Wan (1971, 69), "A large portion of the differences between Mrs. Robinson and Solow (if not the entire neoclassical school) lies in the judgement of whether

6. A good example of the similarity between Robinson's notion of historical time and Kaldor's notion of "stylised facts" is provided by her discussion about the nature of prediction in economics. Robinson observed (1979, 118) that "in 1931, he [Keynes] pointed out that falling prices were putting a great strain on the banks. (In March 1933 the banking system in the USA came to a standstill.) In 1936 (following Keynes) I observed that a period of continuous near-full employment would lead to continuous inflation; and (most remarkable of all) Kalecki predicted in 1944 that after the war we should be living under the regime of a political trade cycle (stop-go). These predictions were not at all exact; they were not derived from studying time series, but from a diagnosis of how the contemporary economic system operated. It seems as though what success economics has had depends more upon insight than upon precision and that its affinity must be with history as much as with mathematics."

7. Joan Robinson's defense of the historical nature of her concept of applied economics could be questioned on the basis that she herself did not conduct much historical analysis. Perhaps, judged according to her own standards, she cannot be considered an applied economist. Alternatively, the historical nature of her applied economics could be found in her emphasis on the use of open-ended models, which purported to avoid the establishment of fixed, long-run relationships. A more flexible scheme of analysis, as argued by A. Bhaduri (1996, 202–3), could perhaps compensate for the absence of more historical analysis in her work, but to discuss that issue would be beyond the scope of this article.

useful empirical results can be obtained by following the Solovian procedures."

The New Growth Theory Period

The period of New Growth Theory, comprising the new developments since the mid-1980s, has seen arise a new concept of applied economics based on the seminal work of Robert Barro (1991). The basic methodology presented by Barro, comprising the running of cross-sectional regressions, has spawned an empirical literature on economic growth that has made econometric topics such as robustness (see Levine and Renelt 1992) the key element in the applied dimension of growth theories. Within this framework, the main problems involved in applying a theory consist in, among others, finding significant variables that fit the cross-sectional regressions, obtaining robust results, using specification tests for nonnested models to assess the goodness of the models relative to a conventional specification, and solving measurement errors and heteroskedasticity problems due to large heterogeneity in countries' structures (see Levine and Zervos 1993 and De Long and Summers 1991). It must be noted that although this literature on empirical growth emphasizes the quantitative aspects of theories, as Solow and Swan did, it follows its own research agenda with much less influence from theoretical quarters than the influence generated by the neoclassical theories on applied studies. For instance, Xavier Sala-I-Martin (1997, 178) acknowledges that "the problem faced by empirical growth economists is that growth theories are not explicit enough about what variables x_j belong in the 'true' regression." Therefore, in order to find the variables that are correlated with growth, economists concentrated on assessing the empirical confidence they could attribute to their statistical estimations. In addition, it is widely acknowledged (see, e.g., Islam 1995) that a significant proportion of the empirical research on growth theories has been a response to the elaboration of large data sets, such as those used by Summers and Heston (1988).

Of course, there are theoretical differences between Old Neoclassical and New Growth models that can explain their emphasis on distinct aspects of their applied economics. In the New Growth models, the incorporation of increasing returns to physical capital and positive externalities produces a permanent effect on growth rates that gives to growth-oriented policies much more importance than they had under

Old Neoclassical Growth models. It is natural that the policy dimension of the New Growth conception of applied economics receives more attention. Nevertheless, the most important distinction between these two sorts of models concerns the relative independent status of applied work in the New Growth models. It might be said, based on Jorgenson 1968 and Endres 1982, that the previous *application by fiat* of the Solovian theories—where measurement and estimation were determined a priori by the conceptual structure imposed by theories—was replaced by an *application independent of theory*—where empirical findings determine the concept of interest behind the use of different models, that is, where significant variables that fit cross-sectional regressions suggest a posteriori a conceptual structure used to formulate new explanations for economic growth.

To conclude this section it must be emphasized that the evidence above suggests there exist different views of applied growth theory by different growth theorists. As argued, these differences are related to distinct styles of argumentation and alternative uses of growth models that have been suggested by growth theorists. Therefore, from the perspective of the theorists' views of the applied dimension of their theories, the picture that emerges is of concepts of applied economics that are historically determined. Yet, this illustration might not be enough to account for the actual application of these concepts. In what follows, a second illustration of the historical nature of the concept of applied economics is provided.

Applied Economics at the Cambridge DAE

In order to investigate the actual application of some of the notions discussed above, the empirical and applied work conducted by the DAE since its founding in 1945 is examined here. Its contribution to the development of applied economics and econometric methods and techniques has been prominent, as pointed out by Roy Epstein (1987) and Christophes Gilbert (1986). More important, perhaps, in the history of the DAE were the variety and diversity of approaches it sponsored. It has been argued that its directors have encouraged different views concerning the application of economic theory. As Geoff Harcourt and Michael Kitson (1993, 435) observe, "Cambridge economics has always been a broad church and it could be even argued that the Directors of the DAE have been patriarchs drawn from different denominations."

The first director of the DAE, Richard Stone (1945–55), believed that applied economics should privilege measurement problems, with a rigorous use of mathematics in order to express precisely the theoretical constraints to be tested by quantitative methods. Research carried out at the DAE during this period included Stone's Nobel Prize work on national accounts (with emphasis on the construction of social accounting matrices), Durbin-Watson and Cochrane-Orcutt techniques (for handling serially correlated errors), and estimation of consumer demand models. Indeed, one of the DAE's achievements, as noted by Ron Smith (1998, 88), was "the establishment of the text-book, single-equation, time-series regression framework with its standard notation and tests as the work-horse of econometrics." This emphasis on quantification and use of econometrics appears in the DAE's view of applied economics, which appears in its *First Report*:

> We see the aims of applied economics to be as follows. Through the processes of observation and testing it should develop economic theories so that they stand established as applicable to the actual world, and on these foundations it should seek to provide the basis for making reliable predictions. The realisation of these aims presupposes a certain degree of progress taking place at one time along a number of different lines. In the first place the theories to be tested must be stated with sufficient exactness to be brought into relation with observations. Secondly, the necessary observations must be brought into being if they are not already available. Thirdly, the procedures for testing hypotheses under non-experimental conditions must be developed so that they are suited to the conditions of economic problems. The Department's research programme has been conceived as a group of interrelated investigations which should yield results along each of these main lines of activity. (Department of Applied Economics 1948, 3–4)

This quantitative dimension of applied economics has been materialized in the development of statistical techniques which allowed theories to be tested by empirical methods. A consequence of this view was that *applied* became synonymous with *empirical* in the sense that what could not be measured should not qualify as applied. Stone has discussed this issue in his paper "The A Priori and the Empirical in Economics" (1964), where he comments that in order to apply William Stanley Jevons's theory of utility as a theory of consumption, it is not necessary to measure satisfaction per se as long as we are able to work out its implications which relate to measurable phenomena. He claims that "a model is of *no practical use* unless a means can be found of estimating the parameters it contains" (1964, 8; emphasis added). It might then be concluded that during Stone's directorship of the DAE, the process of converting the theory into reality focused on measurement problems and development of statistical tools.

Conversely, the second director of the DAE, Brian Reddaway (1955–70), supported a practical, policy-oriented approach to applied economics, encouraging a concern with the idiosyncrasies of statistical series and the use of techniques that were less mathematical and statistical. Harcourt (1997, 20) refers to the "Reddaway Method" to describe the sort of applied projects and institutional encouragement given by Reddaway characterized by "thorough knowledge of data and its limitations, careful statistical analysis of it and what it can be used to show, and what it cannot." As reported by Smith (1998, 99–100), "He [Reddaway] shared the general Cambridge doubts about the applicability of econometrics to complex economic processes, where numerous factors, many unmeasurable, interacted and relationships were likely to change through time." As a result, the DAE was split into two groups, with the first group, under the auspices of Stone and the Growth Project (1960), pursuing econometrics and the second, under Reddaway, emphasizing quantification of economic history[8] and longitudinal databases of company accounts. Harcourt and Kitson have pointed out that

> Brian Reddaway's period as Director was marked by an extremely down-to-earth approach to problem-solving. He emphasised the importance of understanding the strengths *and* weaknesses and limitations of data and the framing of questions in a manner which allowed the data to throw light on the answers. On the whole he encouraged the use of techniques which were less technical than those which were applied in the Stone era, and afterwards. (1993, 436)

The concept of applied economics sponsored by Reddaway emphasized the use of descriptive statistics and institutional and historical

8. Feinstein (1998, 181) comments that *British Economic Growth* (1962) by Phyllis Deane and W. A. Cole is widely recognized as "one of the most influential of all the books to have emerged from research undertaken in Cambridge at the Department of Applied Economics." Indeed, under Reddaway's directorship economic history became an important item in the applied economic agenda of the department.

contextualization of phenomena at the expense of using more sophisticated techniques. There was an awareness of the limitation of statistics well expressed, for instance, by Phyllis Deane (1968) that is very representative of the applied economics carried out by Reddaway's group at the DAE. According to Deane (1968, 171–72), "Most economists and statisticians who have either had a share in compiling national income statistics, or have had occasion to depend on them for analytical purposes, will be constantly aware of the fact that they are ambiguous measures of economic phenomena. . . . In some cases they are based on such inadequate statistical reporting systems that the publication of annual national income aggregates can be only the purest of window-dressing, if not a deliberate instrument of propaganda." The positive side of this criticism—of the nature of data generating systems—was an important contribution to the quality of national income statistics and descriptive statistics during this period.

Finally, during the Wynne Godley (1970–87) period, a balance was achieved between the above views on applied economics. The two large modeling works carried out during his directorship, the Growth Project (based on techniques of statistical inference and disaggregation) and the Cambridge Economic Policy Group (based on a model of the U.K. economy used for policy recommendations), synthesize the coexistence of two different notions of applied economics within the DAE. During this period great emphasis was put on forecasting, short-term policy analysis, and structural-change problems. Godley's own group sided with Reddaway's policy-oriented view of applied economics. Godley himself was very critical of an applied economics where the mechanical interpretation of procedures left little or no scope for the judgment of the practitioner. As he put it (1998, 260), "I think the idea of an econometric model which in any real sense thinks for one is anomalous. The purpose of a model is rather to enlarge the capacity of the mind to encompass a far more complex system of interrelationships than would otherwise be possible." Therefore, he believed that an element of judgment is important for any use of economics. But this appears to be more a word of caution that allowed him to stay between the two different concepts of applied economics that have pervaded the history of the DAE, than a statement of an alternative point of view.

A complementary and more direct way of examining the diversity and evolution of the applied research conducted at the DAE consists in classifying the papers produced by members of the DAE and by others working in direct collaboration with the department. Despite the likely inaccuracies involved in the classification of papers, due to the existence of many fuzzy boundaries, and the limitations involved in a quantification of research, without assessing its academic impact, it might be argued that the table below provides a good illustration of the different institutional guidelines and practices carried out at the DAE during this period. The method followed here comprised a classification of 408 papers in the DAE Economic Reprints series and 118 papers in the DAE New Series of Economic Reprints, covering a period of forty-one years of research activities at the DAE. It is based on the assumption that the elaboration of different papers involves different sets of practices and attitudes toward different views of applied economics. For instance, the elaboration of econometric papers entails practices such as handling data sets, using mathematics and econometric computer models, and so on, that are distinct from other practices related, for instance, to historical studies.

Articles were classified according to their style of argumentation (e.g., mathematical, descriptive, conceptual) and potential uses (quantitative, methodological, historical, theoretical, and institutional). The purpose of this classification is to illustrate the evolution of different concepts of applied economics—related to different practices—under particular institutional arrangements. Many papers defied classification but were arranged according to the following principles:

1. Quantitative articles deal with statistics, tables of statistics, mathematical techniques, and econometrics. An article on the measurement of national income or on the significance of correlation between time series would be classified as quantitative. Titles typical of quantitative articles include “A Sampling Study of the Merits of Autoregressive and Reduced Form Transformations in Regression Analysis” and “A Statistical Study of the Productivity of Cambridgeshire Farms.”
2. Methodological articles deal with conceptual and methodological discussions of applied work and techniques. An article on the reliability of statistical data or on the limitations of the input-output techniques would be classified as methodological. Titles typical of methodological articles include “Scope and Method of Econometrics” and “The A Priori and the Empirical in Economics.”

3. Historical articles are related to the disciplines of economic history and the history of economic thought. There is no clear-cut distinction between this category and the quantitative descriptive category in terms of style of argumentation and potential use. Articles have been classified as historical when they addressed economic history issues. Titles typical of historical articles include "The Construction Costs and the Value of the British Merchant Fleet, 1850–1938" and "Trends in Eighteenth-Century Smuggling."
4. Theoretical articles deal with formal modeling or conceptual issues concerned with generalizations and purely abstract reasoning. An article on models of economic growth or on monopolistic pricing would be classified as theoretical. Titles typical of theoretical articles include "Three Models of Economic Growth" and "Taxation and the Cost of Capital."
5. Institutional articles deal with policy-oriented, case-study, and sociological analyses. During the Godley period they consisted largely of short papers for magazines addressing conjunctural issues, such as employment, trade, and the current situation in the industrial sector. Titles typical of institutional articles include "Elites in the British Class Structure," "Industrial Relations and Uneven Development," and "The Political Economy of Collective Bargaining."

The classification of articles itself raised the conceptual problem of the change in the nature of the activities involved in the writing of these different articles. A mathematical article written in the early 1940s does not have the same features as a mathematical article written in the late 1980s. Indeed, as far as the theoretical category is concerned, the transformation of this category along the years has involved pronounced changes in the style of writing and argumentation that have been ignored here for the purposes of classification. This problem was first pointed out by Roger Backhouse (1998), who discusses some difficulties that arise in this sort of classificatory exercise.

During the Richard Stone period emphasis was given to papers in the area of "mathematical statistics," with quantitative articles representing 71.2 percent of all papers published during this period. Stone's own work, such as "The Measurement of National Income and Expenditure" (1948) and "The Demand for Food in the United Kingdom before the War" (1952), illustrates the nature of the activities carried out at the

DAE that were related to mathematical practices. Stone alone wrote about one out of every five papers published in this series during his period as director. The important thing to note here is that not only did most researchers in this period, such as G. H. Orcutt, S. F. James, D. Cochrane, and G. Tintner, follow a quantitative approach to applied economics, but their views concerning the proper style of argument and uses of economics corresponded to the set of activities and practices in which they were engaged. In other words, they not only carried out formal and quantitative work, but they also supported a quantitative and mathematical approach to economics. Similarly, during the Reddaway period, where the emphasis shifted to a more policy-oriented concept of applied economics, it is possible to see a corresponding integration between the new methods being used and the practices, such as the making of economic history, being pursued. This was the period in which Stone was engaged in the Growth Project and in which less mathematical ways of describing empirical facts started being used by other researchers such as Phyllis Deane, R. C. O. Matthews, and W. A. Cole. The drop in the number of quantitative articles (from 71.2 percent to 30.5 percent of the papers) and the increase in the methodological, historical, and institutional works (from 17.7 percent to 50.5 percent of the papers) provide a good illustration of the change in practices in this period.

It is interesting to see the proliferation of short papers written for magazine readers during the Wynne Godley period, such as Barry Moore and John Rhode's "Economic and Financial Implications of Devolution" (1979), precisely when short-term policy analyses had boomed. Other changes may also be detected in this period such as the increase in applied econometric (from 6.5 percent to 15.5 percent) and descriptive work (8.8 percent of the papers). It seems that during Godley's period a balance was achieved between quantitative and historical activities and practices in the department. Whereas theoretical (from 19 percent to 19.5 percent) and institutional (from 19 percent to 19.9 percent) work remained almost at the same levels, quantitative (40.2 percent) and historical (17.2 percent) activities were carried out within levels established previously by the other directors.

Yet, the most important changes produced by different institutional incentives cannot be assessed from the table above, because they are not constrained by the different uses the applied research has been put to. Instead, these changes have "crossed the border" between different

Table 1 Classification of papers by categories (% of total papers)

	Richard Stone Period (1945–55)	Brian Reddaway Period (1955–70)	Wynne Godley Period (1970–87)
Quantitative	71.2	30.5	40.2
Mathematical	44.5	17	7.9
Pure econometrics	17.8	7	7.9
Applied econometrics	8.9	6.5	15.5
Descriptive	—	—	8.8
Methodological	1.9	10	3.1
Conceptual	—	4.5	—
Historical	10.9	21.5	17.2
Policy-oriented	—	7	8.4
Theoretical	10.9	19	19.5
Conceptual	—	4.5	8.8
Modeling	—	—	7.9
Institutional	4.9	19	19.9
Policy-oriented	—	2.5	1.3
Case study	—	6	3.5
Sociological	—	1	2.2

Source: DAE Economic Reprint Series (numbers 1–408) and New Series of Economic Reprints (numbers 1–118).

uses through different practices and styles of argumentation. This means that when the Stone period came to an end, and the Reddaway period started, the most important change in the conception of applied economics behind the work carried out at the DAE was not merely the increase in one sort of use of economics. It was not simply the case that more economic history was done at the expense of less pure econometrics. Rather, the point is that because the concept of interest changed, applied work changed in its style of argumentation in order to address issues that by then were not receiving much attention. For example, quantitative analyses pursued by W. A. Cole or Phyllis Deane were different from the ones pursued by Richard Stone not only because they had a different sense of purpose but because they were written in a descriptive language very different from Stone's mathematical language. This meant that Stone's interest in policy making and Deane's or Reddaway's work on quantification of economic aspects were (and are) to some extent incommensurable because they assumed alternative conceptions of applied economics which in turn presupposed a different set of practices and patterns of action.

Conclusion

This article was divided into three main parts. The first part presented different uses to which growth models have been put and suggested that they might be related to different styles of argumentation. An illustration of contrasting conceptions of applied economics was provided by an outline of the views of Hahn and Sen. It was claimed that an investigation of the history of growth theories would illuminate the historical nature of the concept of applied economics. With this objective in mind, two case studies were pursued in the second and third parts focusing respectively on how growth theorists have understood the term *applied economics* and on the type of work done at the Cambridge DAE.

The second part outlined the different views of applied economics held by growth theorists. These views were broadly related to their theories and to distinct styles of argumentation and alternative uses of growth models that theorists have supported. Their competing styles and uses might explain why growth theorists have disregarded the applied side of other theories. For instance, while Joan Robinson (1980, 90; [1974] 1979, 58) criticized the neoclassical theory of accumulation for constructing models that "cannot be applied" and that are "useless for the analysis of contemporary problems," Solow (1996, 251) argued that the Kaldor-Kalecki-Robinson-Pasinetti line "was not ever able to muster a body of serious applied work." Similarly, supporters of new (endogenous) growth theory, such as Barro (1991), Scott (1991), and Mankiw, Romer, and Weil (1992), have criticized Solow's (1956) model for not assuming externalities and for assuming diminishing returns to reproducible capital (which implies convergence in levels of per capita income across countries) and therefore for not producing good applied results. And Solow (1997, xvi) has argued against many American economists who believe that "empirical economics begins and ends with time-series."

But how are these different concepts of applied economics in the history of growth theories to be explained? Should we simply accept that there is only one correct concept and that the others are pursuing (or have pursued) misguided lines of research? This explanation is what most theorists quoted above have suggested. The problem with this argument is that it assumes the existence of research activities that are related to universal conceptions of truth rather than to the actions and social practices of the researchers. Instead, it seems more reasonable to accept that there are several concepts of applied economics and that these concepts are historically determined rather than subjected to a fixed and stable relation between "pure" and "applied" economics (as argued by ahistorical conceptualizations of applied economics such as the ones provided by Campbell 1989 and Phelps-Brown and Wiseman 1964). The purpose of applied economics seems to be wider—as illustrated by the history of growth theories—than the use of general laws to explain particular circumstances or predict particular courses of action.

The third part illustrated the existence of different uses, practices, and styles of argumentation in applied economics by examining the work carried out at the DAE from 1945 to 1990. Different conceptions of applied economics were associated with distinct institutional guidelines deduced from the directors' views on applied economics. Under Stone's directorship, a quantitative view of applied economics was developed. Models were considered useless when they did not lead to measurement or estimation of economic variables. A mathematical style of argument was behind predictive and theoretical uses of economics. Reddaway's directorship provided a different sort of institutional encouragement given to applied work. A historical, institutional, and policy-oriented view of applied economics became representative of the work carried out at the DAE. A descriptive style was present in most papers written during this period. Under Godley's directorship, a balance was achieved between different uses and styles of economic theory. Now, the important thing to note along this evolution of views on applied economics is that the history of the research carried out at the DAE seems to support an understanding of applied economics that is different from the conventional view.

Both case studies support an understanding that involves looking at the theorists' views on the applied dimension of their theories and the broader activities and practices into which those theories fit; an understanding that argues that models may be used in a variety of ways, employing a diversity of styles, according to the different purposes and circumstances; and an understanding in which circumstances are defined by the context of activities and institutions in which economists are engaged and with which they work.

References

Backhouse, R. 1998. The Transformation of U.S. Economics 1920–1960, as Viewed through a Survey of Journal Articles. In *From Interwar Pluralism to Postwar Neoclassicism*, edited by Mary S. Morgan and Malcolm Rutherford. *HOPE* 30 (supplement): 85–107.

Barro, R. J. 1991. Economic Growth in a Cross-Section of Countries. *Quarterly Journal of Economics* 106.2:407–44.

Bhaduri, A. 1996. Economic Growth and the Theory of Capital: An Evaluation of Joan Robinson's Contribution. In *The Economics of Joan Robinson*, edited by M. C. Marcuzzo, L. L. Pasinetti, and A. Roncaglia. London and New York: Routledge.

Campbell, M. 1989. Sources of Controversy in Applied Economics. In *Controversy in Applied Economics*, edited by M. Campbell, M. Hardy, and N. Healey. New York: Wheatsheaf.

Deane, P. 1968. Aggregate Comparisons: The Validity and Reliability of Economic Data. Paper no. 287, DAE Reprint Series, University of Cambridge.

De Long, J. B., and L. H. Summers. 1991. The Penn World Table (Mark 5): An Expanded Set of International Comparisons, 1950–1988. *Quarterly Journal of Economics* 106.2:327–68.

Denison, E. F. 1967. *Why Growth Rates Differ: Postwar Experience in Nine Western Countries*. Washington, D.C.: The Brookings Institution.

Department of Applied Economics. 1948. *First Report: Activities in the Years 1946–1948*. Cambridge: University of Cambridge, Department of Applied Economics.

Domar, E. D. 1946. Capital Expansion, Rate of Growth, and Employment. *Econometrica* 14 (April): 137–47.

———. 1957. *Essays in the Theory of Economic Growth*. New York: Oxford University Press.

Endres, A. M. 1982. The Economics of Social Measurement Processes: Some Questions of Public Policy Indicator Design. *International Journal of Social Economics* 9.1:3–39.

Epstein, R. J. 1987. *A History of Econometrics*. Amsterdam: North Holland.

Feinstein, C. 1998. Wage-Earnings in Great Britain during the Industrial Revolution. In *Applied Economics and Public Policy*, edited by I. Begg and S. G. B. Henry, 181–208. Cambridge: Cambridge University Press.

Gilbert, C. L. 1986. The Development of British Econometrics 1945–85. Applied Economics Discussion Paper no. 8, Institute of Economics and Statistics, Oxford.

Godley, W. 1998. Using Figures to Guide Macroeconomic Policy. In *Applied Economics and Public Policy*, edited by I. Begg and S. G. B. Henry. Occasional Paper 63. Department of Applied Economics, University of Cambridge. Cambridge: Cambridge University Press.

Griliches, Z. 1963. The Sources of Measured Productivity Growth: U.S. Agriculture 1940–60. *Journal of Political Economy* 71.4:331–46.

———. 1967. More on CES Production Functions. *Review of Economics and Statistics* 49.4:600–610.
Hahn, F. H., ed. 1971. *Readings in the Theory of Growth*. London: Macmillan.
Harcourt, G. C. 1997. The Kaldor Legacy: Reviewing Nicholas Kaldor, *Causes of Growth Stagnation in the World Economy*. Mimeo.
Harcourt, G. C., and M. Kitson. 1993. Fifty Years of Measurement: A Cambridge View. *Review of Income and Wealth*, ser. 39, no. 4, December, 435–47.
Harrod, R. 1936. *The Trade Cycle: An Essay*. Oxford: Clarendon Press.
———. 1939. An Essay in Dynamic Theory. *Economic Journal* 49 (June): 14–33.
———. 1948. *Towards a Dynamic Economics*. London: Macmillan.
———. 1973. *Economic Dynamics*. Aldershot, England: Macmillan.
Islam, N. 1995. Growth Empirics: A Panel Data Approach. *Quarterly Journal of Economics* 110.4:1127–70.
Jorgenson, D. 1966. The Embodiment Hypothesis. *Journal of Political Economy* 74.1:1–17.
———. 1968. Linear Models of Economic Growth. *International Economic Review* 9.1:1–13.
Jorgenson, D., and Z. Griliches. 1967. The Explanation of Productivity Change. *Review of Economic Studies* 34 (July): 249–80.
Kaldor, N. [1944] 1964. The Quantitative Aspects of the Full Employment in Britain. In vol. 1 of *Essays on Economic Policy*. London: Gerald Duckworth & Co.
———. 1955–56. Alternative Theories of Distribution. *Review of Economic Studies* 23.61:83–100.
———. 1957. A Model of Economic Growth. *Economic Journal* 67.268:591–624.
———. [1958] 1989. Capital Accumulation and Economic Growth. In *The Essential Kaldor*, edited by F. Targetti and A. P. Thirlwall. New York: Holmes & Meier.
———. 1960. *Essays on Value and Distribution*. London: Duckworth.
———. 1964. *Essays on Economic Policy*. 2 vols. London: Gerald Duckworth & Co.
———. [1966] 1989. Causes of the Slow Rate of Economic Growth in the United Kingdom. In *The Essential Kaldor*, edited by F. Targetti and A. P. Thirlwall. New York: Holmes & Meier.
———. [1970] 1989. The Case for Regional Policies. In *The Essential Kaldor*, edited by F. Targetti and A. P. Thirlwall. New York: Holmes & Meier.
———. [1974] 1989. What Is Wrong with Economic Theory? In *The Essential Kaldor*, edited by F. Targetti and A. P. Thirlwall. New York: Holmes & Meier.
———. [1977] 1989. Equilibrium Theory and Growth Theory. In *The Essential Kaldor*, edited by F. Targetti and A. P. Thirlwall. New York: Holmes & Meier.
Kaldor, N., and J. A. Mirrlees. 1961–62. A New Model of Economic Growth. *Review of Economic Studies* 29.3:174–90.
Levine, R., and D. Renelt. 1992. A Sensitivity Analysis of Cross-Country Growth Regressions. *American Economic Review* 82.4:942–62.
Levine, R., and S. J. Zervos. 1993. What We Have Learned about Policy and Growth from Cross-country Regressions? *AEA Papers and Proceedings* 83.2:426–30.

Lucas, R. 1988. On the Mechanics of Economic Development. *Journal of Monetary Economics* 22.1:3–42.
Mankiw, N. G., P. M. Romer, and D. N. Weil. 1992. A Contribution to the Empirics of Economic Growth. *Quarterly Journal of Economics* 107.2:407–37.
Marshall, Alfred. 1920. *Principles of Economics*. 8th ed. London: Macmillan.
Meade, J. 1936. *An Introduction to Economic Analysis and Policy*. Oxford: Oxford University Press.
Mirrlees, J. A. 1973. Introduction to *Models of Economic Growth*, edited by J. A. Mirrlees and N. H. Stern. London: Macmillan.
Moore, B., and J. Rhode. 1979. Economic and Financial Implications of Devolution. Paper no. 32, DAE Reprint Series, University of Cambridge.
Phelps-Brown, E. H., and J. Wiseman. 1964. *A Course in Applied Economics*. London: Sir Isaac Pitman & Sons Ltd.
Ramsey, F. 1928. A Mathematical Theory of Saving. *Economic Journal* 38 (December): 543–59.
Robinson, J. 1956. *The Accumulation of Capital*. London: Macmillan.
———. 1962. A Model of Accumulation. In *Essays in the Theory of Economic Growth*. London: Macmillan.
———. [1971] 1979. The Relevance of Economic Theory. In vol. 4 of *Collected Economic Papers*. Oxford: Basil Blackwell.
———. [1974] 1979. History versus Equilibrium. In vol. 5 of *Collected Economic Papers*. Oxford: Basil Blackwell.
———. [1977] 1979. What Are the Questions? In vol. 5 of *Collected Economic Papers*. Oxford: Basil Blackwell.
———. 1979. History versus Equilibrium. In vol. 5 of *Collected Economic Papers*. Oxford: Basil Blackwell.
———. 1980. Time in Economic Theory. In *Further Contributions to Modern Economics*. Oxford: Basil Blackwell.
Romer, P. M. 1986. Increasing Returns and Long-Run Growth. *Journal of Political Economy* 94.5:1002–37.
———. 1990. Endogenous Technological Change. *Journal of Political Economy* 98.5:S71–S102.
Rostow, W. W. 1990. *Theorists of Economic Growth from David Hume to the Present*. Oxford: Oxford University Press.
Sala-I-Martin, X. X. 1997. I Just Ran Two Million Regressions. *American Economic Review* 87.2:178–83.
Scott, M. 1991. A New View of Economic Growth. World Bank Discussion Papers, no. 131.
Sen, A. 1970. *Growth Economics: Selected Readings*. Harmondsworth: Penguin.
Smith, R. 1998. The Development of Econometric Methods at the DAE. In *Applied Economics and Public Policy*, edited by I. Begg and S. G. B. Henry, 88–103. Cambridge: Cambridge University Press.
Solow, R. M. 1956. A Contribution to the Theory of Economic Growth. *Quarterly Journal of Economics* 70.1:65–94.

———. 1957. Technical Change and the Aggregate Production Function. *Review of Economics and Statistics* 39.3:312–20.

———. 1996. Growth Theory. In *A Guide to Modern Economics*, edited by D. Greenaway, M. Bleaney, and I. Stewart. London and New York: Routledge.

———. 1997. *Learning from "Learning by Doing": Lessons from Economic Growth*. Stanford, Calif.: Stanford University Press.

Stone, R. 1948. The Measurement of National Income and Expenditure. Paper no. 4, DAE Reprint Series, University of Cambridge.

———. 1952. The Demand for Food in the United Kingdom before the War. Paper no. 53, DAE Reprint Series, University of Cambridge.

———. 1964. The A Priori and the Empirical in Economics. Paper no. 223, DAE Reprint Series, University of Cambridge.

Summers, R., and A. Heston. 1988. A New Set of International Comparisons of Real Product and Price Level Estimates for 130 Countries 1950–85. *Review of Income and Wealth* 34.1:1–26.

Swan, T. W. 1956. Economic Growth and Capital Accumulation. *Economic Record* 32 (November): 334–61.

Wan, H. Y. 1971. *Economic Growth*. New York: Harcourt Brace.

Young, W. 1989. *Harrod and His Trade Cycle Group: The Origins and Development of the Growth Research Programme*. London: Macmillan.

Applied Economics in a Political Economy Tradition: The Case of Scotland from the 1890s to the 1950s

Alexander Dow, Sheila Dow, and Alan Hutton

The two most common understandings of the term *applied economics* that have served as an explicit backdrop to this collection of essays refer to empirical (as opposed to theoretical) work on the one hand and policy application of theory on the other. These two conceptions imply a somewhat independent existence for pure theory, even when they are employed in discussions as to how pure theory might more effectively be combined with empirical work or give direction to policy issues. This article deals with a third understanding of applied economics, a practice of economics in which applied work does not have an inferior status to theory, in which a focus on application influences the way theory is constructed, and in which the intertwining of the two may be conditioned by institutional context as well as by methodology more narrowly defined.

Our purpose, therefore, is to consider a further understanding of applied economics as extending across the full range of theory, empirical work, and policy application. This approach sees a powerful role for empirical observation and the nature of policy issues to influence the mode of theory—as well as its content—even though the resulting theoretical principles are then significant in influencing the content of policy proposals. It is appropriately characterized as "political economy."

According to this approach the rigor of theory takes on a particular meaning: *rigor* refers to the capacity to inform policy issues; in other

We wish to acknowledge a number of helpful comments from the editors, an anonymous referee, and other participants in the *HOPE* conference at Duke University, Durham, North Carolina, in March 1999.

words, to the ability of theory to be mapped onto reality. This contrasts with the more conventional notion of rigor, which refers to the mathematical formalism of the theory itself. Thus, for example, while admiring the mathematical rigor of pure general equilibrium theory, Frank Hahn (1991) nevertheless denies its capacity to be applied to real-world issues, since real-world states cannot be demonstrated to be in equilibrium.

Since in the practice of applied economics all economists must use theory as effectively as they can, regardless of its suitability for the purpose, it is not uncommon for applied work to depart from mathematical formalism, to draw on other disciplines—and to show a concern to present economic arguments and results in a form that is accessible to policy makers and other end users. This was particularly the case during the period with which we deal in this essay (1890s–1950s). The approach to applied economics that we have outlined above, however, goes further in taking suitability for application as the starting point, with implications that go beyond the act of application itself.

It is our limited purpose here to consider how such an approach might have arisen in practice. To do so we use as illustration the practice of economics in Scotland from the 1890s up to the 1950s, noting its epistemological foundations and the forms of reinforcement provided by educational and other institutional arrangements. The chosen period is one in which economics emerged as a separate university discipline in Britain, but also one in which we believe it is possible to identify a continuing distinctive Scottish approach.

The Scottish tradition is not the only example of such an approach. Economics at Oxford, both before and after World War I, was characterized by breadth and an openness to cognate disciplines, as well as by an emphasis on applied work. In 1921 "the distribution of lecture topics still favoured history and application while the involvement of historians and philosophers in the teaching of economics and economic history remained strong" (Young and Lee 1993, 12). The approach is reflected in the philosophy, politics, and economics undergraduate curriculum, at least until the 1930s. Interestingly, in this period, there were a number of Oxford/Scottish connections. Influential Scots at Oxford included the philosopher Alexander D. Lindsay and, in economics, David H. MacGregor,[1] and two Oxford economists with Scottish roots moved to chairs

1. G. B. Richardson is an Oxford economist from the postwar period who might be linked with the Scottish tradition.

in Scottish universities between the wars—Sir Frederick W. Ogilvie to Edinburgh and Lindley Fraser to Aberdeen.[2] The political economy approach at Oxford, like that which we find in Scotland, can be contrasted with the more formalistic work that was already developing in the two leading English centers: Cambridge and the LSE (London School of Economics). But we do not attempt to consider the range of examples of this kind of approach to applied economics or their origins and interrelations. Rather, we use the Scottish example simply in order to illustrate the third understanding of applied economics mentioned above.

The notion of a regional or national tradition is itself the subject of some controversy. A recent symposium comparing the European and American traditions explored the difficulties involved in such an exercise.[3] A general view emerged that distinctive differences could be identified. The case for considering Scottish thought in terms of a tradition is strengthened by a long-standing and distinctive institutional structure in Scotland which, it can be argued, had considerable influence on its intellectual history.[4] Further, the Scottish approach has explicit philosophical foundations in the work of the Enlightenment economists, foundations that themselves derived from the nature of the policy questions that arose in Scotland in that period. But this paper focuses on the more recent manifestations of that Scottish intellectual tradition within the discipline of economics as practiced in Scotland from the 1890s to the 1950s.

We first develop further our view of the Scottish political economy tradition. Following that, we examine the organization and outputs of teaching, research, and scholarship in economics in Scotland between the 1890s and the 1950s—a period that takes us from the establishment of political economy as a separate degree subject in the universities to the ultimate eclipse of a political economy approach in teaching and research by modern formal analytical economics—for evidence on the nature and significance of applied economic work. In the final section we conclude that a case can be made, on the basis of our Scottish case

2. Later, as first vice chancellor of the New University of Keele, Lindsay introduced a broad-based four-year undergraduate degree structure drawing directly on Scottish traditions. Regrettably, a fuller treatment of the relationship between the twentieth-century Oxford approach in economics and the Scottish tradition is beyond the scope of this paper.

3. The papers produced for the symposium were published in a special issue of *Kyklos* in 1995 (volume 48, number 2).

4. The case is more fully articulated in Dow et al. 1998.

study, for the possibility of an applied economics of a different character and associated with a tradition of political economy.

The Idea of a Scottish Political Economy Tradition

We have argued elsewhere that the idea of a Scottish tradition in political economy is helpful for the interpretation of the history of economics in Scotland, and, following Alec L. Macfie (1955), Sheila Dow (1987), and Douglas Mair (1990, ix–xv), we have offered a view of the origins, nature, and possible persistence of that tradition (Dow, Dow, and Hutton 1997; Dow et al. 1998). A tradition might include "not simply theoretical, practical and descriptive principles, but the role and organisation of teaching . . . the application of economic knowledge and the establishment of professional and academic associations" (Tribe 1988, 3 n. 6).

The institutional environment is significant for the development of ideas and practice. Indeed, in our sense, a tradition of economic thought and practice is a product of the wider intellectual, cultural, and social environment. Such a tradition can be seen to influence the evolution of institutions, both within the economics community and more widely, and the continuity of its influence will be related to the persistence of the institutional environment in which it arose.

Recent interest in the idea of a Scottish tradition in political economy had its origins in a lecture by Macfie (1955) in which he identified a "characteristic Scottish attitude and method" in economics, describing it as "the philosophical approach" or "the sociological approach." We have argued that the Scottish tradition can be defined by a shared view of how knowledge is generated and of its relation to reality and its role in society (Dow, Dow, and Hutton 1997). It had its roots in the Enlightenment period, and in describing the emergence of political economy as a field of enquiry within the Scottish environment Dow (1987, 341) suggested that the new discipline absorbed in some measure a number of features from its Scottish environment.

Drawing on Macfie (1955) and Dow (1987), Mair sees the Scottish political economy tradition as based on philosophy, history, and law, and including the following characteristics:

- "an acceptance of the limitations of theory"
- "a concern with practical issues"

- "a preference for arguing from first principles"
- "a preference for the breadth of understanding achieved by drawing on a range of disciplines in an integrated way"
- the assignment of a relatively unimportant role to mathematics, "since that language does not sit easily" with an interest in historical and institutional arrangements
- a belief that arguments in political economy cannot be settled "solely by virtue of the internal logic of formal theories" (Mair 1990, xiv).

Macfie claimed that the Scottish approach was especially influential until about 1870 and, although by the 1950s the analytical method was dominant everywhere, "in Scotland the traditional approach [was] still alive and influential" (Macfie 1955, 81). We argue that important elements of continuity in Scottish institutions and attitudes helped to maintain the influence of the traditional approach to the way economics was "done" in Scotland well into the twentieth century.

Perhaps most significant for the continuity of traditions in political economy in Scotland, along with the country's status as a small nation with its own economic problems and administrative structures, have been its separate traditions in university education. Although Scotland conceded her independence as a nation-state through the Act of Union with England in 1707, she has retained separate institutionalized traditions in civil society. Significant differences from England have been preserved in law, religion, and education, together with a national culture and history. Paradoxically, as Lindsay Paterson (1994) argues, those traditions have been more often stressed and more jealously guarded because of the context of union with England. "Scottishness" is most commonly asserted in terms of difference from England and has been used regularly throughout the last three hundred years in opposition to "anglicisation"; indeed, Paterson points out that a number of these legal, religious, and educational traditions have been created within the last century or two. In the face of evolving social and economic predicaments Scotland has retained sufficient autonomy to develop her own institutional responses.

In the nineteenth century the four ancient Scottish universities (St. Andrews, Glasgow, Aberdeen, and Edinburgh) came to constitute a national system with a common pattern of courses. Education was seen to exist for the good of the community as a whole, as well as for individual advancement, and a state-supported system, much more open than the English institutions, was underpinned by "notions of public authority, communal solidarity and collective improvement" (Anderson 1992, 70). The Scottish university curriculum, founded on a general M.A. degree,[5] provided a preparation for a wider range of professions than the English universities. Although the importance of philosophy in the arts curriculum may have been exaggerated (Anderson 1992, 71), in the Scottish version of what constituted a "liberal education" special emphasis was certainly given to a strong philosophical core (Carter and Withrington 1992, 9). A particularly significant historical feature of the Scottish university system was its accessibility. In the eighteenth and nineteenth centuries, in comparison to England, Scotland had a high ratio of university places to population. In Glasgow and Edinburgh in particular many students registered for courses that they saw as particularly valuable for their business careers without attempting a full degree program (Carter and Withrington 1992, 11). Such courses included lectures in "political economy" that were offered throughout much of the nineteenth century in all four Scottish institutions as an aspect of the curriculum in moral philosophy.[6]

If, as Joan Robinson and John Eatwell (1973, 2) assert, "economics has three (interrelated) aspects or functions—to try to understand how an economy operates, to make proposals for improving it, and to justify the criterion by which improvement is judged," then the approach taken to understanding economic society will influence the form of economists' contribution toward its improvement—applied economics. There may be as many approaches in applied economics as in economics, or political economy, more generally.

The linked purposes of understanding the world and attempting to improve it are inseparable in the Scottish political economy tradition.[7] From the characteristics highlighted above, we might expect that economists in Scotland would be particularly likely to take an interest in

5. The general M.A. in the older Scottish universities was (and is) a three-year general undergraduate degree. Honors specialization—a fourth year on top of the general M.A.—was introduced in the 1860s partly in response to the demands of competitive examinations for civil service entry.

6. These classes usually formed part of the duties of the professor of moral philosophy. Following the failure of J. R. McCulloch's attempt to found a chair at Edinburgh in the 1820s, there was no professor of political economy in Scotland before 1870 (Rankin 1955).

7. The social and moral purpose of political economy is often asserted by the leading Scottish practitioners (cf. Smart 1916 and Gray 1949).

economic and social problems and policy issues and, as practitioners of applied economics, would adopt approaches that viewed "the historical background to economic problems as at least as significant as anything contributed by mathematical analysis and (take) for granted that economic forces had to be studied in their social and political context and with due regard to psychological factors" (Cairncross 1996, 141).

Economics in Scotland 1897–1957

An examination of aspects of economics in Scotland in the present century will cast further light on the proposition that practice there—in a way that stemmed, at least in part, from the influence of a Scottish political economy tradition with its central purpose of social improvement—was characterized by a particular emphasis on and orientation within applied work. Scotland was not, of course, isolated from the development of work in economics in England and elsewhere. But if the kinds of economics taught and practiced in Scotland between the 1890s and the 1960s were influenced by general trends and developments in the discipline, and by Scotland's position in the wider world of the discipline, we must also consider whether her own national traditions influenced both those elements of the economics of the day that were emphasized in Scotland and, more generally, the role given to economics and economists within and without the universities. In what follows we consider a number of aspects of economics teaching, scholarship, and research in the Scottish universities, as well as the wider organization of the profession in Scotland.

Economics in the Ancient Universities

Given the significance of the Scottish contribution to the early development of political economy as a separate subject, it is perhaps surprising to find that in their account of British experience, as part of the wider international comparative project on the institutionalization of political economy as an academic discipline, Alan Kadish and Keith Tribe (1993) omitted consideration of Scotland. They place the establishment of economics as a separate subject in England, Wales, and Ireland within the last quarter of the nineteenth century. Although political economy had been taught throughout most of the century as part of the moral philosophy curriculum in all four Scottish universities, and many of those who went to teach philosophy and economics in the new English colleges were educated in Scotland, prior to 1914 chairs in political economy existed only in Glasgow and Edinburgh, and the autonomy of economics as a subject in the Scottish university curriculum was not fully achieved until the 1920s.

Claude W. Guillebaud (1954a, 12) distinguishes three main categories in the teaching of economics: (1) "teaching economics as part of a general education"; (2) teaching economics as part of the educational preparation for professional careers, including business; and (3) "training those who regard economics as their main subject of study" (and who may go on to work as economists). If the institutionalization of economics as a university subject implies doing what is stated in category 3, then it is not clear that economics was fully established in the Scottish universities until after 1945. As we suggest above, political economy teaching as part of a general education and as part of professional preparation was established in all four Scottish institutions in the nineteenth century.

The provenance of the chairs that were set up in Edinburgh and Glasgow reflects a particular link with commerce. The Edinburgh chair, founded in 1870 and named the "Chair of Commercial and Political Economy and Mercantile Law,"[8] was endowed by the Merchant Company of Edinburgh in effect for the commercial education of those involved in commerce and law (Rankin 1955). The Adam Smith Chair in Glasgow followed in 1896[9] with an endowment from a Glasgow ironmaster (Macfie 1952). Throughout the sixty-year period under consideration each of these chairs had only three incumbents.[10] Chairs in political economy were established at Aberdeen in 1921[11] and in 1947 at St. Andrews,[12] where a lectureship had been created in 1900. Honors classes were only established in 1898 at Glasgow, in 1900 at Edinburgh and Aberdeen, and rather later at St. Andrews, and throughout the period it was not possible to take "single honours" in political economy at Glasgow.

8. A name it retained until 1957.

9. Glasgow had given William Smart a university lectureship in political economy in 1892.

10. At Edinburgh: Nicholson 1880–1926; Ogilvie 1926–34; and Gray 1934–56. At Glasgow: Smart 1896–1915; Scott 1915–46; and Macfie 1946–59.

11. Held by Gray 1921–34, Fraser 1934–39, and Hamilton 1939–61.

12. Held until the 1960s by Nisbet.

Right up until the late 1950s staff numbers remained low. At Glasgow prior to 1914 the professor had been joined by two assistants[13] (one in social economics and one in economic history); the number of assistants had risen to four by the 1930s (James Cunnison, Buyers, Nisbet, and Macfie) and to five in 1935 when (Sir) Alec Cairncross returned as lecturer. By the early 1950s there were three lecturers and one assistant in political economy, two in social economics, and two in economic history.

At Edinburgh prior to 1914 Professor J. Shields Nicholson was assisted by a lecturer in economic history and a lecturer in statistics and mathematical economics. The number of lecturers rose to three in the 1920s and to six by the mid-1950s. The total number of university teachers of economics (including economic history and statistics) in Scotland in 1954 was only twenty-eight (Guillebaud 1954b, 221). While the number of honors graduates in economics at Edinburgh from 1902 to 1925 totaled 73 and even in the late 1950s was less than 10 per year, the number taking the ordinary political economy class rose from 267 in 1921 to around 400 in the heyday of Sir Alexander Gray in 1949 (Rutherford 1997).

The Edinburgh honors economics curriculum from 1910 until the late 1950s was made up of political economy (three papers); economic history (three papers); political science (one paper); and one class in either statistics and mathematical economics, economic geography, or mercantile law. As at Glasgow, political economy always featured the history of economic thought and social (or realistic)[14] economics. Edinburgh was, however, distinctive in the establishment (with the strong support of Nicholson) in 1920 of a separate department of commerce with chairs in the organization of industry and commerce and accounting and business methods. The bachelor of commerce degree, which included the political economy ordinary course and two optional economics half-courses, had more than twenty graduates annually by 1923. At Glasgow an economics class for students in accountancy was introduced in 1933, and in the late 1940s evening courses in economics and business-related subjects were added for part-time professional students.

This brief review of economics provision within the two larger ancient Scottish universities suggests a strong bias toward the first two

13. Including, at different times, R. H. Tawney, Thomas Jones, and J. H. Jones.

14. An honors course so labeled was established at Edinburgh in 1920 and described as "a realistic treatment of problems of present day importance."

of Guillebaud's categories of teaching. While the orientation of economics teaching in the Scottish universities might, to some extent, be said to parallel the "political economy" orientation of the discipline in Britain and elsewhere more generally during this period and the textbooks recommended seem relatively orthodox (Dow, Dow, and Hutton 1999), it is not unreasonable to argue that the shape of the curriculum was also influenced by the traditional purposes and characteristics of the Scottish universities—including breadth, wide access, and vocational relevance—and that, within that framework, the particular stress in political economy on economic history, social problems and policy, and the history of political economy reflects the persistent influence of a Scottish political economy tradition. The inherent emphasis within that tradition on applied economics, in the broad sense of an engagement with the real world, is matched by the importance given in the honors curriculum to "social economics" and "economic history" and by the general orientation toward education with vocational relevance. In the early 1950s all third-year economics undergraduates at Glasgow were required to write a paper of 10,000 words on the subject "Enterprise, as illustrated by a West of Scotland firm or industry" (Guillebaud 1954b, 213).

There is clear circumstantial evidence of important differences between academic economics in Scotland and England. In Guillebaud's illustrative review of undergraduate economics education in Britain, Glasgow (along with Oxford) lies at one extreme of the specialist/generalist spectrum with Cambridge at the other and most English institutions probably nearer to Cambridge than to Glasgow. While significant amounts of postgraduate work had developed by the 1950s at the LSE, Cambridge, Oxford, and Manchester, graduate studies were largely absent in Scotland. The relative extent of specialist work is reflected by economics staff numbers: in 1948 there were 192 university economics teachers in England, while in Wales and Scotland there were only 19 and 28 respectively (Guillebaud 1954b, 221). The six Scottish institutions out of the British total of twenty-three contained only 12 percent of university economists.

Further evidence of the relatively distinct character of economics in Scotland emerges from an examination of the scholarly output of the Scottish professors of political economy. Research and scholarship were a rather less important aspect of the work of Scottish academics then than they are now, which is reflected in the quantity of published output.

(Nicholson and William Scott were exceptions; they published extensively.) Most of those who held chairs between 1900 and the 1950s published works of economic history, a field in which Scott (Glasgow) and Henry Hamilton (Aberdeen) were specialists (Scott 1910–12; Hamilton 1932; Smart 1910–17). Work on the history of economic thought and on Adam Smith in particular was common and featured especially in the output of Gray (Aberdeen and Edinburgh), Macfie (Glasgow), and Scott (Gray 1949; Macfie 1967). The majority of the remaining publications focused on economic and social problems and policy (Smart 1900; Gray 1927; Ogilvie 1933). Smart published translations of works by Eugen Böhm-Bawerk and Friedrich Wieser and works codifying economic theory. Nicholson, who, like Scott, Macfie, and, to a lesser extent, Gray, saw himself as a follower of Smith,[15] was the most prolific author in the group and perhaps the most closely integrated into the core of the British economics profession of his day. Along with a monumental three-volume *Principles of Political Economy* (1893–1901) he published in all the fields dealt with here, focusing particularly on issues of money, trade, and empire (Nicholson 1888, 1903, 1909). None of the Scottish professors, however, could be said to have contributed a significant advance to the mainstream corpus of economic theory. The evidence seems to support Macfie's assertion that "there is little doubt that Scotsmen, while acquiescent, have not been entirely comfortable . . . in modern economic theorising. . . . The trend has been to teach the orthodox line, but to do one's special work in historical, social or semi-philosophical research" (1955, 98). That discomfort stemmed from a tradition that was in its philosophical roots both realist and wedded to ideas of social and moral purpose.

Applied Economics at Glasgow University

In a eulogy that seems to catch much of the character of the Scottish approach in political economy, Macfie describes a living tradition in the Glasgow Department of Political Economy that had been "the special achievement of the two menwho had led the Department" before him.

15. With the exception of Scott, who was Irish, all those who held chairs in political economy at the Scottish universities in this sixty-year period were products of a Scottish education.

Smart and Scott were

> humane, widely experienced scholars. Each of them had the firmest grasp of and respect for facts, human as well as industrial. Their sense of history[16] and its constant relevance to any finally valuable economic theory is worthy of the master who was their continual joy and inspiration. And their active part in the affairs of a great industrial city was as inevitable as his. In each of them is found that energetic growth from the core of hard facts to their deeper philosophic meanings which was Adam Smith's most shining gift. And each of them contributed his thinking to the direct service of the State on many commissions[17] and committees, just as did Adam Smith in the more personal, less official manner of his day. (1952, 129)

Here Macfie describes how a particular style of applied economics was integral to political economy in the Scottish tradition. This kind of work developed in Glasgow under Scott's leadership, and a characteristic product of the approach is the *Industrial Survey of the South West of Scotland*, produced by the staff of the Glasgow Department for the Board of Trade (Board of Trade 1932).[18] Applied work was later given a notable boost with the appointment of Alec Cairncross to a new chair in applied economics and to lead a newly created Social and Economic Research Department (SERD). A Glasgow graduate (in political economy and politics), Cairncross returned to his alma mater in 1935 as a lecturer in political economy, after a period as postgraduate student and then lecturer on the Cambridge economics faculty.[19] He left again in 1939 to deploy his skills in wartime service, which led to the post of economic adviser to the Board of Trade from 1946 to 1949.

The objective of SERD was to undertake research on social and economic problems in Scotland (and especially west central Scotland), thereby contributing to policies for economic and social development. Expectations that SERD would generate research commissions from the

16. The importance of history in the Scottish tradition is given emphasis by both Campbell (1976) and Cairncross (1989).

17. Smart was a member of the Poor Law Commission and a major author of its majority report. Scott was "frequently away on some Government Committee" during Cairncross's days as undergraduate and, later, lecturer at Glasgow (Cairncross 1998, 37, 47).

18. In an interview with Alan Hutton and Michael Keaney in 1997, (Sir) Alec Cairncross, who was an undergraduate in the department in 1932, reported participating in housing surveys in the city organized by Cunnison, the lecturer in social economics.

19. Cairncross was the first Scottish economist to earn a Ph.D.

Scottish Office were, in the early years, disappointed,[20] however, and Guillebaud (1954b, 230) suggests that "research on immediate short-term problems (was) only incidental to its main work." As well as "occasional papers" the department produced two series of research monographs under the rubric "University of Glasgow Social and Economic Studies." The "Old Series," published in the 1950s under the general editorship of Cairncross, centered on the kind of applied work that might be expected, although not all of it relating to Scotland. There were accounts of crofting, industrial relations in Glasgow, the U.K. shipbuilding industry, and wage structure in Britain. There were also two volumes of intellectual history on Smith and John Millar.

Perhaps most interesting for us here is "a statistical account of Scottish life" under the title *The Scottish Economy*, comprising contributions by a range of Glasgow University staff and edited by Cairncross. In his preface Cairncross notes that the volume aims to analyze those aspects of Scottish life that can be measured quantitatively, arguing that the approach derives from a long-term Scottish tradition, "that of Sinclair, Cleland and Giffen, to name only three of the distinguished Scotsmen who helped to develop the use of statistics as a technique for the analysis of social and economic structure." At the same time he is clear that it is a partial exercise—a comprehensive picture of the Scottish economy would "require far more historical depth" and "more colour and detail of everyday life" (Cairncross 1954b, xv). Although in an age of increasing specialization the Glasgow tradition may, at this stage, be dividing between the more philosophical approach of Macfie and the practical economics of Cairncross, the latter is concerned to link his applied work to important features of the Scottish tradition of political economy.

The Dundee School of Economics

Evidence for the existence of the Scottish tradition that we describe comes also from those outside it. In the interwar period there emerged an institutional challenge that both indicated the strength of the tradition and sowed some of the seeds of its ultimate demise. There was established in 1931 in Dundee a unique institution that became in the latter part of its twenty-one year life "a foreign irritant in the Scottish oyster"

20. Cairncross received not one request for advice during his first ten years as professor at the SERD in Glasgow (Coats 1979).

(Munby 1957, 60). Immediately after World War I, George Bonar, chairman of the Dundee Chamber of Commerce, offered University College, Dundee (a satellite of St. Andrews), an endowment to establish a Faculty of Commerce. When the college finally rejected his offer of funding because Bonar required an open entrance policy, it was taken up by the local Education Authority, and with help from the University of London and the LSE in particular, a quite separate institution, the Dundee School of Economics and Commerce, was established.

The aim of Bonar and the first principal, James Bowie, was to remedy what they saw as the neglect, in the university system, of practical training for the world of business. The initial vehicle for such training was to be a two-year commercial diploma. Such an aim in itself, involving as it does the practical application of economics, seems to fall within the Scottish tradition. Early on, however, the LSE connection asserted itself. Jack C. Gilbert and Kenneth Eastman, the first two lecturers appointed and, by background, analytical economists from London, were soon joined by Duncan Black (a Glasgow graduate) and Ronald H. Coase, both from postgraduate studentships at the LSE and both destined for considerably higher things. The curriculum and approach evolved to match the University of London's external degree programs, and the institution's name was truncated from the Dundee School of Economics and Commerce to the Dundee School of Economics (Blake and Lythe 1981).

At its peak after the war, and up to its subsumption by the University of St. Andrews as the Faculty of Commerce in University College, Dundee, in 1952, there were more than sixty students taking London University bachelor of commerce and bachelor of science (economics) degrees, a number greater than the total number of honors students in political economy in the ancient universities. Despite a demanding teaching load, its young staff achieved a high rate of publication in the professional journals, little of which was applied economics in the Scottish sense. The school can be seen as an early "missionary" incursion by the new analytical economics in the land of political economy.

From the Scottish Society of Economists to the Scottish Economic Society

An indication of the vision of the nature and purpose of economics that was held by the economics community in Scotland can be gained through a brief review of the history of the two professional associations that have aimed to encourage the study of economics in Scotland. It serves to highlight a further important "applied" aspect of the Scottish tradition:[21] the promotion of the discussion of economic ideas and issues among the professional and business community.

The Scottish Society of Economists was established in Edinburgh under the leadership of Nicholson, its first president, in 1897. In his inaugural address Nicholson proposed that the society should not be concerned to promote any particular set of practical reforms but should consider the whole range of economic research, including statistical and financial aspects (Campbell 1997, 360). But this was not, in fact, a society of professional economists. It was made up in the main of members of Edinburgh professional and commercial society, 108 initially.[22] Although several were leading economists, the speakers covered as wide a range of professional interests as the members. Nicholson remained the leading figure in the society, and after his death in 1927 it lapsed into inactivity.

It was revived in 1954 with a new constitution under the less exclusive title of the Scottish Economic Society (SES) on a proposal from the economists at the four Scottish universities (and the Dundee School of Economics). The constitution stated the revived society's goals as follows:

> The objects of the society shall be:—
>
> a) to advance the study of economic and social problems on the widest basis, in accordance with the Scottish tradition of political economy inspired by Adam Smith;
>
> b) to provide a forum for the discussion of Scottish economic and social problems. (Constitution of the Scottish Economic Society 1957)

The main vehicles for the pursuit of these aims were to include a branch organization in the four main cities, each organizing a syllabus of meetings, an annual general meeting followed by a presidential address, and a new journal—*The Scottish Journal of Political Economy* (*SJPE*).

21. This is an aspect also evidenced, inter alia, in the major role taken by Smart, Scott, Gray, Cairncross, and others in the work of Section F of the British Association for the Advancement of Science.

22. Nicholson was followed in the chair by three lawyers, an accountant, and an actuary (Campbell 1997, 359).

Membership in the SES was intended to extend over the whole field of social science.

> Economics in isolation from other branches of social science tends to be emasculated. . . . "political economy" . . . is the description that appears on the cover of the *Journal*, in token of the wish to make room for politics, sociology, economic history and administration while keeping a firm core of economics. (Cairncross 1954a, 2)

While not neglecting theoretical work and the use of new analytical technique, the journal was to be accessible to an educated, but nonprofessional audience. Indeed Cairncross suggested that the SES (in line with the aims of its predecessor society) "[had] the opportunity to create a more informed public opinion on economic matters and to encourage a wider and more constructive outlook" (1954a, 3). Until the end of our period at least a casual survey of the contents of the *Journal* and of the syllabuses of the four SES branches suggests that the society was fulfilling its objectives. The impact on Scottish public opinion is not, of course, easy to gauge. Branch meetings were addressed by a mixture of academic and business and professional speakers and covered a wide range of topics, with an emphasis on Scottish economic problems and institutions. Most issues of the *SJPE* contained articles on economic history, social problems or policies, and the history of economic thought (or philosophy). Among the economics pieces stress was given to economic problems and policy with a bias toward Scottish issues—altogether a representation of the applied element in the Scottish political economy tradition.

The Waning of the Scottish Political Economy Approach

The years from 1953 until the end of Cairncross's period as editor of the *SJPE* in 1960 witnessed the final significant attempts to preserve a Scottish political economy tradition against the inexorable rise of the analytical economic approach stemming, in Britain, particularly from the LSE and Cambridge as part of a process of "Internationalisation" in the discipline (Backhouse 1996). Of more than symbolic significance in that process was the arrival in 1957 of (Sir) Alan Peacock to replace Sir Alexander Gray in the chair at Edinburgh. It seems as if he was sent from the LSE to bring enlightenment to the benighted northerners. David

Simpson, who at that time was a second-year Edinburgh undergraduate with a mathematical bent, has described to us his excitement (shared by many fellow students) at the change. After Gray's "old fashioned" political economy class based on the history of economic thought, the new "scientific" analytical approaches "brought a breath of fresh air," the feeling of being at the frontiers of a developing discipline.[23] Two years later Simpson was one of eight honors graduates in economics, and, along with two or three fellows, he was able to exploit the department's new international links to undertake graduate work in the United States.

On the occasion of the centenary of the Scottish Economic Society Campbell asked, "How then should the century be celebrated? By going back to roots, and by regarding them as pointers to better ways?" (1997, 367). Scottish economists have continued to argue for the political economy tradition and the broader applied approach implicit within it (see Cairncross 1970, 1984 and Alexander 1975). David Simpson (1988), tracing the roots of both back to Adam Smith, puts the case for a reemphasis on the political economy approach as against the analytical approach in the education of economists. From the late 1950s onward, however, degree structures and economics curricula in the older Scottish universities began to change. In the 1960s four new universities were established and, with the possible exception of Strathclyde, their degree structures and curricula did not reflect the older Scottish tradition. By the 1990s little if anything of the traditional Scottish approach can be detected even in the older universities, and departments of economics in Scotland look no different from their counterparts south of the border (or in many other parts of the world). At Glasgow, where the tradition may have been strongest and the pace of change slowest, "Economics" finally replaced "Political Economy" in the departmental title in 1998.

With the relative demise of the influence of the Scottish political economy tradition has come, in the Scottish universities at least, a decline in the significance of applied work of the kind that we have seen to be associated with that tradition.

Concluding Comments

Our wide-ranging review has produced a range of evidence from the practice of economics in Scotland between the 1890s and the 1950s

23. Interview with Alan Hutton and M. Keaney in 1996.

consistent with the proposition that a particularly Scottish tradition of political economy continued to have a significant influence. That influence, in part perpetuated by traditions in the institutional makeup of the older Scottish universities, inhibited the development in Scotland of the use of abstract, deductive, formalistic economic theory, while valuing the pursuit of particular forms of applied economic work. The applied economics inherent in the Scottish approach reflects a view of the importance of history and the limitations of theory, together with a concern to widen the discussion of economic and social issues in society, and to present policy-related analysis in a form that is accessible to the policy maker.

As Cairncross, perhaps the preeminent British applied economist of his generation, wrote, theory is only valuable if it "does justice to recorded experience"; an applied economics must make provision for "the weaving together of economic and non-economic considerations . . . for . . . there is no such thing as economic policy in isolation from other aspects of policy, there is only policy" (1970, 22). Always conscious of his Scottish roots, Cairncross's practical commonsense approach reflects the experience of half a career spent away from academia in economic administration and policy making as "a highly respected . . . member of the economic/administrative establishment" (Roll 1998).

Although Scotland could not have been wholly insulated from developments in economics elsewhere, the influence of Scottish traditions limited the extent of their impact within Scotland. In our view Scotland was not simply a provincial backwater in the empire of economics which, because of its outdated institutions and ideas, took longer than many other "provinces" to assimilate the developing analytical and formalistic economic "science."[24] Rather, the earlier political economy tradition, which Scottish institutional separateness had helped to forge and to sustain well into the twentieth century, had firmer institutional roots in Scotland than elsewhere in Britain.

In an impressionistic piece Harry Johnson (1973) offers one kind of rationalization for what happened. He argues that by the 1970s members of the economics profession could have been divided into three groups:

24. Without more systematic comparative data we can say little about differences between Scotland and, say, the North of England in this respect. Phelps Brown (1989), who pursued his career "south of the border," provides a critical account of developments in the discipline during his lifetime that has all the hallmarks of the Scottish approach. Indeed, Cairncross (1996) saw him as a kindred spirit. See also Backhouse 1996.

those with top graduate school training in research techniques who pursued a research-oriented career; those with a graduate school training who chose not to pursue such a career; and those without research-oriented technical training. The first group, often resented by their departmental colleagues, constituted the international (though U.S. dominated) elite of the profession, responsible for the advance of its technical core of theory and econometric methods. The other two groups were likely to reflect differences in national traditions that, Johnson argued, were related to national culture, university tenure and promotion systems, and research funding. There would be a tendency for the work of economists in the two "lower" groups to be applied and related to national, or local, economic problems. The issue then might be to what extent is it appropriate to see Scotland as a "national" context separate from the rest of Britain? We believe that the degree of separateness was significant.

This has been an attempt at a history of economics in A. W. (Bob) Coats's (1984) sense: "an exercise in the origins, development, and significance of the changing styles of professional activity." In such an exercise the retrospective assertion of traditions in an interpretation of the past will always involve selectivity—some would say "invention" (Hobsbawm and Ranger 1992)—with the aim of lending support to a particular form of institution or activity on the basis of a suggested lineage. As we have indicated there are clear historical reasons why Scots may wish to differentiate themselves from the English. In arguing for the existence of a particular approach in Scotland up to the 1950s we have used the observations both of Scottish economists—including Macfie, Cairncross, and Simpson—who may be seen as supporters of the Scottish tradition, and of those, such as Munby, who are not. We are clear from our review of data on the nature of economics in the Scottish university curriculum, on the work of Scottish academic economists, and on the constitution and activities of the Scottish Economic Society and the contents of the *Scottish Journal of Political Economy*, that substantive evidence of the pursuit of a political economy–related style of applied economics in Scotland up to the 1950s is not hard to find. The Scottish case in this period is illustrative; such an approach may have existed in other places too.

This paper stems from a larger project in which we address the legitimacy of an identification of a tradition (Dow, Dow, and Hutton 1997; Dow et al. 1998). Our aim here has been the more limited one of providing an account of an approach to applied economics that was present in Scotland from the 1890s to the 1950s and to explain how it was supported by particular educational and institutional arrangements. This account is offered to exemplify an approach to applied economics that differs from the two conventional understandings of the term referred to in our introduction.

References

Alexander, K. J. 1975. The Political Economy of Change. In *The Political Economy of Change*, edited by K. J. Alexander. Oxford: Basil Blackwell.

Anderson, R. D. 1992. The Scottish University Tradition: Past and Future. In *Scottish Universities: Distinctiveness and Diversity*, edited by J. Carter and D. Withrington. Edinburgh: John Donald.

Backhouse, R. E. 1996. The Changing Character of British Economics. In *The Post-1945 Internationalization of Economics*, edited by A. W. Coats. *HOPE* 28 (supplement): 33–60.

Blake, C., and E. Lythe. 1981. Introduction to *A Maverick Institution: Dundee School of Economics Fiftieth Anniversary Commemorative Essays*. London: Gee & Co.

Board of Trade. 1932. An Industrial Survey of the South West of Scotland. Made for the Board of Trade by the Staff of the Political Economy Department of the University of Glasgow. London: HMSO.

Cairncross, A. 1954a. The Scottish Economic Society. *Scottish Journal of Political Economy* 1.1:1–6.

———. 1954b. *The Scottish Economy*. Cambridge: Cambridge University Press.

———. 1970. The Managed Economy. In *The Managed Economy*. Oxford: Basil Blackwell.

———. 1984. Economics in Theory and Practice. Richard T. Ely Lecture. *American Economic Review Papers and Proceedings* 75.2:1–14.

———. 1989. In Praise of Economic History. *Economic History Review*, 2d ser., 42.2:173–85.

———. 1996. Henry Phelps Brown. *Review of Political Economy* 8.2:141–44.

———. 1998. *Living with the Century*. Fife: Iynx.

Campbell, R. H. 1976. Scottish Economic History. *Scottish Journal of Political Economy* 23.2:183–92.

———. 1997. The Scottish Society of Economists: The Scottish Economic Society—1897–1997. *Scottish Journal of Political Economy* 44.4:359–67.

Carter, J., and D. Withrington. 1992. Introduction to *Scottish Universities: Distinctiveness and Diversity*, edited by J. Carter and D. Withrington. Edinburgh: John Donald.

Coats, A. W. 1979. The Changing Role of Economists in Scottish Government since 1960. *Public Administration* 57 (spring): 399–424.

———. 1984. The Sociology of Knowledge and the History of Economics. In vol. 2 of *Research in the History of Economic Thought and Methodology*, edited by W. Samuels. Greenwich, Conn.: JAI Press.

Dow, A., S. Dow, and A. Hutton. 1997. The Scottish Political Economy Tradition and Modern Economics. *Scottish Journal of Political Economy* 44.4:368–83.

———. 1999. Scottish Political Economy, 1850–1950. Mimeo.

Dow, A., S. Dow, A. Hutton, and M. Keaney. 1998. Traditions in Economics: The Case of Scottish Political Economy. *New Political Economy* 3.1:45–58.

Dow, S. 1987. The Scottish Political Economy Tradition. *Scottish Journal of Political Economy* 34.4:335–48.

Gray, A. (Sir). 1927. *Family Endowment: A Critical Analysis*. London: Ernest Benn.

———. 1949. Economics: Yesterday and To-morrow. *The Advancement of Science* 6.23:233–43.

Guillebaud, C. W. 1954a. General Survey. In International Economic Association 1954.

———. 1954b. The Teaching of Economics in the United Kingdom. In International Economic Association 1954.

Hahn, F. 1991. The Next Hundred Years. *Economic Journal* 101.404:47–50.

Hamilton, H. 1932. *The Industrial Revolution in Scotland*. London: Frank Cass & Co.

Hobsbawm, E., and T. Ranger, eds. 1992. *The Invention of Tradition*. Cambridge: Cambridge University Press.

International Economic Association. 1954. *The University Teaching of Social Sciences: Economics*. Paris: UNESCO.

Johnson, H. G. 1973. National Styles in Economic Research: The United States, the United Kingdom, Canada, and Various European Countries. *Daedalus* 102.2:65–74.

Kadish, A., and K. Tribe. 1993. *The Market for Political Economy: The Advent of Economics in British University Culture*. London: Routledge.

Macfie, A. L. 1952. Note on the Growth of Political Economy. In *Fortuna Domus*. Glasgow: University of Glasgow.

———. 1955. The Scottish Tradition in Economic Thought. *Scottish Journal of Political Economy* 2.2:81–103.

———. 1967. *The Individual in Society: Papers on Adam Smith*. London: George Allen & Unwin.

Mair, D., ed. 1990. *The Scottish Contribution to Modern Economic Thought*. Aberdeen: Aberdeen University Press.

Munby, D. L. 1957. The Dundee School of Economics—In Memoriam. *Scottish Journal of Political Economy* 4.1:60–65.

Nicholson, J. S. 1888. *Money and Monetary Problems*. London: Adam & Charles Black.

———. 1893–1901. *Principles of Political Economy*. 3 vols. London: Adam & Charles Black.

———. 1903. *The Tariff Question*. London: Adam & Charles Black.
———. 1909. *A Project of Empire*. London: Macmillan.
Ogilvie, F. W. (Sir). 1933. *The Tourist Movement: An Economic Study*. London: P. S. King.
Paterson, L. 1994. *The Autonomy of Scotland*. Edinburgh: Edinburgh University Press.
Phelps Brown, H. 1989. The Radical Reflections of an Applied Economist. In vol. 2 of *Recollections of Eminent Economists*, edited by J. Kregel. London: Macmillan.
Rankin, M. 1955. The Founding of the Chair of Political Economy. *Edinburgh University Journal* 18:191–99.
Robinson, J., and J. Eatwell. 1973. *An Introduction to Modern Economics*. Maidenhead: McGraw-Hill.
Roll, E. 1998. The Practical Economist. *The Guardian*, 24 October.
Rutherford, D. 1997. History of the [Edinburgh] Economics Department. http://www.ed.ac.uk/econ/General_History.htm.
Scott, W. R. 1910–12. *The Constitution and Finance of English, Scottish, and Irish Joint Stock Companies to 1720*. 3 vols. Cambridge: Cambridge University Press.
Smart, W. 1900. *Taxation of Land Values and the Single Tax*. Glasgow: J. Maclehose.
———. 1910–17. *Economic Annals of the Nineteenth Century 1801–1820, 1821–1830*. 2 vols. London: Macmillan.
———. 1916. *Second Thoughts of an Economist*. London: Macmillan.
Simpson, D. 1988. What Economists Need to Know. *Royal Bank of Scotland Review*, no. 160, December.
Tribe, K. 1988. *Governing Economy: The Transformation of German Economic Discourse 1750–1840*. Cambridge: Cambridge University Press.
Young, W., and F. Lee. 1993. *Oxford Economics and Oxford Economists*. Basingstoke: Macmillan.

Strategic Games from Theory to Application

Robert W. Dimand

In his Clarendon lectures celebrating the pervasiveness of noncooperative game theory throughout the applied fields of economics in the 1980s, David Kreps (1990, 1) noted that "thirty-five years ago or so, game theory seemed to hold enormous promise in economics. But that promise seemingly went unfulfilled; twenty years ago, one might perhaps have found 'game theory' in the index of textbooks in industrial organization, but the pages referenced would usually be fairly dismissive of what might be learned from game theory. And one heard nothing of the subject from macro-economists, labour economists, . . . the list goes on seemingly without end." For Kreps, this past darkness serves simply as a dramatic backdrop to the subsequent triumphant adoption of game theory across the fields of economics. For a historian of applied economics, this phenomenon is of great interest: despite the initial powerful enthusiasm for game theory (including a front-page *New York Times* story on John von Neumann and Oskar Morgenstern's *Theory of Games and Economic Behavior*) and sanguine expectations of its wide-ranging applicability, attempts to use game theory to illuminate applied fields in economics and other social sciences in the first quarter-century after the publication of von Neumann and Morgenstern's book (1944) proved problematic.

Although, as we shall see, early attempts were made to apply game theory in a wide variety of contexts, most of those attempts failed to

Correspondence may be addressed to the Department of Economics, Brock University, St. Catharines, Ontario L2S 3A1, Canada.

inspire further efforts. Apart from military strategy, game theory established footholds only in industrial organization and political science in the 1950s and 1960s, and it remained very much a minority approach even in those fields. Some of the factors responsible for those early disappointments remain highly relevant and resonate in recent protests against the excessive claims made for game theory and related approaches in political science (Green and Shapiro 1994; Udehn 1996). One such factor was (in the terminology of the call for papers of this conference) the tool-driven, rather than problem-driven, nature of early applications of game theory in the social sciences, looking to exciting theoretical developments outside the applied fields for possible insights into applied problems, rather than starting with problems and attempting to develop methods of analysis suited to them. Another factor was the multiplicity of solution concepts in cooperative game theory and the perceived lack of definite results beyond the narrow confines of strictly competitive games.

This paper explores the attempts to make game theory applicable in economics and other social sciences in the first twenty years of game theory as a recognized subject. Although theoretical developments in the analysis of strategic games in the 1950s are recognized as the foundations of later work (e.g., Schmidt 1990) and the influence on the development of game theory of potential military applications has been examined (Mirowski 1991; cf. Brewer and Shubik 1979 and Allen 1987), the attempts at application of game theory in the social sciences in the same period have largely been forgotten. Of the three most immediately relevant articles in Weintraub 1992, William Riker's does, as he states in his second sentence, "necessarily, read a bit like autobiography," concentrating on those applications in which he was personally involved, while Robin Rider's article examines attitudes toward game theory among operations researchers (with a section on some applications related to military strategy), rather than examining applications. Only Angela O'Rand, applying network analysis to the diffusion of game theory in sociology and social psychology, surveys efforts to apply game theory, a very valuable contribution, but one that excludes applications within economics, management, or politics. Although section 2 of Alessandro Innocenti's 1995 article is titled "The Early Years of the Application of Game Theory to Economics," it mentions only two instances of game theory application: Martin Shubik's *Strategy and Market Structure* (1959) and John Harsanyi's proof of the mathematical equivalence of John Nash's and Frederik Zeuthen's solutions to wage bargaining. Instead, Innocenti's section concentrates on arguing that the Arrow-Debreu general equilibrium theory shares little with game theory beyond the use of the Kakuktani fixed-point theorem.

The works surveyed in this article were attempts to use game theory in applied fields of economics and other social sciences. This follows the use of "applied" and "application" by early participants in literature that applied to game theory; their perception of what they were doing is shown, for instance, in titles such as "A Proposed Application of the Theory of Games to Collective Bargaining" (the subtitle of Allen 1956), "The Theory of 'Games' in Stock Selection . . . How It Might Be Applied to Security Analysis" (the title of Hale 1960), and "Application of Game Theory to Some Problems in Automobile Insurance" (the title of Borch 1962). Lawrence Friedman (1958, 706) concluded that "advertising allocation problems may become one of the most useful applications of game theory." The spirit in which the papers just cited constitute applications is illustrated by the abstract of Glasser 1958: "What does the mathematical theory of games offer for the study of personnel decisions? Here is one person's answer." Similarly, the abstract of Chacko 1956 notes that international trade relationships in South Asian regional economic development "seem to suggest certain game situations amenable to analysis by employing the tools of the theory of games." Richard Snyder (1955, 70) wished to "suggest some possible applications and uses of the theory of games for the analysis of political behavior." R. Duncan Luce and Arnold Rogow (1956, 83) described Shapley and Shubik 1954 as "the first actual application of a portion of game theory to a political science problem. The present paper outlines another application, which is in a sense a natural successor to the Shapley-Shubik work. . . . it is a purposely oversimplified illustration of how a part of game theory may be applied to such studies." Lloyd Shapley and Martin Shubik (1954, 787) began by declaring that their "method is based on a technique of the mathematical theory of games, applied to what are known there as 'simple games' and 'weighted majority games.' We apply it here to a number of illustrative cases, including the United States Congress, and discuss some of its formal properties." Luce and Howard Raiffa (1957) discussed such analyses of voting power in legislatures in a chapter titled "Applications of *n*-Person Theory," but directed readers to Shubik's then forthcoming book (Shubik 1959) for "the complex of applications to economic theory." Later this use (which parallels the distinction between pure and applied mathematics, with which the participants in this literature would have been familiar) was followed in such titles as *Applied Game Theory* (Brams, Schotter, and Schwödiauer 1979) and "On the Applications of Game Theory" (chap. 12, vol. 1 of Shubik 1982). The participants in this literature thus expressed themselves as being engaged in application of game theory, in the sense of importing the techniques of game theory into fields within economics, politics, and other social sciences.

The participants in this literature viewed game theory as such, or pure game theory, as the analysis of hypothetical, abstract situations in which players could choose from a set of strategies that led to a certain matrix of payoffs. Applying game theory meant looking for analogues to these previously analyzed situations in the social and economic world. The players, strategies, and payoffs would be redefined as specific actors, actions, and consequences in social settings of interest to the researchers, such as unions and firms bargaining over wages, or competing firms deciding on levels of advertising. Modifying the abstract game to fit the social situation might require changes in the previously analyzed game form.

Moreover, these works were applied in the sense of importing game theory into what were considered applied fields of social science (including economics), rather than in the sense of being empirical. While other economists were taking to empirical data analysis in the form of regression analysis and large-scale simultaneous-equations models in the 1950s and 1960s, game theorists looked elsewhere to confront their theories with evidence: to experimental games, the early history of which in this period is examined in Dimand 1999 (cf. Colman 1982, Leonard 1994a, Roth 1993, and Vernon L. Smith's article in Weintraub 1992).

Despite the high hopes expressed in review articles of von Neumann and Morgenstern's *Theory of Games and Economic Behavior* (1944) about the potential of game theory to revolutionize economics (see Dimand and Dimand 1996, chap. 9; cf. Innocenti 1995, Leonard 1992, 1995, Mirowski 1992, and Schmidt 1990), for decades the applied use of game theory lagged far behind theoretical developments. While in the 1950s the theory of strategic games produced such important innovations as Nash-Cournot equilibrium, the Nash bargaining solution, Shapley value, and core (all developed at Princeton), as well as statistical decision theory (building on the work of Abraham Wald), attempts at application in the social sciences (as distinct from military strategy) were, with a few exceptions, initially tentative and isolated. The most substantial early application, Martin Shubik's *Strategy and Market Structure* (1959), was the most notable of these exceptions: firmly rooted in the work of the Princeton game theory community and staking a bold claim to a game-theoretic reorientation of industrial organization, it was the harbinger of how IO would develop a quarter of a century later (e.g., Tirole 1988). Even today, industrial organization remains the one area of economics in which application of game-theoretic models has more or less kept pace with theoretical developments in the field of game theory. In contrast to IO (and to voting theory), applications of game theory in other areas of economics in the 1950s tended not to be followed up, standing as isolated tours de force. Even military-sponsored research on strategic games tended to produce more theoretical research than applications (as is the case with the recent NATO Advanced Study Institutes on game theory at SUNY Stony Brook, e.g., Mertens and Sorin 1994), although not quite to the point of justifying General LeMay's gibe that the name of the RAND Corporation stood for "Research and No Development" (see Kaplan 1983, Mirowski 1991, and Rider 1992 on game theory and military strategy; Brewer and Shubik 1979 and Allen 1987 on the related topic of war gaming; and Dimand and Dimand 1997, vol. 3, pt. 2, for examples of military applications in the 1950s).

Beyond Market Structure: The Scattering of Early Applications

Early attempts to apply game-theoretic reasoning in other areas of economics and management included business cycles (Shubik 1952), regional development (Chacko 1956), expansion of bank credit (Midutani 1955), international trade agreements (Faxen 1949), collective bargaining (Seligman [1952] 1968; Allen 1956), personnel (Glasser 1958), capital budgeting (Bennion 1956), portfolio choice (Hale 1960), and advertising (Gillman 1950; Friedman 1958), while there were much rarer attempts to apply game theory elsewhere in the social sciences (notably Bernard 1954 and Barth 1959) and biology (Lewontin 1961, a precursor of Maynard Smith 1982). The range of areas of attempted application is wide, but the most striking aspect of this list is the lack of clustering: attempted applications of game theory outside market structure, military strategy, and politics tended to remain isolated, failing to stimulate further work. The lack of clustering across topics contrasts with clustering in another dimension. Several of the applications emerged from Oskar Morgenstern's Princeton seminar, including some that might not on first glance appear due to the Princeton game theory community, such as articles by an Indian economist in the *Indian Journal of Economics* (Chacko 1956) and by a Japanese economist in the *Osaka Economic Papers* (Midutani 1955).

Martin Shubik's "A Business Cycle Model with Organized Labor Considered" (1952) replaced the traditional assumption of a given labor supply curve by a two-person, zero-sum bargaining game between a union and a large industry over the course of the business cycle. Shubik, then a Princeton graduate student in economics, made use of the bargaining solution proposed for two-person cooperative games by John Nash, then a Princeton graduate student in mathematics, two years earlier in the same journal. Nash's solution depended on evaluating threats that determine the size of the side payments and had an advantage over von Neumann and Morgenstern (1944) in that the utilities of the players were not assumed to be comparable. Shubik noticed an interesting feature of this solution in the context of the business cycle: "The value of the firm's threat varies inversely with the period of the cycle, whereas that of the union varies directly" (Shubik 1952, 288). He also "noted that the completeness of the sets of information available to the industry and union decreases directly as the rate of change in the income level increases" (290). Strikes and lockouts, which would not occur in the model with complete information, were possible with incomplete information. "Kickbacks, tributes, strikes, and many other similar phenomena are not necessarily examples of the noneconomic aspects of society" (294) but could result in cooperative game models with side payments and incomplete information. In retrospect, Shubik's article appears as a precursor of applications of game theory to macroeconomics thirty years later and as an intriguing use of the then very new Nash bargaining solution, innovative in taking account of how threat values and completeness of information vary over the course of the business cycle. What is most noteworthy for the theme of the present volume, however, is what the reception of Shubik's paper indicates about the vicissitudes of attempting to apply game theory to economic issues in the 1950s.

Shubik (1992, 158 n) recalled that he "had the amusing experience of receiving from Friedrich Lutz a failing grade for a term paper in economic theory at the same time it was accepted for publication in *Econometrica* (Shubik 1952)." Although Morgenstern was a professor of economics and conducted an economics seminar on game theory, the economics department was not an encouraging environment for game theory. Jacob Viner doubted that game theory could be useful in studying the complex economy when it could not even find the solution to the game of chess, while William Baumol was skeptical of game theory because much of it then assumed measurable utility, following the von Neumann-Morgenstern axiomatization of expected utility maximization. Such attitudes of senior economics faculty did not encourage economics students to take Morgenstern's seminar. Shubik was among four students in Morgenstern's seminar one year: of the other three, one "eventually became paranoid and hung himself," one "went into industry immediately after graduate school, and unfortunately was dangerously alcoholic and died at an early age," and one "decided to leave the graduate program before completing his degree" and went to work at the International Monetary Fund "using more gamesmanship than game theory" (Shubik 1992, 152). Outside the university, John von Neumann was at Princeton at the Institute for Advanced Study, but, although he was willing to contribute to the first two volumes of *Contributions to the Theory of Games* and to the first volume of the *Naval Research Logistics Quarterly* (of which Morgenstern was an editor), by the 1950s his time and attention were primarily taken up by computers and the Atomic Energy Commission rather than by game theory.

Game theory at Princeton was thus centered around the mathematics department, where Albert W. Tucker held a game theory seminar, and the journal *Annals of Mathematics*, which from 1950 to 1959 published as *Annals of Mathematics Studies* four volumes of *Contributions to the Theory of Games*, coedited by Tucker (the first two with Harold W. Kuhn, the third with Morton Dresher and P. Wolfe, and the last with R. Duncan Luce), as well as a 1964 volume titled *Advances in Game Theory* (edited by Dresher, Tucker, and Lloyd Shapley). The atmosphere of mathematics at Princeton and RAND in the early 1950s is recaptured in Sylvia Nasar's biography of John Nash (Nasar 1998, chaps. 3–13; cf. Leonard 1992, 1994b). With the exception of Shubik, the Princeton students most active in game theory and related topics in the 1950s were mathematics students, notably Richard Bellman, David

Gale, D. B. Gillies, John Milnor, John Nash, and Lloyd Shapley.[1] In the early 1950s, this group of scholars developed the concepts of Nash equilibrium for noncooperative games, the Nash bargaining solution for cooperative games, the Shapley value for *n*-person games, and the core, and, beyond game theory, the Kuhn-Tucker conditions for optimization and Bellman's principle in dynamic programming. Much of this research was funded by the United States Air Force through Project RAND (later the RAND Corporation of Santa Monica, California) or the United States Navy through the Office of Naval Research (see Mirowski 1991), but the interest of these game theorists was primarily in the mathematics of the games and solution concepts, not possible military or economic applications. Much of the work on solution concepts to games in this period turned out to be capable of interpretation as rediscovery and generalization of earlier economics, but, as the mathematicians had little background in economics, it was from Shubik that they learned of the affinity of Augustin Cournot's 1838 analysis of duopoly to Nash equilibrium (but see Leonard 1994b for a critical account of Shubik's reinterpretation of Cournot as a supposed precursor of Nash) or of F. Y. Edgeworth's 1881 contract curve to the core (see Dimand 1997 and Schmidt 1990). (Morgenstern had previously drawn attention to the relevance of Eugen von Böhm-Bawerk's analysis of a horse market.) The lack of enthusiasm displayed by the economics department and the focus of the mathematicians on interesting theorems rather than applied problems meant that, while Princeton and RAND together were at the center of developments in game theory in the 1950s, these theoretical developments were accompanied by comparatively few important applied contributions, most notably Shapley and Shubik 1954 on voting power in committees and Shubik's *Strategy and Market Structure* (1959).

"The Maximum Expansion of Bank Credit and the Theory of Games" was presented by Kazuo Midutani of Kobe University in Morgenstern's Princeton seminar in February 1954, the year before the paper appeared in the *Osaka Economic Papers*. Midutani stated that he "would like to express my deep gratitude to Professor Oskar Morgenstern, under whose kind guidance I could study recent developments of the theory of

1. The smaller number of prominent young game theorists outside Princeton also tended to be mathematicians with Princeton connections; for instance, Howard Raiffa, then a Michigan mathematics graduate student, presented his research in Tucker's Princeton seminar in the fall of 1950 (Raiffa 1992, 174).

games at Princeton University." Midutani (1955) addresses the familiar bank deposit multiplier process, in which a loan by one bank generates deposits across all banks, some of which will be held as reserves and the rest lent out, repeating the process, with some deposits returning to the first bank. Midutani treated this as a two-player game (lumping the $n - 1$ other banks together as the second player) with the strategic choice being the selection of the reserve ratio, a continuous variable. The payoff function for each player depends on the two reserve ratios, and the game has a minimax solution. Midutani (1955, 56) states that "the demonstration of the theorem in such a continuous case was given independently by Dr. L. S. Shapley and by Dr. Tetsuya Gonoh." The paper offered a new way of formulating a familiar problem, but the analysis was arbitrary in its assumption that the credit-expansion game is zero-sum (or constant-sum).

George Chacko, who in 1956 argued that game theory was useful in analyzing the jute, tea, and cotton textile exports of India, Ceylon, and Pakistan, stated that he was "indebted to Professor Oskar Morgenstern for the opportunity to work as an Assistant in Research in Economics with the Economics Research Project of Princeton University, in which capacity the first draft of this paper was written" (Chacko 1956, 167 n). Previously he had published in India an enthusiastic review article on game theory as a new theory of economic behavior and an article on the von Neumann-Morgenstern axiomatization of expected utility maximization (Chacko 1950, 1951). Chacko (1956) set up a very general three-player, zero-sum game with two-country coalitions assumed to be able to divide up the market and exclude the third player, with no imputation dominating any other imputation. However, he went on to note that the applicability of the model was limited by the differing power of the players and by the possibility of changes in the value of the game as a coalition's price choice would affect the quantity demanded. He did not discuss how a coalition of two of the three producing countries could exclude the third from the market. Chacko mentioned that since India and Ceylon supplied 98 percent of the tea consumed in Britain, there was scope for the two producers to form a coalition against the consumer or for one producer to form a coalition with the consumer against the other producer, but he did not formalize this game. He referred to a forthcoming book of his, an econometric analysis of the prospects for Indian jute. Given that Chacko had welcomed the work of von Neumann and Morgenstern in his earlier articles and had then gone to Princeton to work for Morgenstern's Economics Research Project, it was natural that working on the jute study would lead Chacko to try to reformulate the problem in terms of game theory, but his 1956 article yielded no definite results and did not lead to further work.

Strategic Games as a Managerial Tool

Martin Shubik (1955) argued in *Management Science* for the applicability of the theory of strategic games in management science (a field at the border of operations research and business administration, overlapping both), and the next year demonstrated in the *Stanford Law Review* the relevance of thinking in terms of strategic interaction among a small number of players to understanding how antitrust laws affect the automobile industry (Shubik 1956). The last two chapters of his *Strategy and Market Structure* (1959) built upon the 1956 article. Shubik's 1959 book (written between 1949 and 1956 at Princeton and then at the Center for Advanced Study in the Behavioral Sciences, before he moved to IBM) was the most successful early application of game theory in economics (matched in mathematical statistics by Wald's minimax approach to statistical decision functions) and was a harbinger of how the study of market structure would subsequently evolve, but for some twenty years Shubik's game-theoretic approach was very much a minority approach within the field of industrial organization. *Strategy and Market Structure* was the largest-scale early application of game theory in economics and the social sciences. Uniquely among those applying game theory to economics in the 1950s, Shubik was at the heart of the Princeton game theory community, collaborating with Shapley (Shapley and Shubik 1954 and numerous later joint articles) and with Nash and John P. Mayberry (Mayberry, Nash, and Shubik 1953 on duopoly), and concentrating on game theory throughout a publishing career that began with articles in *Econometrica* and the *Journal of Political Economy* in April 1952 within three years of entering graduate school and that continues to be highly productive (at Yale in 1960–61 and since 1963).

Other early efforts to apply game theory to economics and management present a completely different picture: small-scale, tentative, and not sustained, outliers in the published work of the authors, who were attracted by the prestige of the highly mathematical theory but were not themselves contributors to the theory. A Harvard Ph.D. who was a consulting economist with Standard Oil of New Jersey, Edward

G. Bennion (1956) discussed capital budgeting and game theory in the *Harvard Business Review*, with regard to minimax choice of oil refinery size given what refinery yields would be in each of several possible future economic conditions. He reused this example in a short textbook titled *Elementary Mathematics of Linear Programming and Game Theory* (1960). Bennion (1956, 123) could muster no stronger claim than that "to say that game theory, in its more rigorous sense, still has no significant business applications does not of course mean that claims for its *potential* have been exaggerated. The day of orthodox game theory may well be on its way, just as the day of linear programming has already arrived in some measure. Meanwhile, businessmen may wish to acquaint themselves with the theory and be on the watch for any practical uses it may have." Bennion (1956, 122–23) held that "game theory still does not deal effectively with situations where there are more than two players or where the loser's losses and the winner's gains do not cancel out." Bennion (1952) had previously attempted a simplified, accessible account of another advance in quantitative technique, the Cowles Commission approach to simultaneous-equations estimation. Bennion's 1956 article inspired a Denver securities analyst, Irving Hale, to a brief application to stock selection, given three possible levels of defense spending that would affect the profitability of three companies (Hale 1960).

Surprisingly, there was little effort to reexamine collective bargaining in light of game theory (apart from Shubik 1952). The institutional economist Ben Seligman's short article, "Game Theory and Collective Bargaining" ([1952] 1968), was primarily concerned to argue that "many of the ideas developed by John R. Commons fit squarely into these theories" so that the new theory of strategic games did not invalidate the insights of Commons's nonmathematical, institutionalist economics into labor negotiations with limited information. L. Allen (1956) proposed to a legal audience that game theory could aid in understanding collective bargaining.

Gerald J. Glasser, an assistant professor of economics at New York University, wrote two short articles suggesting the relevance of game theory to analyzing personnel decisions (1958) and cumulative voting for corporate directors (1959). Glasser (1958, 10–11) provided an introduction at the most basic level: "Action, alternatives, uncertainty and consequences are four of the more important principles of thought that have stemmed from the mathematical theory of games, statistical decision theory, *et al.* But there are similar principles that could be profitably expounded. The notion of strategy is one of these ideas. . . . Other principles of game theory include those of competition, cooperation, information and teamwork. All these ideas, like the ones discussed here, can contribute heavily to a way of managerial thinking about everyday activities." Game theory was applied, considerably more formally, to the allocation of advertising expenditures by L. Gillman in the *Journal of the American Statistical Association* (1950) and by Lawrence Friedman in *Operations Research* (1958), but these were isolated exercises that did not lead to a growing body of work. Friedman (formerly with the Operations Research Group at Case Institute of Technology but by 1958 with M & M's Candies and collaborating on an operations research textbook [Sasieni, Yaspan, and Friedman 1959]) seems not to have been aware of Gillman's article, and, apart from his 1958 article, was not active in bringing game-theoretic methods into operations research. These applications by Bennion, Hale, Glasser, Gillman, and Friedman had such little impact in managerial science and operations research that the only mention of any of them by Robin Rider (1992) merely states that a bibliography of operations research notes the application of linear programming to oil refining in Bennion (1960).

High Hopes, Problematic Applications: Positive Political Theory

The application of game-theoretic models, while solidly established in industrial organization, remains problematic in some of these other areas. The rational choice approach of positive political theory (as distinguished from normative political philosophy), growing from early game-theoretic contributions such as Shapley and Shubik 1954, Luce and Rogow 1956, and Robin Farquharson's 1958 Oxford thesis (published in 1969) and strongly identified with the work of the late William Riker (1962, 1986), has generated an extensive literature, exemplified by Brams 1975, Ordeshook 1986, and Flanagan 1998, and has enriched understanding of political behavior, notably with regard to strategic voting (cf. Robinson 1970 on Soviet interest in game-theoretic analysis of political behavior). It has, however, been subjected to vigorous critiques, such as those by Donald Green and Ian Shapiro (1994) and Lars Udehn (1996). These critiques argue that the scope and fertility of game-theoretic models (and rational choice models more generally) in politics are limited in such instances as explaining voter turnout or showing the extent of observed cooperation.

Shapley and Shubik (1954) used the Shapley value in Shapley 1953 to evaluate a priori voting strength in a committee system, such as that of the U.S. Congress. Using the *Social Science Citation Index*, Angela O'Rand (1992, 179 n) found that Shapley and Shubik 1954 was the most-cited journal article in the game theory literature from 1956 to 1965. Only von Neumann and Morgenstern's *Theory of Games* (1944) and Luce and Raiffa's *Games and Decisions* (1957) received more citations. The application of game theory to politics was also advocated at the same time by Karl Deutsch of MIT and by the Northwestern (previously Princeton) political scientist Richard Snyder (Deutsch 1954; Snyder 1955). These publications were not independent: Deutsch 1954 was presented at Princeton's Center of International Studies, and the lead footnote acknowledges benefiting from discussions with Shubik, Morgenstern, and Snyder, while the lead footnote in Snyder 1955 states that "the author is greatly indebted to Dr. Martin Shubik, friend and colleague. . . . Both Professor Morgenstern and Dr. Shubik have read the manuscript carefully, correcting errors and making valuable suggestions. . . . Gratitude is also due to Professor Karl Deutsch of the Massachusetts Institute of Technology who was among the first to recognize the importance of game theory and who has helped to stimulate the interest of political scientists." Shubik (1992, 158) recalled that Snyder encouraged the submission of Shapley and Shubik 1954 to the *American Political Science Review* and invited Shubik to edit a short book titled *Readings in Game Theory and Political Behavior* (Shubik 1954). Luce and Rogow (1956) extended the power-index analysis of Shapley and Shubik 1954 to reflect some institutional structure (a simplified model of the U.S. Congress) and to analyze the effect of defections on a two-party system. Shubik 1954 reprinted Deutsch 1954, while a later book of readings also edited by Shubik (1964) excerpted Duncan Black 1950, Shapley and Shubik 1956, Luce and Rogow 1956, and RAND memoranda by I. Mann and Shapley applying the Shapley-Shubik power index to the electoral college. Deutsch and Snyder dropped out of the game theory literature after a single contribution apiece. Buchanan and Tullock 1962, a foundation stone of the public choice literature, referred favorably to von Neumann and Morgenstern, but did not make use of formal game theory in its rational choice approach to politics.

The Shapley-Shubik index measures the chance, over all permutations of *n* players, for the indexed player to hold the pivotal position between the winning and losing sides, as the last-added member of the minimal winning coalition, assuming a homogeneous voting population (all have the same probability of voting yes on an issue), while the alternative index in Banzhaf 1965 used the chance, over all possible coalitions, for the indexed player to be on the winning side, assuming each player has an equal probability of voting yes or no. The arbitrariness of choice among alternative power indexes disturbed William Riker, a central figure in using game theory in political science (and, at different times, a coauthor with Shapley, Brams, and Ordeshook). Riker (1992, 211) noted that "much as I was impressed by the Shapley-Shubik paper, it has not in the long run turned out to be of much use in political science. . . . Nevertheless, there remains the fundamental insight of power indexes: particular voters' influence over outcomes in a weighted voting system is not proportional to those voters' weights. Furthermore, various decision rules may advantage or disadvantage weighted voters in nonobvious ways." Shubik (1964, 367) remarked of Riker's *Theory of Political Coalitions* (1962) that "the mathematically inclined game theorist might argue that much liberty has been taken with the various concepts of solution employed here."

William Riker (1992, 214) contrasted "the ultimate failure of the Shapley-Shubik index in political science" with "more promising applications of game-theoretic ideas," of which "by far the most important and interesting . . . was Robin Farquharson's *Theory of Voting* (1969)," a game-theoretic analysis of strategic voting, in which voters, instead of voting for their myopic true tastes, vote strategically to achieve a final outcome they prefer to the one that would result if they voted sincerely. Farquharson began with an undergraduate paper at Brasenose College, Oxford, in 1953, on the U.S. Senate's vote on the League of Nations, and then wrote his D. Phil. thesis at Nuffield College, Oxford, on the theory of voting. One of the two examiners for his thesis was R. B. Braithwaite, a Cambridge philosophy professor whose inaugural lecture had been on game theory as a tool for moral philosophers (Braithwaite 1955). Although accepted as a doctoral dissertation in 1958 and awarded the 1961 social science monograph prize of the American Academy of Arts and Sciences, Farquharson's thesis was not published until 1969 (even though William Riker,reading it for the Yale

University Press in 1962, unreservedly recommended publication). Martin Shubik was eventually able to persuade the Yale University Press to publish the work (together with Basil Blackwell), despite Farquharson's insistence on several expensive three-color plates. Even after publication, the book's impact was limited by its numerous typographical errors (twenty-eight significant ones are corrected in Niemi 1983) and by the difficulty of using Farquharson's method of finding equilibria (first presented in a brief article [Farquharson 1955]; see Niemi 1983 for a simplified exposition). Farquharson was unfortunately not in a position to build further on his contribution himself: Colman (1982, 215 n) reports that "Robin Farquharson was a South African with radical political views, and it is a matter of public record (Farquharson 1968) that he was also a manic-depressive psychotic. . . . By the time his epoch-making work on strategic voting appeared in print, he was living as a tramp in London, and he met a tragic and violent death shortly thereafter." Although the idea of viewing voting as a game in which voters choose strategically with regard to ultimate payoffs, rather than simply expressing their myopic preferences, became a commonplace of voting theory in the 1980s and 1990s, Farquharson's pioneering work in the 1950s on strategic voting had little direct influence, and for a long time exerted indirect influence only through Riker's reading of it. An indication of the limited direct influence of Farquharson's thesis is that critiques of game-theoretic and rational choice approaches to politics by Green and Shapiro (1994) and Udehn (1996) do not mention his name (nor the names of Shapley and Shubik, whose 1954 paper was once so much cited).

Within the field of international politics, game-theoretic concepts (notably the prisoner's dilemma game) were applied to the Cold War, particularly in the *Journal of Conflict Resolution* (see, e.g., Schelling 1957 in the inaugural issue of that journal and, more generally, Schelling 1960). A group of studies by Mathematica Inc. (founded by Oskar Morgenstern and then headed by John P. Mayberry) for the U.S. Arms Control and Disarmament Agency between 1965 and 1968 applied game theory to disarmament and arms races. Unlike earlier applications, these studies advanced the theory in the area of games of incomplete information, but their impact on game theory was delayed because, being classified as confidential, these papers had only limited circulation in manuscript until they were collected and published much later as

Mayberry with Harsanyi, Scarf, and Selten 1992 and Aumann and Maschler with Stearns 1995.

Game Theory and the Sociology of Conflict

Theodore Caplow's *American Sociological Review* article "A Theory of Coalitions in the Triad" (1956) spurred a flurry of interest in game theory among sociologists and social psychologists with his argument that studying initial inequalities of power offered a simpler and more empirically valid alternative to formal game theory as a means of predicting coalition formation among individuals in three-person groups (cf. O'Rand 1992, 197–99). Caplow eventually expanded his five-page article into a book (Caplow 1968). William Gamson (1961) made more formal use of game theory in reformulating Caplow's theory of coalitions in the triad, but found that the multiplicity of solution concepts limited the usefulness of formal, axiomatic game theory as a foundation for a descriptive theory: "In examining the mathematical literature, we found that the von Neumann-Morgenstern solution theory was inadequate for our purposes because of its profusion of solutions for many games. An attempt by Vickrey to limit these somewhat by defining a *strong* solution still left the crucial difficulty of determining which member of a set of imputations would actually occur. [Luce's] concept of psi-stability also left the unique specification of a coalition to extra-theoretical determination" while the Shapley value "still suggests the equal probability of coalitions despite initial differences in resources" (Gamson 1961, 382; cf. O'Rand 1992, 199, and Colman 1982, 169–73).

The sociologist Jessie Bernard of Pennsylvania State University posed the question, "Where is the modern sociology of conflict?" (1950), before she was introduced to game theory by Sidney Siegel, the Penn State psychologist who was a pioneer in experimental gaming. She offered an answer to her 1950 question in the title of her 1954 article "The Theory of Games of Strategy as a Modern Sociology of Conflict," which was commented on by Morgenstern and Shubik before publication. Bernard (1958) invoked games of strategy as a metaphor for thinking about such social problems as crime, and cited Luce and Raiffa 1957 very soon after its publication. Bernard (1990, 331) recalled that "at midcentury I was enormously attracted to the game theorists. They seemed to be the wittiest among all the social science communities. They wrote with a sense of humor." Despite this enthusiasm, she made no use of formal game theory and drifted away from her initial interest in game theory as a sociology of conflict, citing Luce and Raiffa on the undeveloped state of *n*-person game theory and finding the mathematical level of game-theoretic discourse a barrier to communication. As with the participants in the literature on coalitions in the triad, Bernard's initial optimism about the prospects for sociological applications of game theory faded away. Some attempts at mathematical formalization of sociology were received coolly by game theorists: Shubik (1964, 6) remarked that "the somewhat fruitless attempt in the quantification of sociology, *Dimensions of Society* by Stuart C. Dodd, appeared in 1942," adding that "the mathematical sophistication in the works noted ranges from next to nonexistent in the case of Dodd, to the outer bounds of modern mathematics with von Neumann and Morgenstern, and Weiner."

There were also a few early attempts by anthropologists to apply game theory, notably the finding by W. Davenport (1960) that Jamaican fishermen appeared to intuitively follow minimax mixed strategies in choosing their fishing grounds in a strictly competitive game against the fish, which were controlled by currents (cf. Walker 1977). The Norwegian anthropologist Fredrik Barth (1959) suggested a constant-sum majority game as framework for understanding the formation of political alliances among the Yusufzai Pathans of Pakistan's Northwest Frontier Province, among whom the formation of corporate political units was not just a reflection of lineage but also a matter of individual choice among alternative allegiances, an approach that "sees groups as forming through the strategic choices of persons, i.e. the solidarity of groups springs from the advantages which persons obtain from being members of the groups."

Auction Design: Transient Triumph

A more recent practical application of game theory, this time to auction design (McAfee and McMillan 1987; Milgrom 1989), subsequently proved that, as in the 1950s, efforts to apply game theory to the solution of real-world problems may still disappoint overly high expectations. Confidently judged by John McMillan (1994) as "a triumph for game theory," the game-theoretic design of the U.S. Federal Communications Commission auction of broadcasting appeared to finally establish the practical applicability of game theory: the penultimate chapter of Sylvia Nasar's biography of John Nash (Nasar 1998, chap. 49) is titled "The

Greatest Auction Ever," echoing the title of William Safire's *New York Times* article on the FCC auction. This auction, which opened in December 1994 as Nash, Harsanyi, and Selten were receiving the Nobel Prize in economics for game theory and closed the following March, raised more than $7 billion for broadcast spectrum rights. Although Nasar (1998, 377) noted that spectrum auctions in Australia and New Zealand had been "costly flops and political disasters," the success of the U.S. auction seemed to definitively settle the issue of the practical use of game theory. The triumph was only temporary, however. A U.S. auction of frequencies suitable for wireless data transmission in April 1997 (discussed in "Learning to Play the Game," *The Economist*, 17 May 1997) raised less than 1 percent of the predicted sum ($13.6 million instead of a predicted $1.8 billion), as bidders, reflecting on their experience with previous auctions, learned how to circumvent the design of the auction and to achieve implicit collusion through signaling. Because of publication lags, Nasar's celebration of the game-theoretic design of the spectrum auction appeared in print after the cause for celebration had faded. In the design of spectrum auctions, as in a variety of earlier applications, game theory provided interesting insights and aids to clarifying thought without justifying the exuberant rhetoric of some of its proponents. The triumph of game theory in spectrum auction design had neglected the memento mori of the ancient Roman triumphs.

Conclusion

Luce and Raiffa (1957, 10) accepted "that we have the historical fact that many social scientists have become disillusioned with game theory. Initially there was a naive band-wagon feeling that game theory solved innumerable problems of sociology and economics, or that, at the least, it made their solution a practical matter of a few years' work. This has not turned out to be the case. . . . there has not been a plethora of applications in a dozen years." In explaining this phenomenon, Luce and Raiffa found it "worth emphasizing again that game theory is primarily a product of mathematicians and not of scientists from the empirical fields. In large part this results from the fact that the theory was originated by a mathematician and was, to all intents and purposes, first presented in book form as a highly formal (though, for the most part, elementary) structure, thus tending to make it accessible as a research vehicle only to mathematicians. Indeed, we believe that so far the impact of game theory has been greater in applied mathematics, especially in mathematical statistics, than in the empirical sciences" (3). The statistical decision theory of Wald (1945) and David Blackwell and M. A. Girshick (1954) was certainly the most immediately successful application of game theory. While Luce and Raiffa appear to stress the difficulty of nonmathematicians in reading formal mathematical exposition as a barrier to widespread application of game theory, their comments implicitly draw attention to another factor: game theory was not developed by applied social scientists as a response to perceived unsolved problems. Rather, it was developed by a community of mathematicians (primarily at or connected with Princeton) engaged in intellectual puzzle-solving at a high level of abstraction. The isolated position of Morgenstern within Princeton's economics department, as well as the hostility toward game theory of the other senior economists at Princeton (such as Lutz and Viner), meant that the game theorists among Princeton mathematicians did not interact with or influence a circle of economists and other social scientists there (with the exception of Shubik) interested in what game theory had to offer for improved understanding of real-world problems. Even when conducting research at RAND or research sponsored by the Office of Naval Research, the interest of the Princeton mathematicians remained focused on theory, not application (even though the military sponsors hoped for research applicable to military strategy and tactics). The prestige of the theory led to a number of scattered attempts to apply the ready-made theory to topics in economics, management, politics, and sociology. Such efforts to fit the problems to the Procrustean bed of a preexisting mathematical (and therefore prestigious) theory were frequently awkward. Only in a very few areas of economics and social science, notably industrial organization and power indexes in politics, did any sustained body of research result. Even in these instances, game theory remained a minority approach (only much later did works such as Tirole 1988, which incorporates a substantial "Game Theory User's Manual" in an advanced industrial organization textbook, attest to the pervasion of industrial organization by game theory), and it is noteworthy that both of these examples reflected the role of Martin Shubik, the only one of the young Princeton game theorists of the early 1950s who was an economist rather than a mathematician.

Another explanation for the lag of application behind theory in game theory is advanced by John Harsanyi (1976), who notes that von Neumann and Morgenstern's work "in general does not yield determinate solutions for two-person nonzero-sum games and for n-person games" (quoted by Andrew Schotter 1992, 107 n) comparable to the minimax solution to two-person, constant-sum games. In his business cycle model, Shubik (1952, 293) noted that "if the von Neumann-Morgenstern solution is used [as distinct from the Nash bargaining solution] . . . the only comment feasible about the splitting of income is that any one of a set of imputations will be possible, depending on the bargainers. . . . The weakness, and possibly the strength of the von Neumann-Morgenstern solution is that it makes no comment on how long it takes the players to agree upon accepting a given imputation as the final division of spoils in any game; it merely delineates the zone of agreement." As Andrew Schotter (1992, 107–8) remarks, "For Morgenstern, indeterminacy was not something to run from but rather to embrace" because he viewed indeterminacy as a feature of social processes in an uncertain world, not as a defect of the models used to analyze such processes. Many economists, and especially applied economists, were troubled, however, that considerations of rationality only narrowed the range of possible equilibria in game-theoretic models without providing unique, determinate results (apart from the very special case of two-person, constant-sum games), and were even more disturbed by the variety of solution concepts proposed in cooperative game theory. While not ruling out the possibility that a theory of equilibrium selection may someday be developed to resolve the problem of "too many equilibria and no way to choose," Kreps (1990, 102) acknowledges that "it is safe to say that formal game theory has not delivered such a theory as of yet." This was the problem that led Gamson (1961) to lose confidence in formal game theory as an approach to coalition formation in three-person groups.

A contributing factor in the later resurgence of interest in attempting to use game theory in applied fields has been the increasing emphasis in game theory on noncooperative strategic game theory rather than coalitional or cooperative game theory with its disturbing multiplicity of possible solution concepts. Ken Binmore (1992, 13) argues that "what is perhaps most important about the last twenty years in game theory is that all the major advances have been made in *noncooperative* theory." Binmore (1992, viii) also remarks that in his *Fun and Games: A Text on Game Theory* "very little is said about *cooperative* game theory. This is partly because . . . I have to confess to being squeamish about teaching things to undergraduates that might turn out to be wrong." This view is much more widespread than is that of Tatsuro Ichiishi, whose graduate textbook on microeconomic theory "presents game theory as a powerful foundation of economic analysis, which includes the neoclassical paradigm as a special case" and "treats the descriptive noncooperative game theory as a special case of the cooperative game theory" (Ichiishi 1997, xiv; cf. Ichiishi 1983).

Another factor in the delayed acceptance of game theory in applied fields is the strength of the competing approaches: for instance, game-theoretic works such as Shubik 1959 had less impact in industrial organization in the heyday of the structure-conduct-performance (S-C-P) paradigm associated with Joe S. Bain than game theory did later when IO specialists were less satisfied with S-C-P.

This survey of nonmilitary attempts to apply game theory (outside statistical decision theory) in the first two decades after von Neumann and Morgenstern's *Theory of Games* (1944) reveals patterns that help understand why the initial high hopes for the practical usefulness of game theory so often led to disappointment in this period. The efforts at application were tool driven, not problem driven. The prestige associated with a much touted, highly mathematical theory (and with such figures as John von Neumann) led to efforts to use game theory in a wide variety of areas of economics and the social sciences, fitting the problem to the analytical tool. Often these efforts were not followed up and remained isolated. Game theory raised some interesting questions and yielded some important insights, notably into strategic voting and into strategic interaction in industrial organization, but failed to provide a satisfactory method of equilibrium selection beyond the simplest case of two-player, strictly competitive games. Where game theory had insights to offer, disillusionment was courted by inflated claims that raised expectations of the practical applicability of game theory to unrealistic levels (as in the recent case of auction design). A noteworthy factor in the lack of practical application behind theoretical innovation was the situation at Princeton, the center of game theory in the 1950s. Morgenstern was isolated in an unsympathetic economics department, so where game theory flourished at Princeton was in the mathematics department with Tucker's seminar and the *Annals of Mathematics Studies*, among mathematicians whose primary interest was in the mathematical development of the theory. The one exception among the younger

Princeton game theorists, the economist Martin Shubik, was crucially involved in the most sustained efforts at application of game theory, to market structure and to power indexes in politics, while also remaining in close contact with the theoretical advances associated with Shapley, Nash, and Gillies. Apart from Shubik's work, however, applications of game theory to economics and the social sciences in those decades were, although numerous, scattered across fields and mostly isolated from each other, failing to generate on-going bodies of research despite extremely high initial expectations.

References

Allen, L. 1956. Games Bargaining: A Proposed Application of the Theory of Games to Collective Bargaining. *Yale Law Journal* 65:660–93.

Allen, Thomas B. 1987. *War Games*. New York: Berkeley Books.

Aumann, Robert J., and Michael B. Maschler, with Richard E. Stearns. 1995. *Repeated Games with Incomplete Information*. Cambridge, Mass.: MIT Press.

Banzhaf, John F. III. 1965. Weighted Voting Doesn't Work: A Mathematical Analysis. *Rutgers Law Review* 19:317–43.

Barth, Fredrik. 1959. Segmentary Opposition and the Theory of Games: A Study of Pathan Organization. *Journal of the Royal Anthropological Institute of Great Britain and Ireland* 89:5–21. Reprinted in vol. 3 of Dimand and Dimand 1997.

Bennion, Edward G. 1952. The Cowles Commission's "Simultaneous-Equation Approach": A Simplified Explanation. *Review of Economics and Statistics* 34 (February): 49–56.

———. 1956. Capital Budgeting and Game Theory. *Harvard Business Review* 34 (November–December): 115–23.

———. 1960. *Elementary Mathematics of Linear Programming and Game Theory*. East Lansing, Mich.: Bureau of Business and Economic Research, College of Business and Public Service, Michigan State University.

Bernard, Jessie. 1950. Where Is the Modern Sociology of Conflict? *American Journal of Sociology* 55.1:11–16.

———. 1954. The Theory of Games as a Modern Sociology of Conflict. *American Journal of Sociology* 59.5:411–24. Reprinted in vol. 3 of Dimand and Dimand 1997.

———. 1958. Social Problems as Problems of Decision. *Social Problems* 6.3:212–20.

———. 1990. A Woman's Twentieth Century. In *Authors of Their Own Lives: Intellectual Autobiographies of Twenty American Sociologists*, edited by B. M. Berger. Berkeley: University of California Press.

Binmore, Ken. 1992. *Fun and Games: A Text on Game Theory*. Lexington, Mass.: D. C. Heath.

Black, Duncan. 1950. The Unity of Political and Economic Science. *Economic Journal* 60 (September): 506–14.
Blackwell, David, and M. A. Girshick. 1954. *Theory of Games and Statistical Decisions*. New York: Wiley.
Borch, Karl. 1962. Application of Game Theory to Some Problems in Automobile Insurance. *The Astin Bulletin* 2 (part 2): 208–21.
Braithwaite, R. B. 1955. *The Theory of Games as a Tool for the Moral Philosopher*. Cambridge: Cambridge University Press. Reprinted in vol. 3 of Dimand and Dimand 1997.
Brams, Steven J. 1975. *Game Theory and Politics*. New York: Free Press.
———. 1983. *Superior Beings*. Berlin: Springer Verlag.
Brams, Steven J., Andrew Schotter, and G. Schwödiauer. 1979. *Applied Game Theory*. Würzburg: Physica Verlag.
Brewer, Gary D., and Martin Shubik. 1979. *The War Game: A Critique of Military Problem Solving*. Cambridge: Harvard University Press.
Buchanan, James, and Gordon Tullock. 1962. *The Calculus of Consent*. Ann Arbor: University of Michigan Press.
Caplow, Theodore. 1956. A Theory of Coalitions in the Triad. *American Sociological Review* 21.4:489–93.
———. 1968. *Two against One: Coalitions in the Triad*. Englewood Cliffs, N.J.: Prentice-Hall.
Chacko, George K. 1950. Economic Behaviour—A New Theory. *Indian Journal of Economics* 30 (April): 349–65.
———. 1951. The Concept of Utility: A Different Approach to Fundamentals. *Indian Journal of Economics* 32 (October): 99–113.
———. 1956. Certain Game Situations in Regional Economic Development. *Indian Journal of Economics* 37:145, part 2 (October): 167–75. Reprinted in vol. 3 of Dimand and Dimand 1997.
Colman, Andrew M. 1982. *Game Theory and Experimental Games*. Oxford: Pergamon Press.
Davenport, W. 1960. Jamaican Fishing: A Game Theory Analysis. In *Papers in Caribbean Anthropology*, edited by Sidney W. Mintz. Nos. 57-64, 3-11. New Haven, Conn.: Yale University Publications in Anthropology.
Deutsch, Karl W. 1954. Game Theory and Politics: Some Problems of Application. *Canadian Journal of Economics and Political Science* 20.1:76–83. Reprinted in vol. 3 of Dimand and Dimand 1997.
Dimand, Mary Ann, and Robert W. Dimand. 1996. *A History of Game Theory*. Vol. 1, *From the Beginnings to 1945*. London and New York: Routledge.
———, eds. 1997. *The Foundations of Game Theory*. 3 vols. Cheltenham, England: Edward Elgar.
Dimand, Robert W. 1997. Thinking about Solutions to Games: Some Changes in Game Theory 1944–1960. Paper presented to the American Economic

Association/History of Economics Society session, New Orleans, and the European Society for History of Economic Thought, Marseilles.

———. 1999. Experimental Gaming: The Early Years. Paper presented at the 1999 European Conference on the History of Economics, Cachan, France.

Farquharson, Robin. 1955. Sur une généralisation de la notion d'equilibrium. *Comptes rendus hebdomadaires des séances de l'Académie des Sciences de Paris* 240:46–48.

———. 1968. *Drop Out!* Harmondsworth, England: Penguin.

———. 1969. *Theory of Voting*. New Haven, Conn.: Yale University Press.

Faxen, Karl-Olaf. 1949. "Spelteori, Förväntnings-analys och handelsavtal [The Theory of Games, Expectation Analysis, and Trade Agreements]. *Nationaløkonomisk Tidsskrift* 251–64.

Flanagan, Thomas. 1998. *Game Theory and Canadian Politics*. Toronto: University of Toronto Press.

Friedman, Lawrence. 1958. Game-Theory Models in the Allocation of Advertising Expenditures. *Operations Research* 6.5:699–709. Reprinted in vol. 3 of Dimand and Dimand 1997.

Gamson, William A. 1961. Theory of Coalition Formation. *American Sociological Review* 26.3:373–82.

Gillman, L. 1950. Operations Analysis and the Theory of Games: An Advertising Example. *Journal of the American Statistical Association* 45 (December): 541–45.

Glasser, Gerald J. 1958. Personnel Decisions and the Theory of Games. *Personnel Administration* 21:6–11, 56. Reprinted in vol. 3 of Dimand and Dimand 1997.

———. 1959. Game Theory and Cumulative Voting for Corporate Directors. *Management Science* 5.2:151–56.

Green, Donald P., and Ian Shapiro. 1994. *Pathologies of Rational Choice Theory: A Critique of Applications in Political Science*. New Haven, Conn.: Yale University Press.

Hale, Irving. 1960. The Theory of "Games" in Stock Selection . . . How It Might Be Applied to Security Analysis. *Financial Analysts Journal* 16 (March–April): 53–56. Reprinted in vol. 3 of Dimand and Dimand 1997.

Harsanyi, John. 1976. *Rational Behavior and Bargaining Equilibrium in Games and Social Situations*. Cambridge: Cambridge University Press.

Ichiishi, Tatsuro. 1983. *Game Theory for Economic Analysis*. New York: Academic Press.

———. 1997. *Microeconomic Theory*. Cambridge, Mass.: Basil Blackwell.

Innocenti, Alessandro. 1995. Oskar Morgenstern and the Heterodox Potentialities of the Application of Game Theory to Economics. *Journal of the History of Economic Thought* 17.2:205–27.

Kaplan, Fred. 1983. *The Wizards of Armageddon*. New York: Simon & Schuster.

Kreps, David. 1990. *Game Theory and Economic Modelling*. Oxford: Oxford University Press.

Learning to Play the Game. 1997. *The Economist*, 17 May, 86.

Leonard, Robert J. 1992. Creating a Context for Game Theory. In Weintraub 1992.

———. 1994a. Laboratory Strife: Higgling as Experimental Science in Economics and Social Psychology. In *Higgling: Transactors and Their Markets*, edited by Neil De Marchi and Mary S. Morgan. *HOPE* 26 (supplement): 343–69.

———. 1994b. Reading Cournot, Reading Nash: The Creation and Stabilisation of the Nash Equilibrium. *Economic Journal* 104 (May): 492–511.

———. 1995. From Parlor Games to Social Science: von Neumann, Morgenstern, and the Creation of Game Theory, 1928–1944. *Journal of Economic Literature* 33 (June): 730–61.

Lewontin, Richard C. 1961. Evolution and the Theory of Games. *Journal of Theoretical Biology* 1:382–403. Reprinted in vol. 3 of Dimand and Dimand 1997.

Luce, R. Duncan, and Howard Raiffa. 1957. *Games and Decisions*. New York: Wiley.

Luce, R. Duncan, and Arnold A. Rogow. 1956. A Game Theoretic Analysis of Congressional Power Distributions in a Stable Two-Party System. *Behavioral Science* 1.2:83–95. Reprinted in vol. 3 of Dimand and Dimand 1997.

Mayberry, John P., John F. Nash Jr., and Martin Shubik. 1953. A Comparison of Treatments of a Duopoly Situation. *Econometrica* 21.1:141–54. Reprinted in vol. 2 of Dimand and Dimand 1997.

Mayberry, John P., with John C. Harsanyi, Herbert E. Scarf, and Reinhard Selten. 1992. *Game-Theoretic Models of Conflict and Cooperation*. Boulder, Colo.: Westview.

McAfee, Preston, and John McMillan. 1987. Auctions and Bidding. *Journal of Economic Literature* 25.2:699–738.

McMillan, John. 1994. Selling Spectrum Rights. *Journal of Economic Perspectives* 8.3:145–62.

Mertens, Jean-Francois, and Sylvain Sorin, eds. 1994. *Game-Theoretic Methods in General Equilibrium Analysis*. Dordrecht: Kluwer.

Midutani, Kazuo. 1955. The Maximum Expansion of Bank Credit and the Theory of Games. *Osaka Economic Papers* 4.2:53–56. Reprinted in vol. 3 of Dimand and Dimand 1997.

Milgrom, Paul. 1989. Auctions and Bidding: A Primer. *Journal of Economic Perspectives* 3.1:3–22.

Mirowski, Philip. 1991. When Games Grow Deadly Serious: The Military Influence upon the Evolution of Game Theory. In *Economics and National Security*, edited by Craufurd D. Goodwin. *HOPE* 23 (supplement): 227–55.

———. 1992. What Were von Neumann and Morgenstern Trying to Accomplish? In Weintraub 1992.

Nasar, Sylvia. 1998. *A Beautiful Mind*. New York: Simon & Schuster.

Niemi, Richard G. 1983. An Exposition of Farquharson's *Theory of Voting*. *Public Choice* 40.3:323–28.

O'Rand, Angela M. 1992. Mathematizing Social Science in the 1950s: The Early Development and Diffusion of Game Theory. In Weintraub 1992.

Ordeshook, Peter C. 1986. *Game Theory and Political Theory*. Cambridge: Cambridge University Press.

Raiffa, Howard. 1992. Game Theory at the University of Michigan, 1948–1952. In Weintraub 1992.

Rider, Robin E. 1992. Operations Research and Game Theory: Early Connections. In Weintraub 1992.

Riker, William H. 1962. *The Theory of Political Coalitions*. New Haven, Conn.: Yale University Press.

———. 1986. *The Art of Political Manipulation*. New Haven, Conn.: Yale University Press.

———. 1992. The Entry of Game Theory into Political Science. In Weintraub 1992.

Robinson, T. W. 1970. Game Theory and Politics: Recent Soviet Views. *Studies in Soviet Thought* 10:291–315.

Roth, Alvin E. 1993. The Early History of Experimental Economics. *Journal of the History of Economic Thought* 15.2:184–209.

Safire, William. 1995. The Greatest Auction Ever. *New York Times*, 16 March.

Sasieni, Maurice, Arthur Yaspan, and Lawrence Friedman. 1959. *Operations Research: Methods and Problems*. New York: Wiley.

Schelling, Thomas C. 1957. Bargaining, Communication, and Limited War. *Journal of Conflict Resolution* 1.1:19–36. Reprinted in vol. 3 of Dimand and Dimand 1997.

———. 1960. *The Strategy of Conflict*. Cambridge: Harvard University Press.

Schmidt, Christian. 1990. Game Theory and Economics: An Historical Survey. *Revue d'Économie Politique* 100.5:589–618.

Schotter, Andrew. 1992. Oskar Morgenstern's Contribution to the Development of the Theory of Games. In Weintraub 1992.

Seligman, Ben B. [1952] 1968. Game Theory and Collective Bargaining. In *Economics of Dissent*. New York: Free Press.

Shapley, Lloyd S. 1953. A Value for N-Person Games. In *Contributions to the Theory of Games II*, edited by H. W. Kuhn and A. W. Tucker, 307–17. Princeton, N.J.: Princeton University Press. Vol. 28. *Annals of Mathematics Studies* series.

Shapley, Lloyd S., and Martin Shubik. 1954. A Method for Evaluating the Distribution of Power in a Committee System. *American Political Science Review* 48.3:787–92. Reprinted in vol. 3 of Dimand and Dimand 1997.

Shubik, Martin. 1952. A Business Cycle Model with Organized Labor Considered. *Econometrica* 20 (April): 284–94. Reprinted in vol. 3 of Dimand and Dimand 1997.

———. 1955. The Uses of Game Theory in Management Science. *Management Science* 2 (October): 40–54.

———. 1956. A Game Theorist Looks at the Antitrust Laws and the Automobile Industry. *Stanford Law Review* 8 (July): 594–630.

———. 1959. *Strategy and Market Structure*. New York: Wiley.

———. 1982. *Game Theory in the Social Sciences*. 2 vols. Cambridge, Mass.: MIT Press.

———. 1992. Game Theory at Princeton, 1949–1955: A Personal Reminiscence. In Weintraub 1992.

———, ed. 1954. *Readings in Game Theory and Political Behavior*. New York: Doubleday.

———, ed. 1964. *Game Theory and Related Approaches to Human Behavior*. New York: Wiley.

Smith, John Maynard. 1982. *Evolution and the Theory of Games*. Cambridge: Cambridge University Press.

Smith, Vernon. 1992. Game Theory and Experimental Economics: Beginnings and Early Influences. In Weintraub 1992.

Snyder, Richard C. 1955. Game Theory and the Analysis of Political Behavior. In *Research Frontiers in Politics and Government*. Washington, D.C.: Brookings Institution. Reprinted in vol. 3 of Dimand and Dimand 1997.

Tirole, Jean. 1988. *The Theory of Industrial Organization*. Cambridge, Mass.: MIT Press.

Udehn, Lars. 1996. *The Limits of Public Choice: A Sociological Critique of the Economic Theory of Politics*. London and New York: Routledge.

von Neumann, John, and Oskar Morgenstern. 1944. *Theory of Games and Economic Behavior*. Princeton, N.J.: Princeton University Press.

Wald, Abraham. 1945. Statistical Decision Functions which Minimize the Maximum Risk. *Annals of Mathematics* 46.2:265–80. Reprinted in vol. 1 of Dimand and Dimand 1997.

Walker, M. 1977. The Jamaican Fishing Study Reinterpreted. *Theory and Decision* 8:265–72.

Weintraub, E. Roy, ed. 1992. *Toward a History of Game Theory*. Supplement to vol. 24 of *HOPE*. Durham, N.C.: Duke University Press.

Part 3

Applied Fields

Personnel/Human Resource Management: Its Roots as Applied Economics

Bruce E. Kaufman

Personnel management, as the name implies, is a specialty area of the field of management. Broadly stated, the subject matter of personnel management is the acquisition and utilization of labor resources in the business organization, a subject that is usually treated in universities and the business world as largely coterminous with the management of the employment staff function in companies. Thus, important topics in personnel management—now more often called human resource management (HRM)—are employee recruitment and selection, compensation management, training and development, employee relations, and collective bargaining.

Today, research and teaching in personnel/HRM in most business schools and management departments have modest to negligible contact with the discipline of economics. A review of scholarly research in personnel/HRM, for example, reveals that little use is made of economic theory and concepts and few references are made to articles and books by economists. As an example, of the twenty articles in the 1997 volume of *Human Resource Management Review*, eighteen contain no references to an economics journal, and of the total of 1,240 citations in these articles, only 5 were to economics journals (4 of the 5 citations were contained in one article). Also illustrative is the fact that many specialized graduate degree programs in personnel/HRM do not require students to take any economics beyond an introductory course

I wish to acknowledge the helpful comments of George Strauss, Jeff Biddle, and Steven Medema on an earlier draft of this paper.

in economic principles (Way 1996), nor do most textbooks on personnel/HRM include even basic economic models or analysis (such as a demand/supply model of wage determination in the chapter on compensation).

Personnel management and economics have not always been worlds apart, however. To a degree largely unrecognized today, personnel management was in the first fifteen years of its life (1915–30) widely regarded in academe as *applied economics*. Furthermore, during this period the most influential scholarly writers on personnel subjects were labor economists, and the bulk of academic research on personnel management was published in mainline economics journals, such as the *American Economic Review*, *Journal of Political Economy*, and *Quarterly Journal of Economics*. Although economics and personnel management had begun to slowly drift apart by the early 1930s, the two continued to be closely linked for the next thirty years through the bridge field of industrial relations. After the early 1960s this intellectual link also began to seriously weaken, leading by the 1980s to a wide and seldom crossed divide between the two fields. Only in the 1990s have personnel management and economics taken a tentative step toward rapprochement—largely due to the emergence in economics of new specialty areas called *organizational economics* and the *economics of personnel/HRM* and in management of a new subfield called *strategic HRM*. The former are avowedly economic in theoretical orientation and perspective, while the latter imports economics into management in the form of the contributions of economists in developing the strategy concept and the influence product and factor market conditions have on the choice of an optimal strategy.

In this article I endeavor to fill in this missing chapter in the history of the founding and early development of the field of personnel management. Three topics are examined in particular: the early contribution of economists to the founding of the field of personnel management, the leading role played by labor economists and economics journals in personnel research in the 1915–30 period, and the reasons personnel management was viewed as applied economics in many universities. My essay concludes with a summary explanation of the centrifugal forces that caused economics and personnel management to drift increasingly far apart after the 1930s.

Economics and Personnel/HRM in the Early Years: The Prevailing View

Historical accounts of the early history of personnel management give almost no mention to the role of economists and the discipline of economics therein. The authoritative text on the history of management thought, for example, is Daniel Wren's (1994). In chapter 9 on the emergence of the field of personnel management, Wren devotes five pages to the role of Frederick Taylor and the scientific management movement, five pages to the role of Hugo Munsterberg and the emergent field of industrial psychology, and six pages to the role of industrial sociology and human relations and the various writers/researchers therein (e.g., Whiting Williams, Vilfredo Pareto, Elton Mayo). But he does not once mention the discipline of economics nor does he cite any economist as having made a contribution to the founding and early development of the field. The closest he comes is one passing reference to the "noted labor scholar John R. Commons" (176) in a short section on employee representation plans.

Likewise, in their otherwise well-done history of personnel/HRM, James Dulebohn, Gerald Ferris, and James Stodd (1995) divide its development into ten stages. Two of these span the years in which the personnel field germinated and was born (roughly 1890–1925). The first is stage 4, titled "Scientific Management, Welfare Work, and Industrial Psychology"; the second is stage 5 titled "World War I and the Emergence of the HRM Profession." In five pages of text, the authors never once mention the discipline of economics, nor do they acknowledge the personnel/HRM research conducted by labor economists of that era. This treatment stands in sharp contrast to the extended discussion given to the fields of scientific management and industrial psychology and their principal leaders, Frederick Taylor and Hugo Munsterberg.

A third example from the personnel literature is the book *The Management of Personnel Relations: History and Origins* (1965) by Cyrus Ling. Individual chapters are devoted to fourteen sources of "contribution" or "influence" in the development of personnel management. While academic disciplines such as psychology, sociology, management, education, and industrial medicine are covered, no chapter on economics or economists is included.

A similar situation is found among writers on the history of labor economics. The definitive work on the early history of labor economics, for example, is Paul McNulty's *The Origins and Development of Labor Economics* (1980). The period 1880–1920 is covered in the chapter "Labor Problems as an Applied Field." Economists first became involved in research on labor issues, he notes, as an outgrowth of efforts to resolve what were then called "labor problems," such as long work hours, low wages, and frequent incidences of injury and death in the workplace. The "problems" perspective inevitably focused the attention of economists on shortcomings and pathologies of labor markets, and solutions thereto. Of these solutions, McNulty examines in detail one—the institution of trade unionism and the process of collective bargaining—and gives moderate attention to a second—protective labor legislation, such as minimum-wage and maximum hour laws. A third solution—improved methods of personnel management—is not once mentioned. Nor is mention made of any research or writings of labor economists on personnel issues or problems during this period.

Also illustrative are these comments from two economists active in the new "economics of personnel" subfield of labor economics. Arthur Blakemore (1987, i) states, "The business literature on matters of personnel management has existed for quite a long time. It is only recently, however, that economists have taken much interest in the area." This theme is echoed by Edward Lazear—the economist whose writings have most influenced this burgeoning area of research—when he states (1999, 201), "There are a number of [economic] theories that have been proposed over the past two decades that purport to explain a variety of human resources phenomena observed in firms." In an accompanying footnote he comments, "Actually, the work in personnel economics goes back much further. The earliest mention in relatively modern literature is found in Slichter (1928)." As I shall demonstrate below, the work of economists (including Sumner Slichter) on personnel subjects began, in actuality, a decade earlier, when the field of personnel management was born, and quickly came to dominate academic research on the matter.

Involvement of Economists in the Early Years of Personnel Management

A closer examination of the early literature in personnel management reveals that labor economists were, in fact, the first and most prolific academic writers on the subject. Before documenting this assertion, however, a brief description of the origins and early years of the personnel management field provides useful context for what follows.

Birth and Early Development of the Field

The field of personnel management was born in the World War I period both as a management specialization in business and an applied field of study in universities. Before 1915 the term *personnel management* (or *personnel administration* or *industrial relations management*) was practically unknown, and few firms had any form of centralized, professional personnel department or function (Jacoby 1985; Kaufman 1993, 2001).

The initial writings on personnel management were by management consultants (then called "counselors") and business practitioners (see Federal Board for Vocational Education 1920). Prominent names among the former were Robert Valentine, Ordway Tead, and Meyer Bloomfield and his brother Daniel. Valentine and Tead were members of the Taylor Society, an association named after Frederick W. Taylor, the father of scientific management, and dedicated to the advancement of progressive methods of management, while the Bloomfields helped found the Boston Employment Managers Association in 1912 (Eilbert 1959)—the first association in the United States dedicated to the new business specialty area of "employment management" (a term that preceded *personnel management*)—and were authors of a number of articles on employment management in the business periodicals of that period.

In 1918 personnel management suddenly mushroomed in popularity, due to the desperate search of employers for ways to staunch sky-high rates of employee turnover and labor unrest unleashed by the economic and political pressures associated with World War I, and quickly assumed the proportions of a management fad. Personnel also received a boost from the widely publicized success the United States Army had in using intelligence and aptitude tests to screen new recruits drafted for the war (Baritz 1960). Practitioner and consultant writings on personnel management proliferated, first in general periodicals catering to business people, such as *Industrial Management*, and later in specialized periodicals, such as *Personnel* (started in 1919).

Personnel management appeared in university curriculums contemporaneously. The first course in personnel management (but using the earlier label *employment management*) was offered at the Tuck School at Dartmouth University in 1915 (Kaufman 1993). During World War I the federal government recruited a number of universities to teach short courses in personnel management in an effort to stabilize wartime labor conditions in industry. By the early 1920s a dozen or so universities, such as Wisconsin and Columbia, had established new courses in personnel management in the curriculum and the first textbook on personnel, *Personnel Administration* by Ordway Tead and Henry Metcalf, appeared in 1920 (Tead was a consultant and adjunct professor of business at Columbia, Metcalf held a Ph.D. in political science and became involved in personnel through wartime government work). By the mid-to late 1920s the number of universities offering personnel courses had tripled and a number of competing textbooks were on the market (Bossard and Dewhurst 1931; Brissenden 1926).

Involvement of Labor Economists

In the early years of the field writers on personnel management tended to fall into one of three groups. The first group came from the ranks of consultants and businessmen. Their perspective was focused heavily on technique and implementation of personnel practices, although some endeavored to place the practice of personnel in a larger social context (e.g., Lewisohn 1926) and on occasion published articles in academic journals (Tead 1921). The second group, of relatively modest number, was composed of industrial psychologists, such as Walter Dill Scott and C. S. Yoakum, who held academic positions but also did considerable business consulting and in some cases held executive personnel positions in industry (Ling 1965). Their work, as elaborated later, often had a relatively narrow focus on specific personnel practices, such as employment tests. The third group of writers were economists with an interest in labor, referred to here as "labor economists" although the term did not come into general use until the late 1920s (Brissenden 1926; Kaufman 1993). Of the three groups, the economists were without question the people whose writings on personnel were the most intellectually substantive, scholarly, and well represented in the academic journals during the first fifteen years of the field's existence (1915–30).

For example, to the best of my knowledge the first in-depth, evaluative studies of the new practice of personnel management published by academic faculty in scholarly journals were by two labor economists in the year 1919. The first article, "Plant Administration of Labor," was written by Paul Douglas and published in the July 1919 issue of the *Journal of Political Economy*. The second, titled "The Management of Labor," was written by Sumner Slichter and published in the December 1919 issue of the same journal. Douglas and Slichter went on to establish reputations as two of the most distinguished labor economists of the interwar period. In these articles they examine at length the origins of the new personnel management field, the management and administrative practices utilized in personnel management, and the positive impact on profits and employee relations of the new personnel methods.

The first book published by an academic devoted to the new philosophy and practice of labor management was *Industrial Goodwill* in 1919 by noted labor economist John R. Commons (Commons was president of the American Economics Association the previous year). Commons's book was not a "how to" of personnel management (not much "how to" knowledge yet existed) but rather an extended discussion of a new conceptualization of treating labor in which industrial autocracy and "drive" methods of management are replaced with more participative and cooperative methods. *The Bulletin of the Taylor Society* (1919, vol. 5, issue 5) described Commons's book as "in a class of its own" on the subject of industrial relations management (Kaufman 1998).

The beginning part of the book describes the traditional "commodity" approach then used by most firms to the hiring and utilization of labor, and the waste and inhumanity associated with it. Commons goes on to describe a new approach to labor management, which he calls a "goodwill" approach, where firms use positive management methods, rather than fear tactics and coercion, to obtain labor's cooperation and commitment. Part of this new approach, according to Commons, involves transferring responsibility for employment policy and practices from foremen to trained personnel professionals. He describes the personnel function in these terms: "The personnel function . . . is the department that deals with every human relation within and without the establishment. It is the department of industrial goodwill. . . . Raised to its proper place of equality with other departments it is the department that guides the entire establishment in the administration of justice, industrial, welfare, and service to the nation" (1919, 165).

Commons also broaches topics and ideas that years later became staples of writing and research in personnel management. For example, Commons explicitly refers to employees as "human resources" (129); describes how the government and business sectors create these human resources through investments in education and training (130); describes the existence and importance of informal work groups and notes how these groups regulate social behavior in the shop and restrict output (18–19); argues that increased work effort and efficiency must ultimately be obtained, not by use of drive methods and fear tactics, but by positive management practices that develop mutual goodwill and a community of interest between employers and employees (24–28); notes that employment security and fair dealing are crucial ingredients for creating high levels of employee motivation (72–73, 106–7); maintains that providing some form of worker participation in management (he uses the term "voice") is crucial to winning employee loyalty and commitment (110–12); states that scientific application of psychology to the management and organization of work is fundamental to the success of the enterprise (140); and denies that workers are motivated only by economic incentives (148). Also of note, Commons develops in the book a fivefold typology of different human resource management strategies, labeled the "commodity, "machine," "natural resource," "goodwill," and "citizenship" models, which in many respects anticipates efforts of management writers in the 1980s and 1990s to identify conceptually distinct HRM systems (see Wright and McMahan 1992).

Through the early 1930s economists continued to dominate academic research and writing on personnel management. Wisconsin was the center of labor research during this period, and Commons and colleagues were the preeminent names in economics-based research on personnel subjects. The three most authoritative articles by academic scholars on the state of personnel management during this period, for example, were by economists trained at Wisconsin—William Leiserson (1929), Sumner Slichter (1929), and Don Lescohier (1935). But a number of economists at other universities were also active in personnel research, including Joseph Willets and Anna Bezanson at the Wharton School's Industrial Research Unit (established in 1921), J. Douglas Brown at Princeton's Industrial Relations Section (established in 1922), and Paul Douglas at the University of Chicago (Industrial Research Unit 1989; Industrial Relations Section 1986; Kaufman 1993).

Not only were economists the foremost academic experts on personnel management at this time; economics journals were also the major place that leading personnel research was published—by both economists and noneconomists (e.g., Tead and Kornhauser in the list below). In the late 1910s and early 1920s, for example, mainline economics journals (*AER*, *JPE*, *QJE*) carried articles on personnel topics such as the following:

- labor turnover (Douglas 1918; Eberle 1919; Slichter 1920b)
- securing the initiative of workers (Wolf 1919)
- absenteeism (Frankel 1921)
- industrial morale (Slichter 1920a)
- constructing psychological employment tests (Kornhauser 1923)
- the personnel policies of the A. Nash Company (Atkins 1922)
- shop committees (Tead and Valentine 1917; Douglas 1921; Seager 1923)
- graduate training in personnel administration (Tead 1921)
- profit sharing and bonus plans (Ford 1920; Wolfe 1921)
- participative management (Hotchkiss 1920)
- incentives and output (Marshall 1920)
- scientific methods of job analysis (Kitson 1921)
- scientific management and labor welfare (Hoxie 1916)
- promotion from without (Bezanson 1921)

Two pieces of additional evidence on the leading role of economists can be gleaned from the massive 365-page bibliography of literature in personnel management, published in 1925 by William Rossi and Diana Rossi. Of all the authors cited there, economist John R. Commons had citations to more separate studies than any other person—in fact, twice as many as the next leading contender (Ordway Tead). Likewise, at the beginning of the book they provide 342 citations to "general" works in personnel management (as opposed to articles and books on specialized personnel subjects, such as training, safety, etc.). Thirty-five of these citations were to articles in academic journals, and the greatest number of these were in economics journals (13). The second and third contenders were, respectively, the *Annals of the American Academy of Political and Social Science* (8) and the *American Journal of Sociology* (6). The *Journal of Applied Psychology*, now a mainstay of theoretical and empirical research in personnel/HRM, had no articles cited, and the *Journal of Personnel Research* (a publication of the Personnel Research Federation, a nonprofit research organization with an orientation toward industrial psychology) had 1.

Finally, note must be made of two other indices of involvement in personnel management. The first is authorship of textbooks used to teach personnel management. During the 1920s, students could take coursework in personnel management in two different venues—a "labor problems" course offered by an economics department and a personnel administration course offered in a school of business. The large majority of enrollments were in the former (Bossard and Dewhurst 1931, 290), where approximately one-fourth to one-third of the course was devoted to personnel management (the remainder being devoted to a description of labor problems and the subjects of trade unionism and labor law and social insurance). The authors of the labor problems textbooks were in nearly all cases academic economists and some, like Gordon Watkins, were specialists in personnel administration (see Watkins 1922). It is worth noting that persons trained in economics departments continued to write best-selling personnel management texts up until the late 1960s. Examples include Dale Yoder, Charles Myers, and George Strauss.

The second index of involvement is participation in personnel professional associations and meetings. Economist Joseph Willets of the Wharton School, for example, was an officer and frequent speaker in the Employment Managers Association (EMA), while John R. Commons gave a number of addresses to national and local meetings of the Industrial Relations Association of America—the successor group to the EMA and a predecessor group to the American Management Association. Indicative of Commons's stature as a preeminent expert on personnel management is the fact that the editors of the journal *Personnel* (May–June 1921 issue) solicited the opinions of thirty of the nation's leading figures on the future of personnel work in industry. Of the two academics so asked, Commons was one. Economist L. C. Marshall, dean of the University of Chicago's business school, was the other.

Reasons for Economists' Involvement in Personnel Management

A variety of factors account for the active role played by economists and economic journals in the early years of the personnel management field. The two most important are personnel management's role as a solution to labor problems, and the growth of business subjects in universities.

Personnel Management and Labor Problems

The central intellectual concept around which the study of labor was built in the pre–World War II period was that of labor problems (Kaufman

1993). According to writers on the subject, labor problems took many forms and adversely affected employers, employees, and the broader society. Examples included high employee turnover, low work effort, poverty-level wages, excessive work hours, and arbitrary and often autocratic management methods. Labor problems, it was thought, grow out of various imperfections, shortcomings, and maladjustments in workplace organization, labor markets, management methods, and statute and common law. The purpose of academic research on labor was to identify both the causes of these labor problems and the methods, practices, and policies needed to resolve or ameliorate them. Most often the study of labor problems, and their resolution, was seen at that time as the province of the interdisciplinary field of industrial relations (IR)—a new field of study that emerged contemporaneously with personnel management and that subsumed the latter within it (Leiserson 1929; Kaufman 1993).

By the early 1920s a consensus had emerged that the solution to labor problems fell into three separate categories. These were typically labeled the *employers*,' the *workers*,' and the *community's* solutions to labor problems (Watkins 1922; Estey 1928). The employers' solution was personnel management and associated practices (e.g., human relations, a nonunion form of employee representation or "industrial democracy"), the workers' solution was trade unionism and collective bargaining, and the community's solution was social insurance and protective labor law. Scholars who specialized in the study of labor at this time were thus expected to be knowledgeable about three distinct specialty areas, one having to do with unions and collective bargaining, a second having to do with personnel management, and a third having to do with government law and regulation of employment conditions—all of which fell within the corpus of industrial relations.

And who were these scholars of labor problems/industrial relations? Given the interdisciplinary character of labor problems, they could have come from a variety of fields, including sociology, history, political science, management, and law. But, in actuality, the great majority were economists.

Of the three solutions to labor problems, the first one written on in a systematic, thoroughgoing way was the workers' solution of trade unionism and collective bargaining (Kaufman 1998). This line of investigation commenced in earnest with the publication of economist Richard T. Ely's book *The Labor Movement in America* (1886) and was carried forward by a large number of other economists, such as Robert Hoxie, George Barnett, and Jacob Hollander, after the turn of the century. But by popular agreement the single most influential academic person in this area of industrial relations scholarship was economist John R. Commons. Commons was Ely's student, was brought to Wisconsin by Ely in 1904, and proceeded to turn out two decades of research on trade unionism and collective bargaining that was widely acclaimed then—and remains so acclaimed now—as the leading work on the subject. Examples include his *Documentary History of American Industrial Society* (1910), *Labor and Administration* (1913), and *History of Labor in the United States* (1918).

The community's solution to labor problems was the second in chronological order to receive attention, albeit with recognition that several important ideas had been introduced earlier in the nineteenth century by Henry Carter Adams and Sidney and Beatrice Webb. But sustained research and debate on labor law per se did not really begin until the founding of the American Association for Labor Legislation (AALL) in 1906. And just as Commons was to emerge as the leading writer on trade unionism, so also did he do this in the area of labor law. He took a leading role, along with fellow Wisconsonites Richard Ely and John Andrews and several other progressive economists, such as economist Henry Seager of Columbia, in the establishment of the AALL (Moss 1996). He went on to become the nation's leading academic expert on workmen's compensation, industrial safety, unemployment insurance, and the administration of labor law. Likewise, Commons's labor law text, *Principles of Labor Legislation*, published in 1916 with Andrews and revised through four editions, was to remain the leading work of its kind through the mid-1930s.

Last in chronological order with respect to sustained scholarly research was the employers' solution to labor problems. This branch of research did not really begin in earnest until the last half of the 1910s, although important antecedent work was done by Frederick W. Taylor in his early writings on scientific management (e.g., his first published paper [1895] was titled "A Piece Rate System, Being a Partial Solution to the Labor Problem"). But among academic scholars it was again the economists who first wrote extensively on the employers' solution of personnel management, and again the leading role was played by Commons and colleagues from Wisconsin. Commons's interest in personnel management developed during 1913–15 when he served as a member of the seven-person presidential-appointed Commission on Industrial Relations. Its mission was to identify the causes of labor unrest and other labor problems and recommend remedies and solutions. Through extensive testimony of employers, plant visits with Frederick Taylor, and on-site observation of employment conditions at progressive employers, Commons came to realize that improved methods of management and personnel administration—then in their infancy—were yet another valuable approach to solving labor problems and improving industrial relations. This insight led to his book *Industrial Goodwill* (already described) and a second book, *Industrial Government* (1921). The latter is a series of case studies of "best practice" employment practices and labor relations policies at more than two dozen companies.

Not only did the Commission on Industrial Relations stimulate Commons's interest in personnel management, it also introduced other, younger economists to the subject and kindled their interest in it. The commission sponsored numerous research reports on aspects of labor problems, and Commons enlisted students and colleagues to work on them—a cadre of talent that in the next decade became many of the leading academic experts on personnel management (Kaufman 1993). Of greatest influence was Robert Hoxie's report and subsequent book (1915) on the impact of scientific management on labor. Although Taylor's theory of scientific management made little reference to personnel management per se (indeed, the term was barely known when Hoxie wrote on Taylor's system), Taylor's ideas regarding piece rate systems of compensation, functional forms of foremanship, and time and motion study nonetheless drew attention to the potential role new methods of management could play in resolving labor problems. The commission's work also drew attention to other labor problems that had heretofore gone largely unrecognized among academics. Principal among these was the astoundingly high rate of labor turnover in American industry (often 200 to 300 percent annually). Two of Commons's students—Sumner Slichter and William Leiserson—investigated the causes of and solutions to labor turnover in reports for the commission, work which was later published (Leiserson 1915; Slichter 1919b) and helped launch their careers as experts on personnel management. Labor turnover was also the subject of early works by Don Lescohier and Paul Douglas, the other two standout names among economists in the area of personnel management (Lescohier 1919; Douglas 1918).

The concept of labor problems thus provided the entrée for the extensive involvement of economists in the study of personnel management. In part, these economists were attracted to the study of labor problems because they were repelled by existing conditions of employment in American industry and saw the study of labor (including personnel management) as a way to promote reform (Eisner 1967; Douglas 1972). These scholars were also attracted to the study of labor problems for intellectual reasons. Their training was in economics, and the subject matter of economics, as defined by the leading authorities of the period, was the production and distribution of wealth through alternative social institutions (Hadley 1897; Carver 1921). Labor problems were thus within the domain of economics since they influenced the processes and outcomes of both production and distribution, while personnel management was similarly relevant because it was the method used in one particular economic institution—the business firm—to acquire and utilize the factor input labor for purposes of wealth creation.

Business Subjects as Applied Economics in Universities

The extensive involvement of economists in the formative years of personnel management arose from a second factor as well. This factor was the undeveloped state of management and the behavioral sciences (psychology, sociology, anthropology) in business school curriculums and the predominant role played by economics as the foundational discipline for business subjects.

Prior to the mid-1910s, only a handful of universities had established some form of independent, freestanding business school, most often called a school of commerce (Bossard and Dewhurst 1931). Indeed, at the time there was strong sentiment that it was inappropriate for universities to offer specialized degree programs in business, reflecting a belief that (1) business subjects were entirely vocational and lacked intellectual content and (2) proponents of business education had failed to define a coherent body of knowledge and a well-ordered curriculum. Illustrative is the caustic comment of one critic (quoted in Daniel 1998, 48) that business programs were little more than "glorified schools of typing and secretarial science."

Many of the same events and pressures that led to the birth and development of personnel management also led to a dramatic expansion in demand for training in all branches of business. The intellectual shortcomings of business administration had not been resolved, but the strong market demand for college-educated business professionals overcame the qualms of many university administrators, and a host of new programs were established. In 1911, for example, 20 universities had a business program, but by 1918 this number had more than tripled to 65 and by 1922 doubled again to 147 (Daniel 1998, 71).

Up until the 1930s economics served as the principal intellectual discipline around which business curriculums were built. Bossard and Dewhurst, for example, state in their comprehensive review of business education, written in 1931, that "the collegiate school of business is an outgrowth largely of the subject of economics. In the building of business curricula, the general assumption has been that economics is, in a peculiar sense, the foundation or basic subject to be studied" (325). Not only was economics the foundational discipline, most business faculty in this time period were trained as economists—per the comment of Willis Winn (1964, 13) that "faculties of school of business were drawn from a wide variety of academic backgrounds—the classics, mathematics, sociology, psychology, law and economics. The majority, however, held advanced degrees in economics." And, finally, courses in functional areas of business, such as finance, accounting, marketing, and personnel management, were typically viewed as offerings in "applied economics." Writing in the mid-1920s, for example, Brissenden (1926, 443) refers to personnel administration as "applied labor economics," and, looking back on the period, Carter Daniel (1998, 97) states that "business studies had from the first often been referred to as a branch of 'applied economics.'" This fact helps make sense, for example, of the decision of the editor of the *Journal of Political Economy* to publish in the May 1921 issue Ordway Tead's full-length article titled "The Problem of Graduate Training in Personnel Administration."

The foundational role economics played in business education during this time period reflected both the expansive definition given to the study of economics and the underdeveloped state of rival disciplines and fields of study. As previously indicated, economics during this period was typically defined as a science concerned with scarcity of material wealth and how humankind overcomes scarcity through the processes of production and distribution. While markets were portrayed as one institutional device through which production and distribution take place, much greater emphasis than today was also given to the complementary role of firms—illustrated by the large number of chapters in a standard text on the principles of economics devoted to the structure, operation, and management of business firms (Carver 1921). Likewise, economists often treated economics as coterminous with the study of business—per Arthur Hadley's (1897, iii) opening declaration in his economics text that its purpose is to "attempt to apply the methods of modern science to the problems of business," while the process of "economizing" was likewise frequently equated to careful *management* of resources (Carver 1921, 5). It was thus relatively natural at this time to see economics as the foundational discipline for business administration since wealth creation and "economizing" behavior were viewed as generic processes relevant to all forms of economic organization, a perspective that tended to get lost in the post–World War II period with the ascendancy of neoclassical economics and its emphasis on price, equilibrium, and market exchange.

As noted, business subjects such as personnel management were often portrayed as topics in "applied economics." At the School of Commerce at the University of Wisconsin, for example, students in the late 1920s were required to take the following business courses: business letter writing, elements of accounting, business management, marketing methods, business statistics, commercial law, and transportation and public utilities. All had an "Economics" designation (University of Wisconsin 1928). The intellectual rationale for treating these courses as part of economics is indicated in this comment by economist Ralph Heilman (1928, 74): "Economics is to the study of business what biology is to the study of medicine." The idea is that biology and economics identify, respectively, the basic principles underlying the functioning of the human body and the commercial system which provide, in turn, a foundation for the applied tools, techniques, and practical knowledge that make up the large part of the practice of medicine and business. Economist C. O. Ruggles (1928, 81) thus identified economics courses in the business curriculum as the place to learn "general principles" and business courses as the place to acquire more vocationally oriented "tools." Another way writers often made the distinction between economics and business was to identify the former as a "science" and the latter as an "art" (Sidgwick 1901). What economists brought of unique value to the study of business subjects such as personnel management at this time was thus not a body of formal theory as we know it today (microeconomic theory was still in its infancy in the 1920s) but rather a broad perspective and way of thinking about the role of business firms and practices in the production and distribution of wealth.

When the subject and vocation of personnel management suddenly rocketed into public view during and shortly after World War I, universities rushed to add this new subject to the curriculum. Indeed, courses in labor, retailing, and international trade were the three fastest growing segments of business education in the early 1920s (Daniel 1998, 80–81). One issue confronting universities was where to offer courses in labor. Since most had a department of economics (sometimes amalgamated with other liberal arts disciplines, such as sociology or political science), a frequent choice was to have economists teach it. The typical approach was to add a course in "labor problems" and to use a book on that topic, such as Adams and Sumner 1905 (and later editions), Watkins 1922, or Estey 1928. As indicated earlier, the major share of such books were devoted to unions, collective bargaining, and labor legislation and social insurance, but typically several chapters were also included on personnel management and its practice. A second approach was to offer a labor course in a business school, typically in the form of an entire course devoted to personnel management. In the personnel course, a textbook on personnel management, such as Tead and Metcalf 1920 or Scott and Clothier 1923, was most often used—the advantage being that they covered both a much greater breadth and depth of information on personnel subjects than the labor problems text. Choice of faculty to teach the personnel course confronted university administrators with a dilemma, however.

Typically, the business schools could either use a full-time faculty member—usually a Ph.D. labor economist—or a consultant or personnel practitioner hired on a part-time, adjunct basis. Both had their strong and weak points. The economists were long on theory and the "social" point of view but often only modestly acquainted with the "how to" of personnel management and often disdainful of the philosophy and practice of commerce. The typical economists' attitude and set of qualifications elicited this jaundiced comment from Tead (1921, 355): "No thought is more appalling . . . than its [personnel administration's] teaching might some day fall into the hands of the routineer or the conventional college professor of economics equipped only with the erudition which his possession of a Ph.D. betokens." Another writer (Dowrie 1928, 82) implored economists "to come down out of the air of abstract speculation and to tie in their theories with the affairs of the world about them."

The consultants and business practitioners represented the opposite side of the coin—long on the practical and vocational aspects of personnel administration but short on theory and a broader view of the place of business in the nation's social and political systems. Most authors of personnel texts came from the ranks of consultants and practitioners and—to the dismay of the intellectually inclined members of the university faculty—they gave considerable attention to the numerous administrative minutia of personnel administration, such as filling out and filing time cards. The result was that even in business schools, personnel management earned a reputation as a particularly shallow, vocational-oriented subject—per the comment of Robert Gordon and James Howell (1959, 189) that "next to the course in production, perhaps more educational sins have been committed in the name of personnel management than in any other required course in the business curriculum." The opinion of many economists was often even more critical—per the statement of economist Paul Ellsworth (quoted in Lampman 1993, 84) that "many of those courses [in the Commerce School] . . . were intellectual deserts."

Universities could, of course, try to finesse this staffing problem by hiring Ph.D. faculty to teach the personnel course but from disciplines other than economics. But the choices in this time period were thin. Doctorates in business administration—and management in particular—were largely unknown prior to World War II. The other major option was to hire a person with a Ph.D. in industrial psychology or sociology. Sociologists, however, did not become interested in employment issues in any significant degree until the 1930s and 1940s, largely as a result of the Hawthorne experiments and the writings of Elton Mayo (1933). Industrial psychologists, on the other hand, had been active in the personnel field since its birth, and their mother discipline (psychology) had by then acquired a credible standing in the academic community. For psychologists, personnel management represented "applied psychology" much for the same reason it represented applied economics for the economists (Kingsbury 1923).

But three factors caused the industrial psychologists to have less impact and visibility than the economists in the early years of personnel /HRM. One was that they came from a discipline clearly outside of business administration and thus issues of "fit" and relevance loomed larger than for economists. The second was that the research interests predominant in the 1920s in industrial psychology were quite narrow and technique oriented, which tended to keep psychologists on the margin of the personnel field and away from the "big issues" in employment (Baritz 1960). The three big topics in pre–World War II industrial psychology, for example, were employment tests, job evaluation, and work fatigue, a focus that in the words of one participant largely kept the psychologists in a "peripheral technicians' role" (Leavitt 1961, 25). And, finally, psychology as a discipline was not as well developed as economics in terms of either theory or publishing outlets in well-regarded scholarly journals.

Labor economists thus dominated academic-based research and writing on personnel management in the pre–World War II period not only due to their interest in labor problems, labor reform, and industrial relations but also because of the predominant role played by economics and economists in the business schools of that period (Shultz 1959). Personnel management was, like finance, accounting, and marketing, an area of applied economics and thus one they would be expected to teach (albeit often not as their first choice) and, furthermore, write on as a topic of research should their tastes and interests run in that direction. Some labor economists of the 1920s and 1930s, such as Paul Douglas, later abandoned research in personnel in favor of work focused more directly on labor markets and wage determination, but others, such as Sumner Slichter and Dale Yoder, maintained a lifelong interest in personnel and contributed major research works to the field in later years of their lives.

Reasons for the Separation of Economics and Personnel Management

From the mid-1930s onward a gradual separation developed between economics and personnel management, although the connection between the two remained strong until the 1970s. Indicative of economics' preeminent role even in the early post–World War II period is the title of this 1960 article by psychologist Mason Haire on the state of business education: "Business Is too Important to Be Left to the Economists." Over the next four decades, however, economics lost its position as *the* disciplinary foundation for business education, a trend reflected in the subfield of personnel/human resource management. By the late 1970s little intellectual exchange took place between labor economics and personnel/HRM, few new faculty hired to teach personnel/HRM had doctoral degrees or extensive training in economics, and few personnel topics were featured in labor economics journals.

Among the many factors responsible for the separation between economics and personnel/HRM, the following four are particularly important.

Development of Alternative Theoretical Foundations

Economics was the initial disciplinary base for business education and personnel management partly because of a lack of good substitutes. But over the years substitutes appeared and chipped away at the dominant position held by economics.

The first influence was engineering, under the impetus of the scientific management movement. The second was the development of the administrative and organizational sciences in the 1930s and 1940s, a body of knowledge originating in the work of Henri Fayol and Max Weber that sought to identify principles for the design and administration of efficient hierarchical organizations (see Wren 1994). The third and most influential development was the importation of the various behavioral sciences—most particularly psychology and sociology—into management studies. The latter occurred principally through the human relations movement of the 1940s and 1950s, and in later years through the development of organizational behavior (OB). Both subject areas stress the importance of motivation, leadership, and interpersonal and group relations to successful management (Wren 1994).

Human relations and organizational behavior provided an alternative body of theoretical constructs and research methods for teaching and research in personnel/HRM. As a result, personnel/human resource management gradually evolved from "applied economics" to "applied OB," and psychology, not economics, provided the lingua franca for scholars in the field (Strauss 1970; Kaufman 1999a). As this evolution proceeded, research and writing in personnel management became, increasingly, terra incognita to economists, while the behavioral science–trained faculty who came to dominate personnel/HRM had little familiarity with or interest in economic theory.

The Decline of Institutional Economics and the Ascendancy of Neoclassical Economics

Theoretical trends in economics also played a role in the growing split between the two fields. In the years prior to World War II, labor economists came primarily from the institutional school, and the institutional perspective made these economists far more interested in, and conversant with, the literature and concerns of personnel management (McNulty 1980; Kaufman 1993). Not only did institutional economics attempt to integrate psychology and sociology into economic theory—thus providing an intellectual bridge to the study of personnel management—but it also sought to incorporate in its theoretical corpus nonmarket mechanisms of resource allocation, such as management decision-making in business firms. Institutional labor economists were thus interdisciplinary in training and outlook and interested in management processes and methods.

Beginning in the 1940s, and accelerating in the 1960s and beyond, the institutional paradigm in labor economics was supplanted by the neoclassical paradigm. Neoclassical economics, particularly the version popularized by George Stigler and Gary Becker at the University of Chicago, largely purged psychology and sociology from economic theory, focused primarily on the operation of competitive markets, and tended to treat firms and management processes as a "black box" (Kaufman 1993, 1999b). As a result, the theoretical orientation of labor economists became increasingly divorced and even antagonistic to the concerns of personnel management.

The emergence and popularization of the new "economics of personnel" subfield in labor economics have, in the 1990s, partially brought personnel/HRM issues back to the attention of economists, albeit with much greater emphasis in the modern-day literature on theoretical model building and econometric hypothesis testing. The modern economics of personnel literature can also be thought of as applied economics, only *applied* in this case means an application of neoclassical microeconomic theory to an activity outside the core of standard economics analysis (e.g., the market determination of prices and levels of output, business fluctuations, etc.). If *applied* is used, as it was in the 1920s, in the context of art, practice, and problem solving, the new economics of personnel is largely nonapplied in that it remains an effort first and foremost at science building and only secondarily intends to inform and advance the practice of personnel/HRM.

Functionalization and Specialization of Business Education

A third development that promoted a split between economics and personnel management were several evolutionary trends in business school education. The social science "problems" perspective on the study of labor was gradually replaced, for example, by a business perspective that emphasized labor as a functional area of management practice (Daniel 1998)—an approach that tended to exclude economists. A second trend was a growing specialization in business school departments, curriculums, and courses. In the 1920s an economics department was often the organizational home for courses in personnel, finance, and marketing, but over time these subjects were transferred to their own separate departments in business schools. Likewise, while a "generalist" labor economist could adequately staff and teach a single course offering in personnel in the 1920s, over time the course offerings in personnel and related subjects (e.g., human relations) expanded and became more specialized. Increasingly, therefore, business schools found it advantageous to hire faculty who had formal training and research interests in these more specialized subjects, which again tended to exclude economists. Finally, a certain tension or "ill-fit" had always existed between economists and business schools, due in part to the liberal arts training and social science perspective of the former and the more commercial and vocational focus of the latter, and hence both sides breathed a certain sigh of relief when they could pursue their separate interests (Mears 1923).

Decline of the Field of Industrial Relations

A final factor of importance that contributed to the widening split between economics and personnel management was the gradual decline in the intellectual vitality of and faculty participation in the field of industrial relations (Kaufman 1993, 1999a). As economics and management pulled apart in the post–World War II period, the interdisciplinary field of industrial relations served as an important bridge between the two for several decades (roughly 1945–75). After World War II, several dozen universities established interdisciplinary schools and institutes of industrial relations. These programs brought together faculty from a diverse range of disciplines and fields related to the study of labor and the employment relationship, including labor economists and people specializing in personnel management, human relations, and organizational behavior. This arrangement not only provided an opportunity for labor economists to teach personnel courses but also to stay in contact with the latest theories and empirical research in personnel. Ph.D. programs in industrial relations also helped provide a pool of faculty for business schools who were trained in both economics and the behavioral/organizational sciences. Beginning in the 1960s, and accelerating after the mid-1970s, however, was a marked decline in the field of industrial relations—due partly to a narrowing in IR's intellectual boundaries from "all aspects of employment" to primarily trade unionism and collective bargaining and partly to the growing gap that separated the economists who dominated IR and the behavioral science–trained faculty who increasingly dominated personnel/HRM. Thus, as IR declined, the two groups had even less opportunity and incentive to interact, leaving economics and personnel/HRM largely as noncompeting groups after 1980.

Conclusion

For the first two decades of its existence, economics was the major intellectual influence in personnel management, labor economists were the most important and influential participants, and the subject was typically viewed as an element of "applied economics" in business school curricula. The presence of economics in personnel/HRM remained strong until the late 1960s, after which it declined sharply. Today economics and personnel/human resource management have only peripheral contact with each other either intellectually or organizationally in most universities.

The gradual separation that has developed between the two subject areas can be viewed as a product of an ongoing process of specialization and division of labor in the production and dissemination of knowledge. This process carries with it both benefits and costs. Largely lost, for example, is the holistic, problem-solving perspective brought to the study of labor and employment issues by the institutional labor economists of the 1920s. Also ranked as a cost, at least by this author, is the narrowness of perspective and theoretical approach found in most research in both modern-day labor economics and personnel/HRM—in the former case, typified by neglect of both human psychology and internal organizational features and practices of business firms; in the latter case, typified by neglect of external market forces and models of rational behavior. Counterbalancing the costs are a variety of benefits that go with the specialization and division of labor, such as an amazing advance in both the quantity and sophistication of the body of knowledge in the two fields. It would be desirable to keep the benefits and avoid the costs, but such may not be possible. Whatever the case, this essay does demonstrate that a closer relationship between economics and personnel/HRM did exist at one point, albeit now more than six decades ago. Recent theoretical advances in both fields may, possibly, help reintegrate the two fields in the years ahead.

A second conclusion that emerges from this analysis is that the definition of *applied* in economics is historically contingent. Before World War II *applied* in economics meant using economic concepts and ways of thinking to help solve and understand practical problems in life and business. Today, applied work in economics most often connotes that economic theory—generally neoclassical microeconomic theory—is used to model and generate hypotheses about areas of life and business outside of what is now conventionally defined as the corpus of economics, meaning the operation of markets and determination of price and output. Thus, applied economics is now largely an extension of what may be called science building, whereas in earlier years it was largely an exercise in problem solving. Both are illuminating but pursue different ends with different methods.

References

Adams, Thomas, and Helen Sumner. 1905. *Labor Problems*. New York: Macmillan.

Atkins, Willard. 1922. The Personnel Policies of the A. Nash Company. *Journal of Political Economy* 30 (April): 212–28.

Baritz, Loren. 1960. *The Servants of Power: A History of the Use of Social Science in American Industry*. Middletown: Wesleyan University Press.

Bezanson, Anna. 1921. Promotion from Without. *Quarterly Journal of Economics* 36 (November): 154–61.

Blakemore, Arthur. 1987. Preface. *Journal of Labor Economics* 5 (October, pt. 2): i.

Bossard, James, and J. Frederick Dewhurst. 1931. *University Education for Business*. Philadelphia: University of Pennsylvania Press.

Brissenden, Paul. 1926. Labor Economics. *American Economic Review* 16 (September): 443–49.
Carver, Thomas Nixon. 1921. *Principles of National Economy*. New York: Ginn and Co.
Commons, John R. 1910. *Documentary History of American Industrial Society*. Cleveland: Clark.
———. 1913. *Labor and Administration*. New York: Macmillan.
———. 1918. *History of Labor in the United States*. 2 vols. New York: Macmillan.
———. 1919. *Industrial Goodwill*. New York: McGraw-Hill.
———. 1921. *Industrial Government*. New York: Macmillan.
Commons, John R., and John Andrews. 1916. *Principles of Labor Legislation*. New York: Harper.
Daniel, Carter. 1998. *MBA: The First Decade*. Lewisburg: Bucknell University Press.
Douglas, Paul. 1918. The Problem of Labor Turnover. *American Economic Review* 8 (June): 306–16.
———. 1919. Plant Administration of Labor. *Journal of Political Economy* 27 (July): 544–60.
———. 1921. Shop Committees: Substitutes for, or Complements to, Trade Unions. *Journal of Political Economy* 29 (February): 89–107.
———. 1972. *In the Fullness of Time: The Memoirs of Paul H. Douglas*. New York: Harcourt Brace.
Dowrie, George. 1928. Roundtable Discussion: The Relationship between Departments of Economics and Collegiate Schools of Business. *American Economic Review* 18.1:82–84.
Dulebohn, James, Gerald Ferris, and James Stodd. 1995. The History and Evolution of Human Resources Management. In *Handbook of Human Resource Management*, edited by G. Ferris, S. Rosen, and D. Barnum. Cambridge: Basil Blackwell.
Eberle, George. 1919. Labor Turnover. *American Economic Review* 9 (March): 79–82.
Eilbert, Henry. 1959. The Development of Personnel Management in the United States. *Business History Review* 33 (autumn): 345–64.
Eisner, J. Michael. 1967. *William Morris Leiserson: A Biography*. Madison: University of Wisconsin Press.
Ely, Richard. 1886. *The Labor Movement in America*. New York: Thomas Crowell.
Estey, J. A. 1928. *The Labor Problem*. New York: McGraw-Hill.
Federal Board for Vocational Education. 1920. *Bibliography of Employment Management*. Series no. 9. Washington, D.C.: Federal Board for Vocational Education.
Ford, J. 1920. Profit Sharing in Great Britain. *Quarterly Journal of Economics* 34 (August): 777–80.
Frankel, Emil. 1921. Labor Turnover. *Journal of Political Economy* 29 (May): 487–99.

Gordon, Robert, and James Howell. 1959. *Higher Education for Business*. New York: Columbia University Press.

Hadley, Arthur. 1897. *Economics*. New York: Putnam.

Haire, Mason. 1960. Business Is too Important to Be Left to the Economists. *The American Psychologist* 15 (April): 271–72.

Heilman, Ralph. 1928. Roundtable Discussion: The Relationship between Departments of Economics and Collegiate Schools of Business. *American Economic Review* 18.1:73–74.

Hotchkiss, Willard. 1920. Participation in Management—Discussion. *American Economic Review* 10 (March):110–15.

Hoxie, Robert. 1915. *Scientific Management and Labor*. New York: Appleton.

———. 1916. Scientific Management and Labor Welfare. *Journal of Political Economy* 24 (November): 833–54.

Industrial Relations Section, Princeton University. 1986. *The Industrial Relations Section of Princeton University, 1922–1985*. Princeton: Princeton University.

Industrial Research Unit, The Wharton School. 1989. *Report on Progress: The Wharton School Industrial Research Unit and Labor Relations Council*. Philadelphia: The University of Pennsylvania.

Jacoby, Sanford. 1985. *Employing Bureaucracy: Managers, Unions, and the Transformation of Work in Industrial America*. New York: Columbia University Press.

Kaufman, Bruce E. 1993. *The Origins and Evolution of the Field of Industrial Relations in the United States*. Ithaca: ILR Press.

———. 1998. John R. Commons: His Contributions to the Founding and Early Development of the Field of Personnel/HRM. In *Proceedings of the Fiftieth Annual Meeting*, Industrial Relations Research Association, 328–41. Madison, Wisc.

———. 1999a. Evolution and Current Status of University Human Resource Programs. *Human Resource Management Journal* 38 (summer): 103–10.

———. 1999b. Expanding the Behavioral Foundations of Labor Economics. *Industrial and Labor Relations Review* 52 (April): 36–92.

———. 2001. The Theory and Practice of Strategic HRM and Participative Management: Antecedents in Early Industrial Relations. *Human Resource Management Review* (forthcoming).

Kingsbury, Forrest. 1923. Applying Psychology to Business. *The Annals of the American Academy of Political and Social Science* 60 (November): 2–12.

Kitson, H. 1921. Scientific Method in Job Analysis. *Journal of Political Economy* 29 (June): 508–14.

Kornhauser, Arthur. 1923. Scientific Method in Constructing Psychological Tests. *Journal of Political Economy* 31 (June): 401–32.

Lampman, Robert. 1993. *Economists at Wisconsin*. Madison: Board of Regents of the University of Wisconsin System.

Lazear, Edward. 1999. Personnel Economics: Past Lessons and Future Directions. *Journal of Labor Economics* 17 (April): 199–236.

Leavitt, Haorld. 1961. Toward Organizational Psychology. In *Walter Van Dyke Bingham Memorial Program*, edited by B. von Haller Gilmer. Pittsburgh: Carnegie Institute of Technology.

Leiserson, William. 1915. Movement for Public Labor Exchanges. *Journal of Political Economy* 23 (July): 707–16.

———. 1929. Contributions of Personnel Management to Improved Labor Relations. In *Wertheim Lectures on Industrial Relations*. Cambridge: Harvard University Press.

Lescohier, Don. 1919. *The Labor Market*. New York: Macmillan.

———. 1935. Personnel Management. In vol. 3 of *History of Labour in the United States, 1896–1932*, by John R. Commons, David J. Saposs, Helen L. Sumner, E. B. Mittelman, H. E. Hoagland, John B. Andrews, and Selig Perlman. New York: Macmillan.

Lewisohn, Sam. 1926. *The New Leadership in Industry*. New York: Dutton.

Ling, Cyrus. 1965. *The Management of Personnel Relations: History and Origins*. Homewood, Ill.: Irwin.

Marshall, Leon. 1920. Incentive and Output: A Statement of the Place of the Personnel Manager in American Industry. *Journal of Political Economy* 28 (November): 713–34.

Mayo, Elton. 1933. *The Human Problems of an Industrial Civilization*. New York: Macmillan.

McNulty, Paul. 1980. *The Origins and Development of Labor Economics*. Cambridge, Mass.: MIT Press.

Mears, Eliot. 1923. The Teaching of Commerce and Economics. *American Economic Review* 13 (December): 648–51.

Moss, David. 1996. *Socializing Security: Progressive-Era Economists and the Origins of American Social Policy*. Cambridge: Harvard University Press.

Rossi, William, and Diana Rossi. 1925. *Personnel Administration: A Bibliography*. Baltimore: Williams and Wilkins.

Ruggles, C. O. 1928. Roundtable Discussion: The Relationship between Departments of Economics and Collegiate Schools of Business. *American Economic Review* 18.1:79–82.

Scott, Walter, and Robert Clothier. 1923. *Personnel Management*. New York: Shaw.

Seager, Henry. 1923. Company Unions versus Trade Unions. *American Economic Review* 13 (March): 3–13.

Shultz, George. 1959. Personnel Management and Industrial Relations. In *The Education of American Businessmen*, edited by Frank G. Pierson and others. New York: McGraw-Hill.

Sidgwick, Henry. 1901. *The Principles of Political Economy*. London: Macmillan.

Slichter, Sumner. 1919a. The Management of Labor. *Journal of Political Economy* 27 (December): 813–39.

———. 1919b. *The Turnover of Factory Labor*. New York: Appleton.

———. 1920a. Industrial Morale. *Quarterly Journal of Economics* 35 (November): 36–60.

———. 1920b. The Scope and Nature of the Labor Turnover Problem. *Quarterly Journal of Economics* 34 (February): 329–45.

———. 1929. The Current Labor Policies of American Industries. *Quarterly Journal of Economics* 43 (May): 393–435.

Strauss, George. 1970. Organizational Behavior and Personnel Relations. In *A Review of Industrial Relations Research*, edited by Woodrow Ginsberg, E. Robert Livernash, Herbert Parnes, and George Strauss. Madison, Wisc.: Industrial Relations Research Association.

Taylor, Frederick. 1895. A Piece Rate System, Being a Partial Solution to the Labor Problem. *Transactions* 16:856–83.

Tead, Ordway. 1921. The Problem of Graduate Training in Personnel Administration. *Journal of Political Economy* 29 (May): 353–67.

Tead, Ordway, and Henry Metcalf. 1920. *Personnel Administration: Its Principles and Practices*. New York: McGraw-Hill.

Tead, Ordway, and Robert Valentine. 1917. Work and Pay: A Suggestion for Representative Government in Industry. *Quarterly Journal of Economics* 31 (February): 241–58.

University of Wisconsin. 1928. *Bulletin of the University of Wisconsin, 1927–1928*. Madison: University of Wisconsin.

Watkins, Gordon. 1922. *An Introduction to the Study of Labor Problems*. New York: Thomas Crowell.

Way, Philip. 1996. A Survey of Curricula of IR/HR Master's Programs: Common Features, New Directions. *Labor Law Journal* 47 (August): 535–39.

Wolf, Robert. 1919. Securing the Initiative of the Workmen. *American Economic Review* 9 (March): 120–31.

Wolfe, F. E. 1921. A Survey of Profit-Sharing and Bonuses in Chicago Printing Plants. *Journal of Political Economy* 29 (June): 521–42.

Winn, Willis. 1964. *Business Education in the United States: A Historical Perspective*. New York: The Newcomen Society.

Wren, Daniel. 1994. *The Evolution of Management Thought*. 4th ed. New York: Wiley.

Wright, P., and G. McMahan. 1992. Theoretical Perspectives for Strategic Human Resource Management. *Journal of Management* 18.2:295–320.

A Portrait of the Economics of Education, 1960–1997

Pedro Nuno Teixeira

The process of exponential growth has reached the stage where any history of our profession must, in part, be statistical.
—Michael Lovell, "The Production of Economic Literature—An Interpretation"

The economics of education is genuinely economics.
—Mary Bowman, "The Human Investment Revolution in Economic Thought"

The emergence of the economics of education as an autonomous field of study is usually associated with Theodore Schultz's presidential address to the annual meeting of the American Economic Association (AEA) in 1960.[1] In his address, reinforced later by other publications (such as *The*

Correspondence may be addressed to Pedro Teixeira, Faculdade de Economia do Porto, Rua Dr. Roberto Frias, 4200 Porto, Portugal; e-mail: pedrotx@fep.up.pt. An earlier version of this work was presented at the European Conference on the History of Economics that took place in Antwerp in April 1998. I would like to express my gratitude to the participants at the 1999 *HOPE* conference for providing stimulating discussions. A special mention is due to Jeff Biddle, Roger Backhouse, and Robert Goldfarb, whose help enormously improved, in form and in substance, my work. I am also very grateful to my colleagues António Almodovar, Maria de Fátima Brandão, and Rui Pedro Esteves, who provided me with so many valuable suggestions and comments, besides their priceless patience and support. I also thank Professor Mark Blaug for his kind comments. Notwithstanding all this help, the remaining errors and omissions are my responsibility. I would like to acknowledge the financial support of the Luso-American Foundation for Development and the Faculty of Economics at the University of Porto.

1. Reference should also be made to the work of Jacob Mincer (1958). His 1958 article on human capital investment followed his doctoral dissertation on personal income distribution, presented the year before at Columbia University.

Economic Value of Education in 1963), Schultz promoted the importance of educational benefits and of an economic approach to the analysis of education. As a result, during the sixties, a large amount of work was produced aiming at the classification and quantification of the economic benefits and costs of education. This literature usually reflected the conviction that expenditures on education had an important effect on the economic performance of individuals and of society. Therefore, governments were called upon to reinforce their financial effort in education.

In spite of a promising beginning, from the sixties until recent times the economics of education has sometimes faced skepticism from academic and political audiences, with its prestige and scope being seriously challenged. In response, research in this field has attempted to deepen knowledge about the economic value of education and has expanded to address other issues such as educational finance and the estimation of educational production and cost functions. This process of consolidation is indicated by the sustained number of publications on the economics of education and by the frequent inclusion of the economics of education in economics curricula.

The emergence and consolidation of the economics of education will be documented through an analysis of five major economics journals—the *American Economic Review* (*AER*), the *Journal of Political Economy* (*JPE*), the *Quarterly Journal of Economics* (*QJE*), the *Economic Journal* (*ECJ*), and the *Journal of Economic Literature* (*JEL*)—from the sixties until the mid-nineties.

The Economics of Education and the Rise of Human Capital Theory

Some authors claim that the economics of education is a rather old branch of economics. Maureen Woodhall (1987), for example, cites authors such as Adam Smith and Johann von Thünen. On the other hand, writers such as Mark Blaug (1970, 7) associate the field closely with human capital theory, arguing that "ten years ago there was hardly such a subject as the economics of education." In spite of these differences, there is consensus that the field took off in the sixties, following the development of human capital theory.

The attempts to define the economics of education reflect the importance of human capital theory.[2] The economics of education has been defined as the study of the allocation of resources to different types of training and schooling (Cohn 1979, 2). Blaug (1970) distinguished two main themes: the economic value of education (mainly associated with human capital theory), and the economic aspects of educational systems. Elchanan Cohn's popular textbook (1979) considered five major themes: the economic value of education, the allocation of resources in education, teachers' salaries, the financing of education, and educational planning.

For both Blaug and Cohn it is clear that the major concern involves the economic value of education and therefore human capital theory. Cohn, for example, allocates six chapters to the economic value of education, and one to each of the other four themes. In summary, the economics of education as a separate field within economics became closely associated with human capital theory.

Throughout the sixties we find evidence of increasing attention to this new perspective. One of the most important examples was Schultz's presidential address to the American Economic Association, mentioned above. Schultz (1961a) stressed the role of human capital in the promotion of individual and social economic development. Another important example was the *Journal of Political Economy*'s October 1962 supplemental issue, "Investment in Human Beings," edited by Schultz and based on a 1961 conference. Authors included Gary Becker, Jacob Mincer, Burton Weisbrod, and Edward Denison.

In 1964 Gary Becker published his monograph *Human Capital*, which some consider his magnum opus. Indeed this work, with three editions thus far (1964, 1975, and 1994), became a standard reference in all works treating education from an economic perspective. The early seventies saw a burgeoning of textbooks in the economics of education (for a complete list, see Blaug 1976a).

The increasing importance of these issues in the second half of the sixties was visible in the meetings of the American Economic Association. In 1965, the AEA had a session on the economics of

2. Consider that the 1987 *The New Palgrave: A Dictionary of Economics* does not have an entry devoted to the economics of education; rather, the reader is directed to the entry on human capital.

education[3] and a session on labor economics and the importance of knowledge. The 1969 AEA meeting had a session on the economics of education, with papers mainly dealing with higher education.[4]

In Europe attention to these subjects came later. In the forefront was Mark Blaug. In 1965 he published his famous article, "The Rate of Return on Investment in Education in Great Britain," which was "a defense of the investment approach to human resource development" (205). Blaug applies this approach to the British case, attempting to refute most of the existing criticisms of the investment perspective on education and the subsequent calculus of rates of return.[5]

About this time, Blaug also published his readings on the economics of education (1970) and his annotated bibliography of the same name (published in 1964, extended in 1966 and 1976). The former facilitated in the diffusion of some important papers.[6] His annotated bibliography documented the increasing attention to the economics of education as a field of research. In spite of all this, human capital theory and the economics of education remained much less visible in Britain and the rest of Europe.

Although this economic perspective on education seemed promising for a growing audience, some researchers expressed reservations. An example was the resistance to the use of the expression *human capital*, which led some authors to use the expression *human wealth*. This happened even among some authors who supported human capital theory's basic proposals (e.g., Blinder and Weiss 1976). Even Schultz himself sometimes used this expression (Schultz 1959).

3. Three papers were presented at the session on the economics of education: Gary Becker and Barry Chiswick's on the link between education and income distribution, Eugene Smolensky's on the effectiveness of education in the promotion of disadvantaged groups, and one on the measurement of the quality of schooling by Finis Welch.

4. The papers presented at this session focused on the supply and demand of higher education (by R. Rodner and L. S. Miller), on the distributional effects of higher education (by Lee Hansen), and on resource allocation in higher education (by Joseph Kershaw and Alex Mood).

5. A lot of Blaug's argumentation was based on research by American scholars and aimed to show that there was a strong correlation between educational attainment and future earnings. Moreover, Blaug has in mind John Vaizey, who considered that such a correlation was much weaker than the one between ability (and intrinsic capacities of the individuals) and future earnings (Blaug 1965, 217).

6. Among them were Schultz's presidential address, excerpts of Gary Becker's *Human Capital*, Burton Weisbrod's article on the external effects of education, and Lee Hansen's article on the rates of return to schooling in the United States.

An instructive example of these criticisms is Harry Shaffer's comment on Schultz's address. He criticizes Schultz on three main points: the importance of motivations other than economic ones in the demand for education, the mixture of consumption and investment elements, and uselessness of human capital theory for policy purposes (Shaffer 1961). Schultz replied that although economic motives are not the only ones to take into consideration, they are not weak or absent. He admitted that benefits other than the economic ones were also relevant for policy purposes (Schultz 1961b, 1037–39).

Growing acceptance in academic and publishing circles is illustrated by the classification indexes used by the *AEA* and the *JEL*.[7] The classification scheme claimed a distinction between human capital (production side) and the economics of education (consumption side). The former category (human capital) received mainly those works dealing with the labor market, the earnings profile, and training. The latter category included most of the research on schooling, educational production, and the benefits and costs of education.[8]

The Favorable Context of the Sixties

Most of the themes treated by Schultz and the other authors were not entirely new. Indeed, various economists from the classical era on had reflected on the benefits of education for economic growth. The interest in human capital theory and the economics of education led scholars of the sixties to search for the roots of this economic approach to education in the works of the pioneers of economic analysis.[9] One set of debates concerned Alfred Marshall's approach to human capital (cf. Kiker 1966

7. In 1968 the report of the Committee on Classification of the AEA, led by Richard Leftwich, proposed a new system of classification that included the economics of education as a subject. It was placed in the same group as the economics of health, the economics of poverty, social security, and general welfare programs, all in turn included in the group of terms under welfare economics. At the end of the sixties, the *Journal of Economic Literature* (until 1968 the *Journal of Economic Abstracts*) included human capital theory and the economics of education (consumption side) in its index of economic subjects. In 1970, the AEA's classification of themes included human capital under the group heading "Manpower, Labor, and Population."

8. This corresponds to the idea that the human capital theory spread its influence along various fields of economic analysis (Blaug 1970, 7), which is observable either in the articles published or in the listing of doctoral theses presented by the *AER*.

9. Accordingly, B. F. Kiker published, in the October 1966 issue of the *JPE*, an article titled "The Historical Roots of the Concept of Human Capital," later expanded into the book *Human Capital in Retrospect* (1968).

and Blandy 1967). However, the typical view among economists prior to the 1960s seemed to be that the demand for postcompulsory education was a demand for a consumption good (Blaug 1976b, 829).

The authors of the sixties tried to use economic concepts to develop a theory of investment of human capital with a methodology for assessing its rate of return. Hence, "it was not until the work of Gary Becker, T. W. Schultz and their colleagues that the analytical possibilities of this approach began to be realized" (Faber 1973, 1322). But what accounted for the fast and successful development of the economics of education as a field of study in the sixties? That can only be fully understood by considering the theoretical, methodological, institutional, and political frameworks in which it emerged.

A first important element was the momentum in the field of economic growth following World War II (see, for example, Rostow 1990, chap. 15). Moreover, the efforts to clarify the sources of economic growth created a space of convergence between economic growth and human capital theorists. In fact, and from its beginnings, human capital theory suggested an important link between investment in education and economic growth. The early works of human capital theorists contain numerous references to the work of Edward Denison and growth accounting research. Denison tried to identify the contribution of different productive factors to economic growth in the United States and later in other Western countries. His work suggested that the quality of the factors was more important than their quantity. In the case of labor, education represented a major source of improving its quality, hence of improving a nation's potential for growth (Denison 1966). Denison's perspective was often used by researchers on the economics of education and by human capital theorists. This was the case with Schultz, who frequently mentioned Denison's work (see Schultz 1963, 45).[10]

The convergence between economic growth theory and human capital was also visible in the field of development economics. Accordingly, the early phase of development studies gave an important role to human capital in the promotion of growth—"a necessary if not a sufficient condition of economic development" (Arndt 1987, 52). Furthermore, W. Arthur Lewis, one of the most important pioneers in this subject,

10. Schultz restated his position thirty years later by stating that "advances in knowledge are a decisive factor in economic progress" (1993, 15).

emphasized the critical function of education in the development process (Lewis 1955).

The methodological context was also favorable to the emergence of the economic approach to educational issues. It was the time of Milton Friedman's positive economics,[11] according to which economic theory should progress through the empirical testing of theoretical predictions. This would then allow a consensus "on a correct (and widely accepted) economic policy" (Friedman 1953, 6–7). This inspired what could be considered a *loose* approach to realistic assumptions, that is, simpler approaches toward economics that, nevertheless, would be compensated by an increased predictive power. It also promoted the development of an empirical drift in economics (Friedman 1953, 8–17; O'Brien 1991). The straightforward hypotheses implied by human capital theory, and the empirical testing of those hypotheses, appeared to be consistent with this approach to the development of economic theory.

In addition, certain disciplinary conditions were also important in the development of the economics of education, namely the role of the Chicago Department of Economics, as both an internationally recognized collection of economic researchers and a major training center for aspiring Ph.D. economists. In fact, some consider the emergence of the economics of education and human capital theory to be a result of the efforts of the Chicago school.[12] Becker had been trained at Chicago and would soon return there from Columbia, and Schultz had a prominent role in departmental leadership. Hence, human capital theory had at Chicago in the mid-sixties important academic support for its diffusion.

The political context presented also some interesting features that promoted the emergence of human capital theory and the economics of education. On the one hand, the spread of the Keynesian gospel paved the way for higher expenditures, including expenditures on education. In fact, the government was supposed to play, in the Keynesian framework (and based on a skepticism toward market mechanisms), a more visible role in economic management (Skidelsky 1988). In the case of education, the increase in public expenditures seemed to be not only socially popular but also economically meaningful (Svennilson 1966).

11. On the relevance of Friedman's essay and its persistence see, among others, Stewart 1991 and Blaug 1980.

12. "The modern vintage of the human capital theory was conceived and developed largely but not extensively by the Chicago School, starting around the turn of the decade of the 1950s, under the intellectual inspiration of Theodore W. Schultz" (Sahota 1978, 11).

Accordingly, human capital theory attempted to define new criteria for social investment. Resources would be allocated to levels of education and to years of schooling so as to equalize the marginal, "social" rate of return on educational investment. This equalized yield on educational investment would not fall below the yield on alternative private investments (Blaug 1976b). However, at that time there were already some doubts about the viability of defining economic criteria to allocate funds to education (Vaizey 1966).

On the other hand, some international institutions, in particular the World Bank and the Organisation for Economic Cooperation and Development (OECD), rapidly absorbed the human capital mindset. In the OECD's case, there were both political and theory-development implications A political example was the Washington conference (16–20 October 1961) on economic growth policies and educational investment. Among its main conclusions was that *investment* in education was a condition for economic growth (as important as that traditionally ascribed to capital goods). The beneficial character of education, socially and privately speaking, justified increasing levels of public funding. Several participants at this conference already referred to the expression *human capital* and espoused an investment approach to education (OECD 1962).[13]

As for theory-development activities at the OECD, an important event in the dissemination of the human capital approach was the study group on the economics of education created within the OECD. This study group, which was responsible for organizing relevant conferences in this field, worked mainly between 1962 and 1965 (Papadopoulos 1994, 39–43). Among the conferences were ones on the financing of education (September 1964) and the social objectives in educational planning (March 1965) (Papadopoulos 1994, 38).

Indeed, since World War II, but especially in the 1960s, education has increasingly benefited from a favorable attitude from government. During the 1960s governments viewed education as a major instrument for improving and equalizing social opportunities. There was a strong

13. Theodore Schultz was aware of the importance of this conference (1963, vii) and referred to it in what can be considered the first textbook exclusively devoted to the subject, *The Economic Value of Education*, which appeared in 1963. This book was quite important, for it aimed to bring "economic analysis to bear on education" (1963, 1), treating in a systematic way, among other things, the costs of education and the economic value of education.

belief that education could be a powerful force to promote social mobility. This led to what has been called the social paradigm of education (Neave 1989, 214). Accordingly, policies intending to increase access to education were promoted in most Western European countries, as well as in other OECD countries.

The Difficult Seventies and Human Capital Theory under Fire

After a promising beginning, the human capital approach was seriously challenged in the seventies by the appearance of alternative theories. The most important criticisms came from advocates of the so-called screening theories. An extreme version of the screening hypothesis asserts that education merely identifies students with particular attributes, acquired either at birth or by virtue of family background, but does not produce or improve those attributes. Therefore, education and training would not increase the productivity of individuals, but only sort them according to their innate capacities.[14] Education had private benefits but not social ones. As a result, the arguments in favor of public support of education were seriously weakened. Less extreme versions of the screening hypothesis were also proposed. According to some authors, differences in earnings among individuals should not be viewed solely as the result of differences in educational attainment (Taubman and Wales 1973, 29).[15] These criticisms created difficulties for the human-capital research program, because human capital theory tended to take tastes and abilities as given and emphasized the role of present and future earnings as determinants of the education decision (Blaug 1976b, 830).

The seventies were also characterized, in the case of labor economics and the role of education, by the emergence of some critical views, including so-called segmented labor market theories. The supporters of these theories argued that educational and training programs had not benefited poorer classes. They pointed to both the difficulties in

14. Moreover, the more extreme versions of the screening hypothesis implied that there was little reward to an uncompleted degree or certificate (cf. Blaug 1993, 29).

15. Paul Taubman and Terence Wales (1973) showed that, holding education constant, several sociodemographic and background variables were statistically significant determinants of earnings. Two years later, Joseph Stiglitz (1975) argued that education's role as a screening device in a world of imperfect information led to overinvestment in education, which would be both inefficient and inequitable.

translating increased schooling resources into increased educational achievement (e.g., the Coleman report of 1967) and the weak effect of schooling on the promotion of social mobility and in the reduction of income inequalities (Cain 1976).

These theorists also tended to see education as a screening device, because of the evidence of discrimination against minorities (Cain 1976). In an article published in the *Economic Journal*, Nicholas Bosanquet and Peter Doeringer (1973) tested for the existence of a dual labor market in Great Britain. The inclusion in the analysis of variables such as race and sex led to lower returns to education for racial minorities and women. However, in broad terms, their results were consistent with human capital theory (Bosanquet and Doeringer 1973, 421).

Another important challenge to human capital theory came with the problem of surplus schooling and overeducation.[16] This problem emerged during the seventies in the American labor market, when the number of college graduates arriving in the labor market increased at a faster rate than the market could absorb them, leading to lower wages and higher unemployment rates for graduates. Accordingly, the characteristics of a job would determine the returns to one's educational attainments, and schooling would not be rewarded similarly in all occupations. Additional schooling beyond that required for the job was not always rewarded either (Rumberger 1987).

These criticisms of human capital theory were perhaps given additional credibility by the economic context of the late seventies. The sluggish growth rates of the mid-seventies throughout the Western world called into question the inevitability of economic growth and the efficacy of education as a way of promoting that growth. Screening theory provided a theoretical basis for challenging the link between human capital and economic growth, for it held that the only contribution of education to economic growth was that of providing a selection device for employers (Blaug 1976b, 846).

One of the most contentious debates surrounded the concepts of the rates of return to education and externalities. The consideration of education as an investment led to attempts to estimate the yield of that

16. Surplus schooling was defined as workers with educational attainment in excess of that required, while overeducation (a relative concept) referred to workers with educational attainment greater than one standard deviation above the mean for their specific occupation (Verdugo and Verdugo 1989).

investment.[17] This yield, or rate of return to education, was held by human capital theorists to explain people's behavior in seeking educations of different levels and types and could be used as a guide in allocating public resources to education. (Psacharopoulos 1994, 1325). Rate-of-return estimates and calculations were used extensively in discussions of allocative efficiency by considering alternative investments within and outside education.[18]

The rate-of-return estimates were extremely important from an academic perspective, and also from a political one. As far as scholars were concerned, the rate of return was the key parameter of the human capital model of the demand of education. Moreover, the fact that estimation of the rate of return involved the application of some of the best-known instruments in the empirical economists' toolbox (such as the regression approach or the cost-benefit analysis) made it a popular area of research for scholars interested in assessing the individual and social economic impact of education (although it reduced its acceptance in other dis-

17. Indeed, the calculations of the rates of return to investment in schooling have proved to be the bread-and-butter of the human-capital research program (Blaug 1976b, 840; see also Psacharopoulos 1973, 1981, 1985, and 1994). Estimates of the rates of return can be attained by two basic methods: the "full" or "elaborate" method and the "earnings function" method. The adoption of a method depends largely on data availability (Psacharapoulos 1994, 1325). The elaborate method amounts to working with detailed age-earnings profiles by level of education and finding the discount rate that equates a stream of education benefits to a stream of educational costs at a given point in time. The annual stream of benefits is typically measured by (1) the earnings advantage of graduates of the educational level for which the rate of return is calculated and (2) the earnings of a control group of graduates with a lower educational level. The stream of costs consists of the foregone earnings of the individual while in school in a private rate-of-return calculation, augmented by the true resource costs of schooling in a social rate-of-return calculation (Psacharopoulos 1994, 1325). The basic earnings function method was primarily developed by Jacob Mincer and involves the fitting of a semi-log ordinary least squares regression using the natural logarithm of earnings as the dependent variable, and years of schooling and potential years of labor market experience and its square as the independent variables. The coefficient on years of schooling can be interpreted as the average private rate of return to one additional year of education, regardless of the educational level to which this year of schooling refers. An extended version of this method (using dummy variables) allows the estimation of the returns to education at different levels or even to different types of curricula (1325).

18. Key findings of this research were as follows: social and private returns decline over time and by level of the country's per capita income; returns to female education are higher than those for males; different types of curricula yield different returns; there are large variations in returns to higher education; returns change with the employment sector (Psacharopoulos 1994, 1327). Another significant finding was the persistent variance in terms of the private rates of return to successive years of schooling within each cohort (Blaug 1976b, 840–41).

ciplinary contexts). From a political perspective, the estimated rate of return to education provided a straightforward, easily understood, and politically effective way of presenting information on the effectiveness and appropriateness of public expenditures on education.

In spite of the vast amount of work devoted to estimating rates of return, several formal and substantive criticisms were raised.[19]

At the end of the seventies, after vivid debates on the virtues and shortcomings of human capital theory, the result was ambiguous. On the one hand, the theoretical controversy had focused academic and political attention on the economic role of education. On the other hand, the doubts raised by this debate were not yet convincingly answered. Human capital theory had lost its initial impetus, and the process of recognition within the discipline became, during this decade, more complicated than in the late sixties.

Also during the seventies there was a clear retrenchment in social and political support for governmental expenditures, including educational expenditures. The growth of unemployment promoted an increasing skepticism about educational achievements and their economic benefits. The focus of discussions of school finance issues was moving to efficiency and accountability rather than equity and social mobility. In fact, already in the seventies some governments (e.g., the U.S. government) started to reduce investment in education (decreasing funds per student), mainly due to two reasons: disbelief that education could promote economic growth and the necessity of sharing restricted resources with other competing purposes.

19. One of the main criticisms was the deficient amount of attention paid to nonpecuniary returns (either private or social). Another was the inaccuracy of most cost estimates (Leslie and Brinkman 1986, 224) due to difficulties in the computation of the costs (Hough 1994, 93–95). Yet another criticism was that most of the studies provided were cross-sectional and not longitudinal, giving a somewhat static picture. Moreover, calculations of returns were based on past and current situations, and nothing could be taken for granted in terms of future earnings (Hough 1994, 97–99). There was the problem that individuals chose not just schooling but a certain type of schooling, and few studies have attempted (and even fewer have succeeded) to calculate rates of return by type of educational institution (Blaug 1976b, 841). According to differences in the rates of return between academic subjects, some have considered that there was an overstatement of the importance of the rates of return to training and education. The evidence that some shortages of trained personnel (with promising foreseeable returns) seemed to be scarcely satisfied suggested that these rates of return had less impact than expected on individual decisions (Lindsay 1971, 1213–14). Finally, several authors pointed out the lack of consideration of quality factors in calculations of the rates of return.

Reformulations in the Eighties

Human capital theory started the eighties with its academic and political support seriously weakened. The model's seeming inability to provide a solid answer to most questions raised during the controversies of the seventies led to a loss of academic and political credibility. As a result, and following the criticisms and doubts raised by the alternative theories, human capital theorists developed reformulations of some of the model's early propositions. These reformulations, though moving toward a more complex picture of the economic role of education, did not challenge the central elements of that theory—that education was a profitable investment both in private and in social terms, and that individual decisions about how much education to pursue were made on a cost-benefit basis.

One of the most important areas of research in this period of reformulation was that of educational quality: how it should be measured and the link between it and expenditures on education. These studies often focused on educational levels other than the postsecondary level.[20] Their most distinctive character was the claim that efforts should not exclusively aim at increasing resources ascribed to the system (e.g., teachers, equipment), since the quality and effectiveness of resources also mattered (Hanushek 1986).[21] The quality of resources and the efficiency with which they were allocated received increasing attention, as educational expenditures and wealth grew (Solmon 1985). In addition, returns to education appeared to be significantly related to some measures of school quality (Card and Krueger 1992, 14).

The attention given to quality issues reinforced a previous trend toward more caution about the funding of education. An interesting focus was the trade-off between efficiency and equity in funding. This issue, already important during the seventies,[22] attracted even more attention in

20. Some good examples are Behrman and Taubman 1989, Solmon 1985, Hanushek 1986, and Card and Krueger 1992.

21. An interesting finding to emerge was that educational quality was important in the reduction of inequalities in personal income distribution, namely in the case of some ethnic minorities. Indeed, some studies reported that quality of education had to be taken into consideration in the assessment of the impact of education on labor market performance and lifetime earnings of ethnic minority cohorts (Smith and Welch 1989).

22. The importance of this issue during the 1970s was visible in the workshop organized at the University of Chicago (June 1971) that was the main source of articles published in the May/June 1972 supplemental issue of the *JPE* titled *Investment in Education: The*

the eighties.[23] A central theme in the discussion was that tuition should be seen as a price, education as a service, and students and their families as clients. This perspective, already discussed in the *JPE* supplement of 1972 (see, for instance, Schultz 1972), gained increased relevance during the eighties. Furthermore, explorations of this theme flourished during the nineties, with the so-called market approaches to education.[24]

The analysis of funding issues was closely related to the crucial issues of equity and social mobility. The mid-seventies displayed a less confident view of the role of education in the promotion of a more equitable income distribution. This crisis of confidence was strengthened by the emergence of critical views of human capital theory and by disappointing results from analyses of income and wealth effects of education for some disadvantaged groups. Other controversial discussions involved the mechanisms of funding education and their consequences. In fact, some researchers had been arguing since the early seventies that the method used to finance systems of state-supported higher education could lead the net distributional effect of those systems to be regressive (cf. Hansen 1970).

Therefore, with respect to equity questions, the late seventies and most of the eighties were a *reflux* period, displaying a more skeptical and complex attitude. Intensive debate tended to give more importance to noneducational factors and their interaction with educational achievement in the future distribution of income and wealth. The importance of external factors tended to be stressed in the case of unequal access.[25]

In terms of the policy attitude there was also an increasing emphasis on quality (not only or necessarily more money or more quantity) and on evaluation systems (see, e.g., World Bank 1994), an emphasis that goes hand in hand with the *accountability* procedures that have pervaded

---

Equity-Efficiency Quandary. In the same year, this supplement was also published as a book by the University of Chicago Press.

23. See, for example, the collective volume edited by Walter McMahon and Terry Geske and published in 1982, suggestively titled *Financing Education: Overcoming Inefficiency and Inequity*.

24. See the collective volume edited by Elchanan Cohn in 1997 titled *Market Approaches to Education*, which contains various articles published in journals from 1984 to 1997 on the economic rationale for government intervention in education and the performance of public versus private schools.

25. Some authors have, nevertheless, clarified that even equal access does not mean equal opportunities, since family environment and family resources make a substantial difference in children's opportunities (Behrman, Pollak, and Taubman 1989, 399).

public services since the 1980s. Thus, the belief that education was important to economic growth was no longer enough to justify public support for higher education. Educational institutions needed to find (quantitative) ways of proving their economic relevance to increasingly skeptical political decision-makers.

The Renewed Trust of the Nineties in Education's Economic Potential

The turn from the late eighties to the nineties was characterized by an increase in confidence in the fundamental utility of the human capital model. Although it was an important challenge, the screening hypothesis ultimately proved less resilient than the human capital model in that it failed to produce a truly alternative, empirically confirmed theory of the demand for education (Blaug 1976b, 1981).[26] Moreover, the screening hypothesis never really questioned the private benefits of education. It implicitly assumed the investment perspective on education (as the human capital theory), rather than the presixties dominant consumption perspective on education (Lazear 1977, 569–71).

The sorting models developed since the eighties also illustrate this capacity for resistance on the part of human capital theory. These models represented a compromise between the human capital and the screening theories, allowing for a productivity effect due to educational investment and some filtering behavior of educational institutions. In fact, higher productivity was modeled as a joint result of acquired and innate capacities, and education had both a sorting and a learning effect on individuals (Weiss 1983, 1995).

Thus, the human-capital research program has moved steadily away from some of its early naive formulations. The criticisms of the screening theorists tended to show that the relationships between education and income were more complex than any single model had demonstrated (Kodde and Ritzen 1988). The result was the emergence of a picture of the economic value of schooling somewhat more skeptical toward the belief that education makes workers more productive and that employers pay them more because they are more productive (Blaug

26. Richard Freeman (1986, 362) summarized the situation as follows: "The general tone of the findings is supportive of the human capital view. Screening/signalling effects are undoubtedly part of the world, but no empirical study has found them to be a major factor in the demand of education."

1993, 31). These reformulations did not, however, affect the theoretical nucleus of the human capital approach.

This skepticism toward the economic value of education is also manifested in the debate on the issue of externalities and the nonpecuniary benefits associated with education, a debate that was ongoing throughout the period analyzed.[27] More recent empirical research has tried to overcome the main criticisms (the subjective nature of the externality concept and ignorance about their real magnitude). Moreover, they aimed to substantiate the existence and relevance of the nonpecuniary benefits,[28] arguing that, although these benefits were not greatly visible in rates-of-return calculations, their importance should not be underestimated.[29] (For a review of this empirical research on externalities of education, see Haveman and Wolfe 1984 and Wolfe and Zuvekas 1997.) However, and in spite of these efforts, several academics remained skeptical on the issue of externalities and nonpecuniary benefits.[30]

Following the general path of the field, the nineties were also characterized by a recovery of the interest in the equity effects of education, although not to the level of the late sixties and early seventies.

The resurgence of the credibility of human capital theory was also visible in research on the determinants of labor market outcomes.[31] In spite of the criticisms of the human capital approach developed since the mid-seventies, the existence of a link between schooling and earnings

27. Blaug (1976b) pointed out the subjective and qualitative judgments associated, in the education framework, with issues of externalities. Most of the skepticism involved higher levels of education: "There is a kind of cyclical pattern in their beliefs. In the 1960s, the standard view was that these externalities were large in relation to the private benefits of higher education. Later, they were supposed to be negligibly small. . . . the pendulum may now be swinging in favor of higher education" (De Meulemeester and Rochat 1995, 352).

28. This followed Schultz's initial claim (1963) for the need to inquire about the social benefits and their magnitude, one of the best documented being the one existing between education and good health (cf. Kenkel 1991, 287).

29. According to one of the leading scholars in the field, "If people are willing to invest in their education, in spite of low private returns, they must be deriving some value other than monetary" (Psacharopoulos 1994, 1334).

30. This critical stance is obviously more evident in skeptics of the human capital approach: "I am not convinced that the externalities are very important, as contrasted with elementary and secondary education where externalities are undoubtedly consequential. It is somewhat hard for me to visualize what these externalities consist of" (Arrow 1993, 8).

31. This evolution can be illustrated by the assessment that one leading labor economist, Sherwin Rosen, made of the impact of the human capital approach on labor economics. The tone of his writings in the nineties was clearly more benevolent (almost hagiographic in some respects) than that of his writings in the seventies (cf. Rosen 1977, 1992).

continued to be regarded by economists as a robust empirical result and an article of faith.[32] The persistence of a fundamental belief in this link was due mainly to the fact that further research tended to see the empirical evidence of overeducation as the product of a certain historical context, not of a permanent relationship between education and the labor market.[33] In any case, the nineties saw an outpouring of new empirical research on the education/earnings link. This was driven in part by the availability of richer data on individual labor market outcomes, but also perhaps by the more complex picture of the relationship between educational achievement and labor market performance that emerged from attempts to reformulate the human capital model.[34]

The nineties also saw a renewed interest in models of economic growth, in particular those that center on human capital accumulation.[35] The recently fashionable endogenous growth models, for example, gave education and human capital accumulation a place of prominence.[36] The

32. As stated recently in a reevaluation of the link between social mobility and higher education, "While no longer a guarantee for job security or for a guaranteed salary, the link (between educational attainment and employment) still persists" (Nowotny 1995, 75).

33. Nevertheless, the education-earnings relationship is regarded by some authors as more complex than the standard human capital model would suggest. For example, it seems to vary widely across occupational groups (Rumberger 1987). Although the alternative theories failed to produce conclusive empirical support, their criticisms led human capital theorists to reexamine their theory by considering previously omitted variables (Cain 1976) and by enlarging their perspective (which was too concentrated on the educational component) (Sahota 1978, 12).

34. See, for example, the policy forum on the economics of youth training published in the *ECJ* (September 1993), which treated the cases of Britain, Germany, and the United States. Other examples can be found in the notes from the annual meetings of the AEA during the nineties, published as a supplement of the *AER* (see especially the one published in 1993). There were sessions on women and labor market conditions and on the importance of race, age, and sex in employability and income conditions (see also the February 1992 issue of the *QJE*).

35. Although these models of economic growth with emphasis on human capital were already being discussed in the second half of the eighties (cf. Solow 1991).

36. According to most of the endogenous growth theorists, "The engine of growth is human capital" (Ehrlich 1990, S4). This was confirmed by most of the authors who participated in the conference on development (May 1988) that originated the supplemental issue of the *JPE* published in October 1990. The work of authors like Paul Romer, Robert Barro, and Sérgio Rebelo gave again an increasing economic importance to human capital. Accordingly, the *ECJ* published a policy forum in May 1992 on the determinants of economic growth. The *AER* had already published in 1987 what has become one of the classic articles on economic growth, Paul Romer's "New Theories of Economic Growth" (presented at the 1986 meeting of the AEA), as well as articles from a session on the new growth theory (presented at the 1989 meeting of the AEA).

developments of both the Lucas approach (inspired by the work of Gary Becker) and the Nelson-Phelps approach (assuming complementarity of education and R and D activities) converged in their emphasis on the positive effect of educational attainment. This positive effect was visible in the productivity of workers, with an important growth enhancing effect (Aghion and Howitt 1998, chap.10).

These recent theories of economic growth also gave a prominent role to the public authorities and public expenditures, in that public investment in human capital could play an important role in the promotion of intergenerational social mobility, in the avoidance of low-development traps, and in enhancing the mobility of workers, all of which would have positive long-run effects in terms of growth (Aghion and Howitt 1998, chap. 10). Therefore, Schultz could recently reaffirm his view that it was the acquired abilities of people—their education, work experience, skills, and health—that explained most of modern economic progress.[37]

The Economics of Education in Economics Journals (1969–1996)

The analysis of the process of emergence and consolidation of the economics of education will now be complemented with a review of the five economics journals indicated in the introduction.[38] These were chosen since they have been consistently considered as some of the core journals in economic theory.[39] As described above, the emergence of the

37. "It is 'human capital,' not space, cropland, energy or other physical properties of the earth, that is decisive in improving the income and welfare of people in the modernizing economy"(Schultz 1993, 18).

38. The period of analysis was restricted to 1969–96, first because it was only by the end of the sixties that this field of research became distinct, and second because the database used in this analysis (taken from the *Econlit* database) starts in 1969. Due to space constraints, only a summarized view of the results will be presented. More detailed data are available from the author, upon request.

39. In spite of an observed decline in the quantitative importance of the top economics journals over the period 1965–90, their relevance to economics continues. This is supported by factors such as the persistence of inequality among the importance of economics journals, evident in the fact that the inequality in the distribution of citations (and of importance) remained almost constant from 1970 to 1990 (Laband and Piette 1994, 656–57). Some decrease in the relevance of the core journals in economics is possibly related to the increasing importance and influence of a number of specialized journals. Indeed, the success of some may reflect the advantages of specialization (Laband and Piette 1994, 657). This indicates that the information provided by the analysis of these five journals should be, in a future work, complemented by an analysis of other journals, namely those that specialize in the field. Among them, special

Table 1 Articles on the economics of education and on the human capital theory

	Economics of Education			Human Capital Theory		
Period	Total Number of Articles	Articles per Year	Percentage of Total Articles	Total Number of Articles	Articles per Year	Percentage of Total Articles
1969–70	16	8	1.9	13	6.5	1.5
1971–80	72	7.2	1.6	166	16.6	3.7
1981–90	34	3.4	1.0	57	5.7	1.6
1991–96	51	8.5	2.4	127	21.2	6.0

Source: *Econlit* database.

economics of education as a separate field of economic analysis is explicitly linked with the development of human capital theory. Therefore, the analysis looks at not only those articles focusing on the economics of education, but also at those focusing on human capital issues.

The evidence provided by the publishing activity of the major economics journals (table 1) mostly confirms the evolution described above for both the economics of education and human capital theory. The early phase (late sixties and early seventies) was a rather favorable period for the diffusion of this field of study and this theoretical approach, both of which achieved an important visibility in those journals, either in absolute or in relative terms. Most of the comments that follow below apply to the economics of education and human capital theory.

The total number of articles increased from the late sixties to the seventies, decreased in the eighties, then significantly increased in the nineties. This pattern generally holds for the average number of articles per year and the relative weight of both subjects.

---

reference should be made to the *Economics of Education Review* (founded in 1981) and the *Journal of Human Resources* (founded in 1966). One additional element in the perception of the consolidation process of the scope of this field of study is provided by the structure of the main textbooks on the subject. This can be a further source of valuable information about the evolution of the economics of education as a field of study. The emphasis on different areas of interest within this subject changed visibly, reflecting not only the interests and progress of research, but also the changing social and political context. However, in this paper, I decided to concentrate on the core journals.

When comparing the two fields of research, the quantitative importance of human capital theory is frequently higher than that of the economics of education. The human capital field exhibited a more dynamic pattern during the seventies than did the economics of education. The late seventies and the eighties were periods of retrenchment, due to the difficulties faced by human capital theory (inevitably affecting the economics of education). If in the seventies the theoretical debate, led by the alternative theories, promoted visibility, in the eighties doubts about human capital theory reduced academic attention to issues relating to education, among economic circles. However, the economics of education seems to have suffered less from a loss of interest during the eighties. The enlargement of its scope to other themes such as the efficiency of educational expenditures may have prevented a larger decrease. Again, the events of the nineties had a more visible effect on human capital theory than on the economics of education. The reformulations and the complexity introduced into the analysis of economic effects of education since the mid-eighties strengthened the credibility of both the human capital theory (hereafter, HCT) and the economics of education, as reflected in the generally greater attention given to them in these journals in the early nineties.

An analysis of a larger pool of journals complements that of the leading economics journals. In this case we will use the index of economic articles published in current journals (as published in each edition of the *JEL*).

Starting with low values (even when taken together), the importance of both the economics of education and HCT rose rapidly, almost doubling in importance in the articles published in economics journals (table 2). However, this was followed by a steady decrease during the second half of the seventies. The eighties followed this trend and can be characterized as a period of reflux (with a combined value of around 1 percent in some years). The nineties saw a renewed attention to both issues, with values similar to those obtained in the earliest period.

In general we cannot consider the values obtained as high, since the aggregated value is always under 2 percent. Thus, the number of articles devoted to both issues seems to be higher in the case of the main journals (previously analyzed) than in the larger group of journals.

The importance of the economics of education seems to be closer to that achieved by the HCT articles, with the latter presenting a less stable picture (with even wider variations in the annual values). More

Table 2 Relative importance of human capital theory and the economics of education in the index of economics journals

Period	Human Capital Theory	Economics of Education
1970–75	0.77	0.73
1976–80	0.63	0.69
1981–85	0.45	0.52
1986–90	0.41	0.65
1991–96	0.82	0.60

Source: *Journal of Economic Literature*. Values correspond to the ratio between the number of pages devoted to the topics and the total number of pages devoted to all economic subjects covered by the economics journals considered by the *JEL*, and for each period.

specifically, HCT seemed to be more affected by the reflux trend that characterized the eighties, as well as by the increased attention given to the economic effects of education during the nineties. Moreover, HCT finished with its higher values, doubling the score of the preceding period.[40] The economics of education seemed to resist better the difficulties subsequent to the emergence of critical views on the HCT. This capacity of resistance was probably related to its capacity of broadening/diversifying its focus to issues like funding, quality, and efficiency.[41]

Main Themes in the Publication Activity of the Core Journals

The publication activity in the field of the economics of education and HCT, during the period 1969–96, can be analyzed in terms of nine themes, considered the most relevant among the economics of education.

The quantitative analysis (as shown in table 3) of the evolution of the articles published in major journals supports roughly the evolution previously described. Accordingly, the themes reflecting a more positive approach toward the economic role of education and its benefits saw their visibility decrease in the late seventies, after a promising beginning (table 3). The reduced visibility continued through the eighties but

40. Regarding the analysis of this result, bear in mind the changes in the classification index used by the *JEL*.

41. This change was also visible in the main textbooks on the subject. Those published in the nineties tended to emphasize financial, efficiency, and effectiveness issues rather than HCT and cost-benefit analysis, which textbooks in the seventies stressed.

Table 3 Articles in the economics of education and human capital theory, by theme (core economics journals)

	Economics of Education				Human Capital Theory			
Main Themes	1969–70	1971–80	1980–90	1991–96	1969–70	1971–80	1981–90	1991–96
Economic growth and development	1	4	3	18	4	10	3	27
Benefits, costs, and rates of return	1	5	—	5	1	15	2	11
Finance, efficiency	5	20	8	8	—	4	3	1
Screening, alternative theories	—	5	—	2	—	19	3	1
Labor markets	—	2	1	5	—	23	8	43
Human capital	—	12	10	4	4	48	22	32
Equity, minorities, and income distribution	3	7	3	3	—	30	13	16
Quality, special programs	—	—	4	4	1	4	3	1
Others	2	3	5	2	2	5	1	—

Note: The category human capital includes all the articles on the core of human capital theory: that individuals demand (invest) in education and training because they expect this will enhance their future earnings; earnings will be higher since with more education and training individuals will become more productive; being more productive, and under the assumption that the factors are paid at the marginal level, the revenue of those people who are more productive will be higher.

reversed itself during the nineties. The themes that suggest a positive economic role for education are as follows: economic growth and development; benefits of education and externalities; equity, minorities, and income distribution; and labor market issues. The alternative theories were mostly present, as expected, during the seventies, and quite absent after that time. Quality issues appeared only later. The financial issues gained increased relevance in the seventies, probably due to factors external to academia (such as problems with weak economic growth and restricted public funding). Although the financial issues lost some of their previous importance during the following decades, they still remained among the more relevant themes in the economics of education.

The results obtained by the classification of the articles published on HCT in major journals roughly endorse the comments made regarding the economics of education. The improved visibility of the seventies was a joint effect of the diffusion of the HCT and of its alternative theories, being a good period for both. Hence, the theoretical discussion had a positive short-term effect on the disciplinary visibility of HCT (and the economics of education). This was also a good period for issues such as economic growth, the labor market, equity, and externalities related to education. On the contrary, the eighties were characterized by a reflux in the attention given to all these issues. Again, rising doubts about HCT lessened interest in both it and the economics of education. In some cases there were important reductions in the number of articles (mainly those on economic growth and externalities, but also those on screening theories). The nineties were also characterized by increased attention. Special mention should be made of economic growth, labor market issues, and externalities.

Some Methodological Aspects of the Articles in the Core Journals

Finally, in table 4 the articles published on the economics of education in four of the five main journals are classified according to whether their main emphasis is empirical or theoretical.[42] Two main groups were considered. The first group included the articles of a pure theoretical type or those that developed a simulation approach (also on a theoretical basis). The second contained those of the empirical type, either using new data or data already presented in other published applications/articles. New data includes not only surveys developed by the authors, but also those applications (for the first time) to official statistics or data.[43]

As expected there were more papers of the empirical type. These represented half of the papers devoted to the economics of education in four of the main economics journals (and even when ignoring those articles that presented known data). The category of theoretical papers showed an increase in the nineties, namely in the highly formalized articles. This reflected the more generalized trend, among economics, of privileging papers with a higher degree of mathematical complexity. Interestingly,

42. Due to its idiosyncracies, the *JEL* was excluded from this analysis, since its articles survey recent literature or report on the state of the art, rather than present original research, as is typical of other journal articles.

43. This classification was inspired by one used in an article by Daniel Hamermesh, which partially drew from a classical note from Wassily Leontief (Hamermesh 1996).

Table 4 Classification of journal articles in the economics of education

Period	Purely Theoretical	Adopt a Simulation Approach	Empirical, Using New Data	Empirical, Using Data in Articles Already Published	Total
1969–70	1 (0.10)	—	7 (0.70)	2 (0.20)	10 (1.0)
1971–75	14 (0.46)	2 (0.07)	12 (0.40)	2 (0.07)	30 (1.0)
1976–80	3 (0.20)	1 (0.07)	7 (0.46)	4 (0.27)	15 (1.0)
1981–85	5 (0.36)	—	7 (0.50)	2 (0.14)	14 (1.0)
1986–90	3 (0.20)	—	9 (0.60)	3 (0.20)	15 (1.0)
1991–96	17 (0.38)	—	22 (0.49)	6 (0.27)	45 (1.0)
Total	43 (0.33)	3 (0.02)	64 (0.50)	19 (0.15)	129 (1.0)

this was also observable in an applied field such as the economics of education. The third category in terms of the number of papers—empirical articles using data already used by other researchers—also seemed to have more importance in the later years.

The material conditions that allowed an easier application of mathematical models to statistical data can help to explain the growth of empirical papers that use previously analyzed data. In fact, most of the papers presented in the second category were mere applications of statistical and econometric techniques to available data and did not involve the development or use of new data.

The Emergence and Consolidation of the Economics of Education: An Attempt at an Epilogue

Since the early sixties, the economics of education and HCT have gained increased prominence in the economic profession. However, the economic approach to thinking about education did not raise enthusiastic reactions from other social scientists, who, in most cases, remained quite skeptical toward it. Instead, this field of economics tended to consolidate by developing links almost exclusively with other fields inside economics. The strongest links were developed with labor economics and with the theory of economic growth. The empirical techniques employed were those that had already been introduced in other fields of economics, including cost-benefit analysis and regression analysis of both cross-sectional and panel data. Hence, the economics of education consolidated as a field of study by enhancing its economic side.[44]

Early research on the economics of education that tended to place emphasis on the benefits of education soon came to be regarded rather skeptically by others in the field. This was visible in the case of the alleged ability of education to promote equity. Serious doubts were also raised about the effectiveness of education in the promotion of social mobility. Increasing financial pressures faced by governments led to an increased emphasis on research into the quality of education and on efficiency in the allocation of resources to education; less attention was given to questions of access to and the social role of education.

Another interesting aspect of this field of study is its impact on policy circles. The sixties and the early seventies can be characterized by a rapid absorption of the main arguments of HCT into policy discussions, providing some theoretical basis for increased public expenditures on higher education. However, the alternative theories, although they ultimately did not replace the human capital model as the basic conceptual framework employed by economists in thinking about education, did succeed in creating a sense of skepticism about the social and economic benefits of education.[45] This effect, enhanced by increased financial restrictions on public expenditures, created, in subsequent years, a more difficult context for educational expenditures. Moreover, this skepticism remained in spite of the resurgent academic interest in HCT in the late eighties and nineties.

The picture of this field of study that emerges from the analysis of the five core journals at the end of the period is rather different from that of the early days. The optimism of the early phase (the sixties), in which the link between education and economic benefits seemed to be clear and straightforward, was gradually weakened during the following years.[46]

44. The analysis of the main textbooks published on the subject, since the seventies, indicates the increasing role of commonly used economic techniques in the consolidation of this field of study (not only the more generalized econometric practices, but also others borrowed from operational research).

45. The most successful of the alternative theories were the screening ones, probably due to the fact that these competed for the same audience and had a similar approach to economic theory as the HCT (i.e., both human capital and screening theories navigate in neoclassical waters).

46. Arthur Goldberger (1979), who considers it almost impossible to disentangle the genetic and environmental factors affecting human capabilities, impressively discusses this complexity in an insightful paper.

Furthermore, the vivid debates of more than three and a half decades produced a more complex view of the role of education in the promotion of private and social economic progress. However, despite the criticisms and doubts raised through the last three decades, the basic proposition that education and training make individuals more productive (thus, they may expect higher earnings, due to this higher productivity) has persisted and today seems to be as widely accepted as ever by academics, politicians, and the general public.

References

Aghion, Philippe, and Peter Howitt. 1998. *Endogenous Growth Theory*. Cambridge: MIT Press.

Arndt, H. W. 1987. *Economic Development—The History of an Idea*. Chicago: University of Chicago Press.

Arrow, Kenneth. 1993. Excellence and Equity in Higher Education. *Education Economics* 1.1:5–12.

Barr, Nicholas. 1993. Alternative Funding Resources for Higher Education. *Economic Journal* 103 (May): 718–28.

Becker, Gary. 1962. Investment in Human Capital: A Theoretical Analysis. *Journal of Political Economy* 70.5:9–49.

———. 1964. *Human Capital*. New York: Columbia University Press.

Behrman, Jere, and Nancy Birdsall. 1983. The Quality of School: Quantity Alone Is Misleading. *American Economic Review* 73.5:928–46.

Behrman, Jere, and Paul Taubman. 1989. Is Schooling Mostly in the Genes? Nature-Nurture Decomposition Using Data on Relatives. *Journal of Political Economy* 97.6:1425–43.

Behrman, Jere, Robert Pollak, and Paul Taubman. 1989. Family Resources, Family Size, and Access to Financing for College Education. *Journal of Political Economy* 97.2:398–419.

Blandy, Richard. 1967. Marshall on Human Capital: A Note. *Journal of Political Economy* 75.6:874–75.

Blaug, Mark. 1965. The Rate of Return on Investment in Education in Great Britain. *Manchester School* 33.3:205–51. Reprinted in *The Economics of Education and the Education of an Economist*, by Mark Blaug. Aldershot, England: Edward Elgar, 1987.

———. 1976a. *The Economics of Education: An Annotated Bibliography*. 3d ed. Oxford: Pergamon Press.

———. 1976b. The Empirical Status of Human Capital Theory: A Slightly Jaundiced Survey. *Journal of Economic Literature* 14.3:827–55.

———. 1980. *The Methodology of Economics*. Cambridge: Cambridge University Press.

———. 1981. *Educación y Empleo*. Madrid: Instituto de Estudios Económicos.

———. 1985. Where Are We Now in Economics of Education? *Economics of Education Review* 4.1:17–28.

———. 1993. Education and the Employment Contract. *Education Economics* 1.1:21–33.

———, ed. 1970. *Economics of Education 1*. London: Penguin.

Blinder, Alan, and Yoram Weiss. 1976. Human Capital and Labor Supply: A Synthesis. *Journal of Political Economy* 84.3:449–72.

Bosanquet, Nicholas, and Peter Doeringer. 1973. Is There a Dual Labor Market in Great Britain? *Economic Journal* 93.330:421–35.

Bowman, Mary Jean. 1966. The Human Investment Revolution in Economic Thought. Reprinted in *Economics of Education 1*, edited by Mark Blaug. London: Penguin, 1970.

Cain, Glen. 1976. The Challenge of Segmented Labor Market Theories to Orthodox Theories: A Survey. *Journal of Economic Literature* 14.4:1215–57.

Campbell, Robert. 1977. The Keynesian Revolution 1920–1970. In vol. 6 of *The Fontana Economic History of Europe*, edited by Carlo Cipolla. London: Collins.

Card, Davis, and Alan Krueger. 1992. Does Quality School Matter? Returns to Education and the Characteristics of Public Schools in the United States. *Journal of Political Economy* 100.1:1–40.

Chamberlain, Neil. 1967. Some Second Thoughts on the Concept of Human Capital. Reprinted in *Human Capital and Manpower Development*, edited by Ronald Wykstra. New York: Free Press, 1971.

Cohn, Elchanan. 1979. *The Economics of Education*. 2d ed. Oxford: Pergamon.

———, ed. 1997. *Market Approaches to Education: Vouchers and Social Choice*. Oxford: Pergamon.

Cohn, Elchanan, and Terry Geske. 1990. *The Economics of Education*. 3d ed. Oxford: Pergamon.

Colander, David, and A. Coats, eds. 1989. *The Spread of Economic Ideas*. Cambridge: Cambridge University Press.

De Meulemeester, Jean Luc, and Denis Rochat. 1995. A Causality Analysis of the Link between Higher Education and Economic Development. *Economics of Education Review* 14.4:351–61.

Denison, Edward. 1966. Measuring the Contribution of Education to Economic Growth. In *The Economics of Education*, edited by J. E. Vaizey and E. A. G. Robinson. New York: Macmillan and St. Martin's.

Eagly, Robert. 1975. Economic Journals as a Communication Network. *Journal of Economic Literature* 13.3:878–88.

Ehrlich, Isaac. 1990. The Problem of Development: Introduction. *Journal of Political Economy* 98.5:S1–S11.

Faber, Robert. 1973. Consumer Economics: A Survey. *Journal of Economic Literature* 11.4:1303–42.

Freeman, Richard B. 1986. Demand for Education. In vol. 1 of *Handbook of Labor Economics*, edited by Orley Ashenfelter and Richard Layard. Amsterdam: Elsevier.

Friedman, Milton 1953. *Essays in Positive Economics*. Chicago: University of Chicago Press.

Goldberger, Arthur S. 1979. Heritability. *Economica* 46.184:327–47.

Greenaway, David. 1993. Economic Aspects of Youth Training in Industrialised Countries: Editorial Note. *Economic Journal* 103 (September): 1259–60.

Hamermesh, Daniel. 1996. Doing Applied Economics: Positive and Normative Aspects. In *Foundations of Research in Economics: How Do Economists Do Economics*? edited by Steven Medema and Warren J. Samuels. Cheltenham, England: Edward Elgar.

Hansen, W. Lee. 1970. Income Distribution Effects of Higher Education. *American Economic Review* 60.2:335–40.

Hanushek, Eric. 1986. The Economics of Schooling: Production and Efficiency in Public Schools. *Journal of Economic Literature* 24 (September): 1141–77.

Haveman, Robert H., and Barbara Wolfe. 1984. Schooling and Economic Well-Being: The Role of Nonmarket Effects. *Journal of Human Resources* 19 (summer): 378–407.

Hough, J. R. 1994. Educational Cost-Benefit Analysis. *Education Economics* 2.2:93–128.

Jaffe, Adam. 1989. Real Effects of Academic Research. *American Economic Review* 79.5:957–70.

Johnes, Geraint. 1993. *The Economics of Education*. London: Macmillan.

Kenkel, Donald. 1991. Health Behavior, Health Knowledge, and Schooling. *Journal of Political Economy* 99.2:287–305.

Kiker, B. F. 1966. The Historical Roots of the Concept of Human Capital. *Journal of Political Economy* 74.5:481–99.

———. 1968. *Human Capital in Retrospect*. Columbia: University of South Carolina Press.

Kodde, David, and Jozef Ritzen. 1988. Direct and Indirect Effects of Parental Education Level on the Demand for Higher Education. *Journal of Human Resources* 23.3:356–71.

Laband, David, and Michael Piette. 1994. The Relative Impact of Economic Journals: 1970–1990. *Journal of Economic Literature* 32.2:640–66.

Layard, Richard. 1979. Introduction. *Journal of Political Economy* 87.5:s1–s5.

Layzell, Daniel. 1996. Developments in State Funding for Higher Education. In vol. 11 of *Higher Education: Handbook of Theory and Research*, edited by John C. Smart. New York: Agathon Press.

Lazear, Edward. 1977. Education: Consumption or Production? *Journal of Political Economy* 85.3:569–97.

Leslie, Larry, and Paul Brinkman. 1986. Rates of Return to Higher Education: An Intensive Examination. In vol. 2 of *Higher Education: Handbook of Theory and Research*, edited by John C. Smart. New York: Agathon Press.

Levin, Harry, and Carolyn Kelley. 1994. Can Education Do It Alone? *Economics of Education Review* 13.2:97–108.

Lewis, Arthur. 1955. *The Theory of Economic Growth*. Homewood, Ill.: Irwin.

Lindsay, C. M. 1971. Measuring Human Capital Returns. *Journal of Political Economy* 79 (November–December): 1195–1215.

Lovell, Michael. 1973. The Production of Economic Literature—An Interpretation. *Journal of Economic Literature* 11.1:27–55.

Mayer, Thomas. 1993. *Truth versus Precision in Economics*. Aldershot, England: Edward Elgar.

McMahon, Walter, and Terry Geske, eds. 1982. *Financing Education: Overcoming Inefficiency and Inequity*. Urbana: University of Illinois Press.

Mincer, Jacob. 1958. Investment in Human Capital and Personal Income Distribution. *Journal of Political Economy* 66.4:281–302.

———. 1962. On-the-Job Training: Costs, Returns, and Some Implications. *Journal of Political Economy* 70.5:50–79.

Morgan, James, and Ismail Sirageldin. 1967. A Note on the Quality Dimension in Education. *Journal of Political Economy* 75 (September–October): 1069–77.

Neave, Guy. 1989. Foundation or Roof? The Quantitative, Structural, and Institutional Dimensions in the Study of Higher Education. *European Journal of Education* 24.3:211–22.

———. 1995. The Stirring of the Prince and the Silence of the Lambs: The Changing Assumptions beneath Higher Education Policy, Reform, and Society. In *Emerging Patterns of Social Demand and University Reform: Through a Glass Darkly*, edited by David Dill and Barbara Sporn. Oxford: IAU Press and Pergamon.

The New Palgrave: A Dictionary of Economics. 1987. Edited by John Eatwell, Murray Milgate, and Peter Newman. London: Macmillan.

Niklasson, Lars. 1996. Quasi Markets in Higher Education: A Comparative Analysis. *Journal of Higher Education Policy and Management* 18.1:7–22.

Nowotny, Helga. 1995. Mass Higher Education and Social Mobility: A Tenuous Link. In *Emerging Patterns of Social Demand and University Reform: Through a Glass Darkly*, edited by David Dill and Barbara Sporn. Oxford: IAU Press and Pergamon.

O'Brien, Denis. 1991. Theory and Empirical Observation. In *Routledge Companion to Contemporary Economic Thought*, edited by David Greenaway, Michael Bleaney, and Ian Stewart. London: Routledge.

Organisation for Economic Cooperation and Development. 1962. *Politiques de Croissance Économique et d'Investissement dans l'Enseignement*. Paris: OECD.

———. 1990. *Financing Higher Education: Current Patterns*. Paris: OECD.

Papadopoulos, Georges. 1994. *Education 1960–1990: The OECD Perspective*. Paris: OECD.

Psacharopoulos, George. 1973. *Returns to Education: An International Comparison*. San Francisco: Jossey Bass.

———. 1981. Returns to Education: An Updated International Comparison. *Comparative Education* 17.3:321–41.

———. 1985. Returns to Education: A Further International Update and Implications. *Journal of Human Resources* 20.4:583–604.

———. 1994. Returns to Investment in Education: A Global Update. *World Development* 22.9:1325–43.

———, ed. 1987. *Economics of Education: Research and Studies*. Oxford: Pergamon.

Reder, M. W. 1982. Chicago Economics: Permanence and Change. *Journal of Economic Literature* 20.1:1–38.

Rosen, Sherwin. 1977. Human Capital: A Survey of Empirical Research. In vol. 1 of *Research in Labor Economics*, edited by Ronald G. Ehrenberg. Greenwich, Conn.: JAI Press.

———. 1992. Distinguished Fellow—Mincering Labor Economics. *Journal of Economic Perspectives* 6.2:157–70.

Rostow, W. W. 1990. *Theorists of Economic Growth—From David Hume to the Present*. Oxford: Oxford University Press.

Rumberger, Russell. 1987. The Impact of Surplus Schooling on Productivity and Earnings. *Journal of Human Resources* 22.1:24–50.

Sahota, Gian. 1978. Theories of Personal Income Distribution: A Survey. *Journal of Economic Literature* 16.1:1–55.

Schaffer, Henry. 1961. Investment in Human Capital: Comment. *American Economic Review* 52.4:1026–35.

Schultz, Theodore. 1959. Human Wealth and Economic Growth. *The Humanist* 2.19:71–81.

———. 1961a. Investment in Human Capital. *American Economic Review* 51.1: 1–17.

———. 1961b. Investment in Human Capital: Reply. *American Economic Review* 52.5:1035–39.

———. 1962. Reflections on Investment in Man. *Journal of Political Economy* 70.5:1–8.

———. 1963. *The Economic Value of Education*. New York: Columbia University Press.

———. 1972. Optimal Investment in College Instruction: Equity and Efficiency. *Journal of Political Economy* 80.3:s2–s30.

———. 1993. The Economic Importance of Human Capital in Modernisation. *Education Economics* 1.1:13–19.

Skidelsky, Robert. 1988. The Political Meaning of the Keynesian Revolution. In *Keynes and Public Policy after Fifty Years*, edited by Omar Hamouda and John Smithin. Aldershot, England: Edward Elgar.

Smith, James, and Finis Welch. 1989. Black Economic Progress after Myrdal. *Journal of Economic Literature* 27.2:519–64.

Solmon, Lewis. 1985. Quality of Education and Economic Growth. *Economics of Education Review* 4.4:273–90.
Solow, Robert. 1991. Growth Theory. In *Routledge Companion to Contemporary Economic Thought*, edited by David Greenaway, Michael Bleaney, and Ian Stewart. London: Routledge.
Stewart, Ian. 1991. The Role of the Methodologist. In *Routledge Companion to Contemporary Economic Thought*, edited by David Greenaway, Michael Bleaney, and Ian Stewart. London: Routledge.
Stiglitz, Joseph. 1975. The Theory of "Screening," Education, and the Distribution of Income. *American Economic Review* 65.3:283–300.
Svennilson, Ingvar. 1966. Education, Research and Other Unidentified Factors in Growth. In *The Economics of Education*, edited by J. E. Vaizey and E. A. G. Robinson. New York: Macmillan and St. Martin's.
Svanfeldt, Göran. 1993. Higher Education Policy in Sweden. In *Higher Educational Policy: An International Comparative Perspective*, edited by Leo Goedegebuure, Frans Kaiser, Peter Maassen, Lynn Meek, Frans van Vught, and Egbert De Weert. Oxford: Pergamon.
Taubman, Paul, and Terence Wales. 1973. Higher Education, Mental Ability, and Screening. *Journal of Political Economy* 81.1:28–55.
Vaizey, John. 1966. Criteria for Public Expenditure on Education. In *The Economics of Education*, edited by J. E. Vaizey and E. A. G. Robinson. New York: Macmillan and St. Martin's.
Vaizey, J. E., and E. A. G. Robinson. 1966. *The Economics of Education*. New York: Macmillan and St. Martin's.
Verdugo, Richard, and Naomi Verdugo. 1989. The Impact of Surplus Schooling on Earnings. *Journal of Human Resources* 24.4:629–43.
Weale, Martin. 1993. A Critical Evaluation of the Rate of Return Analysis. *Economic Journal* 103 (May): 729–37.
Weiss, Andrew. 1983. A Sorting-cum-Learning Model of Education. *Journal of Political Economy* 91.3:420–42.
———. 1995. Human Capital vs. Signalling Explanations of Wages. *Journal of Economic Perspectives* 9.4:133–54.
Wolfe, Barbara, and Samuel Zuvekas. 1997. Nonmarket Outcomes of Schooling. *International Journal of Educational Research* 27.6:1–18.
Woodhall, Maureen. 1987. Economics of Education: A Review. In *Economics of Education: Research and Studies*, edited by George Psacharopoulos. Oxford: Pergamon.
World Bank. 1994. *Enseignance Supérieure—Les Leçons de l'expérience*. Paris: World Bank.

"Related Disciplines": The Professionalization of Public Choice Analysis

Steven G. Medema

In scholarship it is not perhaps necessity, but prejudice,
that is the mother of invention.
—Mancur Olson, review of *The Calculus of Consent*

The evolution of economic ideas is driven by several forces, including the internal logic of the ideas themselves, the events of the world that economic analysis is said to describe, and sociological forces at work within the profession. If the first of these forces is overplayed in the history of economic ideas, the last has certainly received insufficient attention. In particular, the role that (small) communities of scholars play in the development of particular aspects of economic analysis is often overlooked in tracing out how it is that this analysis comes to occupy an established place in the profession. While there are exceptions to this (e.g., the Cambridge crowd in the 1930s, Cowles, and RAND), there is little doubt that substantial insights can be gained into the development of economic analysis by more deeply probing this facet of the history of economic ideas.

Correspondence may be addressed to Steven G. Medema, Department of Economics, Campus Box 181, University of Colorado at Denver, P. O. Box 173364, Denver, CO 80217-3364. I wish to thank Roger Backhouse, Jeff Biddle, James Buchanan, Craufurd Goodwin, Ana Maria Bianchi, an anonymous referee, and participants at the 1999 *HOPE* conference and the 1999 History of Economics Society Conference session on twentieth-century thought for their very instructive comments on earlier drafts of this article. Special thanks go to James Buchanan, Betty Tillman, and Jo Ann Burgess for their assistance and hospitality during my visit to Buchanan House. Permission to quote from the archival materials is gratefully acknowledged, as is the research support of the Earhart Foundation.

In the present paper, I propose to discuss the early (1960s through the early 1970s) development of the field of public choice analysis—not in terms of the development of the theory itself, but by tracing the development of the community of scholars and the professionalization of public choice as a distinct field within economic analysis. There are numerous relevant issues here: how economists came to be interested in applying the tools of economic science to the analysis of the political process; the professionalization of the field through the establishment of conferences, journals, and associations; the evolution in the definition and boundaries of the field's subject matter and in the types of analyses undertaken; the relationship between economists and political scientists in the development of the field; and the process through which public choice analysis became a component of "mainstream" economics alongside other applied fields. While we can touch on only a subset of these themes in the present essay, it is nonetheless hoped that the reader will get a picture of the processes underlying and driving the emergence of a well-defined scholarly community and the institutions that supported its discourse.[1]

The development of the field of public choice has parallels in the other imperialistic forays by economists into the various social sciences. Law and economics and public choice are the two most successful of these movements and thus constitute the best cases for analyses of the present type. But while the evolution of law and economics has been rather heavily analyzed, the development of public choice has been relatively neglected. Public choice is also particularly interesting as against law and economics because its roots and evolution lie primarily within the economics community, whereas those of law and economics are much more divided between the legal and economics communities.

The next section of the paper will briefly discuss the historical antecedents of modern public choice. Section 2 elaborates the early reactions to the economic analysis of politics within economics and political

1. The reader will notice that this essay focuses disproportionately on the Virginia school of public choice. There are sound reasons for doing so. First, as I hope to establish, the Virginia school was at the forefront of the drive to professionalize public choice. Second, the "social choice" approach of, for example, Kenneth Arrow and Amartya Sen, was largely divorced from public choice from the beginning, and the Chicago school of public choice did not really emerge until the mid-1970s—that is, beyond the time period that concerns us here. Both of these are fruitful subjects for further study. See Reder 1982, Rowley 1993, and Mitchell 1988, 1989 for contrasts of the Virginia and Chicago approaches to public choice, and Wittman 1989 and Rowley and Vachris 1993 for a useful case study in this regard.

science and the voids within these disciplines suggested by these reactions. Subsequent sections will show how economists and sympathetic political scientists attempted to put into place various professional organs that would further the research that was attempting to fill these voids.

1. Coming to Public Choice: Historical Antecedents

Public choice, in the most simple of terms, is the economics of politics—that is, the application of economic methods, and the rational actor model in particular, to the analysis of the political process, including voting, legislative and bureaucratic behavior, interest group activity, constitutional design, and so on. Here, government is analyzed "not as an organization that pursues some 'public interest' or other higher goals, but rather as a somewhat mundane machine for achieving the concrete desires of individual human beings," and "the ultimate results are observed as emerging from the processes of choice made by individuals within alternative sets of rules and decision-making institutions" (Center for Study of Public Choice 1970, 4). Standing with the *homo economicus* postulate in the public choice perspective is catallactics—the science of exchanges. Here, collective action within the political process is considered as a process of "complex exchange or agreement among all members of the relevant community" (Buchanan 1989, 15). While the various strands of the public choice literature utilize the catallactics and *homo economicus* perspectives in different proportions, or with differing degrees of emphasis, it is in the combination of these two ideas that public choice generates both its positive attempts to explain the operation of the political process and its normative suggestions for political reform.

So defined, public choice analysis is a relatively recent phenomenon. Yet both the Marxian and institutionalist traditions have lengthy histories of attempting to link up political and economic processes. These traditions have been all but ignored within modern public choice analysis, owing at least in part to their very different methodological underpinnings and (real or perceived) ideological perspectives. However, there are a number of significant, albeit scattered, historical precursors to the contemporary work in the field. The mathematical analysis of voting processes originated in France in the work of mathematicians

Jean-Charles de Borda, the Marquis de Condorcet, and Pierre-Simon LaPlace in the late eighteenth and early nineteenth centuries, and this line of research was picked up in England more than a half century later in the work of E. J. Nanson, Francis Galton, and Rev. C. L. Dodgson (Lewis Carroll). Yet, these ideas were not developed in any significant way by the mathematical community within which they originated, and the mathematical formulation of these works made them inaccessible to students of political theory. A second significant body of antecedent scholarship can be found in the literature of the Italian "*La Scienza delle Finanze*" tradition[2] and in the work of Knut Wicksell (1896), which focuses on the integration of the political process into the theory of public finance using a marginalist, market-oriented view of the political sector. But this analysis, too, had virtually no impact on economics prior to the middle of this century, owing both to the almost complete absence of translations of these works into English and the firm grip that the Cambridge welfare tradition had on British and American economists.

The development of modern public choice theory dates to the late 1940s and early 1950s and the work of Duncan Black and Kenneth Arrow.[3] Black fleshed out significant aspects of the theory of majority rule and proportional representation in a series of papers in the 1940s and 1950s, including, most famously, the median voter theorem. But Black was a loner; apart from his colleague and coauthor R. A. Newing (a mathematician), there was no one within the United Kingdom who seemed interested in the type of problems he was working on, and it was not until the 1960s that his work began to receive any serious attention. Arrow's place here is intimately connected with the work going on at RAND in the early Cold War period. Much of the theoretical inspiration for modern public choice theory came from the development of the theory of games and hard-nosed rational choice theory. The ability to model relationships among political actors as games of strategy opened up entirely new vistas for the analysis of agent responses to political decision rules and for the analysis of the formulation of the rules themselves. The work going on at RAND at this time figured significantly here; two of the pioneers of public choice theory—Arrow (1951) and his student, Anthony Downs (1957)—were affiliated with RAND, and others

2. The most seminal contributions here came from Maffeo Pantaleoni ([1883] 1958), Ugo Mazzola ([1890] 1958), and Antonio de Viti de Marco (1936). For surveys, see Buchanan 1960 and Medema 1999.

3. See, for example, Black 1948, Black and Newing 1952, and Arrow 1951.

at RAND—for example, Lloyd Shapley and Martin Shubik—although not prominent figures in the history of public choice theory, did devote some efforts to the game-theoretic analysis of the political process,[4] but this line of research was not taken up in any large way until a decade later, by Steven Brams, Peter Ordeshook, and others who developed a highly technical game-theoretic approach to politics.

The works of Arrow and Black had no discernable impact on political science or the development of an economics of politics in the years immediately following their publication. William Mitchell (1999) has suggested that political scientists were largely ignorant of this literature (a hypothesis supported by a perusal of leading political science journals during this period), and that the problem that Arrow and Black addressed—the aggregation of individual preferences into collective decisions—was not of great interest to political scientists. Reflecting this, William Riker, writing in 1961, complained that while "the work of Black and Arrow is of great importance both for political theory and the study of political behavior . . . on the whole political scientists have tended to ignore this literature (Riker 1961, 911). Some evidence for this indifference (apart from the paucity of citations) can be gleaned from the fact that a Northwestern University conference titled "Approaches to the Study of Politics" included not a single economist invitee to talk about what politics can borrow from economics (Riker 1959, 209).

Things began to change a bit in the late 1950s and early 1960s with the publication of several works that were to become seminal in the field: Downs's *Economic Theory of Democracy* (1957), Black's *Theory of Committees and Elections* (1958), Riker's *Theory of Political Coalitions* (1962), James Buchanan and Gordon Tullock's *The Calculus of Consent* (1962), and Mancur Olson's *Logic of Collective Action* (1965). While it has become quite common to regard Buchanan and Tullock's work as the least influential of these—in terms of stimulation of scholarship—early on, the view espoused here is rather different. Specifically, the perspective that will emerge from the following discussion is that

4. See Shapley and Shubik 1954. Buchanan, too, spent some time at RAND, the efforts of which were then devoted to furthering U.S. strategic Cold War interests, but he says that this had no influence on his thinking regarding public choice analysis (interview with the author, 5 November 1998). When the scholars at RAND became aware of Black's work in the late 1940s, they sent a letter to him requesting offprints of his articles. Upon ascertaining the mission of RAND, Black apparently decided not to comply with the request (McLean, McMillan, and Monroe 1998, xxiii).

Buchanan and Tullock were very much responsible for the institutionalization of the field, and their efforts on this score were largely derivative of the reception accorded to *The Calculus*.

To think of public choice analysis solely in terms of the economics of politics, however, is to lose sight of the larger project that Buchanan and others, such as Warren Nutter, commenced upon in the 1950s: the development of what they believed to be a more appropriate theory of public economics. What specifically concerned Buchanan was that public economics raised important issues relating to the process of collective decision making but yet gave no place to the role of political forces within the economic policy-making process. His goal was to reshape public economics in a way that took these forces into account. While Buchanan's project was novel, it was not without precedent. Indeed, he was stimulated to pursue this line of analysis after reading Wicksell's *Finanztheoretische Untersuchungen* and, subsequently, the works of the late-nineteenth- and early-twentieth-century Italian "*La Scienza delle Finanze*" tradition. Ultimately, Buchanan saw his modern political economy approach linking back to Adam Smith and the classical economists and to the study of the market process as it operated within and through "the framework of society, described by the 'laws and institutions' about which Adam Smith wrote" (Buchanan 1983, 6). What would emerge, however, was something far broader than this.

2. Early Reactions

Because of the relative lack of attention paid to the economics of politics in its formative years, the initial reception of this literature must be traced primarily through the reviews of the major early works in the field.[5] It is interesting both to juxtapose the reactions of economists and political scientists to these works and to examine how these views evolved over a relatively short period of time. As one might expect, the debate here centered on the usefulness of the economic/mathematical

5. On Arrow, see reviews by Somers (1952), Baumol (1952), and Houthakker (1952); on Black and Newing, see reviews by Richenberg (1953) and Simon (1952); on Black, see reviews by Harsanyi (1965) and Kort (1959); on Downs, see reviews by Bergson (1958) and Pennock (1958); on Riker, see reviews by Fagen (1963), Hotz (1963), and Matthews (1963); on Buchanan and Tullock, see reviews by Olson (1962), Downs (1964), Meade (1963), and Ward (1963) within economics, and Gertzog (1964), C.M.P. (1963), Riker (1962a), Vines (1963), Milne (1962), Ulmer (1963), and May (1963) within political science, as well as reviews by sociologist McGinnis (1963) and lawyer Manne (1963).

deductive method versus the more inductive approach of political science, and the extent to which the *homo economicus* assumption holds promise for the analysis of the behavior of political agents.

Perhaps not surprisingly, most of the methodological opposition came from within the political science community. Foremost in the minds of these critics was the degree of attachment to the real world of politics evidenced in the economic models. Kenneth Vines (1963, 161) suggested that *The Calculus of Consent* demonstrates limited "political awareness" and that it "derives general propositions about politics according to economic theory but largely outside the political context."[6] This, in turn, led to a great deal of concern regarding the adequacy and usefulness of the results derived from this modeling process. L. J. Richenberg (1953, 131), for example, argued that Black and Newing's models "do not lead to any results that can be interpreted in words: no new propositions emerge about the general relations between private and social choice except at an inescapably mathematical level of abstraction. Mathematical niceties apart, the results are barren." This view was echoed by W. Hayward Rogers (1959, 483), who suggested that while "political scientists drawn to the methodology and techniques of natural science are currently producing some interesting and provocative suggestions[,] . . . in their eagerness to exploit the power of the methodology, sometimes a misapplication or overextension of various techniques occurs and confusion ensues." This, he says, is evidenced in Downs's book, which he finds to be essentially devoid of real-world implications. Reflective of the gulf between economists and political scientists on the methodological front, Rogers argued that a priori deductive theorizing is only relevant to the extent that the underlying assumptions are exactly correct; a useful political theory, he said, must be based upon empirical investigations, and it is only from empirically validated phenomena that further conclusions may be properly deduced (1959, 484–85).

Donald Matthews (1963, 579) sums up the position of many of the political scientist critics when he says that

> even the most sympathetic reader . . . is likely to put down [Riker's] book undecided as to the utility of such highly abstract and formal

6. In fact, this concern was even evidenced on occasion within this new paradigm—for example in Downs's (1959, 212) criticism of what he saw as the narrow internalism of Black's analysis, particularly his failure to relate his analysis of committee processes to the larger political context and a larger economic theory of politics.

> models. How much of our limited time, resources, and imagination should be invested in their construction and perfection? Game theory itself was developed in revolt against the constraints of the elegant but increasingly irrelevant model of classical economics. The realism and utility of models are a function, in part, of their inventors' prior understanding of how the real world operates. Do we know enough about politics to construct useful models now? Or do we need more and better empirical studies first?

Through all of this commentary runs a fear among political scientists that, as R. J. May (1963, 113) put it, this work would promote "the *science* of political science at the expense of politics."

One particularly vexing aspect of the economic approach was the application of the rational actor assumption to the political realm, as a number of commentators either rejected it altogether or at least questioned whether *homo economicus* can move as seamlessly between the economic and political arenas as the theory assumed. Sidney Ulmer's enthusiastic reception of *The Calculus* was tempered by his feeling that the new scholarship had "assumed too hastily that the explicit and implicit assumptions of economic behavior can be carried over to political behavior. The extent to which this can be done with each and every such assumption is a matter to be determined by testable, empirical consequences" (1963, 175). R. S. Milne (1962, 152), who found *The Calculus* to be "like a colonizing expedition," criticized the behavioral assumptions on the grounds that "less well-organized groups, or individuals, may not act wholeheartedly in favour of their interests, in the sense of being fully informed, rational and seeking to maximize utility." Likewise, Irwin Gertzog (1964, 974) suggested that the equation of individual and group behavior makes the theory ill equipped to analyze those aspects of the social process that embody a different, group dynamic. This criticism was even present within the economics literature, where Abram Bergson—whose welfare economics was very much called into question by this literature—criticized the assumption of vote maximization. "Perhaps the economist himself," he wrote, "is often misguided about motives, if not of bakers then of corporate executives, but this is no reason to compound the error in politics" (1958, 437–38, 440).

But a number of political scientists, and most of the economist reviewers, had a decidedly more positive reaction, and, even when disagreeing with the conclusions drawn, were favorably disposed toward the possibilities offered by the new methodology. As several of those offering more positive assessments of this methodology were themselves tilling this or related soils, these reactions are perhaps not overly surprising. Herbert Simon (1952, 638), for example, acknowledged that the assumptions underlying these models "will seem deplorably naïve" to those unfamiliar with them, but both he and John Harsanyi (1965) suggested that there are substantial benefits to treating political theory with the rigorous methods of economics, in no small part because they lend a degree of precision and determinateness to things that are otherwise rather fuzzy. Downs and James Meade were also of the mind that this work had much to offer economics. Downs (1964, 88), in a bit of a slap at both economists and political scientists, noted that "while economists refine the theoretical conditions for perfect competition down to the last gnat's eyebrow, the gigantic problems of economic choice and allocation within our political institutions are left largely to political scientists and to a few economists working on defense-oriented problems." Yet, he said, "government action involves many of the same decision-making processes that economists are so much better tooled to analyze than political scientists." Similarly, Meade (1963, 101) criticized economists for being "much too ready to call in the State as a *deus ex machina* to remove the imperfections of the laissez-faire market without examining the implications of this view for the political, as contrasted with the economic, behaviour of the individual citizen." *The Calculus*, he said, with its "assumption that the individual citizen is wholly selfish in his behaviour in the voting booth and in the market-place," is "a most laudable attempt to close [this] gap"—a somewhat surprising assessment since Buchanan and Tullock's analysis very much calls into question the ability of government to effectively bring off the types of optimal policy solutions that Meade championed in his writings.

These sentiments go some distance toward explaining why this literature received a favorable reception in parts of the economics community. It is fair to say that the theory of economic policy had long neglected to analyze the ability of government to effectively carry out the policies proffered by the theory. For those who were opposed to the interventionist possibilities suggested by the traditional theory, and for those who were simply intellectually curious about the ability of government to effect optimal interventions, the emerging economics of politics had much to offer—particularly given its formalist nature.

But one is still left with the question of why this work—when it was not ignored—was well received, or at least not rejected outright, within certain quarters of the political science community, where no strong opposing camp emerged for two decades. One possible answer is that there was no perceived threat here, since political scientists were not quick to pick up this stream of research en masse. But there is certainly more to it than this, since publications in leading political science journals and citations to works in this area were moving upward as the 1960s progressed.[7] One part of the explanation that emerges is that political science has historically been open to, and even relied upon, the insights of other disciplines in the furtherance of its own, and that this created a degree of receptivity for the economic approach that would not otherwise have been present. As Vines (1963, 160) pointed out,

> An endemic characteristic of political science has been its use of theories and data drawn from other disciplines. Traditional political science used methods and data from history, philosophy, and law. Present day political science has supplemented these with data and theories drawn from modern social science, from psychology, sociology, economics and anthropology, and from mathematics. Definitions and methods may be initiated by political scientists but these original efforts are apt to be either syntheses or else adaptations of data and methods used in the social sciences for the study of politics.

Gertzog (1964, 974), for one, found himself impressed by the perspective of the "sister discipline," economics, and lauded the "extension of economic terminology and orientations to the essential concepts of democratic political theory," particularly the application of the notion of economic or market-place exchange to political organization and the interpretation of voting in terms of its economic value.

Further evidence on this score can be found in a powerful new interdisciplinary movement—the behaviorist approach—that was emerging within political science at this same time (see Mitchell 1999). The behaviorist approach drew heavily upon insights from sociology and psychology to examine individual behavior, including power relationships, within the political realm. While both the behaviorist and economic approaches focused on individual behavior, their methods, the resulting analysis, and the ideological overtones were very different. All of this

7. On publications, see section 4, below.

may help to explain why the invasion of economics into political science generated a less hostile reception than within law: the openness of political science contrasts sharply with the jurisprudential tradition of insularity and the view of law (from the inside) as an autonomous, self-contained discipline (Posner 1987).

Further pieces of the explanation for the reception of this work can be found in the perceived limitations of the extant political science paradigm and in a search for moorings within political science that would create an openness to a new body of theory that offered substantial promise. "The search continues," noted Gertzog (1964, 973–74), "for theoretical frameworks which will give perspective and direction to the study of politics" and "lift political theory out of the abyss of diffused speculation" (Ulmer 1963, 171), and it was thought that the economics of politics offered a potential solution. Indeed, both the behaviorist revolution, where empirical study and statistical analysis played an important role, and the economic approach were responses to the perceived unscientific shortcomings of the existing theory. One particularly significant aspect of this dissatisfaction was the felt need to give the discipline a more scientific, theoretical underpinning—which included, indeed required in the minds of some, working from restrictive and often unrealistic assumptions (Hotz 1963, 295; Banfield 1958, 324). The feeling was that "mathematical approaches to social phenomena . . . are not merely fashionable endeavors, but . . . serve the purpose of discovering or comprehending relationships that cannot be fully explored by exclusive reliance on qualitative interpretation" (Kort 1959, 327). In the process, they would bring "formal elegance to the discussion of matters which are usually very muddy" (Banfield 1958, 325) and "do precisely what good theory ought to do: namely, give guidance to empirical research" (Pennock 1958, 541).

The view of political science held by those more closely associated with these new ideas was even more stridently critical. Henry Manne (1963, 1065), who figured prominently in the development of law and economics during this same period, commented that "it is a commonplace observation that political theory largely failed to develop systematic tools of analysis comparable to those of economics" and "allow[s] neither for quantification nor objective evaluations." Because of this, he argued, political science "has become more and more comparable to descriptive sociology than to a mathematical or logical science." Riker was even more abusive to his colleagues in political science, offering stinging commentaries on the state of the field:

> There is considerable intellectual ferment among political scientists today owing to the fact that the traditional methods of their discipline seem to have wound up in a cul-de-sac. These traditional methods—i.e., history writing, the description of institutions, and legal analysis— . . . can produce only wisdom and neither science nor knowledge. (1962b, viii)[8]

> As numerous writers have pointed out, political theory as a field of academic concentration has been in a confused and unproductive state for at least the last generation. . . . Refusing . . . to theorize themselves, most academicians have been limited to a consideration of intellectual primitives or of, what amounts to the same thing, the rantings and ideological tergiversations of half-educated modern pamphleteers. In almost no other field do the professionals thus abase themselves before the ancients and the amateurs. (1962a, 408)

Meanwhile, economics had been able to broaden its scope as the result of developments within utility theory and the application of the theory of games—the result of which was that nonmarket interactions were being brought under the economist's umbrella. Peter Ordeshook felt that "the success of economic theory, and the relative failure of political science to develop equally satisfactory theories [left] political science at a distinct disadvantage with respect to economics in its ability to conjecture about, advise on, and devise policy" (1969, 1294). Rejecting other attempts then being made to revitalize the field, Riker (1962a, 409) contended that the economic approach to politics appears to be the only thing on the horizon "which offers some hope of a really successful reorientation of political theory."

Here, too, the comparison with law and economics is apposite. Law was engaged in a similar search for moorings during this same period, and some found it in the application of the economic approach. There was a sense within the legal community that lawyers could not solve the problems of the legal system on their own and that the traditional autonomous perspective had little new to say. As a result, legal schol-

8. Even some contemporary critics of the rational choice approach to politics acknowledge that "much of what passes for the scientific study of politics is anything but that" (Green and Shapiro 1994, 10).

ars began to look elsewhere for interpretive principles. Moreover, the increasing prestige and authority accorded scientific modes of inquiry, and the relative decline in prestige and authority accorded to the nonscientific method of legal analysis, pushed legal scholars to adopt more scientific methods. In the eyes of many legal scholars, economics, with its formalist approach, logical interpretive framework, and determinate solutions, offered exactly what was needed to fill the void (Posner 1987). In law, as in political science, economists were more than happy to assist in filling this void.

All of this having been said, the positive to lukewarm reviews of the early works in public choice are almost certainly an upward-biased indication of the general reaction to public choice analysis within the political science community. One gets a hint of the more severely negative undercurrent within certain quarters from Buchanan. "*Successful* invasion of an established discipline by 'outsiders' generates strong emotions,"[9] he said, with the result that "some traditional political scientists of a narrow bent tend to become somewhat violently and irrationally prejudiced against all efforts in public choice theory. They see their own intellectual capital threatened with rapid depreciation, and they are led to resist."[10] Buchanan has suggested that it was not resistance to "economic imperialism" per se that drove the hostility emanating from certain quarters within the political science community, but, rather, conflicts over ideology—individualist versus collectivist.[11]

It is indisputable that much of the public choice literature, both pro and con, has ideological overtones, even if little of the early reaction overtly dealt with this issue. Interestingly, the one place where this does come out strongly is not in the political science literature, but in Mancur Olson's review of *The Calculus* in the *American Economic Review*. Olson (1962, 1217) called the book "a stimulating new addition" to the emerging literature on the economics of politics, but he was critical of what he considered the "implicit ideological emphasis" of the book. This perspective, he argued, distinguishes the book from

9. Letter from James M. Buchanan to Frank L. Hereford, 25 August 1967; emphasis in original. In Buchanan House Archives (BHA), George Mason University.

10. Draft letter from James M. Buchanan and Gordon Tullock to Dr. Leslie F. Malpass (not sent), May 1970 (in BHA).

11. James M. Buchanan, interview with the author, 5 November 1998. Buchanan and Tullock have suggested on several occasions that these forces played a significant role in their departure from the University of Virginia.

most other work in the area, and it at once raises cause for scholarly concern and is the source of scholarly possibilities: "The somewhat eccentric ideological quality that characterizes [the authors'] writing," he said, "unfortunately narrows the appeal and perhaps obscures the objective importance of some of their theories." Yet, he continues, "their right-wing view is . . . also a blessing in that it gives them an unusual perspective that must account for many of their fresh insights."

In a letter to Olson subsequent to the publication of this review, Buchanan took issue with the imputation of "right-wing prejudice," arguing that "the book was devoted to deriving a simple logic of political choice from a position of methodological individualism," and he wondered whether Olson was actually suggesting that "anyone who tries to derive a logical basis for democratic government from a consideration of individual choice is guilty of right-wing prejudice." Buchanan contends that Olson's interpretation was, "fundamentally, a reaction of a strong emotional nature to the ideas, rather than any reasoned position that is based on careful examination of the arguments themselves." He goes on to allow that the book stimulated in others, especially political scientists, reactions similar to those expressed by Olson, but suggests that these reactions actually derived from a confusion of methodology with ideology on the part of the readers.[12]

We have already noted that the impact of these early works on the larger professional communities of economics and political science was by no means instantaneous or widespread. One correspondent lamented to Buchanan in early 1970 that "so few economists are aware that this theory [the economic theory of politics] even exists, much less that it says some interesting things" and found "sadder yet . . . the seeming unawareness of political scientists that exciting insights into collective behavior can be gleaned from simple models employing the behavioral assumption of rationality and the methodology of economics."[13] In fact, it is safe to say that these works provided only a partial stimulus to the development of public choice; it was through other forces that the field really became established and solidified.

12. Quotations in paragraph from a letter from James M. Buchanan to Mancur Olson, not dated (in BHA).

13. Letter from Professor A. James Heins to Buchanan, March 1970 (in BHA), excerpted in Center for Study of Public Choice 1970, 9. On this point, see also Mitchell 1999.

3. Getting "Centered"

Science Meets Ideology: The Thomas Jefferson Center

One cannot properly understand the evolution of public choice analysis without an understanding of the integration of positive and normative elements surrounding its genesis—Buchanan's comments to Olson notwithstanding. Public choice evolved out of the Virginia tradition in political economy that became entrenched in the late 1950s through the founding, by Buchanan and Nutter, of the Thomas Jefferson Center for Studies in Political Economy at the University of Virginia. The center's first brochure states its purpose as follows:

> The Center is organized to promote scholarly discussion of the basic ideals of Western civilization and of the solutions to modern social problems most in accord with those ideals.
>
> The Center is a community of scholars who wish to preserve a social order based on individual liberty. The Center will encourage students to see the philosophical as well as the technical issues entering into problems of social organization. (Thomas Jefferson Center 1957–58, 1)

This overtly normative purpose put Virginia political economy on a course that was consciously at odds with what its founders believed was the left-wing, interventionist tide within academia at that time (Buchanan 1983, 4–5) and served to give it its highly distinctive flavor.

But the center did not see itself simply as a countervailing force against academic radicalism. Fundamental to the center's orientation was a profound dissatisfaction with economic analysis as it was being practiced within the profession. As Buchanan (1983, 6) has noted,

> We were concerned, first of all, by what seemed to us to be a developing neglect of the basics of economics. Both Warren Nutter and I were Chicago economists, and Chicago economists of the Frank Knight, Henry Simons, Lloyd Mints, Aaron Director vintage. The basics of economics were those of price theory, not formal mathematics, and price theory applied to real world issues. The economic organization, the market process, and the working of this organization operating through the pricing structure were the subject matter of the discipline. Political economy was nothing more than this subject matter embedded within the framework of society, described by the "laws and institutions" about which Adam Smith wrote. To us, quite simply,

> political economy meant nothing more than a return to the stance of the classical political economists. Aside from Chicago, we saw programs elsewhere in economics neglecting these very foundations of our discipline.

But this positive stance of analyzing the market process had a larger normative goal, for, as Buchanan (1983, 6–7) has since said:

> Let me now also admit openly and without apology then or now, that we were motivated by our conviction that if these foundations are neglected, a society in which individuals retain their liberties is not sustainable. We had faith that an understanding of the price system offered the best possible avenue for the generation of support for free institutions. We did not feel any need for explicitly ideological polemic.

Their purpose, Buchanan acknowledges, was intentionally "*subversive*" (7). Through research and the training of graduate students, the center hoped to alter the focus of economic analysis and the attitudes of the scholarly community regarding the efficacy of the market system.

The staff of the Thomas Jefferson Center expanded steadily in the early years and included Buchanan, Nutter, Leland Yeager, Rutledge Vining, Ronald Coase, Andrew Whinston, and Tullock (who was brought in as a postdoctoral fellow at its inception and returned on a "permanent" basis in 1962). The financial support for the center in its early years came from organizations such as the Volker Fund, the Relm Foundation, the General Electric Foundation, the Lilly Endowment, and the University of Virginia, and the individual scholars associated with the center received strong financial support for their research from a variety of external sources. Among other things, this financial support allowed the center to establish an active program of visiting scholars, including Frank Knight, Maurice Allais, Duncan Black, Bertil Ohlin, T. W. Hutchison, F. A. Hayek, and Michael Polanyi.

During these early years, it became increasingly clear to the center's scholars that their normative goals could not be accomplished simply through the study of the market process; securing "the intellectual-analytical foundations of a free society" required "a complementary understanding of the political process" (Buchanan 1983, 10). The result was a new focus on the study of political institutions and their interaction with the market system—a major component of which evolved into public choice analysis. In 1963, the center moved to solidify, in an institutional sense, its mission in the area of public choice analysis by forming the Committee for the Analysis of Nonmarket Decision-Making. The purpose of the committee, which consisted of Buchanan, Tullock, and Paul David, was to "coordinate the Center's continuing interest in the research of American scholars in this new and growing area of emphasis"(Thomas Jefferson Center 1963, 6).

But this interest was not limited to America. By the mid-1960s there were significant signs of an emerging internationalization of the field, as scholars from Europe began to inquire about and hold visiting positions at the center to do research in the field, and graduate students from India, Europe, and Japan were in residence. Buchanan and Tullock also coordinated postdoctoral research programs for several scholars who went on to be significant players in the field, including Francisco Forte (Italy), David Chapman (England), and Thomas Borcherding (United States).

However, the center's heyday as a nucleus for the study of public choice was relatively short-lived. By the mid-1960s, Coase and Whinston had been lured away, and a controversy embroiling the center, the economics department, and the university led to the departures of Tullock (in 1967) and Buchanan (in 1968).[14] In a letter to Leland Yeager informing him of his decision to resign from Virginia, Buchanan says that the decision was a difficult one, and that "by any reasonably fair evaluation our whole efforts here must, I think, be judged a success."[15] The question, at that point, was whether this success would continue.

Virginia Redux: The Center for Study of Public Choice

Shortly after the meltdown at Virginia, public choice was reestablished—indeed more defined and solidified—at Virginia Polytechnic Institute (VPI) through the founding of the Center for Study of Public Choice. Charles Goetz, a former student of Buchanan's at Virginia, was on the faculty and spearheaded the push to bring in Tullock (in 1968) and Buchanan (in 1969) to establish public choice at VPI,[16] which made

14. See Buchanan 1983 and Breit 1986 for one perspective on these events.

15. Letter from James M. Buchanan to Leland Yeager, 16 January 1968.

16. James M. Buchanan, interview with the author, 5 November 1998. Today, VPI is more commonly known as Virginia Tech.

"strengthening the program in Public Choice" the centerpiece of its plan to develop a strong emphasis in the social sciences (Center for Study of Public Choice 1970, ii). The center was established in 1968 with Tullock as interim director, and Buchanan assumed the position of general director upon his arrival. Others affiliated with the center from its inception were Goetz, Joseph Bernd, and James Herndon, the latter two of the VPI political science department. The decision to establish a "public choice" center rather than a "political economy" center, as at Virginia, was a logical consequence of the focus of the work being done by those affiliated with the center at VPI (Center for Study of Public Choice 1970, ii).

The plans for the development of the center were substantial, including several new faculty lines, a visiting scholars program, postdoctoral fellowships, summer research fellowships, graduate student fellowships, the development of an experimental laboratory, and efforts at instructional innovations that would introduce the students to fundamental issues in public choice analysis, as well as the regular sponsorship of general and small thematic conferences. VPI committed over $500,000 in funding for the center, and additional funds were secured from other sources.

The economics Ph.D. program at VPI was established in 1968 and, from the outset, emphasized public choice analysis, including allowing students to take a double field in the area—the effect of which was that virtually all of a student's education beyond the core would be in the field of public choice. This course of study involved a yearlong sequence in public finance with a substantial public choice flavor, and a yearlong sequence in "Collective Decisions" that examined the economic theory of democracy, the theory of constitutions, voting models, and so on, as well as incorporating heavy doses of game theory and model building and an original research project. A similar course of study was offered at the undergraduate level. In addition, plans were developed for a Ph.D. program in political science that would allow a concentration in public choice, and students in both the economics and political science Ph.D. programs would be encouraged to take courses across the two departments (Center for Study of Public Choice 1970, 11–12 and attachment 4).

The center grew quickly, with a dozen permanent research associates on board by the mid-1970s and an active and wide-ranging program of research. Even with its overtly public choice emphasis, the Center for Study of Public Choice, like the Thomas Jefferson Center, carried out a broad-based program in political economy—including subjects such as crime, charity and income redistribution, fiscal federalism, and education. It also carried on an active program of publication, including book and monograph series and the housing of the editorial office of *Public Choice*.

The internationalization of public choice continued during this time, as the center received numerous inquiries annually from professors and graduate students, in both economics and political science, from around the world who wished to come to VPI to study public choice analysis. The extent of the attention that this work was attracting is evidenced in an excerpt from the Yugoslavian journal *Ekonomska Politika* in April 1970: "The political sciences have now found an application for electronic computers and mathematical models: at the Virginia Polytechnic Institute, for example, a young team is performing pioneering work in the field of 'the economics of politics' . . . —and that is a field which offers economists a wide area of investigation for the next twenty years."[17]

Molding the Next Generation

Perhaps most important for the long-term growth of the field was the heavy emphasis placed by these centers, from the beginning, on the support and training of graduate students (funded by, among others, the Earhart Foundation). The role of the Thomas Jefferson Center and the Center for Study of Public Choice in turning out strong graduates who went on to make significant impacts in public choice and related areas simply cannot be minimized. The University of Virginia turned out numerous successful graduates during the heyday of the Thomas Jefferson Center, including a number of individuals who went on to become significant figures in the development of public choice analysis: Otto Davis, Charles Goetz, Mark Pauly, Charles Plott, William Craig Stubblebine, Robert Tollison, Richard Wagner, and Thomas Willett (Tollison 1991). This continued at VPI, where the graduate students included Richard McKenzie, James Marchand, Marilyn Flowers, Gordon Brady, Randall Holcombe, Eugenia Toma, and Mark Toma (Tollison

17. Translated from *Ekonomska Politika*, 6 April 1970, pp. 45–46, in Center for Study of Public Choice 1970, 9.

1991). Riker was also training students at Rochester, and several of his students, including Peter Ordeshook, Peter Aranson, and Kenneth Shepsle, went on to make their mark in the field. Vincent Ostrom was doing likewise at Indiana.

The students who came through the programs at Virginia and VPI diffused themselves across the nation's colleges and universities, and a number of them came to hold professorships at leading universities. Many of these scholars have also held temporary appointments in important governmental posts with, among others, the Council of Economic Advisers (as senior staff economist), the Federal Trade Commission, the Department of the Treasury, and the National Science Foundation (NSF), and they have also served as staff economists for the U.S. Congress. Their influence extends throughout the profession, and it may safely be said that these students helped to solidify the place of public choice within the academic culture.

On a broader level, however, public choice's inroads into the formal curricula of economics and political science outside of places like VPI, Rochester, and Indiana proceeded "indirectly and with little uniformity" (Center for Study of Public Choice 1970, 6–7; see also Dow and Munger 1990 and Mitchell 1999). Even so, there were some important early strides made here. The decade of the 1960s saw a broadening of the content of standard public finance courses to include public choice analysis and applications. Courses specifically focusing on public choice were introduced at both undergraduate and graduate levels in a number of institutions, and graduate research concentrations in the field began to emerge, albeit slowly. The introduction of the public choice perspective into political science education proceeded more slowly. The first political science textbook written from a public choice perspective, Joyce Mitchell and William Mitchell's *Political Analysis and Public Policy*, was published in 1969, but did not attract imitators. There were both resistance to the teaching of these new methods and significant barriers to entry on the students' side, owing to the investment costs involved in mastering the requisite economics and mathematics. The much simpler quantitative tools employed by the behaviorists required a smaller investment and offered the additional attraction of being much more welcome within the professional community.

4. Carving Out a Field

Meetings of the Minds

The beginning of the institutionalization of public choice within the larger academic community came through the organization of several scholarly conferences in the 1960s. The first of these conferences, which was organized by Buchanan and Tullock following the initial favorable reviews of *The Calculus*,[18] has variously been referred to as the "Conference on Converging Trends in Politics and Economics," the "Conference on the Pure Theory of Collective Decision Making," and the "Conference on Nonmarket Decision-Making."[19] It was held at the William Faulkner House at the University of Virginia under the auspices of the Thomas Jefferson Center in October 1963 and sponsored by the National Science Foundation. The conference included as participants economists Buchanan, John G. Cross (Institute for Defense Analysis), Otto Davis (Carnegie, and UVA alum), Anthony Downs (RAND), John Harsanyi (Wayne State), James March (Carnegie), Ronald McKean (RAND), Henry Oliver (Indiana), Mancur Olson (Princeton), Jerome Rothenberg (Northwestern), Craig Stubblebine (Delaware, and UVA alum), Gordon Tullock (Virginia), and Andrew Whinston (Cowles and Yale). The political scientists in attendance were Edward Banfield (Harvard), Paul David (Virginia), Gerald Garvey (United States Air Force Academy), Stanley Kelley (Princeton), Gerald Kramer (Rochester), Vincent Ostrom (Resources for the Future), and William Riker (Rochester) (Thomas Jefferson Center 1964, 21–22). The organization was relatively informal, with the participants talking about the research currently underway in the field and what could be done to further the development of this work.[20] Buchanan felt that "a certain community of interest" developed among the participants, and he thought the conference "a great success." He also suggested that, because of the diversity of perspectives present, the conference "takes the right-wing onus off us to an extent, and it establishes our claim to scholarship, so to speak."[21] In fact, the conference was sufficiently successful that the Thomas Jefferson Center formed the Committee for the Analysis of Nonmarket Decision-Making, made up

18. Letter from James M. Buchanan to Sonja Amadae, 26 February 1997 (in BHA).

19. See, for example, Mancur Olson, "The Proposed Interdisciplinary Committee on Nonmarket Decision Making," 1966 (in BHA), and Thomas Jefferson Center 1964, 7.

20. James M. Buchanan, interview with the author, 5 November 1998.

21. James M. Buchanan, journal entries, September and October 1963 (in BHA).

of Buchanan, David, and Tullock, with Banfield, Harsanyi, McKean, Ostrom, and Riker serving the committee in an advisory capacity. It was determined both that continued meetings were in order and that the center should look into the publication of a series of research papers in the area (Thomas Jefferson Center 1964, 6–8).

A second conference was held at the Big Meadows Lodge in Virginia in October 1964, and featured papers by Mancur Olson, John Rawls, and Henry Manne. The general discussion held at the meeting's end suggested that there were several issues "relating to title, formal organization, conference focus, and breadth of participation" that needed to be worked out, and a committee was appointed to deal with these issues (Stubblebine 1964, 17).[22] Thereafter, and reflective of its quick maturation, the group attempted to establish a national organization loosed of its direct ties to the Thomas Jefferson Center. One significant aspect of this was the drive to seek status as a subcommittee under the auspices of the Social Science Research Council (SSRC)—an effort that was ultimately unsuccessful. The SSRC's Committee on Governmental and Legal Processes agreed to sponsor the third conference, which would allow them to scout out this new enterprise, and that conference (organized by Riker) was held in New York City in April 1966. Although the group was growing (the invited participants numbered twenty-three) and evidenced "considerable unity of interest," Buchanan felt that the continued existence of the group was "highly uncertain."[23] A fourth conference, again sponsored by the SSRC, was held in Chicago in December 1967; attendance here numbered thirty-seven—indicative of the group's continued expansion. It was at this meeting that the group adopted the name "Public Choice Society" and began the process of establishing a formal organization, including the designation of Vincent Ostrom as chair and the drafting of a constitution.

Thereafter the field continued to grow and achieve institutional solidity. By 1970, the Public Choice Society had more than five hundred members and the conference had become an annual event (Center for Study of Public Choice 1970, 6). More than eighty scholars attended the 1971 meeting in Blacksburg (the site of VPI), and although the ranks of economists participating exceeded those of the political scientists, there was substantial political science representation on the program. Nearly

22. Graduate students—including Charles Goetz, Charles Plott, and Richard Wagner—were also involved in these early conferences as observers.

23. James M. Buchanan, journal, 23 April 1966 (in BHA).

twenty papers were presented, and a session was held titled "Teaching and Courses Related to Public Choice." While the society had been divided on the issue of whether to retain the small, seminar-type format or attempt to expand the conference in the manner of larger professional societies (Ostrom 1969), this dramatic early expansion makes it quite clear that growth was the order of the day.

The decade of the 1960s also saw increasing acceptance of the study of nonmarket phenomena within the economics profession at large. Sessions on nonmarket decision-making were held at American Economic Association meetings in 1963, 1964, 1967, and 1968 (the last jointly with the Public Choice Society),[24] with papers presented by a number of the individuals who were active in the society's evolution—for instance, Buchanan, Tullock, Downs, Black, and Harsanyi—and discussants ranging from pioneers in the field to a group as diverse as Nathan Rosenberg, A. Allan Schmid, and Benjamin Ward. The topics of the papers ranged from the standard economics-of-politics fare to the analysis of traditional issues in public finance in light of the insights of the economics of politics, and these sessions succeeded in bringing this work to the attention of a wider audience.

The decision of the Committee for the Analysis of Nonmarket Decision-Making at the 1966 New York conference to ask the SSRC "to create an interdisciplinary committee that would organize and finance . . . a series of conferences and publications" on nonmarket decision-making is interesting for the perspective that the group's proposal, written by Mancur Olson, sheds on its thoughts regarding its own work and the state of economics and political science at that time (Olson 1966, 1). We have already mentioned that many political scientists were dissatisfied with the state of their discipline. Likewise, many economists found both economics and political science less than useful for evaluating the government's ability to successfully carry out policy, and they felt that public choice offered the potential to remedy this deficiency. The rationale offered by Olson for the establishment of an SSRC committee reflected this—specifically, "the conviction that certain problems and methods had been neglected in economics and political science, and that the previous meetings of this conference had shown promise

24. Buchanan recalls that they were never invited but still managed to get on the program with some aggressive pushing. James M. Buchanan, interview with the author, 5 November 1998.

of overcoming this neglect" (Olson 1966, 1). Economists, Olson contended,

> have been working with considerable success for more than a century and a half to explain how well or how badly markets function in various circumstances, [but] they have barely begun to consider how governments or other types of organization will perform these functions. Economists will presumably have to draw upon the insights and evidence gathered by political scientists and sociologists as they attempt to develop appropriate models of the economic behavior of governments and other organizations. (1966, 3)[25]

Political scientists, meanwhile, had, in the view of conference participants, "neglected to master certain scholarly methods of extraordinary importance," and only rarely used modeling techniques and statistical testing. The definition of modeling employed here was very specific: "There has been very little (non-trivial) *deductive* theory in political science—almost no model building or theory in the sense in which these words are used in economics" (Olson 1966, 3).[26] The result was that "those political problems that are logically too complex to be feasibly capable of solution unaided by common sense, and which demand properly theoretical or mathematical modes of thinking, have not usually been studied" (Olson 1966, 3). It is interesting to note here both the tool-based nature of the approach being advocated and the argument that these methods would expand the range of problems addressed within political theory—in contrast to the narrowing of scope so often attributed to these tools when their impact upon economics is considered.

Olson's memo reflects a similarly dismissive attitude toward the quantitative side of political science:

> Though not unmindful of the widespread use of quantitative research in political science and sociology, [the political scientists at the conferences on nonmarket decision-making] have been concerned that

25. It is worth noting that the borrowing here has been much more of political science from economics than of economics from political science.

26. This view is echoed in remarks that Tullock made to Buchanan in a letter written sometime in the late 1950s or early 1960s: "I think that you are too kind to the modern political scientist. His position is really based on no line of reasoning at all. Vague feelings and confused emotions, together with a lot of description of institutions and historical development make up the intellectual equipment of this discipline" (letter from Gordon Tullock to Buchanan, no date [in BHA]).

> the emphasis has been on the use of non-parametric techniques for testing what are essentially qualitative hypotheses. This has been due in part to the fact that the existing political theory has not lent itself into ready translation into a specific mathematical model or a specific set of interrelated quantitative hypotheses. Even when a specific theoretically derived hypothesis can be verified or falsified empirically, the overall importance of the empirical test is often unclear because of the non-deductive character of political theory. It is not, for example, clear whether, or how, or how much, the refutation of a specific hypothesis will affect the overall conception of, say, democracy or political stability. (Olson 1966, 4)

This statement is somewhat ironic, in that by the standards of evidence reflected in the Olson memo, the evidence-to-theory ratio in public choice remained very low for a long time, and the lack of empirical validation has long been one of the major charges leveled against public choice by its critics (Green and Shapiro 1994).

Interestingly, Olson urged the SSRC's support not simply because of the benefits of interdisciplinary activity, but because of the novelty of such with respect to economics:

> Economics has been, in Talcott Parsons' words, an "hermetically sealed" discipline, isolated from other social sciences. This lack of communication between economics and the other social sciences has presumably been due, not to any lack of need for such communication, but to the narrowness of the concerns of most modern economists and the unwillingness of many other social scientists to master the relatively rigorous and deductive methods of economic theory. (Olson 1966, 4–5)

Not that this "narrowness" was completely absent from the nascent public choice; the lists of invitees to these early conferences, while perhaps a bit more broad ideologically than the standard caricature, did not evidence extensive methodological pluralism. The rational choice approach was clearly dominant, and heterodox voices were hardly in evidence. In any event, Olson's prediction that the newfound desire of some economists to examine the role and effects of the political process and the adoption by a small number of political scientists and sociologists of the tools of economics "promises to undermine the thick wall that separate [*sic*] economics from the other social sciences" (1966, 5) has proven to be rather prescient, as public choice, law and economics, the economics of the family, and so on, became significant growth areas within economics, and the rational choice approach has gained a great deal of ground within social sciences generally. While none of these so-called imperialistic movements were received with open arms outside of economics, their impacts—measured in terms of scholarly inroads and even eventual rise of strong opposing camps within these other disciplines (most powerfully seen in the critical legal studies movement within law)—cannot be minimized.

Words Written Down

While these various professionalization efforts were stimulating scholarship in the field, this continued growth presented a problem for its dissemination. As Tullock pointed out in 1967, "The field has suffered . . . from the absence of a specialized journal. Articles are hard to place since most learned journals regard them as outside their scope and once published are hard to find. In a new and developing field, rapid interchange of ideas is extremely important. The existing journals are not organized to provide this exchange in an area which lies between (and overlaps) the traditional disciplines of economics and political science."[27] Moreover, he argued, the establishment of such an outlet, particularly as a multi-issue annual journal, would serve as an important stimulus to quality research in the field, owing to the greater publication potential offered by a specialized journal.[28]

Because of this perceived difficulty, the Committee for the Analysis of Nonmarket Decision-Making, in the person of Tullock, decided to take matters into its own hands. The first thrust at this was *Papers on Nonmarket Decision Making*, the initial volume of which was published under the auspices of the Thomas Jefferson Center in the summer of 1966. *Papers II*, which was published in the first half of 1967, evidenced an expanded number of articles, the inclusion of a book review section, and, perhaps as important as any of this, the publication of a bibliography of books and articles in the field (by Mark Pauly)—something that was to be repeated in later issues of the journal and served the very useful

27. Tullock, National Science Foundation proposal for *Papers*, 1967, p. 1 (in BHA). These sentiments were echoed from the political science side by Vincent Ostrom (1969), who was the chair of the Public Choice Society.

28. Tullock, National Science Foundation proposal for *Papers*, 1967, p. 11 (in BHA).

function of keeping scholars abreast of the far-flung publications in this area. By the time that the third volume of *Papers* appeared in the fall of 1967, the operation had evolved to the point that an editorial board had been put into place: Tullock served as editor and Mark Pauly as book review editor; Riker, Olson, Downs, Harsanyi, Black, Coleman, and Buchanan served on the editorial board. Even so, the status of the journal and its operations were by no means settled. While there was an intention to offer two issues in 1968, three in 1969, and four in 1970, the editors were not sufficiently confident of this to be willing to solicit subscriptions paid in advance, choosing instead to bill "subscribers" at year's end for whatever number of issues had been published. In 1968, *Papers* was formally converted to a journal and given a new name, *Public Choice*. The journal was sponsored by the newly founded Public Choice Society[29] and funded from a three-year grant provided by the NSF, after which time it was expected that the journal would become self-supporting. In an editor's note to the maiden issue of *Public Choice*, Tullock opined that, in light of all of this, "we are still a struggling journal, but our struggle will be a bit less desperate in the future."

While we shall not trace in any depth the history of the journal beyond this point, suffice it to say that its progress was quite rapid. In 1973, the journal added a third annual issue, and circulation was approximately 900; in 1976, it was up to four issues per year with a circulation of 1,300; in 1980, the journal was publishing five annual issues.[30] Tullock, who had served both as editor and as the main referee since the journal's inception, stepped aside in 1990 (Rowley 1991). By 1998, the journal was publishing nine issues annually under the editorship of Charles Rowley, Robert Tollison, and Friedrich Schneider (the journal's "European Editor"), and the editorial board had expanded to include forty-five scholars. To accommodate the vast growth in and range of scholarly output, a sister journal, *Constitutional Political Economy*, was established in 1990 under the auspices of the Center for Study of Public Choice, with Viktor Vanberg and Richard Wagner serving as editors. Here, too, the internationalization of public choice has been much in

29. Tullock (1997, 125) reports that the name of the journal was decided by a vote by the members of the society at the 1967 Chicago meeting.

30. The center also inaugurated a new annual titled *Frontiers of Economics* in 1976. The center's annual report indicated that *Frontiers* "deals with applications of economics too far out even for *Public Choice*" (Center for Study of Public Choice 1976, 16).

evidence, with the founding of the *European Journal of Political Economy, Economia delle Scelte Publiche* (*Journal of Public Finance and Public Choice*), and, in Japan, *Public Choice Studies* over the past two decades.

While the rise of specialized journals in a field is certainly one mark of its maturity as a scholarly endeavor, another is the publication of scholarship in the field across a broad spectrum of journals and, in particular, in the best general journals. The extensive bibliographical work done by Charles Plott and Mark Pauly in the early years of the public choice movement is instructive as to the range of literature and the broad spectrum of journals in which it was published—from elite journals such as the *American Economic Review*, *Journal of Political Economy*, *Economic Journal*, *Econometrica*, and the *American Political Science Review*, to second- and third-tier journals; in addition, the public choice movement inspired numerous books and a research annual titled *Mathematical Applications in Political Science*. Well over four hundred books and articles were published in the 1960s alone. In the *American Political Science Review*, for example, roughly 5 percent of the articles published in the mid-1960s embodied a rational choice perspective. By the early 1970s, this had increased to 20 percent, and by the early 1990s to around 35 percent (Green and Shapiro 1994, 2–3). All of this seems to call into question the assertions of Tullock and others regarding the lack of receptivity to this work within traditional professional outlets. Nonetheless, there was undoubtedly much to be gained from the establishment of an outlet such as *Papers/Public Choice*, which was overtly receptive to and encouraging of this work, and which served to bring together in one place work that would otherwise have been widely scattered and thus difficult to keep abreast of.

In an interesting commentary on the economics profession's view of this new scholarly enterprise, and in spite of Buchanan's decade-long effort to expand the scope of public finance to include the analysis of the relationship of the political process to public finance, the *American Economic Review* chose to locate its review of *The Calculus*—written by Mancur Olson—not under "Public Finance" but under "Related Disciplines."[31] But by 1970, the scholarship in the field and its impact had grown to the point where it was given a separate *JEL* classification,

31. This raises the larger question of what constitutes an "application of economics." The evidence here, as well as that in Bruce Kaufman's paper in the present volume, suggests strongly that all of this is determined as part of a historical process.

"025 Social Choice," falling under the heading "020 General Economic Theory." This was changed to "Social Choice and Bureaucratic Performance" in the late 1970s and back to "Social Choice" in the late 1980s—a label that is more than a little ironic given the relative paucity of interaction between social choicers in the tradition of Arrow and Amartya Sen and public choicers within the tradition being discussed in this essay.[32] The generalization and widespread acceptance of the public choice perspective are perhaps best illustrated by the perception that the best work in the field is no longer being published in *Public Choice*, but in the profession's top general journals.

5. Conclusion

The rise of a distinct field or school of public choice analysis owes to the scholarship of a number of individuals over the 1940s, 1950s, and 1960s. The development of the associated scholarly community—and thus in part the form ultimately taken by public choice—however, owes substantially to the entrepreurial efforts of Buchanan and Tullock (singly, together, and at times with others), which were largely responsible for the development of the centers, conferences and publications, and the training of students, and which created the critical mass of human and financial resources to promote scholarship in the field. The demand side of the market, while perhaps not large early on, was present in potential, at least, owing to the increasing willingness of economists to apply (and accept the application of) the tools of economic analysis outside of the traditional boundaries of the field and a degree of openness within political science to the application of new methods of analysis. The supply side was also clearly there in potential, but the loosing of these forces was greatly assisted by the opportunities for scholarly publication and interaction that resulted from these professionalization efforts. The role played by the publication of *The Calculus of Consent* was considerable, as its positive reception led Buchanan and Tullock to begin to organize institutional structures that would promote public choice. Arrow and Downs did not follow up their early efforts, nor did these other pioneers within economics produce the cadres of students turned out by Buchanan and Tullock.

32. The subject is now classified under "D Microeconomics" as "D7 Analysis of Collective Decision-Making," and it has seven subcategories.

The case that the growth of public choice was significantly furthered by these entrepreneurial efforts is supported by a glance at larger professional trends during this time period. While membership in the American Economic Association grew substantially in the first two decades of the postwar period, it remained essentially flat between 1969 and 1980. This suggests that the rapid growth of public choice was not part of a larger professional trend, but, rather, that public choice was attracting adherents from within the profession. It may well be the case that this growth was of a piece with several other "nontraditional" movements that emerged and became to a greater or lesser extent professionalized during this same period—for example, law and economics, institutional and evolutionary economics, post-Keynesian economics, radical political economy, and neo-Austrian economics, each of which emerged at least in part because of a sense of dissatisfaction with the increasing homogenization of economics in the postwar period (see Morgan and Rutherford 1998). Certain of these movements, such as public choice and law and economics, retained fundamental elements of the neoclassical approach, but yet they were perceived, both within and without, as important departures from neoclassical economics.

It has been suggested by some that ideas have a life of their own, that they are born out of nothing and evolve at the whims of the human mind, uninfluenced by external circumstances. Such is clearly not the case here. The developments in game theory at RAND and elsewhere during the Cold War period made possible many of the theoretical constructs at the heart of public choice analysis. The perception on the part of some of a substantial expansion of the state's role in society led certain scholars concerned with individual liberty to focus their efforts on the study of governmental processes. As Dennis Mueller (1993) has pointed out, it was the common methodology and ideology (or weltanschauung) of the Virginia school of public choice that helped it to flourish. The ideology component is particularly interesting given attempts by the Virginia school to both embrace and distance themselves from it—examples of which we have seen earlier in this essay. But the claim by Buchanan that the methodology leads to conclusions consistent with the ideology cannot be sustained. There is no one-way street here; as evidenced by, for example, the differences between Virginia and Chicago public choice, it takes only a bit of tinkering with the assumptions to generate results at odds with the Virginia ideological position. And while some—for example, Mitchell (1999)—have argued that public choice was not self-consciously imperialist in the early years, the evidence presented here suggests the opposite—that the major players in the field were indeed trying to remake or supplant political science, or at least render it irrelevant. While these efforts to transform political science ultimately proved less than fully successful, the diffusion of public choice throughout the economics literature evidences the manner in which this work has forced economists to reexamine the theory of the economic role of government.

References

Arrow, Kenneth J. 1951. *Social Choice and Individual Values*. New York: Wiley.

Banfield, Edward C. 1958. Review of *An Economic Theory of Democracy*, by Anthony Downs. *Midwest Journal of Political Science* 2 (August): 324–25.

Baumol, William J. 1952. Review of *Social Choice and Individual Values*, by Kenneth J. Arrow. *Econometrica* 20 (January): 110–11.

Bergson, Abram. 1958. Review of *An Economic Theory of Democracy*, by Anthony Downs. *American Economic Review* 48 (June): 437–40.

Black, Duncan. 1948. On the Rationale of Group Decision-Making. *Journal of Political Economy* 56 (February): 23–34.

———. 1958. *The Theory of Committees and Elections*. Cambridge: Cambridge University Press.

Black, Duncan, and R. A. Newing. 1952. *Committee Decisions with Complementary Valuation*. London: William Hodge.

Breit, William. 1986. Creating the "Virginia School": Charlottesville as an Academic Environment in the 1960s. Second Annual Lecture in the Virginia Political Economy Lecture Series, April 16, 1986. Fairfax, Va.: Center for Study of Public Choice.

Buchanan, James M. 1960. La Scienza delle Finanze: The Italian Tradition in Fiscal Theory. In *Fiscal Theory and Political Economy: Selected Essays*. Chapel Hill, N.C.: University of North Carolina Press.

———. 1983. Political Economy: 1957–1982. *The G. Warren Nutter Lectures in Political Economy*. Washington, D.C.: American Enterprise Institute.

———. 1989. The Public Choice Perspective. In *Essays on the Political Economy*. Honolulu: University of Hawaii Press.

———. 1990. The Domain of Constitutional Economics. *Constitutional Political Economy* 1 (winter): 1–18.

Buchanan, James M., and Gordon Tullock. 1962. *The Calculus of Consent*. Ann Arbor: University of Michigan Press.

Center for Study of Public Choice. 1970. National Science Foundation proposal. In Buchanan House Archives, George Mason University.

———. 1976. Annual report. In Buchanan House Archives, George Mason University.
de Viti de Marco, Antonio. 1936. *First Principles of Public Finance*. Translated from the Italian by Edith Pavlo Marget. London: Jonathan Cape.
Diamond, Martin. 1959. Review of *An Economic Theory of Democracy*, by Anthony Downs. *Journal of Political Economy* 67 (April): 208–11.
Dow, Jay, and Michael Munger. 1990. Public Choice in Political Science: We Don't Teach It, But We Publish It. *PS* 23 (December): 604–9.
Downs, Anthony. 1957. *An Economic Theory of Democracy*. New York: Harper.
———. 1959. Review of *The Theory of Committees and Elections*, by Duncan Black. *Journal of Political Economy* 67 (April): 211–12.
———. 1964. Review of *The Calculus of Consent*, by James M. Buchanan and Gordon Tullock. *Journal of Political Economy* 72 (February): 87–88.
Fagen, Richard R. 1963. Review of *The Theory of Political Coalitions*, by William H. Riker. *American Political Science Review* 57 (June): 446–47.
Farris, Charles D. 1958. Review of *An Economic Theory of Democracy*, by Anthony Downs. *Journal of Politics* 20 (August): 571–73.
Gertzog, Irwin N. 1964. Review of *The Calculus of Consent*, by James M. Buchanan and Gordon Tullock. *American Political Science Review* 63 (December): 973–74.
Green, Donald P., and Ian Shapiro. 1994. *Pathologies of Rational Choice Theory*. New Haven, Conn.: Yale University Press.
Harsanyi, John C. 1965. Review of *The Theory of Committees and Elections*, by Duncan Black. *Econometrica* 33 (July): 651–53.
Hotz, Alfred. 1963. Review of *The Theory of Political Coalitions*, by William H. Riker. *Midwest Journal of Political Science* 7 (August): 295–97.
Houthakker, H. S. 1952. Review of *Social Choice and Individual Values*, by Kenneth J. Arrow. *Economic Journal* 62 (June): 355–58.
Kort, Fred. 1959. Review of *The Theory of Committees and Elections*, by Duncan Black. *Journal of Politics* 21 (May): 325–27.
Manne, Henry G. 1963. Review of *The Calculus of Consent*, by James M. Buchanan and Gordon Tullock. *George Washington Law Review* 31 (June): 1065–71.
Matthews, Donald R. 1963. Review of *The Theory of Political Coalitions*, by William H. Riker. *Journal of Politics* 25 (August): 578–80.
May, R. J. 1963. Review of *The Calculus of Consent*, by James M. Buchanan and Gordon Tullock. *The Australian Quarterly* 65 (December): 111–13.
Mazzola, Ugo. [1890] 1958. The Formation of the Prices of Public Goods. In *Classics in the Theory of Public Finance*, edited by Richard A. Musgrave and Alan T. Peacock. London: Macmillan.
McGinnis, Robert. 1963. Review of *The Calculus of Consent*, by James M. Buchanan and Gordon Tullock. *The Annals of the American Academy of Political and Social Science* 346 (March): 188.

McLean, Iain, Alistair McMillan, and Burt L. Monroe. 1998. Introduction to *The Theory of Committees and Elections, by Duncan Black and Committee Decisions with Complementary Valuation by Duncan Black and R. A. Newing*, edited by Iain McLean, Alistair McMillan, and Burt L. Monroe. Rev. 2d ed. Boston: Kluwer.

Meade, James E. 1963. Review of *The Calculus of Consent*, by James M. Buchanan and Gordon Tullock. *Economic Journal* 73 (March): 101–4.

Medema, Steven G. 1999. Wicksell's Reconciliation of the Disparate Elements of Italian Public Finance. Mimeo.

Milne, R. S. 1962. Review of *The Calculus of Consent*, by James M. Buchanan and Gordon Tullock. *Political Quarterly* 33 (October).

Mitchell, Joyce M., and William C. Mitchell. 1969. *Political Analysis and Public Policy*. Chicago: Rand McNally.

Mitchell, William C. 1988. Virginia, Rochester, and Bloomington: Twenty-Five Years of Public Choice and Political Science. *Public Choice* 56 (February): 101–19.

———. 1989. Chicago Political Economy: A Public Choice Perspective. *Public Choice* 63 (December): 283–92.

———. 1999. Political Science and Public Choice: 1950–70. *Public Choice* 98 (March): 237–49.

Morgan, Mary S., and Malcolm Rutherford, eds. 1998. *From Interwar Pluralism to Postwar Neoclassicism*. Supplement to vol. 30 of *HOPE*. Durham, N.C., and London: Duke University Press.

Mueller, Dennis C. 1993. The "Virginia School" and Public Choice. In *The Public Choice Approach to Politics*, edited by Dennis C. Mueller. Aldershot, England: Edward Elgar.

Olson, Mancur, Jr. 1962. Review of *The Calculus of Consent*, by James M. Buchanan and Gordon Tullock. *American Economic Review* 52 (December): 1217–18.

———. 1965. *The Logic of Collective Action*. Cambridge: Harvard University Press.

———. 1966. The Proposed Interdisciplinary Committee on Nonmarket Decision Making. In Buchanan House Archives, George Mason University.

Ordeshook, Peter C. 1969. Review of *A Theory of Political Exchange: Economic Reasoning in Political Analysis*, by R. L. Curry Jr. and L. L. Wade. *American Political Science Review* 63 (December): 1294–96.

Ostrom, Vincent. 1969. Memorandum to Members and Prospective Members of the Public Choice Society, 10 September. In Buchanan House Archives, George Mason University.

P., C. M. 1963. Review of *The Calculus of Consent*, by James M. Buchanan and Gordon Tullock. *Ethics* 75 (October): 65–68.

Pantaleoni, Maffeo. [1883] 1958. Contribution to the Theory of the Distribution of Public Expenditure. In *Classics in the Theory of Public Finance*, edited by Richard A. Musgrave and Alan T. Peacock. London: Macmillan.

Pennock, J. Roland. 1958. Review of *An Economic Theory of Democracy*, by Anthony Downs. *American Political Science Review* 52 (June): 539–41.

Posner, Richard A. 1987. The Decline of Law as an Autonomous Discipline, 1962–1987. *Harvard Law Review* 100 (February): 761–80.

Reder, Melvin W. 1982. Chicago Economics: Permanence and Change. *Journal of Economic Literature* 20 (March): 1–38.

Richenberg, L. J. 1953. Review of *Committee Decisions with Complementary Valuation*, by Duncan Black and R. A. Newing. *Economic Journal* 63 (March): 129–31.

Riker, William H. 1959. Review of *Approaches to the Study of Politics*, edited by Roland Young. *Midwest Journal of Political Science* 3 (May): 207–10.

———. 1961. Voting and Summation of Preferences: An Interpretive Bibliographic Review of Selected Developments during the Last Decade. *American Political Science Review* 55 (December): 900–911.

———. 1962a. Review of *The Calculus of Consent*, by James M. Buchanan and Gordon Tullock. *Midwest Journal of Political Science* 6 (November): 408–11.

———. 1962b. *The Theory of Political Coalitions*. New Haven, Conn.: Yale University Press.

Rogers, W. Hayward. 1959. Some Methodological Difficulties in Anthony Downs' *An Economic Theory of Democracy*. *American Political Science Review* 53 (June): 483–85.

Rowley, Charles K. 1991. A Changing of the Guard. *Public Choice* 71 (September): 201–23.

———. 1993. Introduction to vol. 1 of *Public Choice Theory*, edited by Charles K. Rowley. Aldershot, England: Edward Elgar.

Rowley, Charles K., and Michelle A. Vachris. 1993. Snake Oil Economics versus Public Choice. In vol. 3 of *Public Choice Theory*, edited by Charles K. Rowley. Aldershot, England: Edward Elgar.

Shapley, L. S., and Martin Shubik. 1954. A Method for Evaluating the Distribution of Power in a Committee System. *American Political Science Review* 48 (September): 787–92.

Simon, Herbert A. 1952. Review of *Committee Decisions with Complementary Valuation*, by Duncan Black and R. A. Newing. *American Sociological Review* 17 (October): 638.

Somers, Harold M. 1952. Review of *Social Choice and Individual Values*, by Kenneth J. Arrow. *Journal of Political Economy* 60 (April): 170–71.

Stubblebine, W. C. 1964. Proceedings of the Big Meadows Conference, October 12–13, 1964. In Buchanan House Archives, George Mason University.

Thomas Jefferson Center for Studies in Political Economy. 1957–58. Brochure.

———. 1963. Report.

———. 1964. Report.

Tollison, Robert D. 1991. Graduate Students in Virginia Political Economy: 1957–1991. Center for Study of Public Choice Occasional Paper on Virginia Political Economy. Fairfax, Va.: George Mason University.

———. 1992. Visitors to the Center for Study of Public Choice: 1957–1992. Center for Study of Public Choice Occasional Paper on Virginia Political Economy. Fairfax, Va.: George Mason University.

Tullock, Gordon. 1997. Origins of Public Choice. In vol. 3 of *The Makers of Modern Economics*, edited by Arnold Heertje. Cheltenham, England: Edward Elgar.

Ulmer, S. Sidney. 1963. The Role of "Costs" in Political Choice: A Review of James M. Buchanan and Gordon Tullock, *The Calculus of Consent. Conflict Resolution* 7.2:171–76.

Vines, Kenneth. 1963. Review of *The Calculus of Consent*, by James M. Buchanan and Gordon Tullock. *The Journal of Politics* 25 (February): 160–61.

Ward, Benjamin. 1963. Review of *The Calculus of Consent*, by James M. Buchanan and Gordon Tullock. *Southern Economic Journal* 29.4:351–53.

Wicksell, Knut. 1896. *Finanztheoretische Untersuchungen*. Jena: Gustav Fischer. Reprinted in part as "A New Principle of Just Taxation," in *Classics in the Theory of Public Finance*, edited by Richard A. Musgrave and Alan T. Peacock. London: Macmillan, 1958.

Wittman, Donald. 1989. Why Democracies Produce Efficient Results. *Journal of Political Economy* 97 (December): 1395–1424.

Yeager, Leland. 1988. Ethics in the History and Doctrine of the Virginia School. Fourth Annual Lecture in the Virginia Political Economy Lecture Series, 5 April 1988. Fairfax, Va.: Center for Study of Public Choice.

Eclecticism, Inconsistency, and Innovation in the History of Geographical Economics

Stephen J. Meardon

An applied field may be pulled by empirical observation toward one set of questions, yet pushed by available tools and accepted heuristics toward different questions. When economists in an applied field appear to talk past each other, they may be revealing different ideas, held consciously or unconsciously, of how the field should "work." Some may place more importance in letting empirical observation direct their research, while others place more importance in using commonly accepted modeling tools—meaning systematically applied metaphors and styles of abstract reasoning, whether they take the form of systems of equations, mathematical techniques, diagrammatic depictions, definitional taxonomies, or verbal analogies. While empirical observation and application of accepted tools are objectives that are rarely totally incompatible, neither are they always neatly reconciled.

Specifically, when the question researchers want to answer cannot be answered with conventional tools, there are at least four possibilities:

- dump the standard tools and apply a more "discursive" type of theory;
- let the tools be one's guide—even if they lead away from the pressing question;
- try to develop new tools;

Correspondence may be addressed to Stephen J. Meardon, Department of Economics, Williams College, Williamstown, MA 01267; e-mail: stephen.j.meardon@williams.edu. I thank Jeff Biddle, Roger Backhouse, Craufurd Goodwin, Pietro Peretto, Neil De Marchi, Gary Gereffi, John Sheahan, and participants in the Williams internal seminar for helpful comments. Any errors and omissions are my responsibility.

- be (at best) eclectic, or (at worst) of two inconsistent minds—using the standard tools to lay the groundwork and dropping them when the pressing question arises.

Geographical economics—the study of the location of economic activity in geographical space—provides a case study of how applied economists make these choices and the consequences of the choices. In the course of the twentieth century the field has witnessed all four of the above reactions to a single question: Why and where do industries agglomerate? Most recently, a class of models referred to as the "new economic geography" developed in the 1990s to help explain agglomerations of industry on a large geographic scale, has attracted significant attention and some controversy. The new economic geography represents one of the approaches listed above; scholars with different priors who have taken different approaches look upon the literature with varying degrees of skepticism.

A disclaimer: geographical economics is a field *I* construct. The term may be widely (if vaguely) recognized, but few if any economists in the field as I define it have described themselves as geographical economists. Precisely because economists have taken different approaches when confronted with a question not well suited for analysis with available tools, they have seen themselves as aligned with different communities of scholars. Naturally, the different scholarly communities identify their work with different fields: among them international trade theory, location theory, regional science, "growth poles," and economic geography. Conversely, because economists have identified with different fields, they have taken different approaches to the question and focused on variations of it for which their tools of analysis are better suited.

The following is a selective history of geographical economics, an applied field constructed *ex post* from the intersection of a number of other acknowledged fields. The history focuses on selected authors and bodies of thought, with two purposes. One is to shed historical light on what the new economic geography accomplishes and why it is met in some corners with skepticism. A second and more general purpose is to illustrate by historical case study the relationship between methodological priors in an applied field, the questions addressed by scholars in the field, and the cohesion or fragmentation of their scholarly communities.

Alfred Weber's Partial Equilibrium Location Model

Among acknowledged fields at the beginning of the twentieth century, one might expect the topic of agglomeration to fall primarily within the domain of location theory. Yet before the publication of Alfred Weber's 1909 *Über den Standort der Industrien* (English translation, *Theory of the Location of Industries*, 1929), location theory was traditionally either a theory of land rent and agricultural production in the manner of Johann von Thünen or a strictly verbal analysis that relied on descriptions of industry location in particular times and places. In Weber's mind, von Thünen's work did not address what had become the major question of location theory: agglomeration. The verbal analyses of the likes of Wilhelm Roscher and Albert Schäffle, on the other hand, did not address it in the way he thought necessary: with abstraction from the historical and particular, and the precision of an argument formulated mathematically—specifically, geometrically.

Weber's goal was to apply his newly developed geometrical tools to explain the forces that "determine the agglomerations of population. This we sense quite distinctly as the modern 'enigma' which is to be solved" (Weber 1929, 6). More eloquently stated:

> We witness today enormous displacements of economic forces, migrations of capital and human labor such as no other age has ever seen. We see "empires rise, empires fall," apparently as the consequence of such locational changes. . . . We also notice enormous displacements taking place within national boundaries. We observe that certain regions rapidly grow poor in human beings and capital, while others become saturated. We see in metropolitan centers great masses conglomerate, seemingly without end. We philosophize about these matters, talk about the advantages and disadvantages which result, about *Asphaltkultur*, or "decline of morals." . . . [B]ut is it possible for us to arrive at any conclusion about its causes when we do not possess as yet any real knowledge of the general rules determining the location of economic processes—when the purely economic laws which without any doubt somehow influence location are not discovered? (1929, 2–3)

Although Weber apparently did not have in mind the general equilibrium systems of Léon Walras or Vilfredo Pareto, it is tempting to read the introduction of his book as a plan to build first a model of partial equilibrium, in which the location of a "productive unit" (an individual plant or an industry, depending on the context) is determined given the locations of other productive units and raw materials; then to extend the model to a general equilibrium system, in which the locations of all productive units are determined simultaneously. His method, he wrote, was to classify the determinants of location "according to the influence which they exercise (1) into such as distribute the industries regionally and (2) into such as 'agglomerate' or 'deglomerate' industries within the regional distribution" (1929, 20).

Weber believed the factors that distribute industries regionally—that is, in partial equilibrium—consisted of transport costs and labor costs. If there are two sites of raw material inputs and one site where final output is consumed, the location of the productive unit will be somewhere inside the triangle whose apexes are the three sites.[1] In particular, assuming that output is produced with fixed proportions of the two raw materials, and assuming also that transportation costs per unit of the good per unit of distance are identical for the raw materials and the finished product, there will be some point in the interior of the triangle that minimizes the total sum of transportation costs.[2] Weber located this point with a method that was geometric and highly visual. The method was illustrated in numerous figures, among them figure 1, that were variations of the basic "Weberian triangle."

Having found the single point of minimum transport costs, any greater sum of transport costs is represented not by a single point, but by a locus of points encircling the minimum point. Weber called these loci, depicted in figure 2, "isodapanes" (1929, 105). He used isodapanes to introduce labor costs into the analysis. Many different points within the triangle may be possible employment locations, each associated with a different labor cost. Each of these points must lie on an isodapane, so one can compare the savings on labor costs accrued by locating there with the increase in transportation costs incurred by departing from the site

1. Weber used varying numbers of raw materials and consumption sites, but three was the basic case that illustrated the main insights of the model.

2. Transportation costs of both of the raw materials and the output are not in reality likely to be identical. However, given the assumption of fixed proportions of raw materials, a greater transportation cost for, say, one of the materials could be expressed equivalently by raising the proportion of that material required in production. The crucial assumption is linearity of the transport costs in distance.

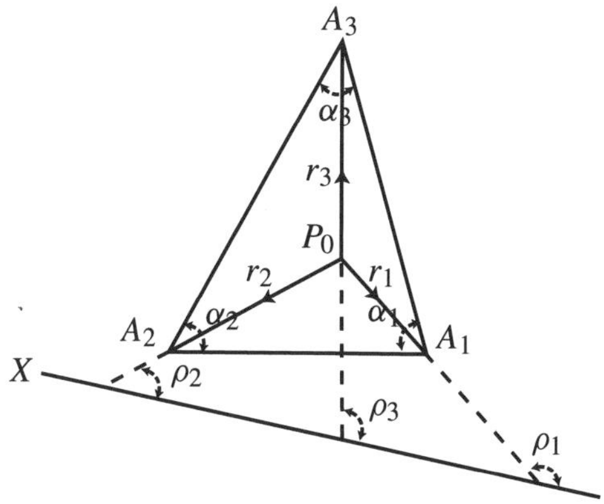

Figure 1 A Weberian triangle (Weber 1929, 228). The input and output sites are at the apexes of the triangle, and the optimal production site is P.

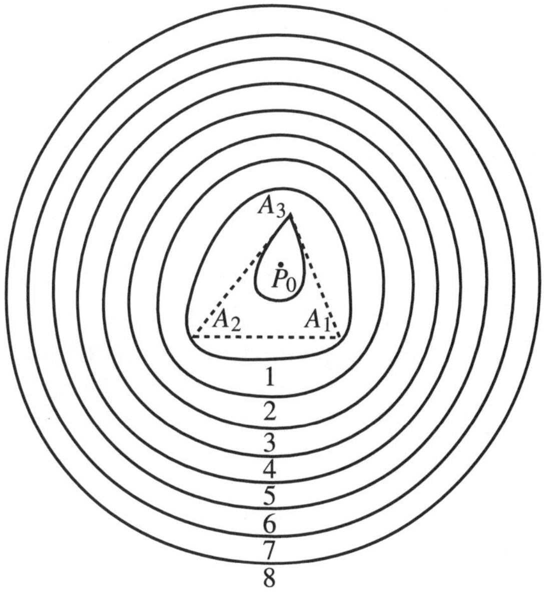

Figure 2 Isodapanes: curves of equal cost incurred by deviating from the point of minimum transportation costs (Weber 1929, 241)

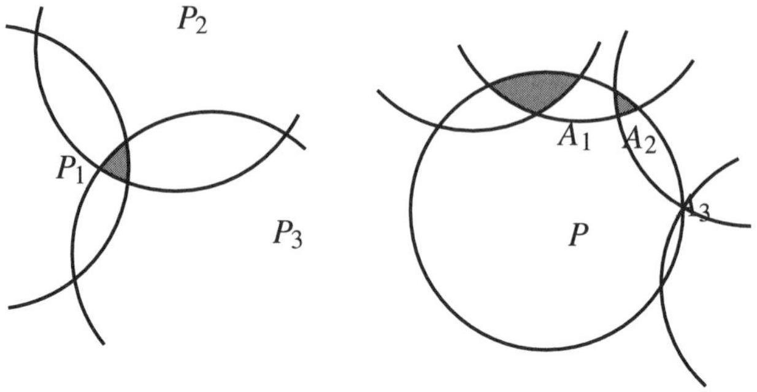

Figure 3 Weberian agglomeration (Weber 1929, 139). Possible agglomeration sites lie in the shaded regions.

of minimum transport costs. Moreover, for every possible employment location there is a "critical isodapane" where the cost of deviating from the point of minimum transport cost is exactly equal to the savings for locating at that employment location. If the location lies within the critical isodapane, it is a possible alternative location of the productive unit; otherwise it can be ruled out.

Therein lay the explanation of the factors that "distribute the industries regionally," holding fixed the locations of all other productive units. As for the factors that "'agglomerate' or 'deglomerate' industries," the temptation to view his approach as one of general equilibrium is not, in the end, supported well by the model. His prose suggests that agglomeration is a phenomenon of the interdependence of productive units: "The groups of locational factors now to be considered are . . . distinguished by the fact that they result from the *social* nature of production, and are accordingly not to be discovered by analyzing an isolated process of production" (1929, 125). In modeling the phenomenon of agglomeration, though, he simply extended the partial equilibrium reasoning he had already developed.

First Weber took as given the locations of productive units determined by the partial equilibrium method. Next, isodapanes of greater costs would be drawn around the actual location of each productive unit. If agglomeration yields cost savings, then there must be another "critical isodapane" where the savings due to agglomeration would exactly balance the increase in total costs due to locating on the isodapane instead of the location already determined. Agglomeration would arise if the critical isodapanes of several productive units intersected, as shown in figure 3: "Whatever the situation and whatever the quantity of output of any individual unit, *if its critical isodapanes intersect with those of enough other individual units to make up a unit of agglomeration, it will be concentrated with these others*" (1929, 137).

Like the model of location for individual productive units, the agglomeration model is also a "partial equilibrium" model in that locations of the productive units are not determined fully endogenously and simultaneously. The model relies on given initial locations, and the initial locations are determined either holding fixed or disregarding the locations of all other productive units. In addition, the cost savings from agglomeration are exogenous, independent of the number of productive units that agglomerate.[3]

Weber's introduction to his 1909 book was admirably ambitious: he sought to address the broad issue of agglomeration, the reason why we "see in metropolitan centers great masses conglomerate, seemingly without end." This was what he did least satisfactorily, though. Agglomeration, he implied, is a phenomenon of interdependent location decisions—and while Weber's contribution to location theory was substantial and influential, his model was fundamentally one of interdependent location decisions. He seems to have been of two minds, posing broad questions about agglomeration but applying his tools in a manner that could not quite answer them.

The Transformation of Trade Theory: Heckscher, Ohlin, and Cassel

The classical theory of international trade, encapsulated in works ranging from David Ricardo's *On the Principles of Political Economy and Taxation* (1817) to Frank W. Taussig's *International Trade* (1927), was

3. Interestingly, Weber did present a version of the model in which the locations of productive units were determined endogenously and simultaneously (1929, 179), allowing production to be broken up into multiple stages and the location of production of each stage to be determined within interdependent triangles. Nevertheless, this variation of the model would have been ill suited to study agglomeration, and Weber did not use it for that purpose. Each interdependent locational triangle is anchored by two exogenous apexes, both of which exert some "pull" on their respective productive units. The productive units could therefore not agglomerate unless their exogenous apexes were in nearly the same places—which would be tantamount to saying that productive units agglomerate because their input and output markets are agglomerated. That would have been no explanation at all, and Weber surely knew it.

built upon international differences in productivity and bound by the labor theory of value. The labor theory of value required the additional assumption of constant factor proportions, which ruled out a satisfactory treatment of migration: if migration did not alter factor proportions, then it would not alter factor returns. In that case, it would be difficult to explain either why factors were induced to move in the first place, or, granted that they did move, why they would not continue to move until one country was emptied. Ruling out migration, however, implied ruling out any treatment of agglomeration.

The definitive break from classical international trade theory made by Eli Heckscher in 1919 provided an opportunity for trade theorists to begin thinking about agglomeration. Factor proportions were allowed to vary both across countries and in the production of different commodities. Differences in factor returns in autarky reflected differences in the relative scarcity of factors, and trade constituted the implicit exchange of the services of a country's relatively abundant factor for the services of its relatively scarce factor. "Thus trade must continue to expand," he wrote, "until an *equalization of the relative scarcity of the factors of production has occurred*" (Heckscher [1919] 1991, 54).

Heckscher observed, however, that the classical assumption of international immobility of factors was patently unrealistic. Nor was factor price equalization to be found in the observable data. His next step was to consider obstacles to factor price equalization. Transportation costs were one such obstacle, and extreme disparities in factor proportions another (58). As these obstacles prevented factor price equalization, they created the incentives for the migration of factors that obviously took place in reality. Heckscher thus shifted focus from international *immobility* of factors to international *mobility* of factors, which he argued was something trade theorists should take much more seriously.

Bertil Ohlin, Heckscher's student at the Stockholm Handelshögskolan from 1917 to 1919, heard his mentor's call. Ohlin was influenced even more strongly, though, by Gustav Cassel, who became Ohlin's adviser after he enrolled for graduate studies at the Stockholms Högskola in 1920. Cassel had just published in 1918 his *Theoretische Sozialökonomie* (translated into English in 1932 as *The Theory of Social Economy*), founded upon a mathematically specified general equilibrium system of price determination. The circumstances were exactly right for Ohlin, by all accounts a precocious and brilliant student, to meld Heckscher's trade model with Cassel's formal general equilibrium model. To that hybrid Ohlin added innovations of his own and conceived a relationship between location theory and trade theory that had not previously been envisioned. He sought a unification of the two fields—attempting to explain, in addition to the pattern of trade, the migration of factors and the agglomeration of industry.

Cassel's influence upon Ohlin's work lay largely in the modeling tools he taught his student to apply. Cassel wrote that "in order to illustrate clearly the mechanism of pricing, it is necessary to present the relation between the various factors in the price-fixing process in mathematical form" (1932, 137). His model involved a system of simultaneous equations with equal numbers of equations and unknowns, similar to that of Walras. For Cassel, the system of equations was not just an alternative method of illustrating the notion of general equilibrium, which some might prefer to express or read in plain text. Rather, the equations were the only means of understanding general equilibrium deeply:

> In order to illustrate clearly the mechanism of pricing, it is necessary to present the relation between the various factors in the price-fixing process in mathematical form. . . . The work is, however, so arranged that these paragraphs may be omitted without interrupting the general connection. The reader, in that case, will simply have to put aside any thought of a deeper study of the problems just mentioned. (Cassel 1932, 137)

Following Cassel, the math came to occupy yet more of the stage; illustration of the interdependence of variables by means of a system of simultaneous equations would become the standard for models to be considered both relevant and persuasive. Ohlin adhered to that standard—both in his 1924 Ph.D. thesis *Handelns Teori* [Trade theory] and in his expansion of it in the 1933 classic *Interregional and International Trade*.

The "Mathematical Illustration" in Ohlin's *Handelns Teori* follows Cassel's style and notation, but extends his analysis to two trading regions. Each region produces multiple goods with multiple factors, but unlike Cassel's model the production coefficients are variable, depending on factor prices. As Heckscher had done with his verbal model, Ohlin used his algebraic model to study the assumptions required for equalization of factor prices across regions to occur, then hastened to relax the assumptions and move in the direction of greater realism.

The foremost barrier he considered to equalization of factor prices was interregional transportation costs (Ohlin [1924] 1991, 103). Transportation costs would drive a wedge between the price paid for a commodity in the region that exports it and the price paid in the region that imports it—and if commodity prices were not equal across regions, neither would factor prices be equal. Furthermore, if factor prices were unequal between regions then there would be an incentive for migration between regions.

Trade theory as Ohlin endeavored to refashion it concerned commerce among various geographical units; between geographical units there existed transportation costs for trade in commodities and partial but incomplete mobility of productive factors. That much he had in common with Heckscher. However, with no apparent antecedent in the work of either Heckscher or Cassel, Ohlin seized upon an idea: there was no reason to assume the geographical units were countries. If international trade theory allowed varying degrees of transportation costs and factor mobility, then the differences between international trade, interregional trade, or "interlocal trade" were just a matter of degree. All ought to be subsumed by the same theory.

Ohlin developed further this idea of "a general localisation theory," as he put it (1933, 243), in *Interregional and International Trade*. He wrote that Alfred Weber's work had "profoundly influenced the material" he presented in at least one chapter, and he discussed the concentration of industry in terms of the opposition of agglomerating and deglomerating forces. It is clear that when he wrote in 1933 that "international trade theory cannot be understood except in relation to and as a part of the general localisation theory" (142), he meant not only, as in his 1924 Ph.D. thesis, that the same theory should apply to international, interregional, and interlocal trade. He meant that the theory should subsume, in addition to trade theory, the existing field of location theory that in 1924 was not familiar to him. The general theory would be one of *trade and agglomeration*.

Ultimately, though, Ohlin was unable to build the theory he envisioned with the tools he had committed himself to using. Insofar as he brought trade theory closer to becoming a special case of location theory, he did it by abandoning the common assumptions of factor immobility and frictionless trade. Having done that, he could take the analysis only so far while remaining anchored to the Casselian general equilibrium framework. A main feature of the real-world space economy that Ohlin thought the "general localisation theory" ought to explain was the inequality of factor prices across space; yet even *partial* factor mobility, meaning mobility hindered by some friction, would eventually equalize factor prices if factor movement continued until an equilibrium was reached. Ohlin concluded that "a study of interregional trade on the basis of partial mobility of some of the productive factors obviously cannot involve the investigation of equilibria. . . . Instead, an analysis of different shocks and their effects must be a description of a process" ([1924] 1991, 103).

"Process" was outside the boundaries of the static Casselian model, but a description of it could at least be grounded on the model. There was another problem, though. In reality factor prices tended to be unequal spatially not just during an "adjustment process" but persistently: such was the case between cities and the surrounding countryside. How then did agglomerations of productive factors in cities, and the consequent persistent differences in factor prices between cities and the countryside, arise? Again the Casselian framework proved limiting for Ohlin. He tried to discuss the problem, mentioning the role of "indivisibilities" (as in fixed costs, which would give rise to increasing returns to scale) in agglomeration—but the more he did so the farther he strayed from his guiding model.

In the end the model could not address adequately a basic question of the general localization theory. In discussing agglomeration Ohlin was forced to resort to a strained eclecticism, at times relying on, and at times departing from, a model fundamentally unsuited for studying agglomeration.

General Equilibrium in Location Theory: Weigmann, Palander, and Lösch

Cassel's general equilibrium system was influential among location theorists during the same time that Ohlin incorporated it into trade theory. Andreas Predöhl, Hans Weigmann, and Tord Palander all struggled to use neoclassical price theory in one form or another to depart from Weber's location theory.

Weigmann and Palander

Of the three, Predöhl (1928) employed the Marshallian partial equilibrium version of the theory. Weigmann (1926) and Palander (1935), on the other hand, used Cassel as their starting point—yet both ultimately saw the Casselian version as too limiting. Like Ohlin, Weigmann decided, as his reviewer put it, "that the Theory of International Trade is capable of a remarkable extension—an extension which renders superfluous a separate theory of International Trade" (Lemberger 1927, 600). Unlike Ohlin, however, Weigmann did not try to express the system mathematically, not even to ground the discussion in general principles before removing the assumptions. Instead he removed them immediately and identified what would be wrong with the application of Cassel's system. Palander followed a similar method. In both theorists' minds there were two problems with Cassel's framework. One problem regarded perfect versus imperfect competition. Weigmann and Palander agreed that modeling a spatial economy must involve modeling imperfectly competitive markets. Space implies friction, limited mobility, and transportation costs, which inhibit equalization of goods and factor prices among spatial units, whether "regions," "localities," or city blocks. If space is defined continuously so that multiple economic units (particularly firms) are not allowed to occupy the same position in space, then the spatial inequality of goods and factor prices implies the presence of rents that cannot be competed away. The Casselian general equilibrium model, with its perfectly competitive market structure, is thus not applicable to the spatial economy (Isard 1949, 490, 494–95).

The other problem was with static versus dynamic modeling. Transportation costs cannot be the only cause of interregional differences in factor prices. As Ohlin showed, if factor prices are not equalized when there are transport costs, it is because *in addition to* transport costs there are limitations to factor mobility. If a model allows interregional differences in factor prices, it cannot allow factors to be freely mobile. Yet Weigmann and Palander agreed that a useful model could not constrain factors to be entirely fixed, either. Factors must be able to move, but mobility must be met with friction and it must take time. In that case, though, the static Casselian system is inadequate—so for that reason too neither Weigmann nor Palander made use of it (Isard 1949, 492–93; Ponsard 1958, 60–61).

While they both appreciated the interdependence of goods prices, factor prices, and the locations of firms and factors, the general equilibrium reasoning of Weigmann and Palander remained verbal. In their view Cassel's model was inapplicable to the spatial economy, so they would not bind themselves to it. Believing the tools at hand to be unsuitable for application to agglomeration, they abandoned the tools.

Lösch

August Lösch (1906–1945) took up the project dropped by Weigmann and Palander. Lösch's magnum opus, *The Economics of Location*, is very wide ranging but remembered most for the mathematical model at its core. The model represents much of what had been eluding Weber and the interwar location theorists: a formal general equilibrium model that was explicitly spatial and that met Weigmann and Palander's criterion of imperfectly competitive markets.

More than any previous location theorist, and more than any author whomsoever since Ohlin, Lösch attempted explicitly to unify trade theory and location theory. Specifically, he sought a theory of location, production, and trade in continuous space that made no prior assumptions about the relevant geographic units. Ohlin's broadening of the discourse in trade theory to include "interlocal trade" and "interregional trade" as well as international trade had made the point that there is something arbitrary and inappropriate about selecting the "nation" as the relevant unit. Lösch argued, however, that it was just as arbitrary and inappropriate to assume that the Heckscher-Ohlin model comprised regions or localities (however those were defined) as nations. Instead of beginning the analysis with assumptions about the size and nature of economic regions, the unified trade and location theory should let the region itself be endogenous. Lösch proposed a model that would allow him to "discover whether and how, under rational assumptions, an economic boundary can be expected to arise" (Lösch 1954, 104). What had to be developed was a theory of "market areas."

Lösch began by assuming a flat and featureless plane upon which raw materials, consumers, and farmer/manufacturers are distributed evenly. Consumers are identical in their demands for goods, and manufacturers are monopolists in the production of their goods within their market areas. Each manufacturer's good has to be transported from his location in two-dimensional space to all the consumers in his market area.

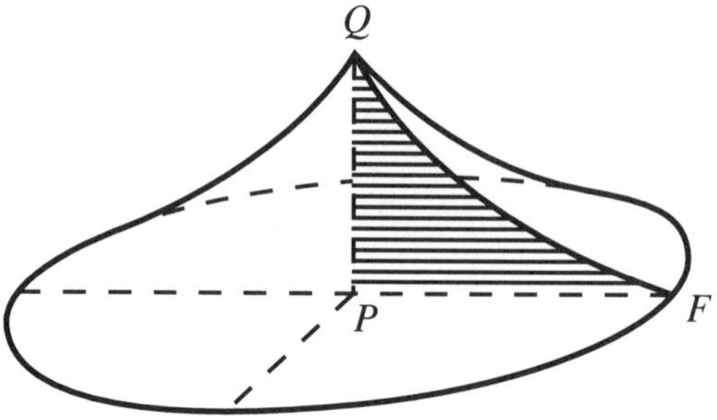

Figure 4 Lösch's spatial demand surface (Lösch 1954, 106)

Transportation costs are proportional to distance. For any given mill price a spatial "demand cone" can be drawn, as in figure 4, with quantity demanded on the vertical axis and spatial coordinates in relation to the manufacturer (who resides at the origin, *P*) on the horizontal plane. Consumers located exactly at the manufacturing site will pay the mill price and demand quantity (*PQ*). Consumers located farther away will pay the mill price, plus transportation costs, and demand a lesser quantity. Beyond a certain distance, represented in figure 4 as *PF*, the manufacturer will have no buyers. The total quantity demanded for any given price is simply the area under the demand cone.

Such is the basic model for individual producers in isolation of each other; it might be considered the "partial equilibrium" model. How does a network of identical producers behave, though?

Lösch showed diagrammatically that if two-dimensional (geographic) space were filled as completely as possible with the circular bases of nonoverlapping demand cones, then no matter how large or small the circles might be there would be some consumers not inside any of them. But that would imply the presence of unexploited profit opportunities. The ideal market area thus *cannot* be a circle. It must be a shape that can form a network exhausting all two-dimensional space: specifically, a hexagon. Lösch's thinking is illustrated by figure 5.

Having determined the general shape of market areas, it was possible to specify the general equilibrium problem. Given that the space economy was composed of a network of hexagonal market areas, the variables to be determined simultaneously were the number of hexagons, their common size, the precise coordinates of their centers, and the price paid for the goods at the centers.

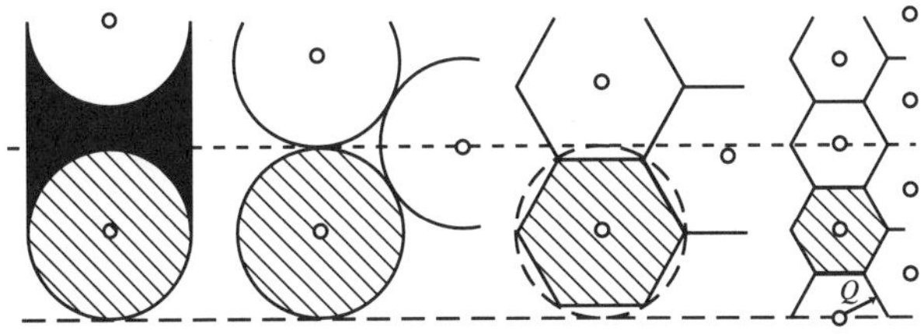

Figure 5 Development of a network of hexagonal market areas, in four stages from left to right (Lösch 1954, 110)

This model informed all of Lösch's book, established his reputation in location theory, and represented very nearly the unification of location theory and trade theory that Ohlin, Weigmann, and Palander had sought. The problems the latter three encountered were in modeling space explicitly, modeling the interdependence of productive units explicitly, incorporating imperfectly competitive markets, formalizing the model as a system of simultaneous equations, explaining spatial variations in equilibrium prices endogenously, and drawing from the model a convincing explanation of agglomeration. Lösch accomplished all but the last of those objectives.

He did try to address agglomeration using the model, but the result, while graphically elegant, was intuitively awkward. Lösch imagined several networks of hexagons superimposed upon one another, each representing market areas for a different good with different transportation costs. Each network consisted of hexagons of a different size, so the centers of its hexagons had spatial coordinates different from those of the hexagons of other networks. A map of all the market centers from all networks would have clusters of centers, as shown in figure 6. The clusters represented agglomerations of production.

This is just agglomeration by chance, with no relationship specified between the agglomerated productive units. It is the best that can be managed with Lösch's model, though: the model achieves all that it does because it assumes evenly distributed productive units. The general equilibrium system is called upon to determine spatially only the density of the distribution. In the end, despite his attempt to address the question of agglomeration, Lösch's commitment to his innovative tools led him

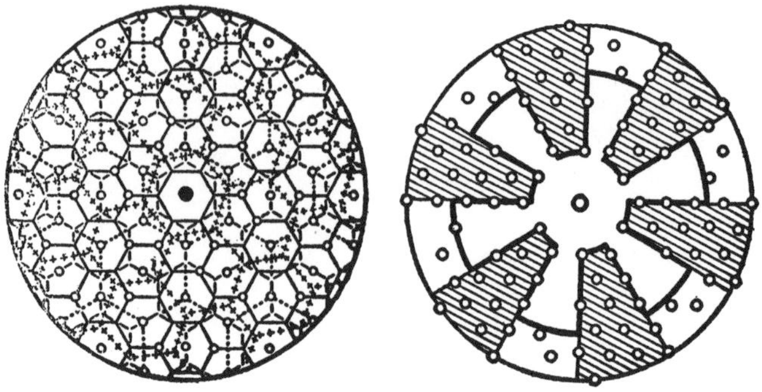

Figure 6 Löschian agglomeration. Left: superimposed networks of hexagonal market areas. Right: market areas in superimposed networks, with hexagonal borders hidden. Shaded areas are relatively agglomerated (Lösch 1954, 125).

away from it; he is remembered instead for his theory of endogenous market areas.

Growth Poles

Beginning in the late 1940s François Perroux pioneered an area of thought that influenced strongly the language and thinking of economists throughout the world eager to apply their work to regional policy. In 1955 Perroux published his seminal article "Note sur la Notion de 'Pôle de Croissance,'" and thereafter subtle distinctions were drawn by numerous authors between growth poles, growth centers, development poles, functional poles, geographic poles, polarized regions, and other terms, all variations on a common theme that will be referred to here simply as growth poles.[4]

4. If this approach seems simplistic, the alternative—a number of finely nuanced definitions—would be cumbersome and yet still unsatisfactory. Growth pole theorists themselves could not agree on the definitions, and a number of them admitted as much: "Too often . . . articles in the development pole literature define (no matter how vaguely) essential concepts and then bring in references to nominally identical concepts from other articles which, unfortunately, have been defined or used in a different manner" (Hansen 1967, 724); "the terms have . . . been used in vague, indistinct, and distressingly over-simplified ways, there being almost as many meanings ascribed to them as authors writing about them" (Darwent 1969, 5).

In barest form a growth pole is an industry which, by way of linkages to inputs and complementary products, generates growth in related industries. To help explain how the pole generates growth, the term is coupled with one or two physics metaphors: centripetal forces versus centrifugal forces, or attraction versus repulsion as with a magnet. *Pole* is evocative of a physical place (thanks, perhaps, to Peary and Amundsen), but Perroux was adamant that he had in mind poles in economic space, not necessarily physical or "geonomic" space. (The latter term foreshadowed ominously the proliferation of vocabulary in the years that followed.) Geonomic space was merely "banal": while "any banal space whatever . . . is a collection of centres and a place of passage of forces," Perroux explained that economic space, in particular,

> consists of centres (or poles or foci) from which centrifugal forces emanate and to which centripetal forces are attracted. Each centre being a centre of attraction and repulsion, has its proper field, which is set in the fields of other centres. (1950, 95)

Notwithstanding the banality of physical space, scholars rushed to develop Perroux's ideas and apply them to precisely that. J. R. Boudeville (1966) was an early and influential practitioner who applied the ideas to advocate and evaluate regional planning in France. In explaining how a growth pole or center translated into physical space, Harry Richardson (1978, 28) revealed why the concept was so seductive to scholars and planners looking for policy applications:

> The underlying idea of growth center theory is that the spatial concentration of economic activity in an urban center of an underdeveloped region will raise the economic performance of the region as a whole more than if activities are either evenly dispersed or distributed randomly.

Growth pole theory provided something very clear for academics to *do*: identify the potential growth centers. It also gave them something to *advocate*: government investment or incentives targeted toward the identified centers. In the decade following the publication of Boudeville's book the literature caught fire—particularly among those interested in regional policy in developing countries, where regional disparities tended to be the worst. To take just two examples, Harry Richardson and Margaret Richardson (1975) discussed the influence of the ideas in regional policy making in Chile, Peru, Venezuela, Colombia, Bolivia,

Argentina, Brazil, and Mexico. A volume edited by Antoni Kuklinski (1972) includes chapters applying the concept to evaluate and advocate regional policy in Canada, India, Libya, Poland, Sweden, and Tanzania. Figure 7 illustrates for the case of Tanzania the common method of empirical study combined with abstract theorizing and policy prescription. "Growth poles," wrote John Friedmann and Yvon Forest (1988, 117) in retrospect, "emerged as the central planning doctrine."

In the later 1970s the growth pole research program degenerated. Its terminology and metaphors remained in the vocabulary of regional economists and planners, but enthusiasm for growth poles as an area of research waned. One reason was that many advocates of central planning became skeptical of growth poles as a wolf in sheep's clothing: since in a larger international context "growth pole theorists, in general, view[ed] as inevitable the dominance of certain advanced national economies or, worse, supranational corporations," it might seem to follow that, even in the subnational context of regional development, growth pole theory was "being forced upon the less-developed countries to explain and convince them of the inevitability of concentration in corporate capitalist expansion" (Conroy 1973, 374).

Other reasons for the loss of momentum were political and practical. Politically, of course, every region could be expected to lobby for recognition as a pole, so the policy strategies would not be undertaken as prescribed by theory but rather in some distorted (and possibly counterproductive) form. Practically, there was the problem of a sort of "Lucas critique" from the left: "identification of 'propulsive' industries and the consequent nomination of related growth centers required heroic assumptions about the determinants of recent growth and the stability of structural relations among sectors and regions when *changes* in those relationships [were] a primary objective of the national development policy" (Conroy 1973, 378). Moreover, regional development strategies informed by growth pole theory seemed not to be working. Citing their case studies of Latin American countries, Richardson and Richardson (1975, 175) admitted that "the analysis of individual countries where growth pole strategies have been considered or tried suggests that experience with these strategies has not been very satisfactory hitherto."

Perhaps most important in the degeneration of growth pole research, however, was a reason internal to the research program itself. Growth pole theorists did not theorize in the Casselian sense—or in the Weberian or Löschian sense, for that matter. Instead, their method involved

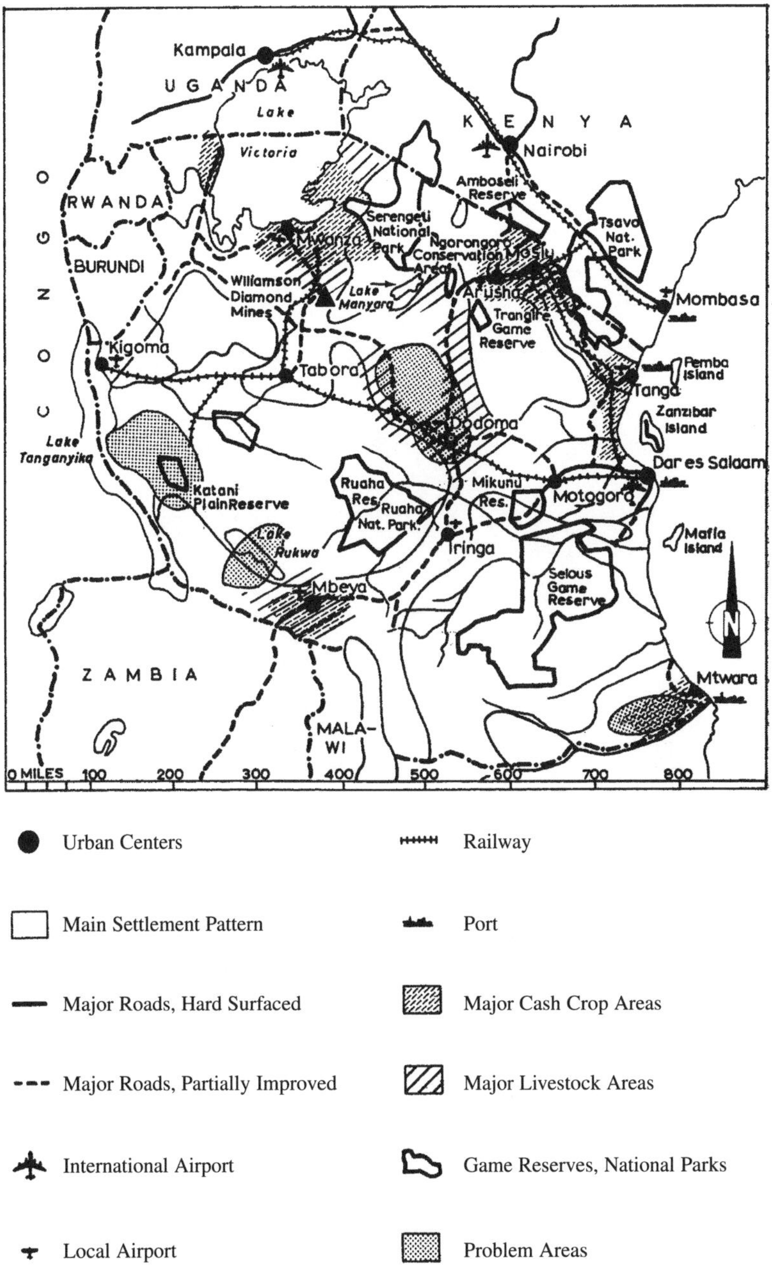

Figure 7 a Growth centers in Tanzania (Pióro 1972, 171).

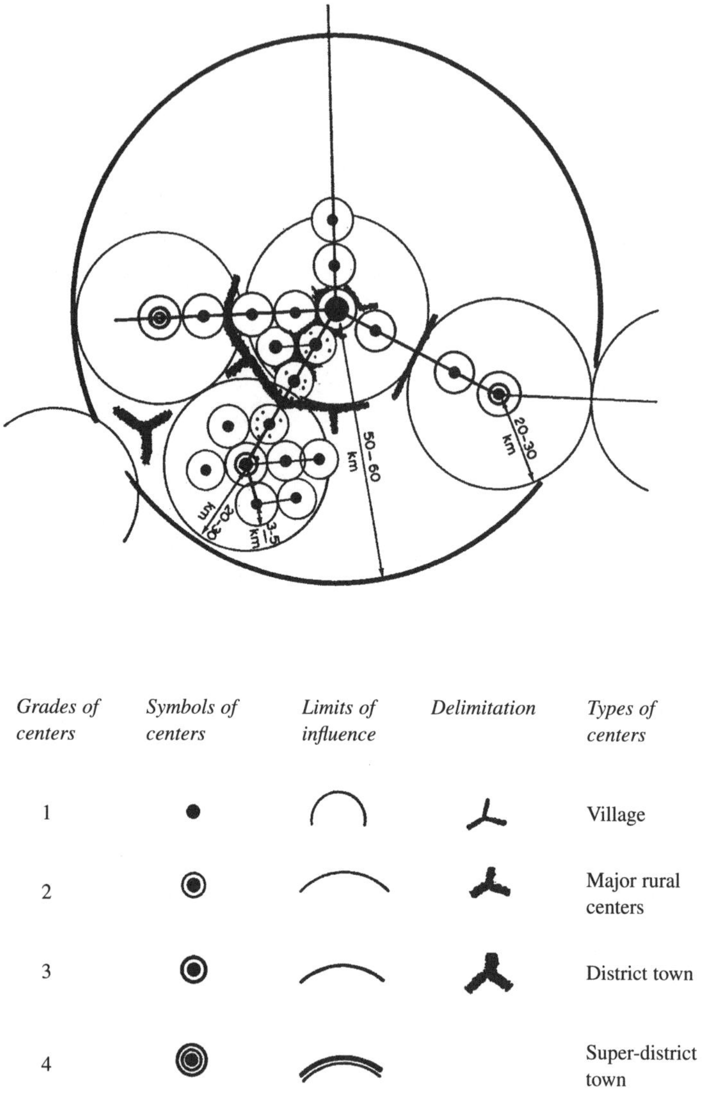

Figure 7b A theoretical network of growth centers (Pióro 1972, 190).

joining mental or visual images with semantic taxonomy, anecdotal evidence, and empirical study. This combination of avoiding standard tools and adopting new ones that conventional economists considered "fuzzy" alienated growth pole practitioners from the rest of the discipline. Even an insider commented, "It speaks volumes for the fuzzy nature of most growth pole research that even simple relationships . . . have never been tested" (Richardson 1978, 29). A well-known outsider put it more bluntly: "Unfortunately, the theory is unsatisfactory . . . , being in principle nonfalsifiable; it is simply a slogan masquerading as a theory" (Blaug 1964, 563).

Growth pole researchers maintained an interest in agglomeration, but in doing so they employed methods and language that were alien to mainstream economists. Isolated from the wider discipline, the research program died—although remnants can still be found in the vocabularies of some regional economists, Marxians, and planners who preserve, inanimate, a few of its parts.

Regional Science: From Location Theory to Neoclassical Urban Systems

To survey the immense regional science literature in a few pages would be impossible. In part that is because regional science is not really a literature so much as a crossroads paved by an interdisciplinary group of scholars, foremost among them Walter Isard, applying in numerous ways the methods of the social sciences to better understand "regions." The Regional Science Association (later the Regional Science Association International) has been meeting annually since 1954. Isard produced two books that helped define the discipline: *Location and Space-Economy* (1956) and *Methods of Regional Analysis* (1960). The first reveals that regional science was intended by Isard to be the inheritor of the tradition of location theory: chapter 2 sets regional science against the backdrop of Predöhl, Weigmann, Palander, and Lösch, as well as Ohlin. Regional science, Isard expected, would close the persisting gap between location theory and mainstream economics (Blaug 1996, 609).

The second book underscores the difficulty in surveying regional science. Unlike trade theory and the location theory that preceded it, the field cannot be pinned down to a prevalent class of models with common premises and tools. *Methods of Regional Analysis* demonstrated that regional science is an amalgam of numerous approaches: economic base models, input-output models, shift-share analysis, gravity models, and (in a revised 1998 edition) regional econometric models and geographic information systems, among other techniques. As Andrew Isserman (1995, 277) wrote, regional science is "a borrower, winnower, adapter, and synthesizer." The present article will examine just one particular strain of regional science, a relatively recent literature that has attempted to model agglomeration with standard tools from economics: neoclassical urban systems.

The neoclassical urban systems literature attempts to explain, as the title of J. Vernon Henderson's (1974) seminal paper puts it, "the sizes and types of cities": the coexistence of cities of different sizes and industry compositions. The work is sufficiently closely related to the new economic geography (to be reviewed shortly) to have compelled Henderson (1996) and Paul Krugman (1996) to hash out between them the differences between the two approaches. Krugman's impulse was to say the difference lies in the imperfectly competitive market structure that, he claimed, is present in the new economic geography but not in neoclassical urban systems. The agglomeration economies determining the sizes of cities in the new economic geography are derived from that market structure in conjunction with transportation costs; in neoclassical urban systems, by contrast, the somewhat different agglomeration economies are an external "black box."

Henderson reminded Krugman that neoclassical urban systems models incorporated imperfect competition, in some cases the very same Dixit-Stiglitz variety, even before Krugman (1991) launched the new economic geography. The difference is that neoclassical urban systems do not have an explicit geometry of space defined in terms of the transport costs between regions. The two literatures do feature different types of agglomeration economies, as Krugman correctly pointed out—but he incorrectly ascribed the difference to the wrong detail.

The neoclassical urban systems modelers do not envy the new economic geography for its ability to model different types of agglomeration economies, however. The choice of agglomeration economies at the heart of the model is an empirical issue:

> The urban systems models assume that agglomeration benefits arise from localized, external economies of scale. . . . In contrast, the new economic geography assumes that agglomeration benefits arise solely from savings on transport costs from concentrating producers and

trade at a point. There is a reality issue here of what is important in modern metropolitan areas. (Henderson 1996, 31)

What the neoclassical urban systems modelers *do* appreciate about the new economic geography is precisely its ability to make geographical space explicit, and by doing so depart from the "wonderland of no [spatial] dimensions" within which most of economics resides.[5] They see their work as compensating for its weakness in this regard in at least two ways: first, as mentioned, they consider the truly relevant agglomeration economies to be entirely external. Second, they believe their work can explain things that the new economic geography cannot: "by introducing space, the new economic geography has been unable to model a system or hierarchy of cities in which cities are of different sizes and specialize in the production of different commodities" (Henderson 1996, 32).

Evaluated by their ability to provide an explanation of agglomeration, neoclassical urban systems models have been more successful than Lösch's model, one of the antecedents of regional science. While it arguably provides a framework for studying agglomeration in greater variety and depth than do other approaches to location theory, however, the neoclassical urban systems framework sets itself apart by sacrificing one of the main features of the other approaches: spatially explicit modeling.

From Heckscher-Ohlin-Samuelson to the New Trade Theory

The general localization theory Ohlin envisioned would have explained both the pattern of trade and agglomeration among numerous locations. But Ohlin did not attain that theory either in his 1924 Ph.D. thesis or his 1933 *Interregional and International Trade*—and a few months before his death he claimed that nobody else had attained it in the intervening forty-six years:

> No one has yet made a serious attempt to build a general location theory and introduce national borders . . . in order to illuminate international economic relations and their development by a method other than conventional trade theory. (Ohlin 1979, 6)

5. This is the longstanding complaint of Isard (1949, 477).

Ohlin's willingness to step away at times from the math allowed him to articulate ideas that could not be formalized well, or formalized at all, with the tools at hand—principally agglomeration. A main benefit of mathematical expression, though, is that it forces one to take a certain care in specifying assumptions. Ohlin was more interested in broad ideas stemming but often departing from the model than in a mathematical statement of the assumptions driving its results. Both are important, but with the increasing mathematical bent of economics it was natural that trade theorists would check Ohlin's assumptions above all.

The foremost question with which trade economists of the 1940s and 1950s approached Ohlin's model was, Under precisely what conditions will factor price equalization take place? Ohlin was interested in the question, although perhaps not to the extent of "precisely": after all, he knew that in reality factor price equalization *did not* take place. It was enough for him to consider the general tendencies of frictionless trade and factor mobility to equalize factor prices internationally, without being very rigorous about it. In reality there were frictions such as transportation costs that prevented factor price equalization, and he was not very rigorous about those, either. For him, the issue could be understood well enough by means of verbal reasoning employing the intuitive insights of the model.

For Paul Samuelson, Ohlin's means were certainly *not* enough:

> Ohlin—like a murderer who returns again and again to the scene of his crime—repeatedly comes back to the point only to leave it elusively hanging in air. There is almost something Freudian in the vehemence with which he asserts the proposition to be true and with which he employs the phrases "clearly," "of course," "obviously," "as a matter of fact," and similar phrases—as if subconsciously he is really a little uneasy about the proposition's validity. . . . At one point he even goes so far as to say, "It is not worthwhile to analyse in detail why full equalisation does not occur; for when the costs of transport and other impediments to trade have been introduced into the reasoning, such an equalisation is in any case obviously impossible." (Samuelson 1948, 167)

Numerous papers were produced assessing the validity of the factor price equalization theorem under various assumptions. Perhaps most important was Samuelson's paper of 1949 that examined the case with two factors and more than two goods, although later authors would revisit the issue with greater generality. Samuelson's finding—that factor prices will be equalized between a pair of countries if they both produce all goods, and if there are no factor intensity reversals—is not as relevant to this essay as his method of getting there. In order to answer his own question, Samuelson had to consolidate and formalize Ohlin's work beyond the degree that Ohlin himself did.

Greater formalization of the model involved, in most cases, making assumptions that Ohlin never took very seriously. For present-day students of international trade it is startling to read *Interregional and International Trade* because one finds Ohlin dismissing out of hand, for example, the assumption of internationally immobile factors. Factor immobility is a basic assumption of what is now taught as the Heckscher-Ohlin model; the student wonders whether he is the victim of a faculty hoax. The truth is simply that mathematical formalism, which has sharpened trade theorists' understanding and has led to numerous valuable applications that Ohlin never considered, comes at a cost. The resulting model cannot address some issues that Ohlin found it impossible to formalize, which he therefore addressed instead in his wider-ranging verbal discussion. One of those issues was agglomeration, for the reasons discussed previously.

By the 1970s the Heckscher-Ohlin model had been thoroughly formalized and extended in myriad directions. While the model was increasingly finely developed, however, it also appeared increasingly questionable empirically. As early as 1953 Wassily Leontief pointed out the "paradox" in light of the model that U.S. imports were capital intensive relative to its exports. More troubling than the Leontief paradox, but related to it, was H. G. Grubel and P. J. Lloyd's (1975) finding of the empirical importance of intra-industry trade in the composition of U.S. imports and exports. The Heckscher-Ohlin model, a model of inter-industry trade, was not at all helpful in understanding the phenomenon. Nor could it explain why the volume of trade among wealthy countries with similar factor proportions was greater than the volume of trade between wealthy countries and countries with dissimilar factor proportions, even after controlling for the correlation between the size of an economy and the volume of its foreign trade. To explain these anomalies, theorists began taking steps that could be better described as departures from the model than extensions of it.

The new trade theory departed from the Heckscher-Ohlin framework by jettisoning the latter's assumptions of a constant returns to scale production technology and perfectly competitive market structure. Firms were instead assumed to produce with an increasing returns technology, usually embodied in a fixed cost. Increasing returns and fixed costs were compatible with more than one market structure. One way of introducing the new assumptions was by means of oligopoly models, specifically Cournot competition.[6] Another way was by means of monopolistic competition.

While the intuition of monopolistic competition was in place forty years prior to the 1970s, the general equilibrium aspect of the model—the way that entry of one firm reduces the demand faced by all firms—had been developed only verbally. The model of monopolistic competition in general equilibrium was not specified mathematically in a manner that allowed comparative statics exercises. In the mid- to late 1970s that changed: Michael Spence (1976), Avinash Dixit and Joseph Stiglitz (1977), and Kelvin Lancaster (1979) all produced models that filled that technical gap in the literature. The Dixit and Stiglitz paper was the most influential in applications to international trade theory. The first among the international trade applications was a model laid out and elaborated by Paul Krugman in three papers (Krugman 1979, 1980, 1981). Closely related models were produced by Dixit and Victor Norman (1980, chap. 9) and Elhanan Helpman (1981).

The early papers of the new trade theory already contained most of the elements of the new economic geography literature that will be surveyed shortly. Krugman 1980 serves as an example. Two countries contain identical consumers with preferences defined over a variety of consumption goods, which are produced by monopolistically competitive firms in both countries. The firms have a fixed cost and their only factor of production is labor. Transportation costs are incurred in "iceberg" form (in the goods themselves) when transporting varieties from one country to another. No matter how high the transportation costs, *some* quantity of all varieties will be traded because of the way consumers' preferences are defined. One result of the model is thus intra-industry trade.

A result of the model that Krugman emphasized even more, however, arises from the interaction of increasing returns and transportation costs.

6. See Brander 1981 and Brander and Krugman 1983.

The interaction produces a "home market effect" wherein the production of certain goods tends to take place wherever demand for them is greatest. The effect had been discussed by earlier authors who thought about increasing returns in the context of international trade, but it could not appear formally in the Heckscher-Ohlin model due to the model's perfectly competitive market structure. In Heckscher-Ohlin the production of goods takes place wherever the factors in which they are intensive are found in abundance, regardless of the location of demand.

With the appearance of the home market effect, there was a hint that the new trade theory could be modified to address an old question. Formalism as represented by Samuelson, a commitment to seeing how far the Casselian framework could be taken, had led trade theory away from the question of agglomeration after the 1930s. Now the appearance of new modeling tools—albeit adopted originally for a very different purpose—was leading it back. More monopolistically competitive producers located in one "country" than in another could be interpreted as agglomeration. Furthermore, and unlike the neoclassical urban systems literature, the presence of transportation costs lent the model a spatial structure. Little more was needed to redirect trade theory toward Ohlin's original objective, a general theory of trade and agglomeration, than a shift of emphasis and some adept marketing.

Krugman provided both, and in addition supplied the two small remaining missing pieces: a serious discussion of factor mobility and a "dispersing" force to counter the agglomerating force. He designated the resulting work "economic geography"—soon to be renamed "the new economic geography" in grudging deference to those already in the field known by that name, all of whom were doing very different work.

The New Economic Geography

It is common for papers in the new economic geography genre to begin by articulating what is known as the "folk theorem of spatial economics." The reader is first asked to imagine a world in which productive factors are spread evenly across space—to abstract away from obvious determinants of industry location like mountains and rivers, and allow the author to explain how concentrations of productive factors might otherwise arise from scratch. The folk theorem states that if productive factors are spread evenly across space, and if transporting goods across space is costly, then increasing returns of some kind must be central to an explanation of spatial agglomerations of economic activity. If instead there were diminishing or constant returns, then in the face of transportation costs for inputs and outputs it would be advantageous to produce all goods in very small quantities wherever factors of production were already located—that is, everywhere. Every agent would be a Robinson Crusoe.

In order to explain spatial agglomeration without relying on geography in the traditional sense (locations of mountains, ports, and so on), the new economic geography must therefore allow some role for increasing returns. The next question is how to represent the increasing returns: for whom will they be internal economies, and for whom will they be external? The answer depends on what sort of spatial agglomeration one is interested in explaining and the modeling tools one uses. By carrying over the Dixit and Stiglitz model of monopolistic competition from the new trade theory, the new economic geography features increasing returns at the firm level that produce pecuniary externalities transmitted through markets. The mechanism of transmission works as follows: if one firm increases production, it demands more inputs, which are produced in part by a second firm. The second firm increases its output and, in doing so, because of firm-level increasing returns, its average cost decreases and its profits rise. The profits will be dissipated by entry of additional firms, but once that happens the first firm will consequently face lower input prices, and its own profits will rise. Thus a modeling tool that allows firm-level increasing returns also allows representation in general equilibrium of economy-wide externalities. This makes the modeling tool well suited for studying the largest and broadest spatial agglomerations.

As in the new trade theory, agglomeration in the new economic geography models means that more monopolistically competitive firms are located in one region than in another. The discussion of the determinants of agglomeration and dispersion is framed in terms of the opposing forces favoring each.

Acting in favor of dispersion is the interaction of transport costs and possibly—this may vary among models—either a dispersed output market (when transport costs are high) or factor market competition (when transport costs are low). To illustrate, assume that some share of the output market is fixed geographically in each of two points, representing two regions in geographic space. If transport costs are high enough, there is almost autarky between the two regions, so industry must be dispersed across regions. The same result may be obtained, however, if transport costs are low enough. Agglomeration bids up factor prices in the more agglomerated region. If factor prices were higher in that region, however, and transport costs low, there would be profit opportunities for firms to enter the less agglomerated region and ship a large portion of their output to the more agglomerated region. The presumed agglomeration would not be sustainable, so again industry will be dispersed across regions.

Acting in favor of agglomeration, on the other hand, are transport costs and the pecuniary externalities arising from firm-level increasing returns to scale. If transport costs are neither too high nor too low, then relative agglomeration in one region may provide its own rationale for further agglomeration in that region. Suppose for example a profit opportunity in one region induces entry there of an additional firm, and hence production of an additional variety. That region now becomes more agglomerated relative to the other region. The price index decreases in the more agglomerated region relative to the other region, because consumers in the more agglomerated region do not have to pay transport costs for the majority of the varieties they consume. Furthermore, nominal wages increase in the more agglomerated region because, as a result of the additional firm's entry, there is greater aggregate production and thus greater demand for labor. Higher nominal wages eliminate the profit opportunity that the firm entered to exploit, but meanwhile something has changed: with a lower price index and higher nominal wages, real wages are now higher in the more agglomerated region than in the less agglomerated region. This induces labor to migrate to the more agglomerated region, which now depresses nominal wages and creates additional profit opportunities. So there is entry of additional firms, and entry of additional firms sets the same process in motion once again.

It may not be immediately clear where increasing returns and pecuniary externalities enter the story. Pecuniary externalities are realized when one firm's entry results ultimately in positive profits for all firms, by means of the effect of real wages on migration and the effect of migration on nominal wages. Without increasing returns there would be no incentive for migration, because the price index would never be lower in the more agglomerated region than in the less agglomerated region. Why should it be, if all the varieties produced in the more agglomerated region (or as many substitutes for them as desired) could just as well be produced on a smaller scale in the less agglomerated region?

Not all new economic geography models work exactly as described in the preceding paragraphs, which were written with the model of Krugman (1991) particularly in mind. Details may vary: the dispersing force may include diseconomies of city size, as in Krugman and Livas 1996; monopolistically competitive firms may use the output of other such firms as intermediate inputs, creating explicit input-output linkages, as in Venables 1996; there may be any number of regions or any number of monopolistically competitive industries, as in Puga and Venables 1996; there may be multiple regions in each of multiple countries, as in Meardon 1999; there may be studies of agglomeration in regions with varying sizes and shapes, as in Stelder 1998. The punch line of most variations, however, is the same. Because firms are linked by pecuniary externalities, the rationale of agglomeration is circular; because the rationale is circular, reinforcing itself, there may be multiple equilibria. If there is to be agglomeration its location is typically indeterminate, depending not on the model's parameterization, but on the initial conditions from which the circular rationale begins. If chance (or arbitrary choice of the modeler, or "history") gives a small advantage to one location, it will become the agglomeration site.

In the introduction to this paper, it was suggested that development of new tools is one possible reaction to a tension between the questions researchers want to address and the questions that available and acceptable tools allow them to address. The new economic geography illustrates how such development may take place in practice. New tools were developed that allowed economists to address agglomeration within a general equilibrium framework. In this case, however, the tools were not developed for that purpose; nor were they even originally borrowed for that purpose.

The Dixit-Stiglitz model of monopolistic competition was first borrowed by international trade theorists who found that it generated a result interpretable as intra-industry trade. In time it was noticed that the model also generated a result interpretable as agglomeration, and this fortuitous discovery launched the new economic geography. New tools were thus developed and applied to a longstanding question intractable by standard techniques—but in fact it was the question of the new economic geography that followed the tools.

Conclusion

The history of geographical economics illustrates the numerous possible reactions in an applied field to a conflict between tools and questions, and the possible consequences to the coherence or fragmentation of the field. Following Alfred Weber's emphatic statement of the importance of agglomeration as a research subject, Ohlin took steps toward unifying trade theory with location theory and building a general theory of trade and agglomeration. The tools Cassel bestowed to him had allowed him to conceive of such a general theory—yet they also prevented him from accomplishing it. Ohlin responded eclectically, basing much of his work on his formal model but departing from it when it proved unsuitable, as it did when applied to agglomeration. Eclecticism largely vanished in the years that followed, though. Cassel's system came to represent a standard of formalization that economists struggled to meet. Trade theorists, led by Samuelson, maintained the standard at the expense of dropping the question of agglomeration for almost fifty years. Location theorists like Weigmann and Palander, on the other hand, preferred to abandon their tools rather than drop the question—while Lösch focused instead on the tangential question of the geographic size of "market areas." The study of geographic economics became fragmented among different fields and different literatures, each representing scholars with different priors speaking essentially in different languages. The project of defining and identifying growth poles, for example, could not have been more different in method, style, and objectives than the project of developing and extending the Heckscher-Ohlin-Samuelson model.

There is now a new literature, the new economic geography, that models agglomeration and trade using a spatially explicit general equilibrium system of equations. The literature was developed almost by accident—or at least without the original motivation of reconciling the fifty-plus-year divorce of location theory and trade theory. Krugman (1993, 1995) does not deny this point in his own historical sketches of geographical economics, but he does assert that other branches of geographical economics attempted to anticipate the new economic geography but failed to achieve that end. "One cannot fault the geographers for their failure to develop full maximization and equilibrium models," writes Krugman (1995, 87), "although one can perhaps complain about their failure to understand how far short of that ideal they were falling." Some practitioners of the other branches, including geographers such as

Ron Martin (1999), dispute Krugman's narrative and are skeptical of the new economic geography. One critical view is that the new economic geography involves the application of tools they rejected long ago to study problems better addressed in other ways. Another is that it is an attempt to market new techniques by questionable historical claims of affinity with Ohlin, Perroux, and other past authors. At the heart of the dispute is a question of the appropriateness of the modeling tools and direction of inquiry of the new economic geography—and one should not expect the dispute to be settled, as it takes place across disciplinary divides created precisely by choices of methods to use and questions to ask.

Putting the new economic geography in historical context and focusing particularly on the fragmentation of scholarly communities within geographical economics sheds light on the methods and historical claims of the new economic geography and on the methodological and historical critiques it has been confronted with. As the new economic geographers and the critics make their claims and critiques in essentially different languages, they reflect long past reactions to the tension between tools deemed acceptable and questions at hand.

References

Blaug, Mark. 1964. A Case of Emperor's Clothes: Perroux' Theories of Economic Domination. *Kyklos* 17.4:551–64.

———. 1996. Spatial Economics and the Classical Theory of Location. In *Economic Theory in Retrospect*. 5th ed. Cambridge: Cambridge University Press.

Boudeville, J. R. 1966. *Problems of Regional Economic Planning*. Edinburgh: Edinburgh University Press.

Brander, James A. 1981. Intra-industry Trade in Identical Commodities. *Journal of International Economics* 11.1:1–14.

Brander, James A., and Paul R. Krugman. 1983. A "Reciprocal Dumping" Model of International Trade. *Journal of International Economics* 15.3–4:313–21.

Cassel, Gustav. 1932. *The Theory of Social Economy*. 2d ed. Translated from the fifth German edition by S. L. Barron. New York: Harcourt Brace.

Conroy, Michael E. 1973. Rejection of Growth Center Strategy in Latin American Regional Development Planning. *Land Economics* 49.4:371–80.

Darwent, D. F. 1969. Growth Poles and Growth Centers in Regional Planning—A Review. *Environment and Planning* 1.1:5–32.

Dixit, Avinash, and Victor Norman. 1980. *Theory of International Trade*. Cambridge: Cambridge University Press.

Dixit, Avinash, and Joseph E. Stiglitz. 1977. Monopolistic Competition and Optimum Product Diversity. *American Economic Review* 67.3:297–308.

Friedmann, John, and Yvon Forest. 1988. The Politics of Place: Toward a Political Economy of Territorial Planning. In *Regional Economic Development: Essays in Honor of François Perroux*, edited by B. Higgins and D. J. Savoie. Boston: Unwin Hyman.

Grubel, H. G., and P. J. Lloyd. 1975. *Intra Industry Trade*. London: Macmillan.

Hansen, Niles M. 1967. Development Pole Theory in a Regional Context. *Kyklos* 20.3:709–27.

Heckscher, Eli. [1919] 1991. The Effect of Foreign Trade on the Distribution of Income. In *Heckscher-Ohlin Trade Theory*, edited by Harry Flam and M. June Flanders. Cambridge: MIT Press. Translation of Utrikshandelns Verkan på Inkomstfördelningen, *Ekonomist Tidskrift* 21 (1919): 1–32.

Helpman, Elhanan. 1981. International Trade in the Presence of Product Differentiation, Economies of Scale, and Monopolistic Competition: A Chamberlin-Heckscher-Ohlin Approach. *Journal of International Economics* 11.3:305–40.

Henderson, J. Vernon. 1974. The Sizes and Types of Cities. *American Economic Review* 64.4:640–56.

———. 1996. Ways to Think about Urban Concentration: Neoclassical Urban Systems versus the New Economic Geography. *International Regional Science Review* 19.1–2:31–36.

Isard, Walter. 1949. The General Theory of Location and Space-Economy. *Quarterly Journal of Economics* 63.4:476–506.

———. 1956. *Location and Space-Economy*. Cambridge: MIT Press.

———. 1960. *Methods of Regional Analysis: An Introduction to Regional Science*. Cambridge: MIT Press.

Isard, Walter, Iwan J. Azis, Matthew P. Drennan, Ronald E. Miller, Sidney Saltzman, and Erik Thorbecke. 1998. *Methods of Interregional and Regional Analysis*. Brookfield, Vt.: Ashgate.

Isserman, Andrew M. 1995. The History, Status, and Future of Regional Science: An American Perspective. *International Regional Science Review* 17.3:249–96.

Krugman, Paul. 1979. Increasing Returns, Monopolistic Competition, and International Trade. *Journal of International Economics* 9.4:469–79.

———. 1980. Scale Economies, Product Differentiation, and the Pattern of Trade. *American Economic Review* 70.5:950–59.

———. 1981. Intraindustry Specialization and the Gains from Trade. *Journal of Political Economy* 89.5:959–74.

———. 1991. Increasing Returns and Economic Geography. *Journal of Political Economy* 99.3:483–99.

———. 1993. On the Relationship between Trade Theory and Location Theory. *Review of International Economics* 1.2:110–22.

———. 1995. *Development, Geography, and Economic Theory*. Cambridge: MIT Press.

———. 1996. Urban Concentration: The Role of Increasing Returns and Transport Costs. *International Regional Science Review* 19.1–2:5–30.

Krugman, Paul, and Raul Livas. 1996. Trade Policy and the Third World Metropolis. *Journal of Development Economics* 49.1:137–50.

Kuklinski, Antoni R., ed. 1972. *Growth Poles and Growth Centres in Regional Planning*. The Hague: Mouton & Co.

Lancaster, Kelvin. 1979. *Variety, Equity, and Efficiency*. New York: Columbia University Press.

Lemberger, J. 1927. Review of *Kritischer Beitrag zur Theorie des Internationalen Handels*, by H. Weigmann. *Economic Journal* 37.148:599–600.

Leontief, Wassily W. 1953. Domestic Production and Foreign Trade: The American Capital Position Re-examined. *Proceedings of the American Philosophical Society* 97.4:332–49.

Lösch, August. 1954. *The Economics of Location*. Translation by William H. Woglom and Wolfgang F. Stolper of *Die räumliche ordnung der wirtschaft*, 2d rev. ed., 1944. New Haven, Conn.: Yale University Press.

Martin, Ron. 1999. The New "Geographical Turn" in Economics: Some Critical Reflections. *Cambridge Journal of Economics* 23.1:65–91.

Meardon, Stephen J. 1999. Trade Liberalization and the Geographic Distribution of Industry in the United States and Mexico. Ph.D. diss., Duke University.

Ohlin, Bertil. 1933. *Interregional and International Trade*. Cambridge: Harvard University Press.

———. 1979. Some Insufficiencies in the Theories of International Economic Relations. Essays in International Finance, no. 134. Princeton: Princeton University Department of Economics, International Finance Section.

———. [1924] 1991. *The Theory of Trade*. In *Heckscher-Ohlin Trade Theory*, edited and translated by Harry Flam and M. June Flanders. Cambridge: MIT Press. Translation of Bertil Ohlin's Ph.D. thesis, *Handelns Teori*, Stockholm, 1924.

Palander, Tord. 1935. *Beiträge zur Standortstheorie*. Uppsala: Almqvist & Wicksells.

Perroux, François. 1950. Economic Space: Theory and Applications. *Quarterly Journal of Economics* 64.1:89–104.

———. 1955. Note sur la Notion de "Pôle de Croissance." *Économie Appliquée* 8.1–2:307–20.

Pióro, Zygmunt. 1972. Growth Poles and Growth Centres Theory as Applied to Settlement Development in Tanzania. In *Growth Poles and Growth Centres in Regional Planning*, edited by Antoni R. Kuklinski. The Hague: Mouton & Co.

Ponsard, Claude. 1958. *Histoire des Theories Economiques Spatiales*. Paris: Librairie Armand Colin.

Predöhl, Andreas. 1928. The Theory of Location and Its Relation to General Economics. *Journal of Political Economy* 36.3:371–90.

Puga, Diego, and Anthony Venables. 1996. The Spread of Industry: Spatial Agglomeration in Economic Development. *Journal of the Japanese and International Economies* 10.4:440–64.

Ricardo, David. 1817. *On the Principles of Political Economy and Taxation*. London: John Murray.

Richardson, Harry W. 1978. The State of Regional Economics: A Survey Article. *International Regional Science Review* 3.1:1–48.

Richardson, Harry W., and Margaret Richardson. 1975. The Relevance of Growth Center Strategies to Latin America. *Economic Geography* 51.2:163–78.

Samuelson, Paul. 1948. International Trade and the Equalisation of Factor Prices. *Economic Journal* 58.230:163–84.

———. 1949. International Factor-Price Equalisation Once Again. *Economic Journal* 59.234:181–97.

Spence, A. M. 1976. Product Selection, Fixed Costs, and Monopolistic Competition. *Review of Economic Studies* 43.2:217–36.

Stelder, Dirk. 1998. Central Places in the Real World: Some 2D Geographic Experiments for Europe with a Krugman Agglomeration Model. Paper presented at the forty-fifth Regional Science Association International meetings, Santa Fe, New Mexico.

Taussig, Frank W. 1927. *International Trade*. New York: Macmillan.

Venables, Anthony. 1996. Equilibrium Locations of Vertically Linked Industries. *International Economic Review* 37.2:341–59.

Weber, Alfred. 1929. *Alfred Weber's Theory of the Location of Industries*. Translated by Carl Joachim Friedrich. Chicago: University of Chicago Press.

Weigmann, Hans. 1926. *Kritischer Beitrag zur Theorie des internationalen Handels*. Jena: G. Fisher.

Contributors

Roger E. Backhouse is a professor of history and the philosophy of economics at the University of Birmingham, United Kingdom. Recent books include *Truth and Progress in Economic Knowledge* (1997); *Exemplary Economists*, coedited with Roger Middleton (2 vols., 2000); and *Macroeconomics and the Real World*, coedited with Andrea Salanti (2 vols., forthcoming). He is an editor of the *Journal of Economic Methodology* and an associate editor of the *Journal of the History of Economic Thought.*

Jeff Biddle is a professor of economics at Michigan State University. His research in labor economics and the history of economic thought has appeared in such journals as the *American Economic Review*, the *Journal of Labor Economics*, and *HOPE.* His current research concerns the development of the economics profession in the United States during the twentieth century.

Flavio Comim is a research associate at Von Hugel Institute, St. Edmund's College, University of Cambridge. He received his Ph.D. from the University of Cambridge in 1999; his thesis was titled "Common Sense Economics: Essays on the Role of Common Sense in the History of Economic Thought." His areas of research are the history of economic thought and development economics (with an emphasis on poverty issues). His most recent works include "Marshall and the Role of Common Sense in Complex Systems," in *Complexity and the History of Economic Thought* (edited by David Colander; Routledge, 2000); "Keynes' Common-Sense Economics: A Criticism of Coates' Argument," in *Keynes, Post-Keynesianism, and Political Economy* (edited by Claudio Sardoni and Peter Kriesler; Routledge, 2000); and "The Scottish Tradition in Economics and the Role of Common Sense in Adam Smith's Thought," forthcoming in the *Review of Political Economy.*

Robert W. Dimand is a professor of economics at Brock University, St. Catharines, Ontario, Canada. His research is on the early history of macroeconomics, the history of game theory, and the history of women in economics.

Alexander Dow is a professor of Scottish economy at Glasgow Caledonian University. He has taught at the University of Manitoba, the University of Toronto, and the University of Stirling. His published articles are mainly in the areas of Canadian economic history, British economic performance, and Scottish political economy.

Sheila Dow is a professor of economics at the University of Stirling. Her research interests are the history of thought and methodology, money and banking, regional finance, and post-Keynesian economics. Her most recent book is *The Methodology of Macroeconomic Thought* (Edward Elgar, 1996).

Robert S. Goldfarb is a professor of economics at George Washington University. His recent research has focused on topics in economic methodology, especially the problem of making plausible inferences from empirical literatures with conflicting results. Another recent research area is the economics of cigarette addiction. Two illustrative publications are "Now You See It, Now You Don't: Emerging Contrary Results in Economics" (*Journal of Economic Methodology*, December 1997); and "An Economic Theory of Cigarette Addiction" (*Journal of Health Economics*, January 1999), written with Steve Suranovic and Thomas Leonard.

Alan Hutton is a senior lecturer in economics at Glasgow Caledonian University. His main research interest is the Scottish tradition of political economy, with a particular focus on relationships between the activities of business and socioeconomic outcomes. Recent publications include articles in the *Journal of Economic Issues* on private business and the public purpose, and on the economic significance of political devolution in Scotland.

Bruce E. Kaufman is a professor of economics and a senior associate of the W. T. Beebe Institute of Personnel and Employment Relations at Georgia State University. His research interests include labor economics, industrial relations, human resource management, and institutional behavioral economics. Publications include *The Origins and Evolution of the Field of Industrial Relations in the United States* (ILR Press, 1993) and *Nonunion Employee Representation: History, Contemporary Practice, and Policy* (M. E. Sharpe, 2000), written with Daphne Taras.

Judy L. Klein is a professor of economics at Mary Baldwin College. She is the author of *Statistical Visions in Time: A History of Time Series Analysis, 1662–1938* (Cambridge University Press, 1997). Her research interests include the experience and comprehension of seasonal commercial rhythms and post–World War II links between control engineering, statistics, and economics.

Thomas C. Leonard is a lecturer in economics at Princeton University. In addition to the history of minimum-wage economics, he investigates the economics of science, including the nature and function of scientific norms and conventions. He also researches foundational and policy issues in rational choice theory, especially as they bear on "addictive" choices. Recent publications include "New on Paternalism and Public Policy" (*Economics and Philosophy*, 2000) and "An Economic Theory of Cigarette Addiction" (*Journal of Health Economics*, January 1999), both written with Robert Goldfarb and Steve Suranovic.

Stephen J. Meardon is an assistant professor of economics at Williams College. His research interests include the history of economic thought, international trade theory, geographical economics, and Latin American area studies. An earlier publication written by him and Craufurd Goodwin, "The International Dimension of American Economic Thought," appeared in *The Economic Mind in America: Essays in the History of American Economics* (edited by Malcolm Rutherford; Routledge, 1998).

Steven G. Medema is a professor of economics at the University of Colorado at Denver. His research interests include law and economics, public economics, and the economic role of government in the history of economic thought. His most recent books include *Economics and the Law: From Posner to Post Modernism* (Princeton University Press, 1997), written with Nicholas Mercuro, and a volume of lectures by Lionel Robbins titled *A History of Economic Thought: The LSE Lectures* (Princeton University Press, 1998), edited with Warren J. Samuels.

H. O. Stekler is a research professor of economics at George Washington University. His interest is economic forecasting, and he has published numerous articles about the evaluation of forecasting methods. He is an editor of the *International Journal of Forecasting*.

Pedro Nuno Teixeira is on the Faculty of Economics of the University of Porto, where he is a lecturer, and a doctoral student at the School of Business and Economics of the University of Exeter. His dissertation topic is the emergence and development of the human capital theory and the economics of education. His main research interests also include the economics and politics of higher education and the history of Portuguese economic thought in the eighteenth and nineteenth centuries.

Warren Young is an associate professor of economics at Bar Ilan University. His current research interests include the economics of nuclear energy and its regulation, the history of the open economy and general equilibrium macromodels, rational and implicit expectations, and the contributions of Roy Harrod and Don Patinkin. His recent publications include *Atomic Energy Costing* (Kluwer Press, 1998) and "The Early History of Rational and Implicit Expectations" (*HOPE*, forthcoming), written with William Darity Jr.

Index

Factions?" He knew he was dealing with professionals, perhaps a department of the government defense? the dept. of the interior as he scoured the sparse appointments of the limo. No door locks. Not even a cigarette lighter. They obviously wanted to insure his safe arrival, wherever that may be.

"Close but no cigar." His promotion was probably out of the question he assumed. The other buffoon turned to him and said learnedly,

"Counter Miniaturization Deterrent Forces." Certainly a mouthful.

"Counter what? well you can count me out."

Under the circumstances, they chuckled at his powerless, defenseless pose. He was in no position to barter, let alone plea bargain.

"You'll be briefed momentarily." They hadn't taken him for a joy ride, he figured. Jubilant to be alive, yet just as nervous, not knowing where or why they were taking him. Whisking across Washington along Pennsylvania Ave, a slight detour and to disorient the passenger, the stretch limousine shuffled through a few deceptive road blocks. Set up to sort the wheat from the chaff, and allow the perimeter police and secret service to allow the carefully selected scientists and specialists access to the secret underground headquarters near the Bethesda naval hospital. Dr Gum was glad they'd come to a stop. He didn't have a clue where he was, he just wanted to get out. As he reached for the door handle, he was startled by a sudden jolt. The limousine began to sink into the ground. He peered out the window at the perimeter of the vehicle. It swiftly sunk several stories below street level inside some sort of maintenance elevator shaft. He peered up through the moon roof. The sparse entrance or porch lighting vanished as they descended toward the center of the earth. Either he was dreaming, still back in bed with the beautiful blonde bombshell, or bewildered drawn into a candid camera type trick. A special effect? Filming a commercial, for Axe deodorant? He entertained every imaginable rational explanation but miscalculated the mark by an immeasurable amount. The long black limo came to a stop at the bottom of the shaft. The pitch black panorama slowly transformed into a sliver than a flash of light. The picture before his eyes